Portraits *of* Women *in the* American West

Portraits *of* Women *in the* American West

Edited by Dee Garceau-Hagen

Routledge
Taylor & Francis Group

New York   London

Cover image: (from left to right) "Sarah Winnemuca in Victorian Dress." Courtesy of the Nevada Historical Society. "Portrait of Mary Fields." Courtesy of the Archives of the Ursuline Convent, Toledo, Ohio. "Portrait of Polly Bemis." Courtesy of the Idaho State Historical Society. "Portrait of Frances Fuller Victoria," 1878, San Francisco. Courtesy of the Oregon State Library (WPA Series 4, General #2741b).

"Mining a Mythic Past: The History of Mary Ellen Pleasant," in AFRICAN AMERICAN WOMEN CONFRONT THE WEST, 1600-2000, edited by Quintard Taylor and Shirley Ann Moore. Copyright © 2003 of the University of Oklahoma Press. Reprinted by permission of the publisher. All rights reserved.

"Reclaiming Polly Bemis: China's Daughter, Idaho's Legendary Pioneer" by Ruthanne Lum McCunn reprinted from FRONTIERS: A JOURNAL OF WOMEN STUDIES, volume XXIV, number 1 (1997) with permission of the University of Nebraska Press. Copyright © 2003 by the Frontiers Editorial Collective.

"Prefiguring the New Woman: Frances Fuller Victor's Refashioning of Women and Marriage in 'The New Penelope'" by June Johnson Bube, Reprinted from FRONTIERS: A JOURNAL OF WOMEN STUDIES, volume XVIII, number 3 (1997) by permission of the University of Nebraska Press. Copyright © 1997 by the Frontiers Editorial Collective.

Published in 2005 by
Routledge
Taylor & Francis Group
270 Madison Avenue
New York, NY 10016

Published in Great Britain by
Routledge
Taylor & Francis Group
2 Park Square
Milton Park, Abingdon
Oxon OX14 4RN

© 2005 by Taylor & Francis Group, LLC
Routledge is an imprint of Taylor & Francis Group

Printed in the United States of America on acid-free paper
10 9 8 7 6 5 4 3 2 1

International Standard Book Number-10: 0-415-94802-9 (Hardcover) 0-415-94803-7 (Softcover)
International Standard Book Number-13: 978-0-415-94802-9 (Hardcover) 978-0-415-94803-6 (Softcover)
Library of Congress Card Number 2005001697

Library of Congress Cataloging-in-Publication Data

Portraits of women in the American West / edited by Dee Garceau-Hagen.
    p. cm.
    ISBN 0-415-94802-9 (acid-free paper) -- ISBN 0-415-94803-7 (pbk. : acid-free paper)
    1. Women--West (U.S.)--Biography. 2. Biography--19th century. 3. Biography--20th century. 4. West (U.S.)--Biography. I. Garceau-Hagen, Dee, 1955-

CT3262.W37P67 2005
305.4'0978'09034--dc22   2005001697

Taylor & Francis Group
is the Academic Division of T&F Informa plc.

Visit the Taylor & Francis Web site at
http://www.taylorandfrancis.com

and the Routledge Web site at
http://www.routledge-ny.com

For my sisters,
Pam, Madelyn, Sarah, and Karla

CONTENTS

ILLUSTRATIONS

PREFACE

This book began as a series of conversations with friends and colleagues about biographical essays as a genre in western women's history. Several of us had found compelling material on a particular woman in the course of doing research broader in scope, but we were unsure of what to do with it. For many of us schooled in gender studies, biography was suspect. It echoed the old "great men" approach to history, in which historical significance was defined by the study of famous individuals recognized for their leadership within institutionalized frameworks of power.

As we talked, it became clear that an alternative existed, albeit largely unexplored, that of writing biography from the perspectives of gender history and the new western history. And so this volume was conceived as a series of biographical essays in which gender is a category of historical analysis that both informs, and is informed by the conceptual boundaries of the new western history. The results are rich in individual detail and interpretive discovery. For this, I thank the contributors to this volume; it was a privilege and a pleasure to work with each one.

My one regret for this anthology is the absence of an essay on a woman from the Hispanic cultures of the American Southwest. There is excellent scholarship in this area and when I put out the call for papers and recruited at conferences, the field was promising. Several scholars I spoke with had intriguing material, but were committed to other projects already in progress, and so the timing was not right for them. In consequence, this collection includes women from the plains, the intermountain West, the Rocky Mountains, the Pacific Northwest, and

California, but not from the American Southwest. I hope to have the opportunity to do a revised edition to remedy this gap.

This project owes much to archivists, the experts upon whom we depend for access to sources that give life to our work. I would like to thank Julianne Ruby, archivist at the Ursuline Center Northwest, Great Falls, Montana; Judy Ellinghausen at the Center for Great Plains Studies in Great Falls, Montana; and Jodi Allison-Bunnell, Director of the Mansfield Library Archives and Special Collections at the University of Montana in Missoula. They provided invaluable help as I researched the life of Mary Fields. In addition, Merrialyce Blanchard at the Nevada Historical Society; Carolyn Bowler at the Idaho State Historical Society; Sister Kathleen Padden, O.S.U. at the Ursuline Convent Offices in Toledo, Ohio; and Richard Collier at the Wyoming State Historic Preservation Office helped locate and secure photographs and illustrations for the essays in this volume. I also would like to thank Terry Bender and Barbara Winters for sharing their memories and photographs with Linda Peavy and Ursula Smith; as well as the staff at the Cascade Historical Society, Cascade, Montana, who generously shared their time and expertise.

Special thanks go to Terry Petersen and Nicki Whearty, who welcomed me to their homes during the course of my research. Their friendship and hospitality are woven into the history of this project. So too, I appreciated the professionalism of my editors at Taylor and Francis, especially Rachael Panthier, Kimberly Guinta, Dan Webb, and Rebecca Condit. Karen Wolny talked over the merits and challenges of biographical essays with me, and for that I am grateful as well. Finally, Susanne Stoeckmann provided valuable research assistance during the early stages of this project.

In closing, I thank my husband, Ron C. Hagen, my partner in life, and my step-daughters, Carrie and Katie, all of whom make life sweet.

INTRODUCTION

Dee Garceau-Hagen

An African-American boardinghouse keeper, a Northern Paiute activist, a California writer, an Ursuline nun, an African-American mail driver, a Chinese immigrant, a Chippewa-Cree basketball player, a Wyoming writer, and a rural Anglo club founder challenge our assumptions about women in the American West, and illustrate the narrative complexity of western and women's history. Nine biographical essays herein present the lives of women on the northern plains, in the intermountain West, the Pacific Northwest, and California. Each of the women profiled offers a window on gender relations in these regions during the late nineteenth and early twentieth century. Taken together, their lives reveal interweavings of race, gender, and class as plural sources of identity, and as unstable categories of power and privilege. For many western women's historians, however, biographical portraits have been suspect. Too often they echoed an old conceptual trap, the study of notable women. If historical significance were defined only in terms of exceptional women whose deeds merited biographical study, then the lives of ordinary women would go unexamined. Much of western women's history, then, has cast a wider net, exploring patterns in the lives of women grouped by cultural identity, region, or era, to create a gendered analysis of the American West.[1] Implicit in these studies is a rejection of the heroic model of western history in which the American West bred remarkable individuals who lived and died larger than life.

1

In keeping with the spirit of those inquiries, this anthology is not a parade of notable women. Though some of the women profiled here became famous within their region, and one became nationally known, others remained obscure. The authors of these essays were not looking for female additions to a heroic narrative of western history. Rather, our focus on individual women allows subtleties of attitude, relationship, and choice to emerge. "Most history," write Susan Armitage and Elizabeth Jameson, "begins with the daily acts of ordinary people."

> As people change their behavior, they transform their relationships with other people. ... They create and recreate families, homes, and communities. In the process, people negotiate who will do what work and what behaviors will be appropriate for each.
>
> The mundane process of personal negotiation is fundamental to how people change their roles and possibilities.[2]

In this volume, each woman's life story reveals dynamics of social change, enacted in daily choices, in shifts of perception, in moments of dislocation or resolution. When an individual woman disrupted, challenged, or redefined gender norms or racial codes, we see the consequences with a human face. When a community reinforced racial-ethnic categories of exclusion or affirmed a gender hierarchy, its effects on an individual woman come into bold relief.[3] Moreover, if a woman did become renowned, or even notorious, the hows and whys of rumor and legend-building call for critical explanation. The life stories within exemplify an adage coined by feminist biographers, "when the subject is female, gender moves to the center of the analysis."[4] These essays explore how individual women in the American West negotiated their place in a landscape of shifting power and privilege.

In recent years, historians of the American West have demystified a region saturated with romantic lore. The familiar trope of the West as an open space where white settlers made a fresh start has been roundly challenged. Frederick Jackson Turner's landmark "frontier thesis" held that the advance of Anglo civilization westward across the continent left democratic institutions and values in its wake.[5] Turner's vision inspired histories of American exceptionalism and progress, in which national character was renewed through masculine struggle on western frontiers. Revisionist historians have since dismantled the Turner thesis, and for good reason. They identified its nationalistic bias and its appeal to antimodernist sentiment.[6] They replaced the master narrative of white advancement westward with multicultural perspectives, through investigation of Native American, Hispanic, Asian, and European immigrant people on their own terms, as well as Anglo-Americans.

Scholars now think of the American West as a meeting ground of cultures, a crucible of inter-tribal history as well as encounters between diverse races and ethnic groups from other continents. In studying encounters between cultures, the new western historians exposed processes of conquest, colonialism, resistance, cultural brokerage and, syncretism.[7] "The Old Western History," writes Rosalina Mendez Gonzalez, "with its misleading emphasis on the 'democratization' of the West, directs attention away from the social inequalities and continuing instabilities in our history."[8] Revisionists replaced Turner's assumption of progress with open questions about contests for control of land, resources, and cultural norms.[9]

Environmental historians further questioned the assumption of progress with regard to the harnessing of natural resources in the West. They weighed the natural as well as cultural history of the extractive industries and remapped the consequences of enterprise. They called attention to the aridity of lands west of the 100th meridian, and explored how this shaped patterns of settlement. They highlighted the role of the federal government in resource management, underscored connections between the West and the rest of the nation, and found the expansion of capitalism to be a driving force in the region's history.[10] Finally, revisionists expanded the history of the American West backward in time, to investigate Native American life before European contact, and forward to include the twentieth and twenty-first centuries.[11]

But if the new western historians recast the West in more complex terms, they rarely addressed gender.[12] "Whether one is male or female," write Armitage and Jameson, "is, for the most part, a matter of biology. But the roles, values, and behaviors different people assign to that natural fact are enormously varied."[13] Gender functions as a category of human organization; concepts of womanhood and manhood shape divisions of labor, family structure, social identity, sexual mores, and political rights. These structures and customs, in turn, define access to opportunity and power. Thus power relations are encoded in gender, and inextricable from the encounters, exchanges, and conflicts between cultures that molded western history.

If one school of new western historians rarely addressed gender, another has taken it up as their charge. Historians of women in the American West ask how gender systems have evolved within the contexts of cultural brokerage, colonialism, conquest, and the expansion of capitalism.[14] The American West emerges as a "laboratory of gender,"[15] where political economy, class interests, and racial-ethnic identities mediate the evolution of gender roles. Gender historians further challenge the myth of an individualistic, masculine West, as women's lives reveal the importance of kin and ethnic networks in migration and settlement, family strategies of economic survival, and the communal values prized within certain cultures.[16] They have exposed the gendered structures of capitalist development in the West, such as women's work in the service industries that sustained workers in the extractive industries.[17] They have demonstrated that race, class, ethnicity, age, marital status, and sexual orientation are sources of identity and discrimination that complicate notions of gender and social change.[18]

Each chapter in this volume addresses a woman whose life story raises significant questions about the late-nineteenth- and early-twentieth-century West. Depending upon whether you read American women's history, African-American history, Native American history, or Asian-American history, scholars will characterize this period in very different terms. American women's historians call it the Gilded Age and the Progressive Era, or an era of New Womanhood.[19] They mark industrial expansion, urbanization, and a groundswell of reform as important developments in women's lives. But historians of American women often base their conclusions on studies of gender in the East or the South, as though the West was disconnected from the rest of the nation. The history of women in the West remains oddly separate from the larger field of American women's history.[20]

Consider the phenomena called New Womanhood. American women's historians coined this term to describe a constellation of trends shaped by a diverse constituency. From the 1870s through the 1920s, increasing numbers of women entered wage labor as factory workers, office workers, retail workers, sex workers, and farmworkers.[21] This held true in the industrializing West as well as in the East. During this period, more women entered higher education,[22] and in the West, land grant colleges led the way by opening their doors to women. As a result, increasing numbers of women developed professional careers as educators, nurses, and social workers. At the same time, legions of married women formed women's clubs, reform groups, and rescue homes.[23] And though thousands of African-American women populated the club movement, women's clubs remained segregated in their membership and programs.[24] Meanwhile, in high schools and colleges, young women found new outlets for physical challenge and competition as women's sports gained acceptance in the curriculum.[25] Women's basketball teams were organized at Indian boarding schools in the West as well as at colleges in the East. In short, while New Womanhood has been associated with the history of the urban East, the same trends were visible through-out the West.

These trends generated a discourse on the "woman question" shaped and enriched by women writers.[26] In chapter 3, June Johnson Bube weighs Frances Fuller Victor's writing in light of her experiences in the West. Victor established herself in San Francisco during the second half of the nineteenth century, where she wrote newspaper columns, researched histories of Oregon and California, and published fiction. Twice married, once divorced, and once widowed, Victor cast a realist's eye on matrimony. She had suffered economic losses with a spendthrift husband, and then endured condescension, sexual harassment, and job discrimination when she left the marriage. But it is Victor's novella, "The New Penelope," that commands our attention. Published in 1877, "The New Penelope," featured a heroine whose adventures in the American West exposed unjust patterns of masculine privilege that hin-dered women's development as mature human beings. Ultimately Victor presented egalitarian marriage as the solution to her heroine's dilemma and redefined the home as a sanctuary for working women, a symbol of their financial independence. Bube finds in Victor's writing a distinc-tively western version of New Womanhood, opening conversation between historians of western women and those who study the broader field of American women's history.

In chapter 8, Natalie Dykstra investigates another western writer, Elinore Pruitt Stewart. Dykstra brings new perspectives to Stewart's life and writing, noting that Stewart overturned the gendered prescription for neurasthenia that held sway in the urban East. During this period, physicians prescribed a dose of the western outdoors for men with nervous debility, but ordered confinement indoors for women with the same illness. Charlotte Perkins Gilman was the most well-known victim of this regimen.[27] Stewart countered this trend by redefining the western outdoors as a curative space for women. Dykstra shows how Stewart domesticated the Wyoming landscape as an extension of her own house-hold, and aimed her celebration of the healing outdoors at invalid women readers. Thus Stewart, too, offered a distinctively western per-spective on "the woman question." Dykstra invites us to rethink Stewart's writing in light of gendered notions about the American West as a place of renewal.

While western women writers critiqued and redefined the bound-aries of womanhood, religious and club women also responded to a landscape of opportunity and limitation. In chapter 4, Anne Butler traces the first year of Sarah Theresa Dunne's commitment to mission work in the American Northwest. Known as Mother Amadeus to the

Ursuline sisters whom she directed, this restless woman migrated to Montana in 1884 to serve the poor and the unchurched. In Montana, the Ursulines ministered to white and Native American communities, focusing on health care and education for children. Butler finds Amadeus to be a study in transition from the sheltered world of a Toledo convent to the secular world of Miles City, Montana. The practicalities of working at a remote outpost eroded habits of deference to masculine authority within the church. Geographically removed from bureaucratic oversight, Mother Amadeus developed a pattern of independent leadership and congregational autonomy. Over time, she turned this self-reliance into institutionalized female authority over a broad sweep of missions in the Northwest. And though we identify the Catholic Church as a participant in Euro-American empire-building in the West, Butler attends to subtle changes in the gendered power structures within this religious institution. Butler's essay calls for rethinking the boundaries of New Womanhood to include the contradictory lives of religious women who challenged gender hierarchy while promoting Euro-American cultural hegemony in the West.

Clubwomen in the West also confronted new environments where they found fields of deprivation and possibility. Elizabeth Layton DeMary was among innumerable women in the intermountain West who formed clubs to improve their local communities. In chapter 9, Laura Woodworth-Ney investigates DeMary's life and club work in Rupert, Idaho, a town born under the aegis of a federal reclamation project. DeMary rejected the popular regional pioneer identity thrust upon her, that of the self-sacrificing woman who met deprivation with cheer and braved primitive conditions with aplomb. Instead, DeMary and her peers opposed the rugged calico image with Progressive ideals aimed at civic improvement and cultural refinement. They promoted intellectual and cultural activity in their small towns, creating a female expression of boosterism. While men trumpeted the potential of irrigation technology to nourish the arid soil, women's clubs promised to nourish the arid spirit. At the same time, DeMary and her female peers articulated the psychic costs of deprivation on sagebrush homesteads. Their clubs gave isolated women a voice and a community of witnesses, as they published women's writings from the irrigation settlements. Like the work of Elinore Stewart, their writings countered the dominant narrative of masculine renewal. Thus Woodworth-Ney presents a gendered analysis of reclamation project culture in the early twentieth century, revealing another distinctively western version of New Womanhood.

Although Mother Amadeus expanded women's authority over western Catholic missions and DeMary's boosterism honored female agency, gender inequities persisted throughout the era of New Womanhood. Historians concur that sex segregation in the workforce continued and women's wages remained far below those of men. Industrial capitalism did not reorganize to accommodate female workers who held responsibility for the care of family members, whether children or elders. And though women gained the vote, they did not vote as a gender bloc any more than men did.[28] New Womanhood, then, was not so much an achievement of something monumental as it was a sea-change, with uneven currents of social transformation apparent in a wide range of female constituencies, from working-class women to college-educated women, from unmarried career professionals to married housewives, from white women to women of color within the club movement, from women's basketball teams at eastern colleges to women's basketball teams at government Indian schools.

Women of color were not isolated from these trends, but the defining themes in their past follow a different logic. Sarah Deutsch writes: "the history of race relations in the West presents intractable problems of periodization. Each group and each subgroup have their own historical dynamics, responding to internal as well as external impulses."[29] A pluralistic history of the West can address these differences, not as sidebars to an Anglo narrative, but as central to a multicultural history of the region.

Scholars of the African-American past mark the late nineteenth and early twentieth centuries as the nadir of black history. In the South, the decades following Reconstruction saw a reassertion of Jim Crow laws, severe economic oppression, and disfranchisement resulting from violence and intimidation.[30] In some instances, these conditions sparked black migration West.[31] In the West, however, the structure of wage labor depended on racial stratification as severe as that in the South. Low paid categories of manual labor fell to minority workers in the West. Racism, expressed through social distance and sporadic violence, reinforced segregated housing and education.[32] African-Americans met these difficulties by building community support in the form of black churches, schools, fraternal organizations, and women's clubs.[33]

Quintard Taylor and Shirley Ann Moore write that black women in the West during this period migrated to urban areas where they found work as domestic servants, chambermaids, cooks, and laundresses. There they formed church groups and clubs for cultural and intellectual development, mutual aid, and better race relations. African-American clubwomen responded to the hostile racial climate by extending services such as safe residence, job placement, and child care to urban working women of color. Some black women's clubs defined legislative goals as well, supporting antilynch law or campaigning for black woman suffrage. Black women's clubs thrived in western cities like Topeka, Denver, Helena, and Great Falls.[34]

But the lives of some African-American women in the West defy neat periodization. Rather than call them exceptional, one can draw fresh insight from their experience. In chapter 1, Lynn Hudson explores the life of Mary Ellen Pleasant, an African-American born in 1814 who migrated west during the California Gold Rush. Pleasant's life becomes most intriguing in the second half of the nineteenth century, after the Civil War. In 1866, Mary Ellen Pleasant and her husband John filed charges of discrimination against a San Francisco streetcar company, expressing the radical spirit of Reconstruction.[35] In 1869, Pleasant opened a boardinghouse in San Francisco's prestigious downtown business district. As the boardinghouse prospered, Pleasant turned her profits into investments. She bought interests in gold and silver mines in Nevada, and speculated in San Francisco real estate. Pleasant amassed a fortune, and gained entrée into San Francisco's elite social and financial circles. Pleasant's success moves Hudson to question the assumption that the post-Reconstruction period was an era "associated solely with African-American defeat."[36] But neither is Hudson sanguine about race relations in the West. Indeed, Hudson finds that Pleasant located herself both within and outside the *Mammy* stereotype of the black female domestic servant. At times, the Mammy figure became Pleasant's camouflage in a society that treated wealthy black women with suspicion. White San Franciscans disparaged the prosperous entrepreneur as a servant or voodoo priestess. Hudson draws a complex portrait that reveals processes of racial marginalization that transcended economic class.

In chapter 5, Dee Garceau-Hagen turns to the rural West and the life of a working-class black woman, Mary Fields. Fields migrated to central Montana in 1885 and remained there until her death in 1914. Contrary to historical pattern, Fields did not participate in building black women's community institutions in the nearby city of Great Falls. She neither belonged to a black church nor joined a black women's club. Instead, Fields lived and worked with white Catholic nuns, though she herself was not especially devout. Later Fields moved to the ranch town of Cascade, where she freighted mail and supplies. A lone black woman in a white town, Fields became the object of rumor and gossip that would become enshrined in regional lore, appearing as *mascot* or gunfighter. Like Pleasant, Fields' public identity raises questions about the use of images like *Mammy* or *mascot*, both by the white community and by black women themselves. Garceau-Hagen traces Fields' life in Montana, and reflects on the regional construction of memory. In doing so, she uncovers the informal processes by which rural Montanans drew race and gender boundaries at the turn of the century.

Historians of North American Indians identify the late nineteenth and early twentieth centuries as an era of intensified federal intervention in Native American life. Bookended by the Dawes Severalty Act in 1887 and the Indian Reorganization Act in 1934, the "allotment era" began with federal division of reservation lands held in common into individual allotments. The goal of the federal government was to transform Native people on western reservations into private property-holding farmers engaged in small-scale capitalist enterprise. Children were to become Anglicized at government boarding schools, and families were instructed to form patriarchal nuclear family households. Husbands were to be sole providers, and wives their economic dependents. But the Anglo model of family structure proved a mismatch to those Native cultures within which women were co-providers, as well as those with traditions of matrilocal residence and female social or political authority. Poverty resulted when extended family households with several providers broke up, and subsistence farming did not revitalize reservation economies in the West.[37]

In chapter 2, Rosemarie Stremlau offers new perspectives on the life of Sarah Winnemucca, a Northern Paiute famous for her work as a Native American activist. Most historians know Winnemucca as a diplomatic liaison between the Northern Paiutes and the United States government after the Nevada silver boom, but few are aware that Winnemucca pointedly addressed the high incidence of sexual assaults on Northern Paiute women. Winnemucca herself had been attacked more than once. In 1875, for example, she discovered an Anglo intruder in her Nevada home, bent on rape. Frightened and angered, Winnemucca fought off her assailant. Not only was sexual violence an affront to her person, it also threatened Northern Paiute economic survival. If women could not travel freely in safety, how could they provide for their families? Sarah Winnemucca spoke out against sexual violence and the ways that white invasion disrupted women's roles as co-providers among the Northern Paiutes. She endorsed allotment as a hedge against economic insecurity caused in part by the violence that interfered with women's work. Winnemucca's experience of sexual assault and her strategies of resistance call attention to the role of sexual violence against women in the United States' conquest of North American Indians, and shed new light on why some Native people endorsed allotment.

As the allotment era wore on, Native Americans developed a variety of strategies in response to reservation poverty and the pressure to assimilate Anglo culture. Some adopted cattle ranching as a viable economic alternative, implemented it through kinship ties, and shaped its rhythms and rewards to fit their own cultural traditions. Others agreed to hold agricultural fairs on reservations, but refashioned them to include Native ceremonies and political initiatives. Still others took wage work as seasonal harvesters, ranch hands, miners, and loggers.[38] A few left western reservations to travel with Wild West shows, where they found both economic opportunity and a space in which to affirm certain cultural traditions.[39] These were syncretic initiatives, transforming opportunity presented by Anglos into Native American agendas, practice, and values.

This also was the era of "maternalism," during which western Native children were separated from their mothers and sent to off-reservation government boarding schools. It was thought they would assimilate Anglo civilization more readily without the interference of parents.[40] Fort Shaw Indian School in Montana was one such government institution; it became home to Emma Rose Sansaver, and it was where she learned basketball. In chapter 7, Linda Peavy and Ursula Smith follow Emma Sansaver's career as a basketball player for the Fort Shaw Indian School at the turn of the century. Emma Sansaver's youth is a story of emergent female athletics and Native American agency. When the Fort Shaw women's basketball team was invited to the St. Louis World's Fair in 1904, competing agendas surfaced. Fair organizers wanted to display Indian students as living proof of the successes of government boarding schools. Indian students' performance of academic, athletic, and artistic feats would show the wisdom of assimilating Native peoples into Anglo civilization. For their part, Indian women students in residence at the fair had other goals in mind. First, the Fort Shaw women could test their basketball prowess against the best teams in the nation. And second, they could tour the world beyond their Montana boarding school. The new sport of basketball became a source of achievement, community, and ethnic pride for Emma Sansaver and her teammates. It augured a national trend in which Indian students would embrace the sport and make it their own. Peavy and Smith's essay prompts us to rethink the consequences of federal Indian education programs during the allotment era. In the hands of Indian women students, government boarding school agendas rebounded in new and unpredictable ways.

Just as African-American and Native American historical experiences create new angles of vision, so too, Asian-American women's history casts the late nineteenth- and early twentieth-century West in a different light. Historian Judy Yung uses the metaphor of *bound feet* to describe the era, meaning that Chinese immigrant women faced numerous restrictions in the nineteenth-century American West. They confronted exclusion and antimiscegenation laws, signs of intense anti-Chinese sentiment in the region. Within Chinese enclaves, women lived by Confucian values that promoted female subordination. Indentured prostitution bound nineteenth-century Chinese women to tongs, business organizations that controlled the skin trade. At the same time, filial piety bound them to serve the needs of elder kin, even if it meant accepting prostitution in order to send money to relatives in China.[41]

Still, Chinese women developed strategies of coping and resistance. If Chinese exclusion law prohibited prostitutes and laborers from entering the country, some maneuvered past it by claiming to be the wives of merchants.[42] Others escaped indentured prostitution by marrying out or fleeing to rescue missions run by Anglo women. There, some Chinese clients saw marriage to mission-approved husbands as a way to improve their social status. And within the Victorian gender norms taught at the rescue homes, some Chinese women found greater leverage for wives.[43] Historians are exploring the complexities of nineteenth-century Chinese women's lives, as they piloted between multiple systems of social control—from Anglo laws limiting female control of wealth, to Anglo reformers bent on converting Chinese women to Victorian morality, to the Confucian values of Chinese relatives.

Judy Yung employs the metaphor of *unbound feet* to characterize the early twentieth century, meaning that Chinese immigrant women found new avenues for social change during this period. Encouraged by Chinese nationalist ideologies of female emancipation and the trend called New Womanhood in the United States, Chinese women entered the wage workforce, sought education, and formed community organizations, such as the Chinese YWCA in San Francisco, which extended social services to Chinese women.[44] In urban areas, Chinese women read and wrote for Chinese newspapers on the woman question.[45] In short, Chinese women in the early twentieth-century urban West began to transform gender relations in their worlds.

Less is known, however, about Chinese women in the rural West. In chapter 6, Ruthanne Lum McCunn traces the life of Chinese immigrant Lalu Nathoy, known in Idaho as Polly Bemis. Through careful sifting of newspaper accounts, legends, oral histories, and archival records, McCunn untangles a welter of stories about the young Chinese woman who came to the mining town of Warrens, Idaho, in 1876. There she married an Anglo saloonkeeper, Charlie Bemis. Together the couple homesteaded in a remote canyon of the Salmon River. McCunn unravels the evidence of Polly Bemis' origins to find Lalu Nathoy, daughter of an impoverished family among the Daur, an ethnic group in Mongolia who settled among Han Chinese during the mid-nineteenth century. The Daur lived in mountainous country, where they grew grains and vegetables, fished, and hunted wild game. In these respects, homesteading in a remote canyon of the Idaho Rockies would have presented familiar challenges to Lalu Nathoy. But anti-Chinese attitudes complicated life in the Rocky Mountain West. In 1894, she faced the threat of deportation without proper credentials. McCunn explains how Lalu Nathoy/ Polly Bemis carved a permanent niche for herself in Warrens, Idaho, and the Salmon River Valley, offering new perspectives on Chinese women in the rural West.

The essays herein are organized chronologically, with those women born before the Civil War appearing first, followed by those whose lives stretched into the early decades of the twentieth century. Their stories create a pluralistic history that defies narrative cohesion but invites thematic contemplation. The lives of Frances Fuller Victor, Mother Amadeus Dunne, Elinore Pruitt Stewart, and Elizabeth Layton DeMary share common threads with New Womanhood in the East insofar as women empowered themselves through writing, religious service, or club work. And yet each woman's vision and work grew out of experiences they identified as distinctively western. Their stories, then, call for dialogue between American women's historians and western women's historians about how Anglo women made meaning out of their western experience, and how this reverberated through the discourse on womanhood nationwide.

So, too, the life stories of women of color in this volume reveal nuances sometimes lost in the effort to create narrative coherence. John Wunder called the new western historians to task for addressing the dynamics of conquest and colonialism in an incomplete fashion. Some of these histories, he wrote, were "like the Old Western History in [their] lack of attention to the specific human dimension of minority individuals or women."[46] The portraits of African-American women herein uncover tensions called forth when a woman of color stepped outside the segregated boundaries of racial-ethnic enclaves. Mary Ellen Pleasant and Mary Fields lived at opposite ends of the economic spectrum, but both moved into currents of white society for reasons of their own. Both became objects of racialized myth-making that subordinated women who challenged conventional race and gender hierarchies. Lalu Nathoy/Polly Bemis lived much of her adult life in the constant company of white settlers in the Idaho panhandle, and she, too, became an exaggerated figure in regional lore. These women's stories should spur further investigation of women of color who formed close and problematic relationships with whites, as well as further inquiry into the processes by which women of color and their white peers contested race and gender boundaries.

The portraits of Native American women within also bring forth subtleties lost in more broadly conceived investigations. When Sarah Winnemucca's autobiography is mined for new insight, the rape of Native American women by Anglo invaders comes into focus as inseparable from the economic marginalization of Indian people in the West. In contrast, Emma Sansaver's story reveals violence against women within the Chippewa-Cree community, and frames her government Indian school basketball team as an escape from family violence, thus confounding the categories of oppressor and oppressed. Historians of women in the American West must continue to address the complexities that arise as they unravel and reweave the past. In studying women of different regional, temporal, and racial-ethnic groups on their own terms, a richer, more authentic history of the West emerges. The life stories of individual women add depth and dimension to these inquiries, and remap our understanding of American women's experience.

ACKNOWLEDGMENTS

I would like to thank Laura Woodworth-Ney, Laura McCall, and Gail Murray for their thoughtful critical readings of this essay in earlier drafts.

NOTES

1. See, for example, Miroslav Chavez-Garcia, *Negotiating Conquest: Gender and Power in California, 1770s to 1880s* (Tuscon: University of Arizona Press, 2004); Lillian Ackerman, *A Necessary Balance: Gender and Power Among Indians of the Columbia Plateau* (Norman: University of Oklahoma Press, 2003); Kathryn Danes, *More Wives Than One: Transformation of the Mormon Marriage System, 1840–1910* (Urbana: University of Illinois press, 2001); Albert Hurtado, *Intimate Frontiers: Sex, Gender and Culture in Old California* (Albuquerque: University of New Mexico Press, 1999); Elizabeth Jameson, *All That Glitters: Class, Conflict, and Community in Cripple Creek* (Urbana: University of Illinois Press, 1998); Dee Garceau, *The Important Things of Life: Women, Work, and Family in Sweetwater County, Wyoming, 1880–1929* (Lincoln: University of Nebraska Press, 1997); Peggy Pascoe, *Relations of Rescue: The Search for Female Moral Authority in the American West, 1874–1939* (New York: Oxford University Press, 1990); Vicki Ruiz, *Cannery Women, Cannery Lives: Mexican Women, Unionization, and the California Food Processing Industry, 1930–1950* (Albuquerque: University of New Mexico Press, 1987); Sarah Deutsch, *No Separate Refuge: Culture, Class, and Gender on an Anglo-Hispanic Frontier in the American Southwest, 1880–1940* (New York: Oxford University Press, 1987); Sylvia Van Kirk, *Many Tender Ties: Women in Fur Trade Society, 1670–1870* (Norman: University of Oklahoma Press, 1980); John Faragher, *Women and Men on the Overland Trail* (New Haven: Yale University Press, 1979). These are but a sample of the rich scholarship on western women that has emerged over the last three decades.

   For anthologies, see James Brooks & Mary Anne Irwin, eds., *Women and Gender in the West* (Albuquerque: University of New Mexico Press, 2004); Quintard Taylor & Shirley Ann Wilson Moore, eds., *African American Women Confront the West, 1600–2000* (Norman: University of Oklahoma Press, 2003); Sandra Schackel, ed.,

Western Women's Lives: Continuity and Change in the Twentieth Century (Albuquerque: University of New Mexico Press, 2003); Theda Perdue, ed., *Sifters: Native American Women's Lives* (New York: Oxford University Press, 2001; Susan Armitage & Elizabeth Jameson, eds., *Writing the Range: Race, Class, and Culture in the Women's West* (Norman: University of Oklahoma Press, 1997); Lillian Schlissel, Vicki Ruiz, and Janice Monk, eds., *Western Women: Their Land, Their Lives* (Albuquerque: University of New Mexico Press, 1988); and Armitage & Jameson, eds., *The Women's West* (Norman: University of Oklahoma Press, 1987). Essays on western women also appear in Valerie Matsumoto & Blake Allmendinger, eds., *Over the Edge: Remapping the American West* (Berkeley: University of California, 1999); and Ellen Carol DuBois & Vicki Ruiz, eds., *Unequal Sisters: A Multi-Cultural Reader in U.S. Women's History* (New York: Routledge, 1990).

For the landmark essay that first called for a multicultural history of women in the American West, see Joan Jensen and Darlis Miller, "The Gentle Tamers Revisited: New Approaches to the History of Women in the American West," *Pacific Historical Review* 49 (May 1980):173–213.

2. Armitage and Jameson, Editors Introduction to *Writing the Range*, 5.

3. Antonia Castenada calls for western women's historians to examine the politics of everyday life and their relationship to the creation or disruption of racial-ethnic or gender hierarchies. See Castenada, "Women of Color and the Rewriting of Western History: The Discourse, Politics, and Decolonization of History," in *Western Women's Lives*, 36–69.

4. Sarah Alpern, Joyce Antler, Elizabeth Isreals Perry, and Ingrid Winther Scobie, eds., "Introduction," *The Challenge of Feminist Biography: Writing the Lives of Modern American Women* (Chicago: University of Illinois Press, 1992): 1–15; 7.

5. Frederick Jackson Turner, "The Significance of the Frontier in American History," (1893) in *The Frontier in American History* (New York: Holt, Rinehart, and Winston, 1947), 1–38.

6. Patricia Nelson Limerick, Clyde Milner II, and Charles Rankin, eds., *Trails: Toward a New Western History* (Lawrence: University Press of Kansas, 1991); William Cronon, George Miles, and Jay Gitlin, eds., *Under an Open Sky: Rethinking America's Western Past* (New York: W.W. Norton, 1992): 3–27.

7. Cronon, Miles, and Gitlin, Becoming West: Toward a New Meaning for Western History" in Under an Open Sky, 3–27; Donald Fbtico, ed. *Rethinking American Indian History* (Albuquerque: University of New Mexico Press, 1997); Margaret Connell Szasz, Between Indian and White Worlds: The Cultural Broker (Norman: University of Oklahoma Press, 1994); Richard White, *'It's Your Misfortune and None of My Own': A New History of the American West* (Norman: University of Oklahoma Press, 1991); Richard White, *The Middle Ground: Indians, Empires, and Republics in the Great Lakes Region, 1650–1815* (NY: Cambridge University Press, 1991); Patricia Nelson Limerick, The Legacy of Conquest: *The Unbroken Past of the American West* (New York, W. W. Norton, 1987); Jennifer Brown, *Strangers in Blood: Fur Trade Company Families in Indian Country* (Vancouver: University of British Columbia Press, 1980).

8. Rosalinda Mendez Gonzalez, Commentary in *Western Women: Their Land, Their Lives*, ed. Lillian Schlissel, Vicki Ruiz, and Janice Monk (Albuquerque: University of New Mexico Press, 1988), 99–109, 99.

9. Ibid.; Castenada, "Women of Color and the Rewriting of Western History," in *Western Women's Lives*, 48–56.

10. William DeBuys, Enchantment and Exploitation: *The Life and Hard Times of a New Mexico Mountain Range* (Alberquerque: University of New Mexico Press, 1985); Donald Worster, *Rivers of Empire: Water, Aridity, and the Growth of the American West* (New York: Pantheon Books, 1985); John Walton, Western Times and Water Wars: State,

Culture, and Rebellion in California (Berkeley: University of California Press, 1992); William Robbins, Lumberjacks and Legislators: Political Economy of the U.S. Lumber Industry, 1890–1941 (College Station: University of Texas Press, 1982).

11. For examples of Native American history before European contact see Alvin Josephy Jr., ed., *America in 1492: The World of the Indian Peoples before the Arrival of Columbus* (New York: Knopf, 1991); Colin Calloway, "American History Before Columbus," in *First Peoples: A Documentary Survey of American Indian History* (Boston: St. Martins Press, 1999), 10–67; Shepard Krech III, *The Ecological Indian: Myth and History* (New York: W. W. Norton, 1999). For examples of twentieth- to twenty-first-century histories of the West, see Hal Rothman, *Devil's Bargains: Tourism in the Twentieth Century American West* (Lawrence: University Press of Kansas, 1998); R. David Edmunds, "Narrative Americans, New Voices: American Indian History, 1895–1995," *American Historical Review* 100 (June 1995):717–40; David Rich Lewis, "Native Americans and the Environment: A Survey of Twentieth-Century Issues," *American Indian Quarterly* 19 (summer 1995): 423–50; Mary Murphy, *Hope in Hard Times: New Deal Photographs of Montana, 1936–1942* (Helena: Montana Historical Society Press, 2003); and Sandra Schackel, *Western Women's Lives: Continuity and Change in the Twentieth Century.*

12. John Wunder, "Whats Old About the New Western History," *Pacific Northwest Quarterly* (April 1994): 50–8; 55. Wunder also quotes Glenda Riley's review of *It's Your Misfortune and None of My Own*, in which she judged White's study "warmed over Old Western History when it comes to the treatment of gender ... the major images of women continue to be the wife, the mother, the civilizer, the suffragist, and the schoolmarm." Riley's review appeared in *Western Historical Quarterly* 23 (1992): 225, and was quoted by Wunder on p. 55.

13. Armitage and Jameson, Editors Introduction to *Writing the Range*, 8.

14. Armitage and Jameson, "Editor's Introduction," 5–13; Castenada, "Women of Color and the Rewriting of Western History," in *Western Women's Lives*, 36–69. For an example of such scholarship, see Albert Hurtado, *Intimate Frontiers: Sex, Gender and Culture in Old California* (Albuquerque: University of New Mexico Press, 1999).

15. In Garceau, *The Important Things of Life*, she writes, "Indeed, if frontiers were like laboratories where a plurality of interest groups met, then multicultural history can sort the ways that regional economy, class identity, and ethic heritage mediated the evolution of gender roles." p. 5. See also Laura McCall, Introduction in *Across the Great Divide: Cultures of Manhood in the American West*, ed. Matthew Basso, Laura McCall, and Dee Garceau (New York: Routledge, 2001): 1–24; 6.

16. Deutsch, *No Separate Refuge*; Judy Yung, *Unbound Feet: A Social History of Chinese Women in San Francisco* (Berkeley: University of California Press, 1999); Dee Garceau, "'I Got a Girl Here, Would You Like to Meet Her?': Courtship, Ethnicity and Community in Sweetwater County, 1900–1925," in *Writing the Range*, 274–97; Deena Gonzalez, *Refusing the Favor: The Spanish-Mexican Women of Santa Fe, 1829–1880* (New York: Oxford University Press, 1999).

17. See, for example, Jameson, *All That Glitters*, 114–39; Paula Petrik, *No Step Backward: Women and Family on the Rocky Mountain Mining Frontier, Helena, Montana, 1865–1900* (Helena: Montana Historical Society Press, 1987), 25–58; Garceau, *The Important Things of Life*, 129–50; Judy Yung, *Unbound Voices: A Documentary History of Chinese Women in San Francisco* (Berkeley: University of California Press, 1999), 99–102, 177–80, 247–50, 329–32, 409–12.

18. Schackel, "Introduction," and "Politics and Power; Theorizing Western History," in *Western Women's Lives*, 1–11 and 14–16. Armitage and Jameson, Editor's Introduction to *Writing the Range*, 3–16.

19. Sylvia Hoffert, "The New Woman and the New Man at the Turn of the Century (1890–1920)," in *A History of Gender in America* (Upper Saddle River, NJ: Prentice

Hall, 2003), 283–317; Robyn Muncy and Sonya Michel, "Progressive Reform and World War I" and "Varieties of New Women," in *Engendering America: A Documentary History, 1865 to the Present* (Boston: McGraw Hill, 1999), 131–60, and 69–88; Joanne Meyerowitz, *Women Adrift: Independent Wage Earners in Chicago, 1880–1930* (Chicago: University of Chicago Press, 1988), 17–23; Robert Daniel, "Approaching the First Hour," in *American Women in the Twentieth Century* (New York: Harcourt Brace Jovanovich, 1987), 4–45.

20. Schackel, "Introduction," *Western Women's Lives*, 4; Scharff, "Else Surely We Shall All Hang Separately," *Western Women's Lives*, 78.

21. Hoffert, "The New Woman," 290–96; Nancy Woloch, "Women at Work, 1860–1920," *Women and the American Experience* (New York: McGraw Hill, 1994), 269–306; Wendy Gamber, *The Female Economy: The Millinery and Dressmaking Trades, 1860–1930* (Urbana: University of Illinois Press, 1997); Susan Porter Benson, *Counter Cultures: Saleswomen, Managers, and Customers in American Department Stores, 1890–1940* (Urbana: University of Illinois Press, 1986); Marjorie Davies, *Woman's Place Is at the Typewriter: Office Work and Office Workers, 1870–1930* (Philadelphia, PA: Temple University Press, 1982); Ruth Rosen, *The Lost Sisterhood: Prostitution in America, 1900–1918* (Baltimore: Johns Hopkins University Press, 1982); Timothy Gilfoyle, *City of Eros: New York City, Prostitution, and the Commercialization of Sex, 1790–1920* (New York: W.W. Norton, 1992).

22. Woloch, "The College Woman; The Professional Woman," *Women and the American Experience*, 276–86; Hoffert, "A New Woman for a New Century," *A History of Gender in America*, 290. Gender historians have also explored manhood during this era, in Gail Bederman, *Manliness and Civilization: A Cultural History of Gender and Race in the United States, 1880–1917* (Chicago: University of Chicago Press, 1995); Anthony Rotundo, *American Manhood: Transformations in Masculinity from the Revolution to the Modern Era* (New York: Basic Books, 1993); Peter Filene, *Him/Her/Self: Sex Roles in Modern America* (Baltimore: Johns Hopkins University press, 1988); and Basso et al., eds, *Across the Great Divide: Cultures of Manhood in the American West* (New York: Routledge, 2001).

23. Robyn Muncy, *Creating a Female Dominion in American Reform, 1890–1935* (New York: Oxford University press, 1991); Pascoe, *Relations of Rescue: The Search for Female Moral Authority in the American West, 1874–1939* (New York: Oxford University Press, 1990); Karen Blair, *The Clubwoman as Feminist: True Womanhood Redefined, 1868–1914* (New York: Holmes and Meier, 1980); Ruth Bordin, *Women and Temperance: The Quest for Power and Liberty, 1873–1900* (Philadelphia, PA: Temple University Press, 1981); Woloch, "Clubwomen and Crusaders," "Social Housekeepers," *Women and the American Experience*, 287–91, 298–301.

24. Evelyn Brooks Higginbotham, *Righteous Discontent: The Women's Movement in the Black Baptist Church* (Cambridge: Harvard University Press, 1993); Rosalind Terborg-Penn, *African American Women in the Struggle for the Vote, 1860–1920* (Bloomington: University of Indiana Press, 1998); Lynda Dickson, "Lifting as We Climb: African-American Women's Clubs of Denver, 1890–1925," *Writing the Range*, 372–92; Peggy Riley, "Women of the Great Falls African Methodist Episcopal Church, 1870–1910," *African American Women Confront the West*, 122–39; Woloch, "Club Women and Crusaders," *Women and the American Experience* 290–92.

25. Susan Cahn, "Mannishness, Lesbianism, and Homophobia in U.S. Women's Sports," *Feminist Studies* 19:2 (summer 1993): 343–68; see 344–6.

26. Charlotte Perkins Gilman, *Women and Economics* (Boston: Small, Maynard & Company, 1898); Kate Chopin, *The Awakening* (1899; Reprint, New York: Avon Books, 1982); Dorothy Richardson, *The Long Day: The Story of a New York Working Girl* (1905), reprinted in *Women at Work*, ed. William ONeill (New York: Quadrangle

Books, 1972): 1–303; Frances Willard, "A Wheel within a Wheel: How I Learned to Ride a Bicycle," (1895); reprinted in *Modern American Women: A Documentary History*, ed. Susan Ware (New York: McGraw Hill, 2002), 17–20; Anna J. Cooper, *A Voice from the South, By a Black Woman of the South* (Xenia, OH: Aldine Printing House, 1892).

27. Charlotte Perkins Gilman's short story, "The Yellow Wallpaper," is widely recognized as a somewhat autobiographical account of her experience with the oppressive rest cure for women. See Gilman, "The Yellow Wallpaper," eds., Thomas Erskine & Connie Richards (New Jersey: Rutgers University Press, 1993).

28. Alice Kessler Harris, *In Pursuit of Equality: Women, Men, and the Quest for Economic Citizenship in Twentieth-Century America* (New York: Oxford University Press, 2001); Alice Kessler Harris, *Out to Work: A History of Wage-Earning Women in the United States* (New York: Oxford University Press, 1982); Joan Zimmerman, "Women's Rights, Feminist Conflict, and the Jurisprudence of Equality," *Journal of American History* 78, no. 1 (June 1991): 188–225; Rosalyn Terborg Penn, "Discontented Black Feminists: Prelude and Postscript to the Passage of the Nineteenth Amendment," in *Decades of Discontent: The Women's Movement, 1920–1940*, ed. Joan Jensen and Lois Scharf (Westport, CT: Greenwood Press, 1983), 261—68; Kathryn Kish Sklar, "Why Were Most Politically Active Women Opposed to the E.R.A. in the 1920s?" in *Women and Power in American History* eds. Kathryn Kish Sklar & Thomas Dublin (Englewood Cliffs, NJ: Prentice Hall, 1991) Vol. II, 175–82.

29. Sarah Deutsch, "Landscape of Enclaves: Race Relations in the West, 1865–1990," *Under an Open Sky*, 110–31; 112.

30. William Harris, "The Nadir," in *The Harder We Run: Black Workers since the Civil War* (New York: Oxford University Press, 1982), 29–50; Jacqueline Jones, *Labor of Love, Labor of Sorrow: Black Women, Work and the Family from Slavery to the Present* (New York: Random House, 1985); Edward Royce, *The Origins of Southern Sharecropping* (Philadelphia: Temple University Press, 1993); Allan Trelease, *White Terror: The Ku Klux Klan Conspiracy and Southern Reconstruction* (New York: Harper & Row, 1971); Rayford Logan, *The Betrayal of the Negro, from Rutherford B. Hayes to Woodrow Wilson* (New York: Collier Books, 1965).

31. Nell Irvin Painter, *Exodusters: Black Migration to Kansas after Reconstruction* (Topeka: University Press of Kansas, 1986); Monroe Lee Billington and Roger Hardaway, eds., *African Americans on the Western Frontier* (Niwot: University Press of Colorado, 1998); Kenneth Hamilton, *Black Towns and Profit: Promotion and Development in the Trans-Appalachian West, 1877–1915* (Urbana: University of Illinois Press, 1991); Philip Durham and Everett Jones, *The Negro Cowboys* (New York: Dodd, Mead, 1965).

32. Richard White, "Race Relations in the American West," *American Quarterly* 38 no. 3 (fall 1986): 396–416; Sarah Deutsch, "Landscape of Enclaves: Race Relations in the West, 1865–1990," *Under an Open Sky*, 110–31.

33. Moore and Taylor, *African American Women Confront the West*; Quintard Taylor, *In Search of the Racial Frontier: African Americans in the American West, 1528–1990* (New York: W.W. Norton, 1998); Glenda Riley, "American Daughters: Black Women in the West," *African Americans*, 160–80.

34. Moore and Taylor, "The West of African American Women, 1600–2000," *African American Women*, 3–21; Riley, "American Daughters," *African Americans*, 160–80; Susan Bragg, "Anxious Foot Soldiers: Sacramento's Black Women and Education in Nineteenth-Century California," *African American Women*, 97–116; Riley, "Women of the Great Falls African Methodist Episcopal Church," *African American Women*, 122–39; Moya Hansen, "'Try Being a Black Woman!': Jobs in Denver, 1900–1970," *African American Women*, 207–27; Lynda Dickson, "Lifting as We Climb," *Writing the Range*, 372–92; Lawrence DeGraaf, "Race, Sex, and Region: Black Women in the American West, 1850–1920," *Pacific Historical Review* 49 (May 1980): 285–313.

35. For discussion of Reconstruction in the West, see Quintard Taylor, *In Search of the Racial Frontier*, 103–33.
36. Lynn Hudson, chapter 1 of this volume, "Mining a Mythic Past: Mary Ellen Pleasant," 20–34.
37. For discussions of the allotment program, dispossession, and the Anglo model of farming and its failures, see Frederick Hoxie, *A Final Promise: The Campaign to Assimilate the Indians, 1880–1920* (Lincoln: University of Nebraska Press, 1984); Janet McDonnell, *Disposession of the Indian Estate, 1887–1934* (Bloomington, IN: Indiana State University press, 1991); Leonard Carlson, *Indians, Bureaucrats and the Land: The Dawes Act and the Decline of Indian Farming* (Westport, CT: Greenwood press, 1981).

    For discussion of federally sponsored Indian boarding schools, see Clyde Ellis, *To Change Them Forever: Indian Education at the Rainy Mountain Boarding School, 1893–1920* (Norman: University of Oklahoma Press, 1996); David Wallace Adams, *Education for Extinction: American Indians and the Boarding School Experience, 1875–1928* (Lawrence, KN: University Press of Kansas, 1995); Robert Trennert, *The Phoenix Indian School: Forced Assimilation in Arizona, 1900–1935* (Norman: University of Oklahoma Press, 1988). See also Tsianaina Lomawaima, *They Called it Prairie Light: The Story of Chilocco Indian School* (Lincoln: University of Nebraska Press, 1994).

    For discussion of attempts to impose Anglo gender norms and the consequences of these programs, see Karen Anderson, *Changing Woman: A History of Racial Ethnic Women in Modern America* (New York: Oxford University Press, 1996), 26–32, 37–66. For discussion of gender norms specific to different tribes, see Laura Klein and Lillian Ackerman, eds., *Women and Power in Native North America* (Norman: University of Oklahoma Press, 1995).
38. Peter Iverson, *When Indians became Cowboys: Native Peoples and Cattle Ranching in the American West* (Norman: University of Oklahoma press, 1994); Peter Iverson, *'We Are Still Here': American Indians in the Twentieth Century* (Arlington Heights, IL: Davidson Press, 1998); William Farr, *The Reservation Blackfeet, 1882–1945: A Photographic History of Cultural Survival* (Seattle: University of Washington Press, 1986); Peggy Albright, *Crow Indian Photographer: The Work of Richard Throssel* (Albuquerque: University of New Mexico Press, 1997); Eric Meeks, "The Tohono O'Odham, Wage Labor, and Resistant Adaptation," *Western Historical Quarterly* 34, no. 4 (fall 2004): 1–18; Peter Iverson, "When Indians Became Cowboys," *Montana: The Magazine of Western History* 45 (winter 1995): 16–31; Andrew Denson, "Muskogee's Indian International Fairs: Tribal Autonomy and the Indian Image in the Late Nineteenth Century," *Western Historical Quarterly* 34, no. 3 (summer 2004): 1–17.
39. Joy S. Kasson, "American Indian Performers in the Wild West," *Buffalo Bills Wild West: Celebrity, Memory, and Popular History* (New York: Hill and Wang, 2000): 161–220; L. G. Moses, *Wild West Shows and the Images of American Indians, 1883–1933* (Albuquerque: University of New Mexico Press, 1996).
40. Anderson, *Changing Woman*, 37–66; Lisa Emmerich, "'Save the Babies!': American Indian Women, Assimilation Policy, and Scientific Motherhood, 1912–1918," *Writing the Range*, 393–409.
41. Judy Yung, *Unbound Voices: A Documentary History of Chinese Women in San Francisco* (Berkeley: University of California Press, 1999), 99–176. See also Yong Chen, *Chinese San Francisco, 1850–1943: A Trans-Pacific Community* (Palo Alto: Stanford University Press, 2000); Huping Ling, *Surviving on Gold Mountain: A History of Chinese American Women and Their Lives* (Albany: SUNY Press, 1998); Ruthanne Lum McCunn, *Chinese American Portraits: Personal Histories, 1828–1988* (San Francisco: Chronicle Books, 1988); Lucy Cheng Hirata, "Chinese Prostitutes in Nineteenth-Century America," *Signs* 5 (fall 1979): 3–29.

42. Yung, *Unbound Voices*, 9–16; Andrew Gyory, *Closing the Gate: Race, Politics, and the Chinese Exclusion Act* (Chapel Hill: University of North Carolina Press, 1998); Judy Yung, *Unbound Feet: A Social History of Chinese Women in San Franciso* (Berkeley: University of California Press, 1995); Sucheng Chan, *Entry Denied: Exclusion and the Chinese Community in America, 1882–1943* (Philadelphia: Temple University press, 1991); George Anthony Peffer, "Forbidden Families: Emigration Experiences of Chinese Women Under the Page Law, 1875–1882," *Journal of Ethnic History* 6 (fall 1986): 28–46. See also Arnoldo DeLeon, *Racial Frontiers: Africans, Chinese and Mexicans in Western America, 1848–1890* (Albuquerque: University of New Mexico Press, 2002).

43. Benson Tong, *Unsubmissive Women: Chinese Prostitutes in Nineteenth-Century San Francisco* (Norman: University of Oklahoma Press, 1994); Peggy Pascoe, "Gender Systems in Conflict: The Marriages of Mission-Educated Chinese American Women," in *Unequal Sisters: A Multicultural Reader in U.S. Women's History*, ed. Ellen Carol DuBois and Vicki Ruiz (New York: Routledge, 1990), 123–40.

44. Judy Yung, "Unbound Feet: From China to San Francisco's Chinatown," in *Women's America: Refocusing the Past*, ed. Linda Kerber and Jane Sherron DeHart (New York: Oxford University Press, 2004), 302–9; Judy Yung, "Unbound Feet: Chinese Immigrant Women, 1902–1929," *Unbound Voices*, 177–246; Victor Low, *The Unimpressible Race: A Century of Educational Struggle by the Chinese in San Francisco* (San Francisco: East/ West, 1982).

45. Judy Yung, "The Social Awakening of Chinese American Women as Reported in *Chung Sai Yat Po*, 1900–1911," *Unequal Sisters*, 195–207.

46. Wunder, "What's Old About the New Western History," 55.

Fig. 1.1 Mary Ellen ("Mammy") Pleasant at 87 years of age. The first and only photograph taken since she was 13 years old. Courtesy of the Bancroft Library of the University of California, Berkeley.

1

MINING A MYTHIC PAST: THE HISTORY OF MARY ELLEN PLEASANT

Lynn M. Hudson

More than any other African-American woman who lived in the nineteenth-century West, San Francisco entrepreneur Mary Ellen Pleasant (1814–1904) left a tangled legacy. She was called a mammy, madam, voodoo queen, and sorceress during her life, and after her death was celebrated as the "mother of civil rights in California."[1] Weeding fact from fiction in the life of this remarkable California pioneer proves nearly impossible. Virtually every detail of Pleasant's history has been contested: her birthplace, her parents, her name, her occupation, and her wealth. The latter especially has been the subject of intense speculation on the part of journalists, novelists, folklorists, and historians. Although she figures at critical junctures in United States history— the Gold Rush, John Brown's raid on Harper's Ferry, the Civil War, and the urbanization of the West—she is largely absent from the annals of American history.

Historians have traditionally looked to churches, families, slave quarters, and female societies and clubs to trace nineteenth-century black women's history.[2] But these are not the spaces and institutions where Pleasant is most visible. As an abolitionist and businesswoman, much of Pleasant's work remained secretive and hidden. Pleasant chose to

21

mask many of her endeavors, and in so doing obscured her allegiances and her wealth.[3]

In an era when wealthy African-American women were anomalies, Pleasant's fortune and her subsequent interaction with San Francisco's financial elite inspired controversy throughout her life. Her San Francisco business activities ranged from so-called women's work, such as operating boardinghouses, to male-centered endeavors such as investing in quicksilver mines and real estate. She helped finance major enterprises that shaped the Western economy in the second half of the nineteenth century, often employing tactics common to this era of robber barons: stock speculation and inside trading. But while utilizing the tactics normally associated with the Rockefellers and Carnegies of the era, Pleasant also used strategies that fell outside the realm of traditional business practices—strategies most often practiced by those on the margins of the economy.[4] Parlaying businessmen's secrets revealed in her boardinghouses into capital became one of her most successful techniques.

Pleasant published her autobiography in 1901 in the short-lived journal, the *Pandex of the Press*. In this brief narrative, she carefully revealed select details of her past:

> I was born on the nineteenth day of August, 1814. Some people have reported that I was born in slavery, but as a matter of fact I was born in Philadelphia, at number 9 Barley Street. My parents, as nearly as I know, must have been a strange mixture. My father was a native Kanaka and my mother a full-blooded Louisiana negress. Both were of large frame, but I think I must have got my physical strength from my father, who was, like most of his race, a giant in frame.[5]

Pleasant's focus on race and physical characteristics and the vagueness about her youth sparked tremendous speculation. Some biographers claim she masked her slave status, while others believe that she was freeborn. It was not unusual for African-Americans to conceal their slave past. Fugitive slaves in particular had to hide, steal, and conceal themselves and their identities after the passage of the Fugitive Slave Act in 1850.[6] Pleasant's relationship to slavery remains a strong, if uncertain, part of her legacy: she is purported by some to have been born a slave, to have alerted slaves to John Brown's raid, and to have hidden escaped slaves in California. Although we can be fairly sure of the last two points, there is no evidence available that confirms Pleasant's status at birth.[7] Given the multiplicity of tales that surface regarding Pleasant's birthplace and slave status, it seems safe to assume that she did not want the details revealed or did not know the details herself.

As a young girl, Pleasant worked on the island of Nantucket for a woman named Mary Hussey. In her autobiography, Pleasant invested these years with tremendous significance in terms of shaping her future in business:

> I was a girl full of smartness and quick at coming back at people when they tried to have a little fun talking with me. I suppose I got in the habit of talking too much, for when young people find they can raise a laugh they are liable to talk too much. ... All this brought customers to the shop, and I would call people in and get them to buy things of me. I was always on the watch, and few people ever got by that shop without buying something of me.[8]

Although Pleasant highlighted her skills and business acumen, it is also the case that she, like many free and enslaved African-Americans, struggled to educate herself.

Pleasant bemoaned the fact that she was refused a formal education. "When my father sent me to live with the Husseys, he also gave them ... plenty of money to have me educated, but they did not use it for that purpose," she explained, "and that's how I came to have no education."[9] Although there were schools for girls on the island in the 1820s and 1830s, they were not open to African-Americans.[10]

Pleasant married in the late 1830s or early 1840s.[11] In an 1895 interview she described her first husband, James Smith, as "a foreman, carpenter and contractor, who had a good business and possessed considerable means."[12] There is little agreement about James Smith's identity and background; some described him as European, others claimed he was Cuban born.[13] One characteristic of the first husband, about which all the sources agree, however, is his penchant for abolitionist work. Whatever his background, Smith committed himself to the fight against slavery. When he died in 1844, he was a wealthy man whose will left at least $15,000 to his wife, Mary Ellen, for the purpose of continuing their abolitionist endeavors.[14]

Between the death of her first husband and her arrival in San Francisco during the Gold Rush, Mary Ellen met and married a man named John James Pleasants. Stories about his background are as murky as those about the first husband. Mary Ellen testified in court in the 1860s that she had married John in 1847 in Nantucket.[15] Census records reveal that John was born in Virginia and that he was a waiter in New Bedford, Massachusetts, in 1850. It is possible that Mary Ellen and John met in New Bedford, a hotbed of abolitionist activity where others, including Frederick Douglass, took refuge.[16]

With the discovery of gold in California in 1848, the possibilities for African Americans seemed limitless. Like thousands of other migrants, the Pleasants were tempted by stories of riches that could be had in the new territory of the United States. The dangers of the Fugitive Slave Law of 1850 also propelled them west. Stories of free blacks being harassed or enslaved were common after the bill became law. Certainly the fact that California became a free, rather than slave, state in 1850 made it more attractive to abolitionists like the Pleasants, who were leaving the East. The combination of economic opportunities and sweeping social changes may have encouraged the Pleasants to seek a new home in the far West.[17]

Mary Ellen and John may not have always lived together during their marriage. She set up house with John Pleasants—later the "s" was dropped—in California. By 1865, John was listed in the San Francisco directory as a resident and cook on the steamship *Orizaba*. Whatever their precise arrangement, Mary Ellen and John Pleasant would set up house together intermittently for over twenty years, work together as abolitionists in Canada, and launch a legal battle against discrimination in California in the 1860s.

In 1866, Mary Ellen and John Pleasant initiated a lawsuit against the North Beach & Mission Railroad Company (NBMRR). They accused NBMRR of refusing to allow people of African descent to board their streetcars. By initiating this lawsuit, Mary Ellen Pleasant also joined a concerted effort on the part of black San Franciscans to end discrimination and harassment on the city's streetcars. Pleasant's litigation against NBMRR lasted for nearly two years. The first hearing resulted in a victory; the Twelfth District Court determined that Pleasant was "willfully and purposefully deprived by the defendant of the exercise of a plain legal right," and awarded Pleasant $500 in damages. The company appealed and the case was heard before the California Supreme Court. Reversing Pleasant's victory, the state supreme court ruled in favor of the streetcar company, finding that the damages awarded in the lower court had been excessive. Although Pleasant argued that she had suffered damages to mind and body, the court was not convinced. In the post–Civil War era, damages inflicted on African-Americans by Jim Crow laws and white supremacy were immense, and Pleasant's effort to draw attention to these was successful, if not legally sanctioned.[18]

Pleasant's insistence on equal treatment on public transportation in the 1860s politicized public space during the era of Reconstruction. Throughout the next three decades, Mary Ellen Pleasant would fight several battles in San Francisco's public arenas—especially the courtrooms. Demanding her rights as a citizen remained a constant focus of Pleasant's life. Her public appearances in court made headlines throughout the century. This is the place, paradoxically, where her power and status were most visible; it is also the place where she would be stripped of both.

The year that the state supreme court overturned Pleasant's streetcar case (1868) was also the first year that she listed herself as a boarding-house keeper in the city directory. In previous years, she described her occupation as a "domestic." This indicates an important shift in Pleasant's occupation, but also in her self-perception and in the way she presented herself to the public. Pleasant transformed herself from a worker to an entrepreneur—a transition very few black women of her day experienced. Most San Franciscans knew Mary Ellen Pleasant as a boarding-house keeper, a role not unusual for African-American women of the era.[19] The occupation of boardinghouse keeper was the one most San Franciscans recognized as the role that best described Mary Ellen Pleasant. It also meshed nicely for some with the stereotype of the mammy—the other role with which she is most often associated.

In 1869, Pleasant moved to 920 Washington Street, where she established a boardinghouse that would be her most successful and most elaborate business enterprise.[20] Its proximity to San Francisco's central plaza meant that Pleasant's business and her presence were public entities. The plaza, officially called Portsmouth Square, bordered Washington, Kearny, Clay, and Dupont (now Grant) Streets; Pleasant's establishment was on the corner of Washington and Dupont. Her property was strategically placed near the city hall, the opera, and the largest gambling house, to attract the city's businessmen, politicians, and investors.[21] Pleasant's forays to the markets, banks, shops, and courts, could be easily observed from the city center, as could the galas and meetings that took place at 920 Washington Street.

Although operating boardinghouses was a common occupation for women in San Francisco, Pleasant, more than any other female inn-keeper or boardinghouse operator, maintained high visibility among the city's elite. According to one source, 920 Washington Street was known for its "fine food and wines and its mysterious, lavishly furnished upstairs rooms."[22] This house, temporarily the home of several of the state's leading politicians, brought Pleasant political as well as financial capital. When Newton Booth, one of Pleasant's admirers and a boarder at Washington Street, was elected the new governor of California in 1871, Pleasant threw a party and boasted, "this is Governor Booth who has been elected from my house."[23]

According to the 1870 census, Pleasant owned at least $15,000 worth of real estate and had $15,000 in personal assets. While she invested in both gold and silver mines, Pleasant also profited by providing a private venue for the most successful investors of the day: the Bonanza Kings and their compatriots who demanded exclusive establishments in which to conduct their business transactions.[24] These men frequented her boardinghouses and revealed information—financial and social—that Pleasant used to further her own enterprise. Pleasant's use of information heard within these private spaces to further her own businesses played on the naive assumptions of her clientele, that "domestics" would not understand financial affairs.[25] The ways Pleasant exploited gendered and racialized codes of behavior constituted one of her most profitable strategies.

Pleasant entered into a new phase of her life in the 1870s. She continued to buy property and appear at philanthropic functions associated with the city's African-American institutions, but moved her home and headquarters to a hill above the city center.[26] At a time when many African-Americans across the nation experienced a retreat from civil rights and the promise of citizenship, Pleasant reached her financial zenith. Pleasant's experience, and that of other black female entrepreneurs like banker Maggie Lena Walker, shifts the traditional periodization that interprets Reconstruction as an era solely associated with African-American defeat.[27]

Pleasant benefited directly and indirectly from the huge profits made during the Comstock mining boom in the 1860s and 1870s. The San Francisco Stock Exchange opened in 1862 in response to Nevada's emerging silver industry, and profits from the Comstock transferred directly to San Francisco bankers and investors.[28] Pleasant's rise to prominence in financial and philanthropic circles can, in part, be attributed to this general economic trend. A keen manipulator of real estate and mining stock, Pleasant also associated with members of the elite investors in the Comstock and other silver mines. Her fortune and her livelihood became linked with one banker in particular: Scottish immigrant Thomas Bell, the vice president of the Bank of California, the financial institution that amassed the greatest profits from the Comstock.[29] Pleasant and Bell had met earlier, and by the 1870s they had become financial partners while he took quarters in her new mansion.

The house that Pleasant built straddled the corner of Octavia and Bush Streets just west of the city's business district. This opulently furnished, multistoried Victorian mansion inspired fantastic speculation regarding its worth. Historian Lerone Bennett values the house at $100,000 at the time of construction, sometime in 1877. This seems likely, given the size of the house which boasted over ten rooms, and the fact that the property encompassed two city blocks.[30] Pleasant's mansion and Thomas Bell's residence in it made for intense speculation by her contemporaries. The press quickly labeled her residence the "House of Mystery" and never ceased remarking on its secrets. Long after her death in 1904 the Pleasant mansion continued to fascinate San Franciscans. In 1939, San Francisco author and newspaper columnist, Charles Dobie, wrote:

> Just to pass this house inspired me with an exquisite terror. Its mystery was not the mystery of ghosts but the mystery of flesh and blood enchantment. People were reputed to live beneath its frowning mansard roof but the only person I ever saw emerge was the black witch who held them all enthralled.[31]

Typical of much popular culture that takes Pleasant as its subject, this passage associates her with witchcraft and danger.[32]

Speculation about a sexual liaison between Pleasant and Bell subsided when he married a young protégé of Pleasant's, Teresa Clingan. After 1878, the three of them, and eventually the Bell children, all lived in the house Pleasant built on Octavia Street. Pleasant was assumed by many to be the "mammy" of the household, with Thomas and Teresa Bell serving as master and mistress. This masquerade proved to be advantageous for Pleasant, at least for a time. Disguising herself as the household servant, Pleasant in fact managed a vast economic enterprise involving multiple properties, tenants, and investments.

Pleasant's account books from this period reveal the vast sums required to maintain the Octavia Street house. She spent exorbitant sums on supplies for the house including lumber, water, dairy products, and meat, as well as finery like lace and jewelry.[33] San Franciscans watched Pleasant bargain and trade all over town. Customarily, Pleasant would travel in her carriage driven by coachman James Allen, "dressed in a livery of a long black coat, white breeches, and a top hat."[34] Pleasant's visits to town with liveryman and horses in tow were familiar sights in Gilded Age San Francisco; they would become even more so as she entered into the most publicized role of her life: witness and confidante of Sarah Althea Hill.

Although Pleasant's streetcar case had generated statewide notoriety among civil rights advocates, her courtroom appearances in the 1880s would attract the attention of columnists and legal pundits across the country.[35] Sarah Althea Hill, an Irish-American woman, sued William Sharon, one of the West's wealthiest men, for divorce. The resulting litigation, in which Pleasant played a central role, took on a circuslike atmosphere.[36] Pleasant's status, her place in San Francisco society, and her financial power became fodder for columnists for the rest of her life.

The first case, *Sharon v. Sharon*, hinged on the question of whether or not Sharon and Hill had been legally married in August of 1880. Mary Ellen Pleasant testified that she had seen the marriage contract. Sarah's relationship to Mary Ellen Pleasant proved a substantial issue for Sharon's defense team, led by attorney William Barnes. In March of 1884, Barnes's opening statement including the following declaration:

> We will show how [Sarah] visited the sanctums of fortune tellers, negroes, Germans, French and every race. We shall show how she obtained a pair of Sharon's dirty socks and had them charmed by a negro. ... She disclosed her secrets to a colored woman and did not confide in a relative.[37]

This legal strategy of linking African-Americans with the occult and using Sarah's contact with Pleasant, in particular, to discredit her, was the premise on which the defense built its case. Sarah Hill's choice of Pleasant as her chief confidante proved her singular lack of judgment, argued Sharon's attorneys. "Will anybody tell me," asked Barnes, "why it was that this unfortunate woman confided the secret of her marriage to not one respectable person of her color, class, or rank in life?"[38]

Pleasant's role in the divorce case carried considerable weight, as demonstrated by Sharon's efforts to discredit her. Attorneys summoned her to the witness stand on at least five occasions. Although accused of operating a ring of voodoo practitioners to trick Sharon into marriage, Pleasant's testimony had nothing to do with potions or charms, but focused on the viability of the marriage contract.

Descriptions of Pleasant's significance in the case varied; in the early days of the trial Barnes described her as peddler of "luxurious articles of female underwear."[39] After a full year of legal battles, however, Barnes reasoned that Pleasant was "the sole financier of the anti-Sharon syndicate."[40] The shift in emphasis is noteworthy; initially the defense employed slavelike imagery of a lace-peddling mammy to describe Pleasant. But by 1885, this image had been replaced by one of a crafty manipulator of the legal system.

On December 24, 1884, the judge ruled that the marriage contract was valid and Sarah was thus entitled to a divorce and alimony. He awarded Sarah $2,500 a month and $55,000 in attorneys fees.[41] A federal decision soon overturned Sarah's brief victory, marking the end of Pleasant and Hill's effort to wrest Sharon of his fortune.[42] Following Sharon's death in 1885, Sarah married one of her attorneys, former California Supreme Court Justice David Terry. When Terry was murdered in 1889, Sarah's health rapidly declined. By 1892, journalists described her as "hopelessly insane." Pleasant attended to Sarah at the house on Octavia Street. Mrs. Sarah Terry told reporters that Pleasant's house provided her sanctuary.[43] And although Mary Ellen Pleasant survived the Sharon trials with person and property intact, members of the Bell household were waiting in the wings to divest her of both. In addition to the mansion on Octavia Street, Pleasant in 1891 bought Beltane, a sprawling ranch in the Sonoma Valley where she spent weekends and holidays.[44] Then in her eighties, Pleasant experienced long periods of illness, as evidenced by the house calls of her physician, Peter A. Kearney.[45] Friends and well-wishers traveled to the ranch and to her San Francisco home for regular visits. But Pleasant's relationship with her boarders and co-mortgage holders, the Bells, deteriorated in these years, as did Pleasant's mask as the Bells' servant.

After nearly two decades of living in the mansard-roofed mansion on Octavia Street, the family and business enterprise of Thomas Bell, Teresa Bell, the Bell children, and Mary Ellen Pleasant collapsed. In 1897, five years after Thomas Bell had died, the eldest of the Bell children, Fred, petitioned the courts to have his mother removed as legal guardian of the children.[46] The petition charged that Teresa Bell's business affairs were "being controlled and directed by … M. E. Pleasant, who is a negro woman at the age of eighty-three years or thereabouts, and neither fit or a proper person to guide, control, or direct any person other than herself."[47] The petition forced Pleasant, once again, to appear before judges, reporters, and onlookers. Angered by the accusations, she told reporters what she thought of Fred's case: "this suit has been brought by Fred because some enemies of ours have urged him on, and his action is too shameful to speak about."[48]

Fred Bell's legal action brought Pleasant's financial and personal relationship to the Bells under extensive scrutiny for the first time. As in the Sharon trials, her name was splashed across newspaper headlines and, once again, the press scrutinized her relationship to a white woman— this time Teresa Bell. The issue of Pleasant's control over Teresa drove Fred's case from the beginning. As Fred's attorney explained, "[Fred] wants to destroy the power of 'Mammy' Pleasant and show her up to people in her true colors."[49] Previously described as the servant of the Bell household, newspaper accounts now characterized her in more sinister terms. One headline captured the new interpretation of Pleasant's role: "Porterhouse for Mammy, Soup Meat for the Family." According to one of the servants, Pleasant and Teresa Bell "fared sumptuously on Oysters, terrapin, chickens, quail, and porterhouse steaks," while the children were fed stale bread. Pleasant, explained the servant, "ran the whole house to suit herself."[50] There was more than a grain of truth to this depiction since the house in question belonged to Pleasant.

Pleasant's description of herself in this case varied little from the one she gave during the Sharon trials: she characterized herself as a servant of the Bell household. When questioned about Teresa Bell's presence, she described Mrs. Bell as her "mistress," and "the noble woman." Pleasant's reputation as a simple servant, however, repeatedly came under attack during the litigation.

The courtroom was not the only place Pleasant took center stage in the 1890s. She was also the subject of several press exposés, most notably a two-page feature article in a Sunday edition of the *San Francisco Chronicle* titled "Queen of the Voodoos." This piece appeared as Pleasant's creditors whittled away at her fortune and successfully rendered her an "insolvent debtor" in the city's courts. In addition to describing bizarre voodoo rituals that Pleasant supposedly used on unsuspecting victims of her greed, the article questioned Pleasant's poverty, thus exacerbating her financial problems. The author by all accounts, James E. Brown Jr., a former employee of Pleasant's, drew attention to Pleasant's efforts to dodge her creditors.[51] With such knowledge coming from someone close to Pleasant, it is hardly surprising that her fortune dwindled quickly in the years to come.

Pleasant responded to the various allegations as best she could. While contesting the claim that she practiced voodoo, Pleasant through a letter to one of the judges in Fred Bell's lawsuit attempted to explain her role in the financial affairs of the Bell family. "Mr. Bell would have soon silenced those who said I had too much influence," she wrote, "I have a good deal to say about the executors and lawyer for the Bell estate— selling [the] assets to pay their own debts."[52] Determined to rescue her diminished fortune and tarnished reputation, Pleasant lashed out at the courts, lawyers, and creditors. "I have said to them, to the principals themselves … I would rather be a corpse than a coward!" She wrote the judge, "now this woman who has respect for the right and the truth would like to have you use your influence." The judge quickly silenced Pleasant, deeming her role in managing the financial affairs of the Bell estate inappropriate given her status as a "servant."[53] Moreover, having disguised for years her ownership of the Octavia Street house as well as mining stocks and other assets by commingling her property with the holdings of Thomas Bell, it was now impossible for her to establish her rightful claim to the mansion. After a series of subsequent lawsuits and a dramatic break with Teresa Bell, Mary Ellen Pleasant lost control of her Octavia Street house and moved to her other properties.

Pleasant lived the last five years of her life at Geneva Cottage, her residence on San Jose Road, just south of San Francisco, and in a house she owned on Webster Street. The *San Francisco Examiner* claimed that she raised chickens and pigs at Geneva Cottage during these years as part of her effort to feign poverty.[54] In November 1903, Pleasant moved to the home of friends, Olive and Lyman Sherwood, who resided on Filbert Street. On January 11, 1904, at ten in the morning, Pleasant died at the home of her friends. Peter A. Kearney, her longtime physician, signed the death certificate. Pleasant's estate, when it was finally settled six years later, was valued at $10,000—a far cry from the millions she once owned.[55]

By the end of her life, Mary Ellen Pleasant had lost a considerable amount of property and capital to creditors and lawyers. Due to the tangled nature of the Bell and Pleasant finances, and the fact that she owned much of her property in partnership with others, the exact amount of her estate will never be known. Given that Thomas Bell was worth over $30 million when he died in 1892—and Bell and Pleasant owned stock and property in common—we can assume that Pleasant was at least a millionaire, making her unusual among nineteenth-century black women, and certainly among black women in the West.[56]

Mary Ellen Pleasant continues to fascinate San Franciscans and the press. This powerful financier provided fodder for novelists, filmmakers, and columnists throughout the twentieth century. Pleasant thought she had a better chance at holding onto her enterprise by claiming the mask of mammy—the one role most white Americans recognized as appropriate for black women in Victorian America. But the few wealthy African-American women of the era were easy targets for those concerned with maintaining white supremacy and, in this regard, Pleasant's mask provided no protection.

NOTES

1. Lerone Bennett, "An Historical Detective Story: The Mystery of Mary Ellen Pleasant, Part I" *Ebony*, April–May 1979, 90–96, 71–86.
2. Darlene Clark Hine, "Lifting the Veil, Shattering the Silence: Black Women's History in Slavery and Freedom," in *The State of Afro-American History: Past, Present, and Future*, ed. Darlene Clark Hine (Baton Rouge: Louisiana State University Press, 1986), 223–249.
3. For an incisive discussion on African-American women and self-fashioning, see Nell Irvin Painter, *Sojourner Truth: A Life, A Symbol* (New York: W. W. Norton, 1996).
4. On black entrepreneurship, see Juliet E. K. Walker, "Racism, Slavery, and Free Enterprise: Black Entrepreneurship in the United States," *Business History Review* 60 (autumn 1986): 343–82.
5. Mary Ellen Pleasant, "Memoirs and Autobiography," *Pandex of the Press* 1 (January 1902): 5.
6. For an example of slaves who disguised themselves to escape, see the chapter on William and Mary Craft in R. J. M. Blackett, *Beating against the Barriers: The Lives of Six Nineteenth-Century Afro-Americans* (Baton Rouge: Louisiana State University Press, 1986), 86–137.

7. Pleasant lived for a time in Chatham, Canada, where John Brown and other abolitionists planned the raid on Harper's Ferry. She became a part of this community and donated her time and probably her resources to Brown's cause. See Sam Davis, "How a Colored Woman Aided John Brown," *Inquirer and Mirror* 26 (December 1901); Earl Conrad, "She was a Friend of John Brown," *Negro World Digest*, November 1940, 6–11; and J. Peter Ripley, *The Black Abolitionist Papers II* (Chapel Hill: University of North Carolina Press, 1986), 393, 398.

8. Pleasant, "Memoirs," 5.

9. Ibid., 6.

10. Barbara Linebaugh, "The African School and the Integration of Nantucket Public Schools, 1825–1847" (Boston: Afro-American Studies Center, 1978).

11. Some believe Pleasant and Smith were married in St. Mary's Church in Boston. Pleasant claimed she sang in the choir of Saint Mary's. See Sam Davis, "How a Colored Woman Aided John Brown."

12. *San Francisco Examiner,* 13 October 1895.

13. Bennett, "An Historical Detective Story, Part II," 72–73.

14. The sum of money bequeathed to her by her first husband is also the subject of wild speculation. Many claim that it was as much as $30,000; one source claims it was $40,000. And one San Francisco author alleged that the amount was $45,000. Pleasant told a reporter that she brought $15,000 in gold coin with her from the East when she traveled to California in 1850. Even the latter amount would have been a tremendous sum for anyone to invest in the Gold Rush era. See J. Lloyd Conrich, "The Mammy Pleasant Legend," unpublished manuscript, no date, California Historical Society, 19; and Bennett, "An Historical Detective Story, Part II," 74.

15. *Pleasants v. North Beach and Mission Railroad Company,* Appeal, 1867, California State Archives, Sacramento. Pleasant said that after her first husband died, she went back to Nantucket to live with Edward and Phoebe Gardner. See Helen Holdredge letter to Edward Stackpole, 9 April 1951, Nantucket Historical Association. This letter, like many of Holdredge's notebooks, indicates that Holdredge had access to Pleasant's diaries or letters, which are now missing or destroyed.

16. 1850 Bristol County Census, roll 309: 272; New Bedford was the destination of many fugitive slaves on the Underground Railroad, including Frederick Douglass. Douglass first took refuge at the home of David Ruggles in New York, who suggested he might find New Bedford more hospitable for fugitive slaves. See Frederick Douglass, *Narrative of the Life of Frederick Douglass,* in *The Classic Slave Narratives,* ed. Henry Louis Gates Jr., ed., (New York: Penguin, 1987), 323–26.

17. To date, one of the studies that best illuminates the intricacies of the process of conquest in California is Lisbeth Haas, *Conquests and Historical Identities in California, 1769–1936* (Berkeley: University of California Press, 1995).

18. See *John and Mary Pleasants v. NBMRR,* June 20, 1867, California State Archives, Sacramento. Several other cases of streetcar discrimination in San Francisco occurred before Pleasant's case. See the *Pacific Appeal,* 10 May 1862, and 14 March 1863. When, nearly a century later, California revised its civil rights legislation, Pleasant's case was brought to the fore. A 1958 article in the *Stanford Law Review* cited *Pleasants v. NBMRR* to demonstrate that "an aggrieved party faces an almost insurmountable burden of proof in seeking to show that a refusal to admit him to, or a discrimination in the use of facilities of, or entertainment resulted in measurable damages for which he is entitled to compensation." See Ronald P. Klein, "Equal Rights Statutes," *Stanford Law Review* 10 (March 1958): 253–73.

19. On the role of African-American women as boardinghouse keepers, see Michael Coray, "Blacks in the Pacific West, 1850–1860: A View from the Census," *Nevada Historical Society Quarterly* 28 (summer 1985): 109–10; Mikel Hogan Garcia, "Adaptation Strategies

of the Los Angeles Black Community, 1883–1919," (Ph.D. dissertation, University of California, Irvine, 1985), 50; and Elizabeth H. Pleck, *Black Migration and Poverty: Boston 1865–1900* (New York: Academic Press, 1979), 191.

20. *San Francisco City Directory*, 1869–1870.

21. For a description of the plaza, see, Philip J. Ethington, *The Public City: The Political Construction of Urban Life in San Francisco* (Cambridge: Cambridge University Press, 1994), 6–7.

22. Gunther Barth, *Instant Cities: Urbanization and the Rise of San Francisco and Denver* (Albuquerque: University of New Mexico Press, 1988), 298; Margaret S. Woyski, "Women and Mining in the Old West," *Journal of the West* 20 (April 1981): 44; Conrich, "The Mammy Pleasant Legend," 46.

23. The U.S. Census of 1870 lists Newton Booth as a resident of 920 Washington Street, San Francisco; Bennett, "An Historical Detective Story, Part II," 79.

24. Much of Pleasant's mining activities must be inferred from the sources due to her complicated financial relationship with Thomas Bell. See Mary Ellen Pleasant Collections, San Francisco Public Library (SFPL) and the Bancroft Library, University of California, Berkeley, California.

25. For a fascinating, although fictional, account of this particular strategy of Pleasant's, see Frank Yerby, *Devilseed* (Garden City, NY: Doubleday, 1984), 175–76.

26. For information on Pleasant's philanthropic activities, see, for example, the *Pacific Appeal* 10 September 1870, 19 November 1870, 1 January 1871, 2 September 1871, 30 August 1873, and 9 May 1874.

27. Elsa Barkley Brown, "Womanist Consciousness: Maggie Lena Walker and The Independent Order of Saint Luke," *Signs* 14 (Spring 1989): 610–33.

28. William Issel and Robert W. Cherny, *San Francisco: Politics, Power, and Urban Development, 1865–1932* (Berkeley: University of California Press, 1986), 23.

29. Bennett describes Pleasant as "that brilliant and knowing manipulator of Western mining stock," and claims that she turned Bell into a "financial tiger." Bennett, "An Historical Detective Story, Part II," 84.

30. Bennett, "An Historical Detective Story, Part II," 84; Mary Ellen Pleasant Collection, SFPL.

31. Charles Caldwell Dobie, *San Francisco: A Pageant* (New York: D. Appleton-Century, 1939), 316.

32. See Lynn M. Hudson, "When 'Mammy' Becomes a Millionaire: Mary Ellen Pleasant, an African-American Entrepreneur," (Ph.D. dissertation, 1996, Indiana University), chapter 5.

33. Mary Ellen Pleasant Papers, Bancroft Library, University of California, Berkeley, and SFPL.

34. Interview with Charlotte Downs, Mary Ellen Pleasant Collection, SFPL. Downs knew Pleasant when she was a little girl and told author Helen Holdredge, "I was in and out of the Bell house from the time it was built."

35. Robert Kroninger, *Sarah and the Senator* (Berkeley, CA: Howell-North Books, 1964), 15. Kroninger notes that "with the aid of the new nationwide wire service," newspapers across the country followed the trials.

36. For the purpose of clarity, I will refer to Sarah Althea Hill as Hill, although she claimed to be "Mrs. Sharon," and was eventually Mrs. Terry. Soon after Hill sued Sharon for divorce, resulting in *Sharon v. Sharon*, Mr. Sharon countered with a suit in federal court, *Sharon v. Hill.*

37. Transcript of W. H. L. Barnes, *Sharon v. Sharon*, San Francisco Superior Court, 1884, Bancroft Library.

38. Ibid.

39. Ibid.

40. Transcript of argument of William M. Stewart, *Sharon v. Hill*, Ninth District, 1885, Bancroft Library.
41. Kroninger, *Sarah and the Senator*, 158.
42. See Transcript on Appeal, *Sharon v. Sharon*, California Supreme Court, 1885, California State Archives.
43. *San Francisco Chronicle*, 14 February 1892.
44. Mary Ellen Pleasant Collection, SFPL. See also Thomas and Teresa Bell papers, California Historical Society, San Francisco.
45. Teresa Bell Diary, Mary Ellen Pleasant Papers, SFPL.
46. There were six Bell children, ranging in age from 22 to 13 years of age, at the time of the trial.
47. As quoted in the *San Francisco Call*, 15 September 1897.
48. *San Francisco Chronicle*, 9 September 1897.
49. Ibid.
50. *San Francisco Chronicle*, 10 September 1897; *San Francisco Chronicle*, 16 September 1897.
51. *San Francisco Chronicle*, 9 July 1899.
52. As quoted in *San Francisco Call*, 9 November 1899.
53. Ibid.
54. *San Francisco Examiner*, 12 January 1904.
55. *San Francisco Call*, 16 April 1910; Conrich, "The Mammy Pleasant Legend," 177.
56. By comparison, the estate of Los Angeles entrepreneur Biddy Mason, also a black woman, was valued at $300,000 in 1896. See Lawrence B. De Graaf, "Race, Sex, and Region: Black Women in the West, 1850–1920," *Pacific Historical Review* 49 (May 1980): 285–313; see also, Loren Schweninger, "Property-Owning Free African-American Women in the South, 1800–1870," *Journal of Women's History* 1 (winter 1990): 13–44; and Willard Gatewood, *Aristocrats of Color: The Black Elite, 1880–1920* (Bloomington: Indiana University Press, 1990).

Fig. 2.1 Sarah Winnemucca in Victorian dress. Reprinted by permission of the Nevada Historical Society.

2

RAPE NARRATIVES ON THE NORTHERN PAIUTE FRONTIER: SARAH WINNEMUCCA, SEXUAL SOVEREIGNTY, AND ECONOMIC AUTONOMY, 1844–1891

Rosemarie Stremlau

In April 1860, while Northern Paiute elders and leaders met in council at Pyramid Lake to determine how best to respond to the non-Indian invasion of their homeland and the destruction of their resource base, Northern Paiute families carried on their day-to-day subsistence work as best they could. Searching for one of their most important food sources, two young Northern Paiute women gathered roots near Williams's Station, a settlers' trading post. Several white men seized the girls, dragged them into a barn, and repeatedly gang raped them. The men, Oscar Williams, David Williams, Samuel Sullivan, and John Flemming, held the young women captive, and when the girls' families came searching for them, the men denied having seen them and threatened to shoot whoever continued to scout around their homestead for evidence of the girls. Their posturing was ineffective, however; the Northern Paiute men heard their women's screaming, and they would retaliate.[1]

In Sarah Winnemucca's autobiography, such stories of sexual victimization are as much a part of the Northern Paiute experience as their

37

seasonal hunting and gathering cycle. In particular, Winnemucca described how sexual violence characterized many white men's relations with the Native American women and girls whom they considered racially and culturally inferior and economically marginal. But Winnemucca's life story should not be read as a police blotter detailing individual crimes. Her vivid descriptions of sexual violence suggest how Native people experienced and responded to interracial rape, and her stories of rape point to larger themes in Northern Paiute adaptation. Winnemucca posited that the Northern Paiutes' best chance at survival lay not in assimilation to white culture but in the restoration of their economic autonomy, symbolized by women's ability to work without fear of sexual assault.

Born in approximately 1844 near the Humboldt River in what is today western Nevada, Sarah Winnemucca grew to adulthood in a world turned upside down by rapid, unprecedented change. While the Northern Paiutes had never met an American until the late 1840s, by 1859, non-Indians outnumbered her people in their own homeland. Winnemucca lived her life at an interchange of power relations that would confound even the brightest of us. As a young girl, she keenly perceived that gender roles functioned differently in white society than in her own. From her earliest contacts with Americans, she described a culture infused with masculinity and violence and in which the combination of the two equated to power. As an American Indian woman, Winnemucca had no claim to power in the rough West of non-Indian miners, soldiers, and settlers. But in her culture, she did have power, in part because Northern Paiutes valued the work that women did.

Prior to the non-Indian settlement of the Great Basin, the Northern Paiutes practiced an extremely flexible gendered division of labor that enabled them to adapt rapidly to changes in their environment. Their homeland covered over 70,000 square miles in present-day southeastern Oregon, southwestern Idaho, northwestern Nevada, and northeastern California. Microclimatic variation caused environmental diversity, and across the Great Basin, arid, desert landscapes blended into fertile, lush valleys and waterfronts. These Great Basin hunters and gatherers adapted to their environment by diversifying their sources of food and establishing extended kin relations, which enabled communication and cooperation among groups in times of abundance and need. While lean periods were common, starvation was not because Native people utilized such a wide variety of natural resources.[2]

The Northern Paiutes migrated from food source to food source in small families and family groups or clusters. Depending on the availability of resources, a married couple or a set of married siblings and their children composed the core of groups that expanded to include a handful of families and then contracted back to the immediate family group. Households joined together for particular communal subsistence activities, especially the pine nut harvest and rabbit drives, or in particularly rich areas, such as near fisheries. Due to the limited food supplies throughout much of the Great Basin, however, the collective labor of larger groups usually proved a disadvantage over that of an individual or couple. Throughout most of the year, then, families functioned as self-contained units, and the gendered division of labor within families enabled the efficient exploitation of their environment.[3]

Married couples comprised the basic unit of production and social reproduction. Among the Northern Paiutes, marriage was not a private concern between a man and a woman. Instead, married couples produced food and children, and the relationships between husbands and wives also bound kin groups together.[4] Marriage among the Northern Paiutes was a mutually beneficial process rather than an event. When a man visited a woman's home at night and eventually moved his belongings into her home with her consent, the family recognized the couple as married and integrated them into the gendered, adult world of production and reproduction. Marriages ended as informally as they began when husbands moved out of, or were removed from, their wives' homes. Anthropologist Judith Shapiro emphasizes that "it is important to distinguish between the perpetuation of particular unions and the importance of the conjugal bond itself." She explains that while Great Basin societies lacked the economic, social, political, or religious institutions that bound wives to husbands and ensured the permanence of marital unions, these societies valued the economic and social complementarity that husbands and wives provided each other.[5]

At the same time, it would be a mistake to describe marriage among the Northern Paiutes solely as an economic agreement. In lieu of extended families, spouses provided each other with social companionship. In her autobiography, Winnemucca emphasized the bonds of affection between husbands and wives; reciprocity, it seems, was emotional and physical as well as economic. Many relationships lasted for a lifetime. She explained, "They not only take care of their children together, but they do everything together; and when they grow blind, which I am sorry to say is very common, for the smoke they live in destroys their eyes at last, they take sweet care of one another. Marriage is a sweet thing when people love each other."[6]

Married couples divided some tasks and shared others in order to maximize their utilization of local resources. Both spouses' labor was essential to a family's survival, and families formed self-sufficient

Fig. 2.2 Sarah Winnemucca in traditional Native dress. Reprinted by permission of the Nevada Historical Society.

economic units. Men usually hunted, trapped, and fished, but men also worked alongside their female relatives gathering when the needs of the family demanded it. Individually or in small groups, men stalked large game including deer, pronghorn, and bighorn sheep. Alternately, several hunters sometimes worked together to corral a herd of animals and to net rabbits and other small mammals and fish. Northern Paiute men developed a variety of ways to kill: they shot game with poisoned arrows; tracked them with dogs; prayed and sacrificed for them; ambushed them; enchanted them with spiritual power; netted them; snared them; charged at them in disguises; tricked them into entering traps with noises; and set out fishing lines with specified hooks. Winnemucca explained that because they avoided warfare, Northern Paiute conceptions of masculinity were bound up solely with the skills of hunting and fishing, which provided food for their families.[7]

Women typically gathered plants, roots, and nuts, but they also hunted small animals and fished. Their selective utilization of natural resources and development of many specific subsistence technologies for procuring and processing food suggest that Northern Paiute women were skilled laborers. They developed, transmitted, and continuously perfected systems of knowledge that made edible and palatable piñon nuts, acorns, cattails, rice grass, many species of seeds, camas, swamp onion, biscuit roots, bitterroots, other types of roots, buckberries, wolfberries, other fruits and berries, leaves, stalks, and greens. Women also prepared meat and fish for consumption through a variety of techniques, including roasting and making pemmican. Northern Paiute women did not simply harvest the resources in their environment, however; they manipulated it to produce more abundant harvests in the future. They burned unwanted vegetation, pruned and plucked plants, and broadcast seeds. Just as importantly, they prayed and gave offerings to the spirits of the plants and animals that they consumed to ensure plentiful seasons in the future.[8]

Northern Paiute women may have provided the majority of food consumed by their families. Anthropologist Catherine S. Fowler's description of the immediate precontact diet of the residents of Pyramid Lake, including the Northern Paiutes, suggests that women likely provided over half of their families' livelihood and perhaps the most important part. Plants provided a significant percentage of nutrients, and nuts provided valuable fat and protein in a diet otherwise prone to deficiencies.[9] Women were accustomed to spending a significant amount of their time gathering away from men's supervision and protection. These women were independent workers unaccustomed to being sexually harassed.

Northern Paiute women's economic contributions accorded them high status as they wielded both spiritual and political power, often seen as interrelated. Because of their ability to provide food, women had a political voice. Female and male leaders attained spiritual power in one of three ways: through dreams, through inheritance from a powerful, deceased relative, and through visiting foreign, unknown places. Male and female elders made decisions for family groups, and as Winnemucca explained, "The women know as much as the men do, and their advice is often asked. We have a republic as well as you. The council-tent is our Congress, and anybody can speak who has anything to say, women and all." While a political scientist might quibble with her use of the term "republic," her assertion that the entire community participated in decision making through consensus emphasized the egalitarian nature of Northern Paiute society. Notably, Winnemucca went on to explain that women and men sat in different circles in council, but she did not consider this a sign of inferiority. Rather, it was a sign of complementarity and social order.[10]

Northern Paiutes correlated women's productivity and reproductivity, and motherhood also accorded Northern Paiute women status. Whether from the earth or their bodies, women brought forth life, and they were valued for it. Beginning with their first menstruation, young Northern Paiute women underwent a period of seclusion involving fasting, laboring, and bathing in preparation for the roles of wife and mother. Once pregnant, both men and women followed specific taboos intended to insure the well-being of mothers and babies. For men, according to Winnemucca, this included assuming much of women's domestic labor. She wrote:

> If he does not do his part in the care of the child, he is considered an outcast. … All this respect shown to the mother and child makes their parents feel their responsibility, and makes the tie between parents and children very strong. The young mothers often get together and exchange experiences about the attentions of their husbands; and inquire of each other if the fathers did their duty to their children, and were careful of their wives' health.

This attention demonstrates the status accorded to women because of their reproductivity, considered essential to the economic and social health of family groups.[11] Such complementarity fostered a culture of respect between Northern Paiute men and women, one in which violence had no place.

The sudden, unexpected influx of non-Indians into their homeland compromised the Northern Paiutes' natural resources and rendered their seasonal rounds impossible. While they had obtained horses and European goods by the mid to late eighteenth century, Northern Paiutes did not directly contact Europeans or non-Indian Americans until the early nineteenth century. They paid these trappers and traders little mind until the opening of the Oregon Trail and the discovery of gold in California during the 1840s brought thousands of migrants through the heart of their territory. Beginning with the Bidwell-Bartleson party in 1841, the wagon trains and their livestock overtaxed the basin and range ecosystem. Hoping to make a quick profit, traders established posts throughout Northern Paiute territory, and some of these seasonal sites evolved into permanent settlements. In 1859, the discovery of gold and silver in Northern Paiute territory along the Virginia Range and the Owyhee Basin attracted thousands of settlers to the area. The Comstock Lode shifted the demographics of their territory within a few months as a minority population of a few hundred whites exploded into a majority of many thousands. As ethnohistorians Martha C. Knack and Omer C. Stewart explain, "Despite the initial trickle of transients, this onslaught of white domination was sudden, complete, and irreversible. The opportunity for natives to respond and resist was nearly gone before they could even comprehend the threat." Seeking rapid profits, these non-Indians destroyed Native hunting and gathering lands; miners cut down groves of piñon trees for shoring and building mine shafts and diverted streams for flumes; ranchers seized grasslands and water; and town dwellers seized timber and the choicest land.[12]

Women's contributions to the family pot may have taken on increasing importance as non-Indians consumed the natural resources most familiar to them, particularly game, and limited the Northern Paiutes' access to other resources, such as fisheries, by locating their settlements near the rivers and lakes. In response, women's skilled gathering of resources with which non-Indians were unfamiliar became vital to Northern Paiute survival. Thomas Morgan, a white settler, called the Northern Paiutes "seed gatherers" and explained that fishing and hunting were of secondary importance to families who relied instead on gathered, wild food and pemmican made of camas, a root, for survival.[13]

Northern Paiutes responded to the invasion by trying to maintain their seasonal hunting and gathering cycle, but they did so in different ways; some fled away from non-Indians and onto reservations where they tried to survive by supplementing their traditional food sources with rations and agriculture. Others relocated to the margins of non-Indian communities and combined the seasonal cycle with wage labor. Neither response enabled women to adequately gather, fish, or trap to feed their families. Regardless of their choices and however well they adapted to the new extractive, market-oriented economy of the Great Basin, many Northern Paiutes suffered from a new social ill—chronic starvation.

Most Northern Paiutes could not get far enough away from the newcomers. As early as the 1830s, the Northern Paiutes altered their hunting and gathering cycle by going to the mountains in the summer instead of the valleys where they usually gathered in order to avoid contact with non-Indians. In 1859, as miners flooded into the Great Basin, Northern Paiutes began relocating onto reservations. The Pyramid Lake reservation was established in 1859 and the Malheur in 1873, but poverty stalked the reservations, too.[14] Even under the best of circumstances reservations wanted for funding and capable leadership. Sarah Winnemucca, like her father and many other Great Basin leaders, considered reservations no better than death camps. Unable to continue their seasonal hunting and gathering cycle with the necessary regularity, unprepared to farm, often swindled by the agents charged to care for them, and unsupplied with the rations promised in treaties, Great Basin Indians starved on reservations. Winnemucca wrote her autobiography as a condemnation of the corrupt reservation system, and she recalled a heated exchange between Chief Egan and Agent William Reinhart. When Egan begged for the food locked in the agency storehouse: "My children are dying with hunger. I want what I and my people have worked for, that is, we want the wheat." Reinhard replied, "Nothing here is yours. It is all the government's." Like prison camps, reservations condemned Native people, even those who wanted to work to feed their families, to dependency on the government for food. According to Winnemucca, this dependency was emotionally, spiritually, physically, and mentally intolerable to men and women who had been self-sufficient adults just a few years earlier.[15]

Northern Paiutes who settled among non-Indians struggled, too. Forced to adapt and utilize non-Indians as another available resource, Northern Paiutes balanced their seasonal cycle with barter or wage labor in menial jobs. Men cut trees, hauled goods, and tended livestock. Because of the shortage of white women, Indian women easily found domestic work as housekeepers, seamstresses, and laundresses. Northern Paiute women also continued to gather in non-Indian communities, albeit under modified circumstances that hinted at their desperation. In the early 1860s, Pyramid Lake agent Warren Wasson reported that Northern Paiutes survived on barley they "panned" from manure piles in stables. In the Indian shantytown that bordered Virginia City, Northern Pauite women with their gathering baskets rose early to pick rotting food from non-Indian trash piles. Others waited outside the mines for workers to empty the leftovers from their lunch pails into their baskets. Despite their meager resources, Northern Paiute women continued to provide a significant portion of their families' livelihoods through their adaptation of the subsistence round. Still whether they lived on the reservations or in towns, Northern Paiute women were vulnerable to poverty and exploitation.[16]

Winnemucca exemplifies how Northern Paiute women put traditional skills to use at non-traditional work as they adapted to survive in the new Great Basin economy. During her early childhood, Winnemucca learned Northern Paiute women's customary domestic and subsistence tasks; she came to understand a woman's role by helping her mother care for her siblings and their household. For example, she prepared food like cattail pollen cakes and practiced crafts like weaving cattails and sage-brush into baskets for gathering and mats for clothing and shelter. As a teenager, her skill at handiwork enabled her to live by selling needle-work door-to-door in Virginia City. In her early twenties, she worked as a laundress on the reservation. By her thirties, she had saved enough money to purchase a wagon and team, and when not working as a maid, she hired herself out as a teamster, not an unlikely job for a woman who grew up migrating and moving her home among campsites. In the 1870s, as the speaker of five languages; English, Paiute, Shoshone, Spanish, and Washoe; she translated and taught on the reservation. In the late 1870s, having gained familiarity with the territory through the seasonal round, she scouted for the United States Army. Beginning in the 1870s and through the rest of her life, Winnemucca, member of a chiefly family who had attained power in her own right, served as an ambassador and spokeswoman for her people: she wrote letters, visited American political leaders, gave lectures, and wrote her autobiography to obtain provisions and ensure safe communities for the Northern Paiutes. In the late 1880s, she established and ran a school that educated Northern Paiute children in their own and Anglo-American culture. Throughout her adult life, Winnemucca was performing new tasks to achieve the same results that Northern Paiute women had always worked for: to provide for their families.[17]

Poverty was not the only challenge that Northern Paiute women faced; their work as providers for their families also made them vulnerable to sexual assault. Hunting, gathering, and wage work took women beyond the protection of brothers, fathers, and husbands. In this new world following the non-Indian invasion, women's work became particularly unsafe. The influx of whites brought a disproportionate number of non-Indian men without families to Northern Paiute territory. The mining industry created several new types of communities: only corporations had the assets to transport the equipment necessary to procure minerals from bedrock, and these large mines sparked the establishment of towns, such as Virginia City. Other miners worked alone or in small groups and migrated from base camp to base camp. Mining also attracted supporting industries, such as trading and ranching. Bandits and outlaws roamed the basin looking for easy targets to plunder. Soldiers manned military posts established throughout the territory to protect mining interests and keep the peace between Indians and non-Indians. Many of these new non-Indian communities lacked permanent female residents. Northern Paiutes, who had no standing army or labor system that kept men away from women for long periods of time, noted the preponderance of men without women and families with disapproval. In describing the non-Indian settlers of the Carson Valley, Winnemucca identified which men had wives and children and which men lived with other men or alone. As an adult, she also claimed to have traveled for days across the Great Basin without seeing a white woman among all the households at which she stopped for food or rest.[18]

Newcomers to the Great Basin did not appreciate the Northern Paiutes' egalitarian gender roles, and, often without women of their own, they considered Native women to be subject, sexual resources. While they had never seen a Northern Paiute woman before, many white male newcomers to the Great Basin believed that they were experts on the subject of Indian women. Since the colonial era, Anglo-American culture had adopted the image of the "Indian princess" to symbolize virtue, but Americans associated overt, primitive sexuality with her "darker twin," the "squaw." As folklorist Rayna Green has suggested, as far as white men were concerned, "squaws [were] understood as mere economic and sexual conveniences." According to the stereotype, Native women worked like slaves and had sex like animals. Moreover, like their European forebears, Americans claimed sexual access to women, along with other forms of property, as a right of conquest.[19] These beliefs were not limited to men of low status. While recognizing that not all Indian women were "wanton," General Oliver O. Howard, under whom Winnemucca served as a scout and with whom she developed a mutually respectful friendship, commented that he understood why "squaw men" took Indian wives: allegedly the women were compliant and sexually eager.[20]

Some Northern Paiute women utilized their sexuality as another resource that enabled them to survive during this tumultuous period. Many Northern Paiute women, including Sarah Winnemucca and her sister, married white men, perhaps in an effort to broaden their resource base through extending kin ties as Northern Paiutes had always done.

Others worked in a nontraditional industry—sex work. Indian women worked as prostitutes in frontier towns across the West during the Gold Rush. Regardless of whether or not particular Indian women actually were working as prostitutes, the predominance of stereotypes about Indian women's sexuality enabled whites to come to the conclusion that they were. For example, referring to her attempted rape in March of 1875, *The Nevada State Journal* accused Winnemucca of having "been on a jamboree" and receiving visitors late at night. In other words, pointing to behavior they considered to be unladylike, they suggested that she was perhaps prostituting herself because she did not conform to Anglo-American standards of femininity.[21]

The discovery of Comstock Lode sparked a frenzied competition for resources in the Great Basin and created an environment particularly conducive to violence against American Indian women. Historians of rape have argued that sexual violence often occurs at societal flashpoints, places were diverging groups struggle over power and status. In particular, historians have suggested that men rape women whom they consider racially or culturally inferior and economically dependent.[22] In the Humboldt Sink in the 1850s and 1860s, white men looked down on Northern Paiute women, and their economic vulnerability made them more readily accessible. Dismissed by the American legal system, Northern Paiute women were also not likely to bring charges against rapists.

Northern Paiutes, particularly women, competed with settlers and miners for access to the land's resources, and newcomers asserted their claims to the Great Basin by attacking those who claimed it first. As whites became increasingly land-hungry, Native people became more defensive and vocal in demanding protection from the army and the federal government. Each resented the other's claim to the land and what grew on it or lay below the surface. Northern Paiute women could not gather roots in the same land that white men mined for silver. When they occupied the land and raped women who came near their camps and posts, these newcomers discouraged women from continuing their subsistence gathering cycle. White men did not simply rape to satisfy sexual urges; they raped Northern Paiute and other Great Basin Indian women to assert their dominance over them and the kinsmen unable to protect them. It worked. The Northern Paiutes were intimidated. Winnemucca explained, "My people have been so unhappy for a long time they now wish to disincrease, instead of multiply. The mothers are afraid to have more children, for fear they shall have daughters, who are not safe even in their mother's presence."[23]

It is historically and morally important to acknowledge that non-Indian men raped Indian women as part of the conquest of the American West. The Anglo-American West bred a *rape culture,* or a "complex of beliefs that encourages male sexual aggression and supports violence against women." Rape cultures equate domination and violence with sexuality, and in rape cultures women experience sexual violence along a continuum of behavior from economic marginalization to rape and murder. Perpetrators in a rape culture assume their behavior is a normal, inevitable aspect of life. While coined by activists working to end rape in contemporary culture, the term *rape culture* is useful to historians because it reminds us that sexual violence is culturally constructed: not all men across time and place have raped women, and when and where men have raped women, they have not committed rape for the same reasons. Likewise, while they may endure similar physical acts, women experience rape differently in cultures that provide for alternative frameworks for understanding rape other than victimization.[24] That we remember the role of rape in conquest is important, but it as just as important to understand the extent and meaning of Native women's resistance if we want to understand how Native people and their cultures adapted and survived.

Women and men's resistance to sexual violence and retaliation against sexual predators were tied to the Northern Paiutes' efforts to maintain their seasonal cycle and economic self-sufficiency. While they adopted some aspects of American culture, Northern Paiutes rejected non-Indian redefinitions of sexually appropriate behavior, such as female economic dependence and male sexual aggression. They disapproved of sexually aggressive behavior and labeled men who raped as deviant. Northern Paiutes distinguished among non-Indians based, in part, on their treatment of Native women, and many white men behaved quite badly according to Northern Paiute conceptions of masculinity. Throughout her autobiography, Winnemucca alluded to the ever-present threat posed by "bad white men who might harm us" and noted that she and other Northern Paiute leaders complained about the frequency of sexual assaults to American leaders in the hopes that they would take steps to prevent them.[25]

But Winnemucca and the Northern Paiutes did more than plead to outsiders for assistance; they adapted their own lifestyles to prevent sexual attacks on Northern Paiute women and girls. Because they often experienced sexual violence together as family groups, Northern Paiutes rearranged their domestic relationships to better ensure the safety of female family members. Winnemucca described in detail how her family prevented the gang rape of her sister. During her early childhood, her grandfather, Truckee, moved part of her family cluster to California where he and several of her brothers worked for a rancher. Several white ranch hands repeatedly tried to gang rape Winnemucca's older sister, a young teenager. Each night the family fled their camp as the men came for her sister. Fearing violent retaliation themselves, her kinsmen felt that they could not physically defend the girl. One evening, five men came into their camp, and two entered their darkened tent and closed off the exit behind them. Winnemucca's uncles and brothers attacked the men and scared them off, and the family then boarded with their employers away from the rest of the workers. Finally, after the men asked Truckee for the girl outright—a request he scornfully refused—the family decided the terrified girl would no longer work alongside her mother but would spend her days under the direct supervision of her grandmother in camp and away from the dangers women faced as they worked away from the safety of their base camps. The memory of an evening that she lay down sobbing next to her sister and heard the other girl's heart beating through her chest epitomized the ongoing terror that Winnemucca's family felt. Winnemucca recalled, "I as usual began to cry. My poor sister! I ran to her, I saw tears in her eyes." Northern Paiute families experienced sexual violence as a process and a persistent threat instead of as single events.[26]

Just as they had always turned to others for food in times of scarcity, Northern Paiute families looked to established and newly formed social networks for protection from violence. Above all, as exemplified by the above account, Northern Paiute women relied on kin for protection. In her autobiography, Winnemucca offered several examples of Northern Paiute men ensuring the safety of their female relatives. Before Natches, her brother, left her alone at Camp McDermitt, he personally requested that the commanding officer ensure that no soldiers would "abuse her." Winnemucca's cousin Joe accompanied her on part of that trip, in particular, past a house known for its "very bad" residents because "sometimes they would throw a rope over our women, and do fearful things to them." Joe Winnemucca lamented, "Oh, my poor cousin, my heart aches for you, for I am afraid they would do something fearful to you. They do not care for anything. They do most terrible outrageous things to our women."[27] But women also took care of each other. Winnemucca only left her sister-in-law, Mattie, at a military post because she knew her brother would arrive shortly. Families worried about their female members, and they tried to prevent sexual violence.

Northern Paiutes also relied on some newcomers for protection from others. When traveling, Winnemucca took every opportunity to stay in homes occupied by white women, although this was not always possible because of the gender imbalance of the non-Indian community. Winne-mucca emphasized when her hosts were white women and when they were not, and she demonstrated her familiarity with Anglo-American gender conventions by expecting that white women's presence would prevent unwanted sexual attention. Winnemucca also recognized that some white men posed no threat. When traveling, she commented, "No white women on all the places where we stopped—all men—yet we were treated kindly by all of them, so far."[27]

While fearing common soldiers, the Northern Paiutes sought protection from army officers against miners, settlers, and soldiers. Winne-mucca and other Northern Paiute leaders developed close relationships with officers whom they identified as friendly and powerful allies. While scouting for them, Winnemucca accepted the escorts of officers who worried for her safety, but she was more proactive than that: she demanded protection when she felt vulnerable. Perhaps playing into her readers' expectations of feminine vulnerability, she recalled having once pleaded: "Colonel, I am all alone with so many men, I am afraid. I want your protection. I want you to protect me against your soldiers, and I want you to protect my people also."[28] Unable to always prevent attacks, Northern Paiute women resisted sexual assaults the best they could with the options posed by their cultural worldview. Winne-mucca's Anglo-American readers expected women to avoid rape by maintaining a virtuous appearance and reputation, a process that included keeping their bodies fully covered in clothing, appearing in public with appropriate male escorts, and not working outside their homes. While adapting some aspects of their dress, Northern Paiute women did not embrace constrictive gendered expectations of Anglo-American women concerning sexual violence. They continued to work alone or in small groups with other women and without male escort. They continued to gather outside their camps; they had to in order to eat. For Northern Paiute women, to do otherwise, such as send men to gather, made no sense.[29]

When threatened, Northern Paiute women attempted to outrun rapists. Winnemucca recalled an incident that occurred while she and Mattie, her sister-in-law, scouted for Lieutenant Wilkinson. When Wilkinson reluctantly left the women behind to rest, he feared that "something might happen," and something indeed did happen. Three solders noticed the two women alone and remarked, "Catch them, boys, let us have a good time." Feeding her readers' taste for adventure, Winnemucca described her and Mattie's desperate race "over the rocks and down the hills" away from the men, whom she claimed General Howard discharged as a result of the incident.[30] Later, when traveling with her sister, non-Indian men followed the women. The two women resolved to go down fighting if overtaken:

> Away we went, and they after us like wild men. We rode on till our horses seemed to drop from under us. At last we stopped, and I told sister what to do if the whole three of them overtook us. We could not do very much, but we must die fighting. If there were only two we were all right,—we could kill them; if one we would see what he would do. If he lassoed me she was to jump off her horse and cut the rope, and if he lassoed her I was to do the same. If he got off his horse and came at me she was to cut him, and I would do the same for her. Now we were ready for our work.[31]

In the end, Winnemucca and her sister escaped their would-be rapists. Other potential victims sought escape of another kind. Another woman, elderly, sick, and unable to defend herself from the white man who murdered her husband and whom she believed would rape her, prayed for death.[32]

When unable to outrun perpetrators, however, Northern Paiute women attacked them or outsmarted them, proving that successful resistance did not necessarily correspond with physical strength. Winnemucca suggested that Northern Paiute women verbally threatened would-be rapists with physical violence and implied that Northern Paiute women were often armed, and thus, that retaliation could hurt. Winnemucca bragged of breaking an offender's nose. The man, a fellow traveler bunked down near her, suggestively laid his hand on her in the middle of the night, and with one straight punch to his face, Winnemucca shunned his proposition. She bloodied his nose and sent him running for the door while she shouted, "Go away, or I will cut you to pieces, you mean man!"[33] Winnemucca sliced another attempted rapist's face with a knife. On a March evening in 1875, Julius Argasse, a white man, either approached Winnemucca on the street or, according to another account, entered her home. Either way Winnemucca refused him with her knife. She was subsequently arrested, but the judge dismissed the charges against her.[34]

When other options for prevention and redress failed, Northern Paiutes and other Great Basin Natives killed rapists. Military doctor George M. Kober recalled a conversation he had with Winnemucca's father in which the chief blamed the ongoing violence on miners and prospectors who "had no regard for the chastity of Indian women."[35] Winnemucca explained that the rapes of Native women and girls prompted the outbreak of the two Indian wars that she experienced.

The Paiute War of 1860 began when the tribe retaliated against the men who kidnapped and raped the two young women who had been gathering roots. Outraged at the treatment of the young women and the men's initial denial of having seen them, the Northern Paiutes killed the four men. Some local whites considered the men upstanding citizens and led a campaign against the Northern Paiutes that resulted in their confinement at Pyramid Lake reservation by the end of the summer. Others, such as settler Richard N. Allen, believed that the Northern Paiutes' retaliation was justified and clearly in response to a wrong committed by these brothers since nearby settlers were unharmed by the Northern Paiutes.[36]

Winnemucca's account of the Bannock War of 1878 had a similar beginning and an equally short duration. A misunderstanding of an 1868 treaty resulted in stockmen grazing their herds on the Bannock's camas prairie, or as whites called it, the "Kansas Prairie." Tension simmered until May 30, 1878 when, after several white men snuck up on a group of women gathering camas roots and gang raped one of the younger women, several warriors, including the brothers of the victim, retaliated by shooting the suspected rapists. The agent responded by seizing the men's guns and horses, in order to prevent them from going to war, but this also kept them from hunting and thus placed a greater burden on women for gathering.[37] Great Basin Indians fought these wars with the very specific intent of punishing outsiders who violated their sexual mores, undermined women's work, and prevented them from feeding their families.[38]

Winnemucca began her account of the 1860 war with a story suggesting the extent of the Northern Paiutes' refusal to accept non-Indian violence against them. Winnemucca told of a tribe who lived along the Humboldt River hundreds of years before. The Northern Paiutes tried to live alongside them, but these people were fierce warriors—and worse yet, they were cannibals. They were violent and destructive, and Winnemucca concluded, "My people took some of them into their families, but they could not make them like themselves ... So at last they made war on them." Winnemucca explained that her ancestors destroyed these disgusting people.[39] By the late nineteenth century, the Northern Paiutes were in no position to destroy invading non-Indians, but that does not mean they did not resist their own destruction as fiercely. The story of the cannibals suggests the Northern Paiutes' revulsion toward the violence foisted on their world by non-Indians. Far from trying to be like them, they dreamed of exterminating them.

However, by the late 1850s, the Northern Paiutes were unable to purge these offensive outsiders from their homeland, and for many Northern

Paiutes, distance from non-Indians provided the best protection from violence. The Northern Paiutes' rapid acceptance of reservations must be considered in this context. As Leggins and Egan, two chiefs, explained when the government threatened to open part of their reservation land to non-Indian settlement, "And another thing, we do not want to have white people near us. We know what they are, and what they do to our women and daughters."[40]

While accounts of and allusions to rape permeate her autobiography, Winnemucca revealed little information about the victims. The details she provided suggest that sexual violence threatened all Northern Paiute women. Victims were old and young. Some were women that she did not know while others were family. Winnemucca herself survived sexual violence. Notably, nearly all victims were working, somehow trying to provide food for their families, or in Winnemucca's case, for her people. While she appealed to her readers' belief in women's vulnerability, Winnemucca never questioned the chastity or moral character of victims, and she refused to engage in non-Indian culture's debate over Native sexuality or pander to their stereotypes of Native women. Winnemucca's accounts of rape suggest what experts on contemporary sexual violence confirm: rape is not an act of sexual pleasure reflective of the victim's sexual appeal according to societal standards of beauty; rather it is an act of power, domination, and conquest inseparable from its social, economic, racial, cultural, and gendered context. In other words, sexual violence was intertwined with racial and economic oppression.

And Winnemucca understood the connection between them. She told stories about rape to critique American society and to rally outsiders to the Northern Paiutes' cause. More than that, however, Winnemucca's narrations about sexual violence enabled her to envision a return to a world without it. While other members of her tribe took up arms against invaders, Winnemucca waged a war of words in defense of Northern Paiute lifeways.

Beginning in 1870 with a letter that ended up in the hands of the commissioner of the Bureau of Indian Affairs, Winnemucca repeatedly brought the Northern Paiutes' suffering to the attention of outsiders and demanded redress. In the letter, Winnemucca criticized the Bureau of Indian Affairs' plans to relocate the Northern Paiutes to the Malheur reservation. They had fled the Pyramid Lake reservation searching for food, and they took refuge at Fort McDermitt, where they supplemented their gathering with army rations. Because the army provided food and protection, the Northern Paiutes resisted efforts to return to any reservation. At her people's request, Winnemucca wrote letters to influential military and civilian leaders, and then traveled to San Francisco to lecture and to Nevada to lobby politicians. She continued her letter and speaking campaigns following their removal to Malheur and subsequent removals and relocations. Always she pleaded with her readers and listeners for food and land for the Northern Paiutes. In 1880, Winnemucca led a Northern Paiute delegation to Washington, D.C. to meet with Secretary of the Interior Carl Schurz, who directed Indian affairs, in order to obtain the Northern Paiutes' release from their reservations and to secure the allotment of their land into 160-acre plots for each family. Once she returned west and was no longer the subject of stories in eastern newspapers, Schurz failed to deliver on his promises to her. So Winnemucca turned to western newspapers to attack the Bureau of Indian Affairs. In 1883, with the support of Protestant reformers, Winnemucca moved East where she lectured and wrote her autobiography.

Expecting to hear and read titillating accounts of indigenous cultural practices, audiences instead felt their heartstrings pulled by Winnemucca's account of the abuse of Northern Paiute women and girls. By recounting the Northern Paiutes' story, including stories about rape, she generated an enormous amount of sympathy for the Northern Paiutes and aroused anger against the Bureau. Instead of responding to her criticism, the Bureau of Indian Affairs countered with attacks on her character, particularly her chastity. Winnemucca responded by including character references in the conclusion of her autobiography.[41]

Winnemucca's stories of rape did not just generate public sympathy for the Northern Paiutes; they posited solutions to the Northern Paiutes' problems. Historian Miranda Chaytor argues that women's accounts of rape reveal more than the details of their violation because in them, women name the violence, contain it, and identify the people and things that will enable their recovery. When describing rape in the Great Basin, Winnemucca emphasized the vulnerability of women at work, whether gathering for their families' subsistence, like most women, or negotiating and lobbying for food and resources for the whole tribe, like her. For all these women, labor ordered their lives and accorded them status by enabling them to sustain their families. Winnemucca's accounts of rape, therefore, point to what she felt her people had lost that made them so sexually vulnerable—their economic self-sufficiency and autonomy.[42]

Winnemucca lobbied for allotments, therefore, not to enable the Northern Paiutes to assimilate but to facilitate the restoration of their economic self-sufficiency. During the late nineteenth century, reformers endorsed allotment, or the subdivision of communal land and resources among individual male heads of households, as a means to rapidly assimilate Native Americans into Anglo-American culture. They sincerely believed that private land ownership would destroy the extended families that characterized most Native cultures and replace them with patriarchal, nuclear families, complete with a husband in the fields and a wife in the home. Though she recognized that their seasonal cycle was destroyed, Winnemucca did not believe that it was irreplaceable, and she looked to allotment to restore the economic autonomy of Northern Paiute families through ranching and farming. On allotments, Northern Paiute husbands and wives could work sometimes together and other times apart as they had always done in order to maintain their families in the Northern Paiute way.[43]

Winnemucca spent her final years attempting to prove that Northern Paiute families could survive and even thrive on their own small farms. In 1885, her brother, Natches, purchased a 160-acre ranch, and while Natches farmed, Winnemucca established a school. She taught Northern Paiute children reading, writing, and arithmetic, and the children helped Natches with the farming and domestic chores. Most importantly, she treated the children kindly according to Northern Paiute custom and schooled them in Northern Paiute culture. The Peabody Institute, named after an eastern donor, was enormously popular with Northern Paiute students and parents, who abhorred the militarized boarding schools that the government forced Indian children to attend. Natches and Winnemucca's ranch and school blossomed for several years until their financial burden and poor health forced them to close in the summer of 1889. Financially and emotionally exhausted, Winnemucca moved to her sister Elma's ranch where she died in 1891.[44]

During her life and since her death, Winnemucca has been the subject of much controversy. Literary and academic audiences honor Winnemucca as the first Native American woman to write her autobiography, *Life among the Piutes*, but many Native people criticize her for her more ambiguous accomplishments, such as scouting for the United States Army and endorsing assimilationist federal policies, particularly allotment. Some Northern Paiutes disown her for her inability to force the federal government to keep its promises to them, and pointing to her notoriety, they dismiss her as a self-serving opportunist. But other Northern Paiutes emphasize her devotion to their sovereignty and culture, generations before whites recognized the value of indigenous ways of life.[45]

Perhaps Winnemucca remains so controversial because she was a leader ahead of her time. In the 1880s, she denounced the disproportionately high incidence of sexual violence against Native American women, and worked to ease their poverty and dramatize the relationship between sexual and economic oppression. Over a century later, the percentage of Native Americans living below the poverty line is over twice that of other Americans, and Native American women still experience sexual abuse in disproportionately high numbers—3.5 times that of other American racial groups. Moreover, unlike other racial groups, someone of another race assaults 90 percent of American Indian rape victims.[46] But Winnemucca also remains controversial because she defied stereotypes of Native American women as sexually lax and available. She personified their power, rooted in cultures that have not totally adopted American culture's attitudes toward women and their sexuality. Through her autobiography, she made Northern Paiute women's power intelligible to white readers during an era when Anglo-Americans were struggling with the question of women's rights themselves; she provided them with an alternative model of gender relations other than male dominance. Winnemucca proclaimed: "I know what an Indian woman can do. ... My dear reader, I have not lived in this world for over thirty or forty years for nothing, and I know what I am talking bout."[47]

ACKNOWLEDGMENTS

I would like to thank all those who read and commented on this essay, particularly Mike Green, Barbara Hahn, John Hall, Malinda Maynor, Paul Quigley, Theda Perdue, Anna Smith, and Montgomery Wolf.

NOTES

1. Richard N. Allen, *The Tennessee Letters: From Carson Valley, 1857–1860*, comp. David Thompson, compiler (Reno: Grace Dangberg Foundation, 1983), 137–41, 157, 159–60. Myron Angel, *History of Nevada* (Oakland, CA: Thompson and West, 1881; New York: Arno Press, 1973), 150–58. Dan DeQuille, *The Big Bonanza: An Authentic Account of the Discovery, History, and Working of the World-Renowned Comstock Lode of Nevada* (New York: Alfred A. Knopf, 1947), 81–82. Angel identified these men as those killed, but Allen identifies the men killed as the ones guilty of provoking the Northern Paiutes.

2. For a description of the Northern Paiute seasonal cycle, see Catherine S. Fowler and Sven Liljeblad, "Northern Paiute," in *The Handbook of North American Indians, Great Basin*, vol. 11, ed. Warren L. D'Azevedo (Washington, DC: Smithsonian Institution, 1986), 435–65. Martha C. Knack and Omer C. Stewart, *As Long as the River Shall Run: An Ethnohistory of the Pyramid Late Indian Reservation* (Berkeley: University of California Press, 1984), chapter 1. In his memoir, George M. Kober remembers a discussion with Old Winnemucca, Sarah Winnemucca's father, during which the elderly man remarked that the Northern Paiutes were rarely hungry prior to permanent contact with white settlers, beginning in approximately 1863 to 1865. *Reminiscences of George Martin Kober, M.D., LL.D.* (Washington, DC: Kober Foundation of Georgetown University, 1930), 252–54.

3. Judith Shapiro, "Kinship," in *The Handbook of North American Indians, Great Basin*, vol. 11, ed. Warren L. D'Azevedo (Washington, DC: Smithsonian Institution, 1986), 620–29.

4. Great Basin people practiced cross-cousin marriage, which often reflects the need for a more secure resource base by broadening kinship networks through multiplying the

conjugal bonds among families. The Northern Paiutes practiced a bilateral kinship system that recognized blood relationships and the benefits and obligations those relationships entailed. Compared to patrilineal systems that trace ties through male lines, bilateral systems that recognize kin through both male and female lines tend to be more egalitarian. While marriage to immediate kin on the maternal or paternal side was forbidden, endogamous marriages to second or third cousins was the norm. As both husbands and wives commonly initiated divorces, most Northern Paiutes practiced serial monogamy although some formed polygamous and, more rarely, polyandrous marriages. Even in these plural marriages, the preferred forms were sororal and fraternal, further interrelating family groups (Shapiro, 622–24).

5. Ibid. In her autobiography, Winnemucca suggests that Northern Paiute families strongly influenced a young person's choice of a mate and kept an eye on courting young people by limiting flirting and sweet-talking to public events in full view of the community, such as their annual Festival of Flowers. *Life Among the Piutes: Their Wrongs and Claims*, by Sarah Winnemucca Hopkins, ed. Mrs. Horace Mann (New York: G. P. Putnam and Sons of New York, 1883; reprint, Reno: University of Nevada Press, 1994), 45–51. Most scholars believe that Winnemucca wrote her autobiography with minimal editing by Mrs. Horace Mann. Her biographer, Sally Zanjani notes that Winnemucca's autobiography is remarkable in its historical accuracy.

6. Hopkins, 53.

7. Catherine S. Fowler, "Subsistence," in *The Handbook of North American Indians, Great Basin*, vol. 11, ed. Warren L. D'Azevedo (Washington, DC: Smithsonian Institution, 1986), 64–97. Hopkins, *Life Among the Piutes*, 50–51.

8. Fowler, "Subsistence."

9. According to Fowler, "it can be estimated that the lake and riverine-based peoples of Pyramid Lake and Walker River in Nevada probably obtained 50–60 percent of their livelihood from fish, 20 percent from large and small game, and 20–30 percent from wild plant products." Men hunted and fished, but women gathered, hunted small game, and fished. Fowler emphasizes the importance of plants and nuts in particular, "Subsistence," 91–93. Also see Knack and Stewart, chapter 1.

10. Fowler and Liljeblad, 450–52. Knack and Stewart, 230, and Hopkins, 52–54. Historians have long debated whether Native women's economic contributions equated to political rights. The matrilineal Iroquois and Cherokee, among whom women produced and controlled access to corn, have proven to be convincing examples. For Iroquois women, see Judith K. Brown, "Economic Organization and the Position of Women Among the Iroquois," *Ethnohistory* 17 (1971): 151–67; Elisabeth Tooker, "Women in Iroquois Society," in *Extending the Rafters: Interdisciplinary Approaches to Iroquoian Studies*, ed. Michael K. Foster, Jack Campisi, and Marianne Mithun (Albany: State University of New York Press, 1984), 109–23; and Nancy Shoemaker, "The Rise or Fall of Iroquois Women," *Journal of Women's History* 2 (winter 1991): 39–57. For Cherokee women, see Theda Perdue, *Cherokee Women* (Lincoln: University of Nebraska Press, 1998).

11. Hopkins, 45–51. For the significance of motherhood, see, for example, Mary E. Black, "Maidens and Mothers: An Analysis of Hope Corn Metaphors," *Ethnology* 23 (1984): 279–88 and M. Jane Young, "Women, Reproduction, and Religion in Western Puebloan Society," *Journal of American Folklore* 100 (1987): 436–45.

12. Fowler and Liljeblad. Knack and Stewart, chapter 2.

13. Knack and Stewart, chapters 1–3. Thomas Morgan, preface to *My Story of the Last Indian War in the Northwest: The Bannock, Piute, Yakima, and Sheep Eater Tribes, 1878–79* (Forest Grove, Oregon: New-Times Publishing Co., 1954).

14. Ibid.

15. The spelling of the Malheur agent's name varies between "Reinhard" and "Reinhart" in the sources. Richard O. Clemmer and Omer C. Stewart, "Treaties, Reservations, and Claims," in *The Handbook of North American Indians, Great Basin*, vol. 11, ed. Warren L. D'Azevedo (Washington, DC: Smithsonian Institution, 1986), 536–37. Hopkins, chapters 5–8. Knack and Stewart, chapter 4.

16. Eugene M. Hattori, "'And Some of Them Swear Like Pirates': Acculturation of American Indian Women in Nineteenth Century Virginia City," in *Comstock Women: The Making of a Mining Community*, ed. Ronald M. James and C. Elizabeth Raymond (Reno: University of Nevada Press, 1998), 229–45. Knack and Stewart, chapter 2. Dorothy Nafus Morrison, *Chief Sarah: Sarah Winnemucca's Fight for Indian Rights* (New York: Altheneum, 1980), chapter 6.

17. For detailed accounts of all of Winnemucca's various jobs, see Hopkins; Morrison; and Sally Zanjani, *Sarah Winnemucca* (Lincoln: University of Nebraska Press, 2001).

18. Hopkins, 58–59 and 231. Knack and Stewart, chapter 2.

19. Rayna Green, "The Pocahontas Perplex: The Images of Indian Women in American Culture," in *Unequal Sisters: A Multicultural Reader in U.S. Women's History*, ed. Ellen Carol DuBois (New York: Routledge, 1990), 15–21. John D' Emilio and Estelle B. Freedman, *Intimate Matters: A History of Sexuality in the United States*, 2nd edition (Chicago: University of Chicago Press, 1997), 85–108.

20. Oliver O. Howard, *My Life and Experiences among Our Hostile Indians* (New York: Da Capo Press, 1972), 214, 222–23, and 524–33.

21. Knack and Stewart, 47. Hattori does not mention whether or not he has evidence that Northern Paiute women worked as prostitutes and states that they rarely intermarried. *The Nevada State Journal*, 28 March 1875. While chiefs marry their daughters to outsiders to cement relationships in many Native cultures, there is no evidence suggesting that either of the men Winnemucca married were in any way important.

22. For example, in her study of working-class white men's rape of African-American women during the Memphis Riot of 1866, Hannah Rosen argues that these men raped as the continuation of a larger struggle over the meanings of citizenship and freedom following the Civil War. "'Not That Sort of Women': Race, Gender, and Sexual Violence during the Memphis Riot of 1866," in *Sex, Love, Race: Crossing Boundaries of North American History*, ed. by Martha Hodes (New York: New York University Press, 1993), 267–93. In "Violent and Violated Women: Justice and Gender in Rural Guatemala, 1936–1956," Cindy Forster concludes that while many men considered Indian women racially inferior and therefore dishonorable, working women were more vulnerable to attacks. She argues that race and class are as essential to understanding rape as gender. *Journal of Women's History* 11 (1999): 55–77.

23. Hopkins, 3–4. Knack and Stewart, chapters 2–8. For accounts of the rape of Indian women during the California Gold Rush, see Albert L. Hurtado, *Indian Survival on the California Frontier* (New Haven: Yale University Press, 1988), chapter 9. Clifford E. Trafzer and Joel R. Hyer, eds., *Exterminate Them!: Written Accounts of the Murder, Rape, and Enslavement of Native Americans during the California Gold Rush* (East Lansing: Michigan State University Press, 1999).

24. Emilie Buchwald, Pamela Fletcher, and Martha Roth, preamble to *Transforming a Rape Culture* (Minneapolis, MC: Milkweed, 1993), iix.

25. Americans' reputation for violence preceded them. In 1844, when John C. Fremont's party passed through Pyramid Lake, the Native men kept their weapons at hand while feasting the newcomers. Knack and Stewart, 39–40; Kober, 280. Winnemucca wrote that even before they met whites face to face, her people associated them with killing Indians with guns and poison, beating children, and engaging in cannibalism. Hopkins, 5–44, 100–104, 116, 167, 181–82, 188, 228, 231, and 280. Other Native people also

characterized Europeans and Americans as sexual miscreants. See Theda Perdue, "Columbus Meets Pocahontas in the American South," *Southern Cultures* 3 (1997): 4–21.

26. Ibid. Accounts of rape in California suggest that rapists often violated women in front of their husbands, fathers, and brothers. See also Hurtado, chapter 9.
27. Winnemucca, *Life Among the Piutes,* p. 228.
28. Hopkins, 94, 120–21, 137, 182–83, and 231.
29. Ibid, 100–04, 167, 178, and 188.
30. Hattori, 233–35. Knack and Stewart, chapters 4 and 5.
31. Hopkins, 182–82. In his account of the Bannock War, Howard does not mention the attempted rape or the men's dismissal.
32. Hopkins, 180–82 and 228–30. Suggesting how insignificant rape was to white officers, Howard does not mention the attempted rape or the men's dismissal in his memoir.
33. Hopkins, 182–83.
34. Hopkins, 231.
35. *Nevada State Journal*, 28 March 1875. *Silver State*, 27 March 1875. Sally Zanjani, 126.
36. Kober, 280.
37. Fowler and Liljeblad, 457. Hopkins, 70–73. DeQuille, 81–82. While DeQuille confirms Winnemucca's account of the outbreak of the war, Myron Angel's compiled *History of Nevada* claimed that the Northern Paiutes attacked the men because they were mean but not because they were rapists. (Oakland, CA: Thompson and West, 1881; New York: Arno Press, 1973), 150–58. Allen, 110–11, 136–41, 154–55, and 159–60.
38. Hopkins, 139. Howard, 378. Robert M. Utley, *Frontier Regulars: The United States Army and the Indian, 1866–1891* (New York: Macmillan, 1973), 323–34. According to Utley's account, based on military sources, no particular incident sparked the war—only the struggle over the camas prairie.
39. Recalling a conversion with Old Winnemucca, Sarah Winnemucca's father, settler George M. Kober stated that Winnemucca explained that the Northern Paiutes attacked settlers because they were destroying their resource base (Kober, 252–54). For warfare as a corrective measure, see Frederick W. Gleach, *Powhatan's World and Colonial Virginia: A Conflict of Cultures* (Lincoln: University of Nebraska Press, 1997).
40. Hopkins, 73–74.
41. Ibid, 116.
42. For detailed descriptions of Winnemucca's campaigns, see Morrison and Sally Zanjani.
43. In her study of seventeenth-century England, Chaytor concludes that survivors often contextualize their attack within their daily work and those that they worked for, routines and people that brought them safety and security, comfort and status—those very things and people that enabled them to recover from their violation. Miranda Chaytor, "Husband(ry): Narratives of Rape in the Seventeenth Century," *Gender and History* 7 (1995): 378–407.
44. Siobhan Senier argues that Winnemucca supported allotment to protect *tribalism.* Considering the socioeconomic aspects of Northern Paiute culture, I think Winnemucca's goals were not as communal as Senier's suggests. *Voices of American Indian Assimilation and Resistance: Helen Hunt Jackson, Sarah Winnemucca, and Victoria Howard* (Norman: University of Oklahoma Press, 2001), 73–120.
45. For a detailed account of the Peabody Institute, see Morrison and Zanjani.
46. Catherine S. Fowler, foreword to *Life among the Piutes: Their Wrongs and Claims,* by Sarah Winnemucca Hopkins, ed. Mrs. Horace Mann (New York: G. P. Putnam and Sons of New York, 1883; reprint, Reno: University of Nevada Press, 1994). Most scholars believe that Winnemucca wrote her autobiography with minimal editing by Mrs. Horace Mann. Zanjani notes that Winnemucca's autobiography is remarkable in its historical accuracy, and while I agree with her, I believe that Winnemucca embellished some accounts in order to appeal to her readers.

47. U.S. Department of Justice, Bureau of Justice Statistics, February 1999 for the period 1992–1996, http://www/vday.org/ie/index2cfm?articleID+864. United States Department of Commerce, *We the First Americans* (Washington, DC: Government Printing Office, 1993).

48. Hopkins, 228.

Fig. 3.1 Frances Fuller Victor. Reprinted by permission of the Oregon State Library (WPA Series 4, General #2741b).

3

FRANCES FULLER VICTOR'S PROMOTION OF STRONG, INDEPENDENT WOMANHOOD: WOMEN AND MARRIAGE RECONSTRUCTED IN "THE NEW PENELOPE"

June Johnson Bube

Mind is the same, whether it resides in a man's form, or a woman's. All the laws of the mind, the soul, the affections, are the same in men and women, so far as observation and science can determine. What affects the one, affects the other, and in exactly the same way.[1]

— Frances Fuller Victor

In 1874, Frances Fuller Victor made this bold declaration of women's equality in the *New Northwest*, a suffragist newspaper published in Portland, Oregon. She had traveled far geographically and experientially from her early life in the Midwest and East. Born in 1826 in Rome, in western New York, Frances Fuller was the eldest of five daughters. During her childhood and youth, her family moved to Erie, Pennsylvania, and then to Wooster, Ohio—both towns along stage lines important for trade, travel, and her father's business as an innkeeper. Frances and her sisters were educated at a female seminary in Wooster, and they also attended political and social debates at the Wooster Lyceum. By her mid-teens, Frances was publishing poems and an occasional story in Ohio weekly papers. Her sister Metta, five years younger, also displayed talent as a poet and fiction writer. As young women, both sisters became regular contributors to Nathaniel Willis's *New York Home Journal*, a popular mid-nineteenth-century women's magazine. In the early 1850s, to help support the family after their father's early death, both sisters worked as assistant editors of the *Monthly Hesperian and Odd-Fellows' Literary Magazine* in Detroit. Their reputations as talented, but nevertheless conventional, poets continued to grow, and in 1849, their poetry was anthologized in Rufus Griswold's *The Female Poets of America*; later in 1860, William Goggeshall included their work in *Poets and Poetry of the West*.[2]

If recognition as a woman poet from the Midwest shaped her identity as a young woman, Frances's first marriage and pioneering in Nebraska Territory deepened her understanding of both women's social and economic status and of the country's westward expansion. In 1853, Frances Fuller married Jackson Barritt, a young man from a well-educated, prominent pioneering family in Michigan. Participating in the country's restless growth in 1855, Frances and Jackson made their way across the country to Chicago, St. Louis, and up the Missouri River to Omaha, the capital of Nebraska Territory, traveling by railroad, stern-wheeler, and stagecoach. From this remote western settlement, Frances wrote travel letters and poems for Midwestern and eastern journals and newspapers. As her later writing reveals, she was profoundly affected by her observation of land speculation, the removal of the Omaha Indians, the grave-marked tracks of wagon trains, and the beauty and loneliness of the prairie. Although Frances envisioned owning a business in town, Jackson purchased land for farming and built a log cabin twenty miles north of Omaha, a conflict of goals that led to their separation. In her divorce from Jackson, granted later in 1862, she charged him with "grossly neglect[ing] his duty toward her,"[3] but never explained publicly the full nature of their rupture.

From the isolation of Nebraska, Frances moved to Manhattan in 1858 to join the New York literary scene in which both her sister Metta and Metta's second husband, Orville Victor, were very active.[4] Orville was editor of several publications, including the newly launched Beadle Dime Library while Metta edited and wrote for *The Home* and soon became one of the foremost women writers of Beadle Dime Novels.[5] For the next four years, Frances helped them edit these publications and raise their growing family. In 1862, Frances herself published two dime novels about western settlement, *East and West; or, The Beauty of*

Willard's Mill and *The Land Claim, A Tale of the Upper Missouri*. Her novel *East and West*, with its depiction of economic competition and social discord in territorial Iowa, foreshadowed the complexities and realism of her later western fiction.[6] In 1862 she married Orville's brother, Henry Clay Victor, an officer in the Engineer Corps of the U. S. Navy. When Henry's ship, which was blockading Southern ports at the start of the Civil War, captured a valuable blockade-runner, Henry chose as his reward to be assigned to the Pacific Squadron and Frances accompanied him to California.

The adventurous thirty-seven-year-old Victor, who enthusiastically embarked for the Panama Isthmus, Mexico, and San Francisco in spring of 1863, was already an accomplished writer, a well-traveled woman, and a lively intellect. By August of 1863, she was contributing articles to San Francisco's *Evening Bulletin* and writing witty social columns for the *Golden Era* under the pen name Florence Fane to supplement her husband's pay. For the next thirty-nine years until her death at seventy-six in 1902, Victor worked as a poet, journalist, historian, and fiction writer in the far West. Her steady work and prolific writing were motivated by her intellectual curiosity, creative energy, astute analysis of social problems, and financial necessity.

Despite a promising beginning, after six years, Victor's second marriage also crumbled, undermined in part by the peculiar opportunities and stresses of the West. In 1869, Victor separated from Henry and found herself thrust into what she called "the position of 'lone woman.'"[7] Henry Victor had became enamored of western possibilities and continuously lost money in economic ventures: speculations in St. Helens' town sites, Santiam gold mines, and coal, iron, and salt mining. Some of Victor's poems and her 1874 pamphlet, *The Women's War with Whisky; or Crusading in Portland*, documenting the temperance movement in Portland, Oregon, also reveal her familiarity with spousal alcoholism. Then in 1875, she found herself a widow when the ship Henry was sailing on sank off the coast of Washington. Restrained in her public comments about Henry, Victor's fiction nevertheless portrays willful, selfish husbands unilaterally exercising their social and economic prerogatives to the detriment of the couple and the wife, particularly. Victor inherited legal and financial problems from Henry incurred through his irresponsibility and bad luck. Thus, personal experiences in the West continued to mold her ideas of women's identity and social status.

The opportunity to write for western dailies and weeklies enabled her to earn some money and to develop her views on gender. Particularly during the 1870s, Victor wrote regularly for a number of western newspapers: editorials for Abigail Scott Duniway's Portland suffragist paper, the *New Northwest*; her social column for San Francisco's *Daily Morning Call* written under the pen name "Dorothy D." in 1875; and articles for Portland's *West Shore* between 1876 and 1878.

During the 1860s and 1870s, Victor also published travel sketches, poems, and a number of short stories, a novella, and a novel in various western literary magazines such as the *Lakeside Monthly* of Chicago, the *Overland Monthly* of San Francisco, the *West Shore* of Portland, and the *New Northwest*. Between December 1873 and May 1874, the *New Northwest* serialized her novel *Judith Miles; or, What Shall Be Done with Her?* Much of her 1870s western fiction centers on women in the West, exhibits a moral complexity, and reflects how Victor increasingly contested cultural norms of femininity. These stories articulate some of her most profound historical and experiential insights. In 1877, Victor collected a body of her poetry and ten of her short stories, many of them published formerly in the *Overland Monthly*, in *The New Penelope and Other Stories and Poems* published by Bancroft of San Francisco.

Victor's work as a professional historian constituted yet a third career. Avidly embracing historical research in the late 1860s and 1870s, she sought "to peer into the past, present and the future" and to ensure that things "which were speedily becoming extinct will now be matters of history."[8] She documented the early fur trade in her 1870 biography of Joe Meek, *The River of the West*. In her book *All over Oregon and Washington*, published in 1872, she undertook to "correct false impressions [of the Pacific Coast] in the minds of the people of the East."[9] From 1878 to 1890, she worked for Hubert Howe Bancroft on his monumental series, *History of the Pacific States*. Her professional, intellectual contribution to this series was far greater than her contemporaries knew as she asserted in her "Autobiographical Sketch" in 1895: "Thus my work on the Bancroft histories aggregates six full volumes of from 700 to 800 pages each. If I had been able to place my name where it belongs on these six volumes I should have made an international reputation."[10] Victor's voluminous historical writings are impressive because they are the work of a woman competing in a male field and because of her research methods. In contrast to some of her contemporaries engaged in writing historical accounts of the West, Victor believed that historians had a responsibility to resist pleasing factions and supporters, to confront controversy, and to question and weigh conflicting "facts" about early settlement. At age sixty-four, Victor emerged from Bancroft's literary industry to take on more historical projects of her own, to give journalistic support to women's contributions to early California literature, and to take an active part in the Women's Press Association of California and the Woman's Congress Association of the Pacific Coast.

Any assessment of Victor's contribution to women's social progress must consider her various careers, her prolific production of historical, journalistic, and literary texts, and the richness and complexity of these texts themselves. In the 1870s, at the time when an increasing number of young women of her class were attending college and grappling with decisions about careers and marriage,[11] Victor, then in her late forties and early fifties, exemplified a professional and personal life that came to be identified with the New Woman. Her profession as an historian continuously immersed her in a male world and pitted her intellect and her resources against male writers, scholars, and publishers. She abandoned two discordant marriages and constantly worked to make a place for herself in the West as an intellect, poet, and professional writer. A roving historian gathering primary documents, she journeyed by stagecoach and steamboat to the headwaters of the Columbia River, to the rim of Crater Lake, and to Indian reservations, a "lone woman" having adventures, studying the West and supporting herself. At her death, she was called the "Historian of the Northwest" and the "Mother of Oregon History," and indeed she had played a prominent public role in capturing the historical development of the far West.[12] But her most striking achievement is her novella "The New Penelope," remarkable for its synthesis of her personal experiences, for its literary qualities, and for its depiction of a strong, independent womanhood that came to be associated with the New Woman.[13]

URGING WOMEN TO BREAK OUT OF CONVENTIONAL MOLDS

Unlike her historical writing, Victor's western journalism overtly focused on women's issues and her commitment to improving women's status. In these newspaper columns and articles, Victor avoids polemics yet fuses her keen observations of contemporary western society and her historical understanding of social change into an incisive social critique of "woman's sphere," that cherished nineteenth-century concept that identified women with marriage and the home. Historian Joan Smyth Iversen explains the dominant trend in nineteenth-century sexual politics in these terms: Women conducted their "search for power and authority in home and nation" based on sexual difference and a belief in innate female morality.[14] For Victor, though, woman's sphere was an oppressive social construct that was unworkable, especially as a base for social power. She also questioned the ability of woman's sphere to nurture gender solidarity. The disturbing question she posed in her western journalism and fiction was, How can women expect to have power in the world or even in the home when, as she said, men "claim for themselves all the privileges of life" and those women who are socially protected and economically provided for by men accept this gendered allocation of power?[15]

In her journalistic writing, Victor's challenge to the ideology of woman's sphere emerges as a group of themes that encourage women to work toward gender equality. As an historian, Victor keenly perceived that women as a group were molded by society to accept marriage as their primary social destiny. In "Cultivated Women," one of her Dorothy D. columns for the *San Francisco Daily Morning Call*, she noted that because many men were killed during the Civil War, many women were left without the option of marriage. In opposition to domesticity's notion of womanhood, Victor argued that marriage and children, far from being a biological destiny, cannot be regarded as women's only purpose.[16] Indeed, she argued that this conventional view of gender roles for women failed to develop women's real abilities. Her articles advocated education reform for women, particularly the need to promote practical education designed to prepare women for self-support, and the search for a better way of making "intellectually cultivated women."[17] She frequently emphasized the necessity for more economic opportunities for women in light of the failure of marriage and, conversely, the need for women actively to embrace the pursuit of self-support to avoid being "moneyless, tradeless, professionless, and thoroughly helpless."[18]

Although she was involved in woman's suffrage organizations in Oregon and eventually in California, Victor, like Charlotte Perkins Gilman later, believed that women's problems went deeper than suffrage; they were rooted in gender consciousness and in the historical institutions and social customs that shape the way men and women think about themselves and each other.[19] She believed that women, individually and as a group, needed to undergo a transformation of consciousness. To that end, she exhorted women to break out of conventional molds. She advised them to resist the "inferior position" in which they have had to "submit themselves to the wishes and opinions of others," and actively to engage in "establish[ing] the precedent of an intelligent, independent womanhood."[20] She underscored the acceptance of woman's "right to be a thinking, observing, reasoning creature with an identity of her own."[21] Her journalistic writings point toward the division in Victorian social conceptions of gender that would become more pronounced with public discussions of the New Woman in the 1890s. These ideas, prominent in Victor's newspaper columns, compose the philosophical-social vision of her western fiction.

MORE THAN A COMPELLING STORY

Victor's seventy-page novella, "The New Penelope," the title story in her 1877 collection, is an artistically sophisticated hybrid of women's sensational western adventure tale, vivid regionalism, historical insight, and social critique. "The New Penelope" is first of all an exciting narrative that engages readers' interest in the appealing main character, Mrs. Anna Greyfield, an Oregon pioneer woman who struggles against the marital bonds that circumscribe her social identity and personhood and who challenges these constraints. The story is structured as a frame within a frame within a frame, with a feminist focus on all three levels. On the first narrative level, an unnamed, middle-aged woman narrator, obviously a persona of Victor, opens and closes the story. The second narrative level, the immediate past, dramatizes a companionable evening spent by the narrator and her close friend, Mrs. Anna Greyfield, at the latter's home in the Sierra Nevada Mountains of northern California. The third narrative level, which comprises most of the story, reaches back twenty years into the past. In this flashback, Mrs. Anna Greyfield tells how the wagon train that she, her husband, and son were traveling with left her husband behind on the Overland Trail, believing he had died from cholera. She recounts the hardships she faced when she ended up in Oregon, and struggled to maintain her integrity and support herself and her young son in Portland in the 1850s. Then she unravels the spicy mystery of her reputed multiple marriages. Now in her late forties, having achieved a comfortable life by running a high-class boardinghouse on the mining frontier in California, Mrs. Anna Greyfield is confronted by the reappearance of the husband of her youth. Although Mrs. Greyfield remarries her husband, she does so on her own terms.

This lively story dramatizes women's grappling with social, economic, psychological, and sexual problems. It exposes the contradictions inherent in nineteenth-century society's prescribed roles for women. Influenced by Victor's own marital tensions, it expresses her mature, complex views of marriage, women's social status, and female identity. The story explores the dynamics of social power between women and men and between women and women; criticizes cultural norms of masculinity; proposes more equal terms for marriage; envisions a new basis for women's support of women; and depicts the emergence of a new, well-rounded female identity that prefigures the New Woman who strove for social position and identity based on equality with men.[22]

"The New Penelope" functions as an imaginary arena in which Victor wrestles with the specific historical gender problems preoccupying her at this time and seeks symbolic solutions to them. In this story, Victor's view of the problems facing women is informed by John Stuart Mill's theory of the corruption of power expounded in *The Subjection of Women* published in 1869.[23] In accordance with Mill's social theories, Victor depicts marriage and the home as powerful inhibitors of women's achievement of full personhood. She portrays women's need for economic independence and dramatizes women's right to self-determination and self-fulfillment.[24] "The New Penelope" also asserts women's right to be fully developed persons and sexual beings. Thus, Mrs. Greyfield, Victor's protagonist, presages the early twentieth-century feminists. New Women, said Marie Jennie Howe, organizer of the 1914 New York "feminist mass meetings," were "sick of being specialized to sex" and sought to be their "whole, big, human selves."[25] Victor's novella explores these issues of women's identity, blending historical realism with a feminist utopian solution.

A WOMAN'S REWRITING OF THE OLD WESTERN NARRATIVE

In "The New Penelope," Victor revises literary and historical paradigms by substituting a western woman hero for a male hero. New western historian Richard White has summarized the generic old western narrative encoded by Frederick Jackson Turner as "the story of a journey, a challenge, and a dual transformation of land and people."[26] "The New Penelope" encompasses Frederick Jackson Turner's thesis and adapts it to a tale of a woman's heroic survival. Like the Greek Penelope, Mrs. Anna Greyfield, the abandoned wife, is a resourceful survivor who repulses male aggression. This new Penelope, through quiet heroism and sheer perseverance, demonstrates how the adversity of frontier life can become for women, too, a forging ground for opportunity.

However, Victor's feminist historical consciousness also revises the tale of western individualism. She depicts a conflicted, socially complex West and raises issues that resonate beyond individual heroism. In "The New Penelope," Old Western History narratives intersect with New Western History narratives. New Western Historians envision multiple frontiers and multiple western experiences: a "variety of gender ideologies held in the West"[27] as Elizabeth Jameson says, and a West that Donald Worster describes as "a scene of intense struggles over power and hierarchy, not only between races but also between classes, genders and often groups within the white majority."[28] When the narrator comments, "I had heard so many stories of deserted Eastern homes, and subsequent illegal marriages in California,"[29] she situates Mrs. Greyfield's experiences within the widespread social upheaval of western settlement, focusing on its effects on women. Victor, the historian turned fiction writer, forges her prototypical New Woman within a perceptively drawn social context.

A second major male influence appears in the literary paradigms borrowed from Bret Harte, who dominated the San Francisco publishing scene in the late 1860s and whose popularity was at its height when Victor was writing "The New Penelope."[30] Just as Harte "concentrated the irregularities of early California life,"[31] Victor capitalized on the distinctive, most exciting mid-century features of the far West. In the preface to her volume containing "The New Penelope," Victor recommends her sketches of Pacific Coast life for their "scenes and characters having the charm of newness and originality, such as belong to border life."[32] One strain running throughout her western fiction is the desire to capture for old-time residents, newcomers, and outsiders, a place and passing era that are fascinating because of their uniqueness and evanescence.[33]

Again, though, Victor transforms male regional writing and creates a critique of gender relations in a narrative that does much more than romanticize the West.[34] Prefiguring what Peggy Pascoe has noted as New Western History's double interest in regional differences and national connections,[35] Victor's historical knowledge enables her to complicate regional writing by linking western social history to nineteenth-century social historical issues and even to world history.[36] Victor shows how the frontier aggravates and exposes the deep, omnipresent disparity in men's and women's social status: life in the West betokens the socially oppressive state of gender *everywhere* in the mid-nineteenth century. The story questions and reconceptualizes the equation of women and home. It illuminates both the regionally specific, and wider class- and gender-specific conflicts women must negotiate to create new personal and social identities.

Victor changes and reworks these male literary and historical influences through a clever artistic strategy in "The New Penelope." In this story, she plays with a style of western writing, popularized by Harte and others, that borrowed images from Greek heroes and legends, yet she reinvests the literary allusion to Homer's *Odyssey* with historical content and social critique. The opening paragraph of the story establishes the Homeric echoes but also boldly intimates its feminist revisionist approach. The first-person woman narrator adopts the empowering role of epic singer in likening herself to Homer: "In the early life of the Greeks, Homer found his Penelope; in the pioneer days of the Pacific Coast, I discovered mine" (*TNP*, 9). Thus, Victor substitutes a woman's voice and a woman's experiences for Homer's narrative of male adventure. In addition, in this story, women venture out into the world; the narrator appropriates for herself an identity as worldly-wise traveler and roaming bard when she announces "[m]y wanderings up and down among the majestic mountains and sunny valleys of California and Oregon had made me acquainted with many persons." (*TNP*, 10). Furthermore, Penelope is the focus of this western version of the deserted wife and mother and the moral and social conflicts that result from her uncertain social status as wife or widow. Unlike Homer's dominant, questing Telemachos, Mrs. Greyfield's son appears mainly as an emotional and physical burden to the young mother and otherwise remains offstage in the story; the husband's adventures also receive scant attention. Throughout the story, Victor ironically compares and contrasts the Greek Penelope's besieged home and uncertainty about her long-absent husband with Anna Greyfield's involvement with boardinghouses and bigamy in frontier Portland in 1850. In short, Victor gives new meaning to a literary allusion in order to expose nineteenth-century gender inequality. Defying literary paradigms and social scripts, the successful Anna Greyfield, who emerges from hard, transformational experiences, is neither resocialized into a simplistic, conventional nineteenth-century femininity nor punished by the narrative for failing to do so.

"MOST PERSONS ... SAID I SHOULD MARRY"

"The New Penelope" brings Victor's personal experiences and her incisive social observations to bear on the institution of marriage in the West. It addresses the connection between women's identity and the dynamics of power in male–female social and sexual relationships. Unmasking nineteenth-century gender relations in her rewriting of the Greek epic, Victor employs the allusion to Penelope, the faithful, threatened wife/ widow as a means to problematize the whole issue of marriage as central to women's social identity and value. The story's constant reference to the characters as "Mrs. Greyfield," "Mr. Greyfield," and "Mr. Seabrook" underscores Victor's concern with marriage and with the discrepancy between the public dimension of marriage and its private realities. The story asks: When men exploit their social and economic power and self-indulgently pursue their dreams, what happens to the women legally and emotionally bound to them? Are Penelope and Mrs. Anna Greyfield still wives? If they are widows, how should they support themselves? Finally, this story compels readers to ponder how far the social condition of women has progressed from Homer's Greece to the nineteenth-century West when this new Penelope also discovers just how entirely "a woman's social position depended on her relationship to men" (*TNP*, 40).

Like Penelope, Mrs. Anna Greyfield's social status is uncertain. As a woman alone, she represents an economic and sexual prize. First, her vulnerable, besieged position exposes the large economic component of marriage. Upon her arrival in Portland, she faces enormous social pressure: "Most persons—in fact everybody that I talked with—said I should marry" (*TNP*, 18). The passage of the Donation Act in 1850 granting double land to a man with a wife, leads to repeated, intrusive marriage proposals from mere acquaintances and total strangers seeking economic gain:

> He told me that he had no "woman," and that I had no "man," a condition that he evidently considered deplorable. He assured me that I suited him "fustrate"; that his children ... "liked my victuals;" ... He also impressed upon me that he had been "considerin" the "rangement of jinin" firms for some time [sic]. To close the business at once, he proposed that I should accept of him for my husband then and there. (*TNP*, 22)

Mrs. Greyfield experiences how laws collapse the distinction between women and property, and depersonalize and objectify women; like Penelope's social world, Mrs. Greyfield's western community identifies her primarily as owned or as ownerless property.

Besides representing an economic asset, an attractive, unmarried woman is a desirable sexual object. The solicitations "of men who did not care to marry" disturb Mrs. Greyfield the most, filling her with self-doubt and disgust: "I know it is constantly asserted, by men, that no woman is approached in that way who does not give some encouragement. But no statement could be more utterly false" (*TNP*, 24, 25). Mrs. Greyfield suffers humiliation and guilt to the point of sickness, believing that "there must be something wrong in my deportment" (*TNP*, 25). Here Victor refutes a popular cultural belief, the idea that women's moral purity shields them from male sexual aggression. Instead, the story reveals that this view of gender casts the blame for men's behavior on women, doubly oppressing women as offenders and victims.[37] Widows, as Mrs. Greyfield discovers, are unprotected property and fair game.

"AN AWFUL POWER"

If widowhood, the state of being unattached to and unsheltered by a man, is dangerous for women, marriage provides questionable sanctuary. Victor, agreeing with Mill's analysis, views nineteenth-century marriage as domestic slavery, a state in which the unequal distribution of social and legal power is fraught with potential for abuse of that power. As widow but also as wife, the young Mrs. Anna Greyfield finds herself caught within a male-dominated social order. Finally worn down by constant social pressures, Mrs. Greyfield agrees to marry Mr. Seabrook, who has frequently offered friendly advice concerning her sickly son, and who has helped her start a boardinghouse. Only when she has married him does she discover that he is a bigamist with a wife and children back in Ohio. When she chooses not to consummate the marriage, the Portland community does not credit her accusation of Mr. Seabrook's bigamy, does not believe that she has not slept with him, and never condones her ungracious conduct toward him. In her isolation and entrapment, Mrs. Greyfield discovers that marriage itself is exploitive and morally reprehensible:

> Although there is nothing in the wording of the marriage contract converting the woman into a bond-slave or a chattel, the man who practices any outrage or wrong on his wife is so seldom called to account. In the eyes of these men, having entered into marriage with Mr. Seabrook, I belonged to him, and there was no help for me. (*TNP,* 51)

Mrs. Greyfield concludes that the husband's position represents "an awful power to be lodged with any human being" (*TNP,* 51). She also recognizes men's investment in perpetuating this marital power.

The distinction between socially sanctioned "sacred" marriage and illegal, immoral relations between men and women is blurred by the confounding of "good" husbands and bigamists. Victor rewrites Homer, completely undermining male heroism, in order to show the corrupting socialization of men and husbands. She unmasks male behavior in Mill's terms: "How many are the forms and gradations of animalism and selfishness, often under an outward varnish of civilization and even cultivation."[38] Whereas Homer boldly distinguishes between the greedy, cowardly, lustful suitors besieging Penelope and her heroic husband, Victor shrinks this distance. The seeming gentleman is really a bigamist; the good husband also makes himself a bigamist through his second marriage. The behavior of both men pushes Mrs. Greyfield into "illegal marrying" (*TNP,* 76).

Mill writes, the family "is still oftener, as respects its chief, a school of willfulness, overbearingness, unbounded selfish indulgence, and a double-dyed and idealized selfishness."[39] Victor embodies this insight in her troubling depiction of the inequitable psychological dynamics between husbands and wives. When Mrs. Anna Greyfield describes her first marriage before and during the move west, the emphasis interestingly is not on woman as "reluctant pioneer"[40] but on the subtle abuses of power within marriage. She says: "I deceived myself expecting Mr. Greyfield to give up anything he had strongly desired"; "My husband was strong and cheerful now that he was having his own way" (*TNP*, 13, 15). These statements echo what Mrs. Greyfield later says about Mr. Seabrook: "He was one who would be kind to man, woman, or child who would be governed by him; yet resistance to his will, however just, roused a tyranny" (*TNP*, 55). Male power shows its longevity when the dying Mr. Greyfield consigns her to his friend. This arrangement forces her to end up in Oregon instead of California, to lose her property, and to be vulnerable to Mr. Seabrook. Good men and bad men, the story testifies, exhibit a selfishness grounded in their assumption of rightful dominance.

In fact, although Mrs. Greyfield herself insists on the difference, the story draws other disturbing likenesses between Mr. Greyfield and Mr. Seabrook. Self-interest and selfish materialism dominate the motivations of both. When Mr. Greyfield apologizes and reintroduces himself to his wife twenty years after his apparent death, he writes:

> You may wonder, dear Anna, that I did not go to Oregon when I had the barest suspicion of your being there. The distance and the trouble of getting there were not what deterred me. I was making money where I was, and did not wish to abandon my claim while it was producing well, for an uncertain hint that might mislead me. (*TNP*, 74)

The disparity between Mr. Greyfield's vision of his wife's situation and the reality mark an immense gulf between the perceptions and experiences of the sexes. Mrs. Greyfield's disgust and anger reveal that she ultimately judges her "good" husband to be the cause of all the suffering she has experienced:

> Who suffered all this to come between us? ... Does it not seem to you that if Mr. Greyfield had done his duty, all this terrible trouble and illegal marrying would have been avoided? Do you think a man should consider anything in this world before his wife and children or fail of doing his utmost in any circumstances for them? How else is marriage superior to any illicit relation, if its duties are not sacred and not to be set aside for anything? I could never have done as he has done, blameless as he thinks himself! (*TNP*, 77)

Victor shows that men and women are conditioned to embrace divergent views of marriage to the wives' detriment. Furthermore, when men and women are not equally bound to marital commitment, marriage cannot be regarded as sacred. Mrs. Greyfield's experience demonstrates that laws and social customs validate husbands' abuse, neglect, and devaluing of wives while they promote male privilege.

OVERCOMING "THE INERTIA OF WOMEN"

Besides refuting the idea "that women were idealized and idolized" (*TNP*, 12) in early frontier days, Victor also writes this story to address women's oppression of each other. In Mrs. Greyfield's words, "The inertia of women in each other's defense is immense" (*TNP*, 50). Throughout "The New Penelope," the frame story vies with the flashback story for the readers' attention; indeed, we are not allowed to forget that a woman is telling her story to a compassionate and like-minded woman. The effect of foregrounding this female friendship is to encourage readers to think about women as a social group. However, rather than follow the convention of celebrating gender difference as the basis of the bonds among women, Victor's new Penelope exposes the hollowness of this solidarity and proposes a new foundation for women's relationships with women.

Once again Victor finds Mill useful in examining the divisions among women. Mrs. Anna Greyfield's social estrangement from women dramatizes the idea that because of gender inequality, middle-class women's social status is always insecure. Even women's bonds with women are warped and contaminated by women's social and economic dependence on men. In "The New Penelope," the early urban frontier has few women, but the real problem is that these women don't stick together. In fact, the story challenges the concept of woman's sphere formulated by Carroll Smith-Rosenberg: that is, of woman's sphere as a nurturing female world where women "turn[ed] automatically to other women for support and intimacy."[41] The narrator comments: "For, among the vices of women I had long counted uncharitableness; and among their disadvantages want of actual knowledge of things—the latter accounting for the former" (*TNP*, 10). By exposing the suffering that women experience at the hands of *women* as well as men, Victor hopes to increase women's solidarity.

Similarly, in her *New Northwest* article "Some Thoughts About Ourselves," Victor explores "the curious question ... why women so rarely stand by women in any undertaking," "why they do not *sustain each other*" [Victor's italics]:[42]

> But why enumerate the disabilities of the "lone woman"? What-
> ever she might have been with liberty to use her natural God-
> given abilities, she is nothing now. And why? Primarily, because
> men claim for themselves all the privileges of life; and secondly,
> because more fortunate women agree to sustain men in the
> assumption, and become the most merciless critics of their help-
> less sisters. By a singular and most illogical mode of reasoning,
> a woman is womanly in proportion as she forsakes all allegiance
> to her own sex, and devotes herself to the other.[43]

Mrs. Anna Greyfield and the narrator discuss how women's economic
dependence on men intensifies women's self-interest and leads them to
excuse and abet male culpability: "We are born and bred to this narrow
view of ourselves, as altogether the creatures of sex." (*TNP*, 58). The
women in the community exert social control through their gossip,
compelling Mrs. Greyfield to marry Mr. Seabrook, who has contrived
through his familiar behavior to make himself and Mrs. Greyfield appear
engaged. Nor do the women help Mrs. Greyfield after she has discovered the existence of his other wife and family. The women she consults
tell her, "that I 'should have thought of all that before I married!' They
treated it exactly as if, having gone through the marriage ceremony,
I was bound, no matter how many wives Mr. Seabrook had back in
Ohio" (*TNP*, 50). Mrs. Greyfield remarks that all the women she sought
for help counseled her to "submit quietly"; "not one encouraged me
to resist Mr. Seabrook" (*TNP*, 51). The helplessness and indifference of
these women illustrate Mill's idea that "In the case of women, each
individual of the subject-class is in a chronic state of bribery and intimidation combined."[44] This story reveals that gender inequality builds
barriers between women that trap some women within socially accepted
bonds and shut other women out.[45] It shows that women will be truly
supportive of each other and able to achieve a new personhood only
when they recognize and resist the social forces that subjugate them
individually and as a group.

On the second narrative level, the story embodies a significant corrective to women's troubled relationships with women. Victor suggests
that the first step toward changing women's social behavior toward
each other is raising their awareness of their real condition as "human-
ity held in intellectual [and] personal subjection."[46] The narrator of
"The New Penelope" introduces herself to the reader as "that anomalous creature—a woman who loves her own sex" (*TNP*, 9), and she tells
Mrs. Greyfield's story in order to cultivate respect and sympathy for
single, divorced, independent women. She demonstrates compassion in

her relationship to this western Penelope and hopes to elicit a similar empathy from the readers.

The second narrative level also exhibits the new appreciation and friendship that can exist between independent women. Like the narrator, Mrs. Anna Greyfield has acquired worldly knowledge through her life experiences. The narrator describes her seasoned friend as, "[i]ntellectual and intelligent without being learned or particularly bookish; quick in her perceptions and nearly faultless in her judgment of others; broadly charitable, not through any laxity of principle but through knowledge of the stumbling-blocks of which the world is full for the unwary" (*TNP*, 10). It is this enlarged experiential knowledge of society possessed by these two women that the narrator shares with her readers. Also like the narrator, this Penelope has been mobile, on her own initiative eventually relocating herself and her son from Portland to the Sierra Nevada in Northern California. According to Victor, expanded female consciousness molded by the world outside the conventional home can form a foundation for new bonds between women.

DOMESTICITY UNHOUSED AND REHOUSED

"The New Penelope" moves beyond criticizing marriage to constructing a new image of womanhood. In the character of her enlightened Penelope, Victor portrays a woman who exerts her agency in resisting oppressive social forces. Mrs. Greyfield's heroism includes bravery in the face of physical dangers and endurance amidst inequitable conditions. Most of all, it is defined by a healthy assertion of self often against diverse, powerful social pressures. Embodying the new heroism that Victor has proclaimed in her journalism, Mrs. Anna Greyfield breaks out of dependent, subservient molds: heroism "is when a good woman dares to loose all her claims upon the man popularly known as her protector, and to go out into the world alone, to make her way as best she can rather than live in constant association with vices she is powerless to restrain."[47] Victor's new basis for moral character for women claims that "you must first be true to yourself before your devotion to another is morally of any consequence."[48] Thus, this story explores the transformative process of forging new female selves, exemplifying potential choices for other women. And it explores the product—a new female identity that resembles historian Louise Michele Newman's description of the New Woman—who "aspired to individuality and autonomy, claiming the right and ability to decide how to best employ her talents in living her own life."[49] As Mrs. Anna Greyfield moves from conformity to eventual resistance, she follows a path from innocence and submission through disillusionment to worldly wisdom, self-possession, and economic self-sufficiency to become an independent New Woman.

Therefore, Victor's reimagined Penelope is more active in her suffering and in her resistance, more engaged and responsible, less prize and more participant than the Greek heroine: She is a new Penelope. In Homer, it was Odysseus's house and stock and Telemachos's inheritance that the unscrupulous suitors were devouring. Victor's Penelope, on the other hand, is viewed as both property and as the exploitable producer of property: "Just think of it. There were three years I had supported, by my labor, a large family of men, for that is what it amounted to. My money purchased the food they all ate, and I had really received nothing for it except my board and the clothes I worked in. The fault was not theirs; it was Mr. Seabrook's and society's" (*TNP*, 62). Mrs. Greyfield refers to the law whereby a husband is entitled to all his wife's earnings. In portraying the suffering this law exacts from women, Victor reveals its extreme inequity.

Rescued by no heroic male relatives, Mrs. Greyfield must extricate *herself* by managing *herself* and *her* own property. Sexual threats push her more and more toward active resistance when she has to continue living in her boardinghouse with Mr. Seabrook while refusing "to live with Mr. Seabrook as his wife" (*TNP*, 38). She experiences prolonged psychological torture and eventually physical threats. First, Mr. Seabrook tries to arouse her passion for him, then he tries to force himself on her. After months of sleepless nights lying in fear of him, she tells him that if he ever touches her, she will shoot him. Ultimately, she rescues herself by deciding to act against custom, public opinion, and social pressure. Knowing that the Portland community will call her a bad wife and a failure as a business woman, she decides to let her boardinghouse run down and to starve out her boarders, including Mr. Seabrook. Mrs. Anna Greyfield also accepts that she has to work within society's rules; she finally curbs her pride and dissolves her "nonmarriage" to Mr. Seabrook through a divorce.

Just as the novella attacks the failings of the institution of marriage, so it also complicates that other cherished Victorian notion, the home. The story proclaims that making a home is more problematic than social ideals maintain, and that the West, which presents men with numerous enticements, makes it even harder for women to have homes. Mrs. Greyfield herself bemoans the group of deserted, economically oppressed middle-class women whose husbands have gone off in search of mining adventures or employment. These women are left "in the sunless backrooms of San Francisco boarding-houses," "doing a little fine sewing for the shops" to supplement their meager teacher's pay

(*TNP*, 13). Unfortunately, a large number of middle-class women in the West find themselves homeless with no means of acquiring homes of their own. In one of her *Daily Morning Call* columns, Victor pinpoints two main obstacles to women's self-support. Women as well as men prevent women from attaining a livelihood on their own: "Women despise the business woman; men half contemptuously patronize her, and totally set her aside when looking for a woman to marry, as being 'out of her sphere.' As if woman's sphere was to be a beggar!"[50] But lack of opportunity also discourages women, necessitating unusual fortitude to persist against real barriers: "How few things there are she is permitted to do."[51] As Mrs. Greyfield comments, "Men talk about our getting out of our places [whenever] we clamor for paying work of some kind, for something to do that will enable us to live in half comfort by working more hours than they do to earn lordly livings" (*TNP* 13). Throughout her writing, Victor acknowledges that men hold more social and economic power, but she urges women to protest this distribution of power and not to be deceived by class and gender expectations that render them dependent. Mrs. Anna Greyfield models successful revolt from within a specific class of women.

First, this character represents a practical feminist perspective on women's social and economic problems. After eking out a living sewing men's clothes when she first arrives in Portland, Mrs. Greyfield turns her substantial domestic abilities to running a boardinghouse, one of the few, respectable channels by which some energetic, unmarried, middle-class women could make a social place for themselves and earn a comfortable livelihood. Yet this story reconceptualizes woman's nature and woman's work and offers domestic talents as commodifiable skills. Victor challenges the idea that managing and beautifying a home are part of woman's nature and indisputably women's role. Years in advance of Charlotte Perkins Gilman's concept of professionalizing housework, through Mrs. Greyfield, Victor dismantles the idea of innate domestic skills: "Did it never strike you as being absurd, that men should expect, and as far as they can, require all women to be good housekeepers? They might as well expect every mechanic to carve in wood or chisel marble into forms of life" (*TNP*, 24). Although Mrs. Greyfield happens to be unusually talented in the domestic realm and fortunate in her ability also to capitalize on her skills, Victor's point in emphasizing her talents is to suggest that society should give women the same opportunities as men to exercise their various abilities.

The story also exhibits a wistful, utopian element in its vision of "lone women" achieving the independence and economic security represented by having their own homes.[52] Again the feminist rewriting of the Greek epic appears in Victor's emphasis on female action. Whereas Penelope holds off her suitors by weaving and unraveling her shroud for her father-in-law, Mrs. Greyfield builds a new life and succeeds financially by marketing her domestic talents. The second narrative level of the story accentuates the elegance and refinement of the middle-aged Mrs. Anna Greyfield's home: "two elegant goblets," "the air of substantial comfort," "the dainty cakes and confections," "the charming views," "a bright wood fire in an open fireplace" (*TNP*, 23, 24, 10). In this female-dominated space, provided, furnished, and sustained by her own earnings derived from the running of her second boardinghouse in a mining town in California, Mrs. Anna Greyfield and the narrator share their ideas and experiences.

This image of a comfortable home resembles conventional middle-class notions of domesticity; however, Victor's point is that a home established through women's economic accomplishments and artistry and enjoyed free from male domination is something new and different. Women should have homes, not because they are innately domestic, but because homes symbolize and represent social independence and economic security. Women, like men, should have the means to provide themselves with homes. Victor has identified, separated, and demystified three different ideas embedded within normative ideas of domesticity: the ideology that associates women exclusively with the home and caring for others, domestic talent to manage and beautify a home, and the right to have a home. In short, Victor redefines home as an institution free from patriarchal assumptions.

REFASHIONED GENDER RELATIONS?

So why, then, does this independent new Penelope take back her wandering husband, who far from being a "long-suffering" Odysseus,[53] has been happily married to another woman, now deceased, with whom he had a daughter, Nellie, in the intervening years? The story suggests several answers, intriguing for their social and psychological complexity. Mrs. Anna Greyfield's magnanimity dramatizes a new basis for women's bonds with women; her sympathy for illegitimate and orphaned Nellie leads her to adopt her husband's daughter by his second "wife": "She is a charming girl, and I could not bear to leave her motherless" (*TNP*, 77). Demonstrating how women should uphold and love other women, Mrs. Greyfield transcends jealousy and vindictiveness toward her husband and focuses her attention on a young woman in need: Mrs. Greyfield remarries, in part, to legitimize Nellie.

Furthermore, women's relationship to men is also complicated by women's own emotional, sexual needs. Throughout the story the narrator comments on the unusual beauty of Mrs. Anna Greyfield; even in her late forties she is still remarkably attractive, lovely and lovable, and a theme of passionate attraction between the sexes runs throughout the narrative. Earlier in the story, Mrs. Greyfield reveals how her own longings confused her thinking, making her wish Mr. Seabrook truly was the intelligent, handsome, affectionate gentleman he had initially appeared to be: "There *was* a yearning desire in my heart to be petted and cared for" (*TNP*, 40). Now years later, the still handsome, middle-aged Mrs. Greyfield admits that in Mr. Greyfield's second courtship, she is being influenced by "passion and romance" (*TNP*, 77). Thus, sexuality and physical desire play a recognized role in this new womanhood.

The ending of the novella poses yet another critical riddle. Although the story concludes with a remarriage, it does not follow the conventional nineteenth-century love plot. Instead, it redesigns marriage and raises disturbing points. The story suggests that Mrs. Anna Greyfield remarries to satisfy personal and sexual needs and not to achieve a social identity or to provide for herself financially. In addition, she reestablishes the marriage on her own terms from a position of strength. Having achieved a comfortable, independent home, she can accept Mr. Greyfield's companionship and share his wealth. By her decision, their pasts will remain undiscussed and their future will begin with a European trip. This trip testifies to their financial success and their social status as wealthy, cultured people, but it is also a new experience for both of them on neutral territory. Mrs. Anna Greyfield intends to play a large role in making decisions and in determining the character of the relationship. This marriage will be an equal partnership in which the parties agree on the conditions, resembling the redistribution of power within marriage that Mill recommends.

Furthermore, the nuanced and ambiguous ending of "The New Penelope" suggests complicated female and male realities. Mrs. Anna Greyfield's veiling of the past shows a mature approach to painful facts; she doesn't want to know about her husband's contented second marriage. The story's ending also bespeaks a sad, realistic need to compromise. Her choice to withhold her own experiences, not "to inflict" her story upon her husband, intimates that a perceptual, experiential distance exists between them (*TNP*, 78). She states that men like Mr. Greyfield are unprepared for such a dose of reality, leaving readers to guess whether he would doubt her purity, fume jealously, or blame her. In contrast, Mrs. Anna Greyfield has conveyed this story in detail to her woman friend, the narrator. Victor implies in the writing and publishing of this narrative that men as well as women *need* to hear this female story. Thus, this story and especially its ending portray the emotional and psychological untidiness of life and the difficulty of transforming gender consciousness. Mrs. Anna Greyfield finds that once she has transgressed gender norms through her sensationally disruptive bigamous "marriage" and her independent entrepreneurship, she has come to see these norms as dysfunctional but has realized she must compromise to obtain a qualified happiness. The achievement, then, in this tempered vision is that Victor, always practically aware of the slowness of social change, portrays a new female self creating and asserting herself within the limits of social and historical conditions while also seeking to redefine those limits.

EXEMPLIFYING NEW WOMEN

"The New Penelope" appeared during the 1870s, a decade of renewed contention over women's sexuality and gender identity. Contemporary historians have examined the late 1800s as a time of increasing divergence in the terms through which women sought to validate their bids for new social power. At stake was the issue of whether gender difference or gender equality should form the foundation of social, economic, and political power for women. In 1873, in his widely read book *Sex in Education: or, A Fair Chance for Girls*, Harvard-affiliated Dr. Edward Clarke articulated the medical profession's determinism based on the physiological fact of gender differences. He and other doctors scientifically asserted that biological forces limit women's intellectual capacity, make the pursuit of the mental and physical rigor of male education dangerous to women's reproductive system, and thus "naturally" establish distinctly different social roles for men and women, upholding women's connection to the home and motherhood.[54] Meanwhile, women responded to these scientific pronouncements with competing ideas of women's nature and social roles. While women who remained within the confines of home and those who expanded its boundaries to include civic housekeeping and the right to vote both grounded their idea of womanhood in the concept of women's distinct nature, New Women sought economic independence, professional opportunities, and a sense of selfhood based on equality with men. Victor's fiction, much more than her historical writing and even more powerfully than her journalism, participates in this exploration of gender equality through its portrayal of mature, independent womanhood and its fashioning of a new social script for women's lives.

Not only does Victor's fiction stand in an interesting relationship to its historical moment of production, but also its recent recovery has an intriguing and timely connection to the late twentieth century. In questioning the nineteenth-century social concept of woman's sphere as a natural, biologically determined social space for women and as a social position where they can securely live their lives, Victor anticipates the recent historical studies that show us a West of intra- and inter-gender struggle. In *The Legacy of Conquest*, historian Patricia Limerick has warned against the tendency "to project a sentimentalized hope for women's essential solidarity into the past."[55] In Victor's stories we can glimpse the socially embattled and fragmented West increasingly recreated for us in the 1990s by revisionist historiography of the New Western History. Victor helps us to resist the temptation to stress the cohesion of middle-class white women in the West. Revealing the external and internalized webs of social control that set women in conflict with themselves and with each other, Victor dramatized the directions women could take toward self-liberation, support of other women, and gender equality.

Like their creator, Victor's women characters, Mrs. Anna Greyfield and the female narrator, wrestle with the problem of women's independence and affirm women's rights by openly staking a claim to personal, sexual, social, and economic power for women. The central theme of "The New Penelope" is the discovery of the need for new female selfhood and power, women's empowerment through self-assertion, and the subsequent remaking of female identity. One of the keys to that selfhood is economic independence. Mrs. Anna Greyfield does not pursue a college education, but she does succeed in her own business. She also exemplifies "intelligent, independent womanhood." She is a woman who chooses to reenter marriage from a position of economic autonomy and psychological strength. In "The New Penelope," Victor's roles as independent western woman, historian, social critic, and fictionist converge. Both Victor's life and her characters in this story anticipate that late-nineteenth-century gender identity, the New Woman.

NOTES

1. Frances Fuller Victor, "Some Thoughts About Ourselves," *Portland (Oregon) New Northwest*, 27 February 1874, 1.
2. As a young woman, Metta had earned a reputation as a writer of popular reform novels while Frances preferred editing, writing poetry, and writing history. Metta wrote three popular reform novels: *The Senator's Son; or, the Maine Law, a Last Refuge* in 1851, a temperance novel; *Mormon Wives: A Narrative of Facts Stranger Than Fiction* in 1856 against Mormon polygamy and Utah's statehood; and *Maum Guinea and Her*

Plantation "Children"; or Holiday-Week on a Louisiana Estate. A Slave Romance in 1861 in favor of abolition.

3. Quoted in Jim Martin, *A Bit of a Blue: The Life and Work of Frances Fuller Victor* (Salem, Oregon: Deep Well Publishing Company, 1992), 9.
4. Metta also had a disastrous first marriage and got a divorce. However, unlike Frances, Metta's second marriage was emotionally and professionally fulfilling. She and Orville had nine children.
5. Beginning in 1860, Metta wrote fourteen novels for the first dime novel series.
6. *East and West. The Beauty of Willard's Mill* was Dime Novel #35 and appeared on 1 February 1862. *The Land Claim. A Tale of the Upper Missouri* was Dime Novel #39 and appeared on 31 May 1862.

    Although Frances felt ambivalent about having written these dime novels, *East and West*, the more original and artistically successful of the two, memorably portrays the harsh conditions of frontier life especially for women and features a spunky female hero.
7. Victor, "Some Thoughts," 2.
8. Hazel Emery Mills, "The Emergence of Frances Fuller Victor—Historian." *Oregon Historical Quarterly*, 62 (September 1961) 316, 317.
9. Frances Fuller Victor, "Autobiographical Sketch," *Daily Oregon Statesman*, 16 June 1895, 2.
10. Victor, "Autobiographical Sketch," 2.
11. Sara M. Evans, *Born for Liberty: A History of Women in America* (New York: The Free Press, 1989), 147.
12. "Talented Writer Dies in Oregon [:] Frances Fuller Victor, Known as 'The Historian of the Northwest' Passes Away," *San Francisco Chronicle*, 26 November 1902, 8; Mills, "The Emergence of Frances Fuller Victor—Historian," 300.
13. Victor's story "The New Penelope" and four other stories from that collection have recently been reprinted in a paperback: Egli, Ida Rae, ed. *Women of the Gold Rush: "The New Penelope" and Other Stories* (Berkeley, California: Heyday Books, 1998).
14. Joan Smyth Iversen, "A Debate on the American Home: The Antipolygamy Controversy, 1880–1890," in *American Sexual Politics: Sex, Gender, and Race since the Civil War*, ed. John C. Fout and Maura Shaw Tantillo (Chicago: University of Chicago Press, 1993), 130. Historian Peggy Pascoe has also studied the popularity of sexual politics based on gender difference in her *Relations of Rescue: The Search for Female Moral Authority in the American West, 1874–1939* (New York: Oxford University Press, 1990). She writes:

    > "In identifying and playing on the Victorian "women's values" of purity and piety, nineteenth-century Protestant mission women tapped a vein rich with strategic advantages. Their search for female moral authority allowed women to turn familia—even culturally approved—ideas about female nature into tools to challenge male power. So appealing was this approach that missionary groups were the largest women's organizations in the country from the 1870s to 1900." (xviii)

15. Victor, "Some Thoughts About Ourselves," 2.
16. Victor [Dorothy D.], "Cultivated Women" *San Francisco Daily Morning Call*, Sunday 27 June, 1875, 1.
17. Victor, "Cultivated Women," 1.
18. Victor [Dorothy D.], "Poor Ladies," *San Francisco Daily Morning Call*, Sunday, 25 April 1875, 1.
19. The paths of Charlotte Perkins Stetson [Gilman] and Frances Fuller Victor crossed at the Woman's Congress, a weeklong meeting held in San Francisco from April 30 to May 6, 1894. The Congress covered a range of topics of interest to women, among them, dress for women, education, women in business, women's pioneer experiences,

and social reform. The *San Francisco Chronicle*, reporting on the proceedings of May 1st, commented, "'The Physical Evolution of Woman,' written by Frances Fuller Victor of Salem, Or., was read by Mrs. Charlotte Perkins Stetson" (Wednesday, 2 May 1894, p.7, c. 4). Victor was one of three delegates from Oregon. Both Victor and Stetson were active in the Pacific Coast Women's Press Association in the mid-1890s. In January of 1895, Mrs. Charlotte Perkins Stetson wrote an article for the *Impress*, the magazine of that organization, featuring Victor's accomplishments as a western journalist and historian.

20. Victor, ["Dorothy D."], Contrasts Masculine and Feminine Nature," *San Francisco Daily Morning Call*, Sunday, 1 August 1875, 5; Victor, "Some Thoughts," 2.

21. Victor [Dorothy D.], "Common-Place Women," *San Francisco Daily Morning Call*, Sunday, 25 July 1875, 1.

22. Victor's stories anticipate the fiction of Mary Austin and Willa Cather. These western women writers share with Victor similar sexual politics; female characters who defy social norms, and a focus on strong, independent, self-assertive women. Mrs. Anna Greyfield has affinities with Cather's Alexandra Bergson of *O Pioneers!* (1913) and Thea Kronborg of *The Song of the Lark* (1915) and with Austin's the Walking Woman in *Lost Borders* (1909) and Dulcie Adelaid of *Cactus Thorn* (written in 1927).

23. In Victor's novel *Judith Miles: or, What Shall Be Done with Her?* (Portland [Oregon] *New Northwest*. December 5, 1873 through May 8, 1874), the narrator briefly mentions John Stuart Mill and his contribution to women's equality. One theme of *Judith Miles* is women's need to be socially and economically free to discover their own potential.

24. Victor was not unique among early feminists in unmasking the flaws in nineteenth-century marriage. For example, in an article entitled "The Man Marriage," Elizabeth Cady Stanton criticized marriage: "Marriage, today, is in no way viewed as an equal partnership, intended for the equal advantage and happiness of both parties" (*The Revolution* 8 April, 1869, 218). Stanton proposed to rectify the problem by empowering women to employ their innate qualities "for everyone knows that morally and spiritually woman is superior to man" (217). Stanton imagined an enlarged life for women: "Exalt woman, make her the sovereign and not the slave of the fireside. ... Help her to be an independent, virtuous, self-supporting being, by giving her a free pass in the world of work and thought wherever she has the power to stand. Then she will no longer degrade marriage, by accepting it as a pecuniary necessity" (218). These ideas resemble Victor's except that she emphasizes cultural conditioning and gender equality over essentialist traits and underscores women's right to independence from marriage. In *Women in Economics*, published in 1898, Charlotte Perkins Gilman also objected to marriage as women's destiny and argued for economic independence for women.

25. Judith Schwarz, *Radical Feminists of Heterodoxy: Greenwich Village 1912–1940* (Norwich, Vermont: New Victoria Publishers, Inc., 1986), 29.

26. Richard White, "Trashing the Trails," in *Trails toward a New Western History*, ed. Patricia Limerick, Clyde A. Milner II, and Charles E. Rankin (Lawrence: University of Kansas Press, 1991), 32.

27. Elizabeth Jameson, "Women as Workers, Women as Civilizers: True Womanhood in the American West," in *The Women's West*, ed. Susan Armitage and Elizabeth Jameson (Norman: University of Oklahoma Press, 1987), 159.

28. Donald Worster, *Under Western Skies: Nature and History in the American West* (New York: Oxford University Press, 1992), 15.

29. Frances Fuller Victor, "The New Penelope," in *The New Penelope and Other Stories and Poems* (San Francisco: A. L. Bancroft & Company, 1877), 11. Subsequent references to this story are cited in the text with the abbreviation *TNP.*

30. Although Harte was a regular contributor to the San Francisco *Golden Era* between 1860 and 1863 (Gary Scharnhorst, *Bret Harte* [New York: Twayne Publishers, 1992], 4–7), and Victor wrote her column for the *Era*, slightly later, between April 1863 and January 1865, she most likely met Harte at this time and read his stories. Between 1868 and 1870, as the first editor of the *Overland Monthly*, Harte published his own western stories and invited Victor's stories and historical articles, especially encouraging her to pursue the latter.

31. Franklin Walker, *San Francisco's Literary Frontier* (New York: Knopf, 1939; reprint; Seattle: University of Washington Press, 1969), 264.

32. Frances Fuller Victor, preface to *The New Penelope and Other Stories and Poems* (San Francisco: A. L. Bancroft & Company, 1877).

33. "The New Penelope" also represents a culmination of Victor's ideas of female heroism and western conflicts that she had experimented with in her dime novels, *East and West* and *The Land Claim*. From these earlier westerns, Victor brought a number of colorful sensational, adventurous elements that selected and exaggerated realistic features of the West: specific western geographical and environmental conditions; specific western conflicts; the sense of a rapidly changing region and thus a highly charged historical moment; a view of women's sexuality under assault by the minimally restricted powers of men; and female identity poised on the border of respectability, between the need and opportunity for expanded action and the physical, social, sexual risks incurred by such actions.

34. Victor's western fiction, while remaining class and race bound, emerges from a thriving, unique, sophisticated western literary scene and also contributes to women's nationwide artistic conversation on women's identity and social status. Within this large dialogue, Victor's fiction incorporates elements of women's polemical writings about women's wrongs and the anguished, artistically complex fiction of mid-nineteenth-century eastern writers such as Alice Cary, Fanny Fern, Rebecca Harding Davis, Elizabeth Stoddard, Elizabeth Stuart Phelps, Rose Terry Cooke, and Harriet Prescott Spofford. Her argumentative discussions of women's economic and social degradation seem to align her with women's rights fiction, that political genre that David S. Reynolds says "dramatized the need for legal and social change on behalf of women" (*Beneath the American Renaissance: The Subversive Imagination in the Age of Emerson and Melville* [Cambridge: Harvard University Press], 387). Yet her stories never seem driven by issues. They also evince some of those dark themes, psychological probings of feminine identity and marital relations, and examples of those strange, stark images found in the body of eastern women's writing that Reynolds has labeled "the literature of misery" (*Beneath the American Renaissance*, 395). But neither the label women's rights fiction nor "the literature of misery" can categorize Victor's stories, which also bring together dime novel western conventions and western local color features.

35. Peggy Pascoe, "Western Women at the Cultural Crossroads," in *Trails Toward a New Western History*, ed. Patricia Nelson Limerick, Clyde A. Milner, II, and Charles E. Rankin (Lawrence: University of Kansas Press, 1991), 43.

36. Even though Ella Sterling Mighels states that Victor's stories were sometimes, when copied in the East, credited to Bret Harte, her most ambitious stories refashion male regional writing (*The Story of the Files: A Review of Californian Writers and Literature* [San Francisco: Co-operative Printing, 1893], 160). Whether we interpret Harte as a sentimentalist who "adapted the perennially successful romantic formulas to the Western scene" (Walker, *San Francisco's Literary Frontier*, 264) as Franklin Walker does, or as a western humorist who infused his stories with biblical parody and harsh irony as Gary Scharnhorst does, Victor's characterization and narrative purpose show a marked difference from Harte's. For Harte's stereotypical gamblers, drunkards, mining partners, prostitutes, and illegitimate babes, Victor substitutes middle-class wives, mothers,

and widows, respectable but threatened girls, intemperate, irresponsible husbands and military officers, tyrannical fathers, gentlemanly bigamists, and cultured land agents. Exhibiting both playful and risque elements, Victor's stories lack Harte's deadpan humor and strive for more psychological and social realism than Harte's stories do.

37. In this story and also in her journalistic writing, Victor addresses the topic of sexual harassment as the subtle and overt ways that men abuse their social privilege and exert their power to intimidate women. Her arguments and examples sound eerily contemporary.

38. John Stuart Mill, *The Subjection of Women* (1869, reprint; New York: Prometheus Books, 1986), 41.

39. Mill, *The Subjection of Women*, 42.

40. Susan Armitage, "Reluctant Pioneers" in *Women and Western Literature*, ed. Helen Winter Stauffer and Susan J. Rosowski (Troy, NY: Whitston Publishing, 1982), 40.

41. Carroll Smith-Rosenberg, *Disorderly Conduct: Visions of Gender in Victorian America* (New York: Oxford University Press, 1985), 65.

42. Victor, "Some Thoughts About Ourselves," 1.

43. Victor, "Some Thoughts About Ourselves," 2.

44. Mill, *The Subjection of Women*, 17.

45. One theme that emerges in Victor's journalism is the economic and social barriers women erect against other women by their adherence to class and gender prescriptions. She writes: "But just so long as women content themselves to be parasites, no matter how graceful or beautiful in their dependence, so long will they degrade the idea of work for their less fortunate sisters, make more thorny the path of the honestly struggling of their sex, reduce the wages that woman receives for her work, and perpetuate their own moral enslavement" ([Dorothy D.], "Poor Ladies," *San Francisco Daily Morning Call*, Sunday 25, April 1875, 1).

46. Frances Fuller Victor, "Dorothy D. Contrasts Masculine and Feminine Nature," *San Francisco Daily Morning Call* (Sunday, 1 August, 1875), 5.

47. Victor, "Women as Know Nothings," *Portland (Oregon) West Shore*, February 1876, 2.

48. Victor, "Women as Know Nothings," 2.

49. Louise Michele Newman, *Men's Ideas/Women's Realities: "Popular Science," 1870–1915* (New York: Pergamon Press, 1985), 298.

50. Victor [Dorothy D.], "Poor Ladies," *San Francisco Daily Morning Call*, Sunday, 25 April 1875, 1.

51. Victor [Dorothy D.], "Poor Ladies," 1.

52. In a letter written from the East to her Oregon friend, Judge Matthew P. Deady, 27 October 1872, Victor, who was now separated from her husband, applied for the job of librarian in the Portland Library and included this remark: "I have no *home*—never shall as long as I am alone in the west—and it is a very ardent wish of mine to set up my lares and penates somewhere soon, as I observe the gray beginning to show among my auburn locks" (quoted in Hazel Emery Mills, "Travels of Lady Correspondent," *Pacific Northwest Quarterly* 45 [37 October 1954], 114). Victor's longing for a steady job and a home suggest that Mrs. Anna Greyfield's attractive home is a feminist fantasy of self-sufficiency. Throughout her thirty-nine years in the West, Victor actively pursued a means of providing as adequately for herself; unfortunately, her intense, rigorous writing career never yielded financial compensation commensurate with her efforts and achievements. Although Victor's six volumes for Bancroft "were pronounced the best in the series," Bancroft, profited from their success rather than Victor ("Talented Writer," 8). Her life continued to testify to the economic vulnerability of a lone woman, and she spent the last four years of her life as a tenant of a boardinghouse in Portland (Alfred Powers, *The History of Oregon Literature* [Portland, Oregon: Metropolitan Press, 1935], 312).

53. See Homer, *The Odyssey*. A Norton Critical Edition, trans. Albert Cook. (New York: W. W. Norton & Company, 1974).

54. For a detailed discussion of the social and cultural force of Clarke's writings and other supposedly scientifically based rationalizations of women's roles, see Rosalind Rosenberg, *Beyond Separate Spheres: Intellectual Roots of Modern Feminism* (New Haven: Yale University Press, 1982); Louise Michele Newman, *Men's Ideas/Women's Realities*; and Carroll Smith-Rosenberg, "The New Woman as Androgyne: Social Disorder and Gender Crisis, 1870–1936," in *Disorderly Conduct*, 245–296.

55. Patricia Nelson Limerick, *The Legacy of Conquest: The Unbroken Past of the American West* (New York: W. W. Norton & Company, 1987), 50.

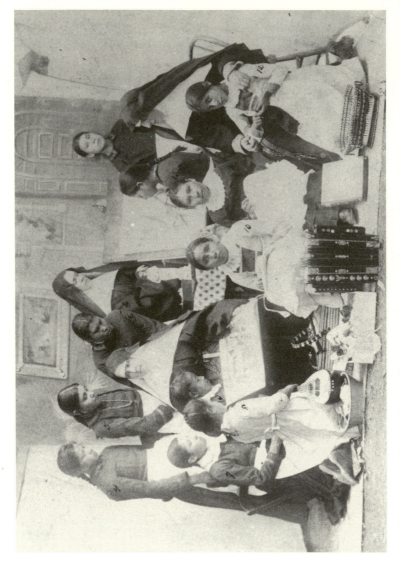

Fig. 4.1 *Left to right:* Mother Amadeus with two of the early St. Labre's Mission teachers, Sister Ignatius and Sister Francis, in the sewing and crafts class with Cheyenne girls. Reprinted by permission of Archives, Ursuline Convent of the Sacred Heart, Toledo, Ohio.

4

"WE HAD NO ASSISTANCE FROM ANYONE–HAPPIER TO DO IT ALONE": MONTANA, THE MISSIONS, AND MOTHER AMADEUS

Anne M. Butler

On a cold January day in 1884, six Ursuline nuns, led by Mother Mary Amadeus of the Heart of Jesus, stepped from the train at Miles City, Montana. These members of the Order of Saint Ursula, leaving the familiar shelter of their Toledo, Ohio, convent, had traveled three days and nights on the Northern Pacific railroad, its tracks only recently extended to this western hinterland. Here, in an uninviting town wedged between the Tongue and Yellowstone Rivers, the women planned to take up life as Roman Catholic missionaries in the Rocky Mountain West.

The move launched the thirty-eight-year-old mother superior out of two decades of privacy as a teacher and convent administrator to a public career, ultimately rewarding her with both acclaim and censure.[1] This essay examines the first year (1884) that Mother Amadeus, a single, middle-aged woman with problematic health, spent in Montana. It argues that the West allowed Amadeus to exercise new aspects of personal agency, resulting in a complex western presence for her and the Ursuline nuns.[2] Inspired by what was, for white women, a frontier environment, as well as by commitment to her religious order and the strength of her own work ethic, Mother Amadeus carved out opportunities to pursue female authority, unusual adventure, and congregational autonomy. Deep inside a zone known to Catholics as the Rocky Mountain Mission, Mother Amadeus Dunne blended the exigencies of frontier living with the goals of the Ursuline sisterhood.[3] For the remainder of her long life, Mother Amadeus Dunne, who died in 1919, immersed herself in the women's West, especially within the context of Catholic religious sisterhood.

In January of 1884, Mother Amadeus brought her sisters to one of the lesser villages of the American West. Miles City had lurched into existence as a military campsite, shortly abandoned for the construction of the nearby Fort Keogh. No particular civic planning marked the transition from military to civilian oversight, and the town stumbled through a series of short-lived economic ventures. Miles City followed the financial path of many a frontier urban settlement—several different booms, driven by masculine labor performed in the open air, which generated prosperity, only to fold, leaving the citizens without an alternate industry for economic support. Soldiers, buffalo hunters, cowboys, mule skinners, and railroad laborers infused some life into the local economy, but a steady job with a steady income was hard to come by. Accordingly, although a few families lived in Miles City and at Fort Keogh, the area population tilted disproportionately toward single males. As a result, the economy depended on the presence of a high number of saloons, brothels, and gambling halls. But this nineteenth-century entertainment industry fell short as a base on which a western town might build lasting commerce, as Miles City came to understand.

Its bonanza days collapsed, Miles City may have hoped that America's pioneer farm folk would fill the economic vacuum with their plows and plantings. However, the stony dry soil of the region discouraged even the most enthusiastic farmers. Stock grazing emerged as the best long-term and profit-bearing agricultural use of the countryside.

Further, although the location between two rivers should have encouraged transportation development, such did not prove to be the case. While the rivers might have been a boon, instead they were a threat. On nearly an annual basis, the winter sequence of freeze and thaw brought unpleasant floods through the center of town. Soil erosion along the river was extreme, with huge portions of the bank lost each year. The rivers, their color dulled by mud, were never easy to cross; their meanders forced travelers to ford several times a day, inhibiting progress and promoting frustration. When the rivers engorged with spring floods, they presented yet another problem, even to experienced drivers.

Well-entrenched cattle rustlers and horse thieves moved around on the broad lands in surrounding eastern and southeastern Montana. For a brief time, their successful raids against the grazing cattle and horses prompted irate stock owners to gather in Miles City to consider ways to halt the exasperating losses. The first of these conversations resulted in the organization of the Montana Stockgrowers Association, which appreciated the city's lavish hospitality to the visiting cattlemen. The businessmen soon found they quarreled as much among themselves as with the rustlers, so despite the efforts of Miles City to be an alluring conference spot, by the late 1880s, the meetings fell off, as ultimately did the open range husbandry of stockgrowers.[4]

Poorly crafted wooden shacks of one story gave the town a shabby appearance. The threat of fire hung in the air, especially along the most congested streets, and on a regular basis, spectacular conflagrations swept through, leaving behind smoldering piles of ash. In these early years, there was no municipal infrastructure: streets were not paved, no water delivery system was in place, and there were no city services. Miles City, with its out-of-the-way location, harsh geography, and shallow economy did not appear destined to draw large numbers of western settlers to add to its population of approximately two thousand. Indeed, the combination of all these factors served to make Miles City a rather dreary place, limited by its past, dissatisfied with its present, and tentative about its future.

The once-cloistered Mother Amadeus, born Sarah Theresa Dunne in 1846, must have struck seasoned Montanans as a peculiar figure to join the grim and soggy world around Miles City. With her arrival in Montana, Amadeus reentered an America she had last known in the midst of civil war. But she did not return as a shy nun or western greenhorn. Despite her long absence and the changes of twenty years, she adjusted quickly to a nation now investing much of its collective energy in political and economic development in the West. Amadeus joined other Anglo-Americans from the East and Midwest who gazed across western lands, seeing better lives for individuals and potential growth for the country. Accordingly, Amadeus, with slight preparation but a healthy measure of confidence, led her companion nuns to make their contribution as community builders on the rugged frontier of Montana.

Such a positive outcome might not have been predicted based on the chilly reception the nuns received at the Miles City train depot, where silent bystanders reacted to the new residents by gawking at their black habits and long veils. Amadeus ignored their coolness and accepted with composure the near boisterous greetings of the Montana bishop John Baptist Brondel, Father Joseph Eyler (the Ursulines' mission escort),

Father Eli J. W. Lindesmith (the Fort Keogh chaplain), and a pair of Catholic laywomen. Mixed opinions of Catholicism, which perhaps explained the oddly friendly and unfriendly scene at the railroad station, as well as the bleak surroundings in this cattle and cowboy town, did not appear to bother Amadeus any more than the uninviting January temperature.

Salutations exchanged, Amadeus and her companions left in carriages for a short tour of Miles City and then on to the inn of Bridget McCanna, arrangements made for them by Bishop Brondel. The sisters could have stayed across the street from the train depot at the Macqueen House, a somewhat upscale hotel that catered to bachelor cattlemen. However, with its partylike masculine atmosphere, ongoing games of chance, and proximity to Kitty Hardiman's dance hall, the Macqueen seemed a poor choice for nuns, who among other reasons could ill afford the room rates in Miles City's lone attractive hotel.[5]

Once inside the McCanna household, Amadeus must have thought Macqueen's with dining service and private rooms more suitable, regardless of the cost or the clientele. The dilapidated McCanna home, with its cracked doors and missing windows, was more unsettling than the nuns had expected, but it introduced them to the typically deep poverty of Irish Catholics in the West.[6] Stale air, chicken droppings, and grease-stained walls surrounded the sisters, who struggled to remain in the stench-filled house. While waiting for supper, the nuns perched uneasily on an assortment of broken furnishings. Bridget McCanna's poor pantry yielded an unappetizing dinner of boiled codfish and potatoes, a taste of jelly cake, and all washed down with tea. The owner's rambunctious and numerous grandchildren added to the general disorder, ricocheting about the main room, tripping over the bishop, dropping firewood, bumping into cook pots.

On retiring to the upstairs, the sisters found more of the same squalor. Amadeus pronounced the sleeping quarters unfit, the bedding filthy, and the snow, drifting through cracks and windows, intolerable. The six nuns, wrapped in their shawls and an overcoat, spent a night without heat, huddled together on the floor, separated from male lodgers by a few pieces of dirty calico and canvas.[7] Through the sleepless night, Mother Amadeus, at last feeling the bite of the Montana cold on her arthritis, later reported to the Toledo superior, "says I to myself, 'this will be our last night at Bridget McCanna's.'"[8]

Daylight saw Amadeus ready to assert herself as superior of the newly arrived nuns. Although her every decision, within the context of a patriarchal faith, required permission from the clergy, Amadeus knew her way around negotiations with male superiors. She had not served two terms as the elected head of the Toledo convent and several years as the mistress of novices for naught. She set forth for Bishop Brondel's quarters fueled by the Ursuline congregation's tradition, which meshed contemplative religious life with an active ministry, fully prepared to use the skills she had learned in her executive positions in Toledo. This complicated background armed her with a strategy for approaching the bishop and building her place in Miles City.[9]

Presenting herself to Brondel, Amadeus declared Bridget McCanna's household "too promiscuous" for the sisters. By employing this language, she called on widely held perceptions of sisterhood to explain her displeasure with the McCanna boardinghouse. No clergyman would try to argue away such a statement or suggest it desirable that nuns, even briefly, take their room and board in a public house that rented open dormitories to laborers, cowboys, and bartenders.

Amadeus refrained from confronting the bishop with the obvious. Because he had anticipated the arrival of the Toledo nuns for at least a month, he might have directed someone to find them an inhabitable residence.[10] Amadeus sidestepped that point, as well as the extreme filth, boisterousness of the McCanna family, or the strain on nuns just from the cloister. Instead, she concentrated on presenting her case in positive language, telling the bishop, "without giving him any of the details, that we were not in the right place ... on account of the ... lodgers."[11]

She also understood the importance of diplomacy, when acting as the spokesperson for an entire convent of sisters, who depended on her leadership for their day-to-day survival. A mother superior who appeared to be a complainer with unrealistic demands, especially to an over worked bishop with few monetary resources, would be off to a rocky start, jeopardizing future relationships for herself, her sisters, and her congregation. The result could be the denial of material and spiritual support for the community, a circumstance that had seen more than one pioneer group of nuns withdraw from a frontier mission.[12]

In addition, Brondel himself had made a difficult journey to Miles City, so that he might personally welcome the Ursulines, a fact that Amadeus knew and appreciated. Amadeus certainly did not care to risk the possibility that the saddle-weary bishop would think her too assertive in manner, ungrateful for his hospitality, or insensitive to his own physical exhaustion. She knew exactly how to weigh these factors, as well as the nunlike tone with which to communicate so that a clergy superior would proclaim, as did Bishop Brondel, "I will say 'Yes' to everything as long as you are good children."[13]

Despite her deference to the bishop and her understanding of his parental role, this decidedly unchildlike woman extracted from her male superior precisely the terms she sought, that is, authorization to engage the town on her own. Amadeus offered to assume for Brondel or his agent the burden of house hunting, assuring the bishop that she could identify desirable and useful apartments more quickly than a third party. Willing to be relieved of the chore, the bishop agreed to both her requests: the nuns could leave Bridget McCanna; and Amadeus, accompanied by a sister of the Sacred Heart of Jesus, could make a public canvas of the available rental properties in Miles City.[14]

Armed with ecclesiastical consent, Amadeus and her companion plunged into the commercial district of Miles City. They walked along its muddy streets, conversed with local citizens, stopped at various stores, and engaged shopkeepers. Here and there, Amadeus stretched the bishop's permission, apparently deciding she might conclude any related business without seeking further approval.

By nightfall, Amadeus had leased, for twenty-five dollars a month, a modest five-room house on the corner of Seventh and Palmer Streets, outfitted it with stoves, installed them, and purchased coal. Mother Amadeus infused the humble rental house with new dignity, naming the unlikely building the "Ursuline Convent of the Sacred Heart."[15] Although the dwelling, furnished only with a couple of boxes and a makeshift table covered by newspapers, hardly suggested the dignified ambiance of a convent, the superior, in a brisk move, transformed its identity from empty rental property to respectable church icon. Now satisfied that the sisters had an appropriate shelter, Mother Amadeus wrote to Mother Stanislaus in Toledo, "We had no assistance from anyone—happier to do it alone."[16]

Within the first day of her arrival in Montana, Mother Amadeus had placed an Ursuline mark on Miles City. Amadeus did so by acting on her congregational authority as the convent superior, taking her role as a decision maker to the public, circulating through town, negotiating for real estate, making purchases, shopping for groceries, and in general, acquainting herself with the business community and it with her. Overnight, Amadeus added to the process of building institutions in Miles City, publicized the Ursuline congregation, redefined a secular structure as a religious space, and increased the material presence of the Catholic Church, within the unquestionable domain of women—a convent.

The nuns brushed aside the stilted events at the train depot and did not look on them as attitudes typical of all their neighbors. Instead, through symbolic behaviors, personal conversations, and business transactions, Amadeus had demonstrated that the Ursuline sisters intended to be part of Miles City, run down and dispirited though much of it was.

After their initial setbacks, Mother Amadeus judged their circumstances to be quite good, declaring, "It is a miserable little town, but the people are fine."[17]

Although the Ursulines seemed saddened, rather than offended or shocked, by the prevalent vice industry in the city—one sister commenting, "not Catholicity but Christianity is at its lowest ebb here"—the poverty and adversity, greater than anticipated, concerned them more.[18] Consequently, the nuns approached their new mission without inflicting moral judgments on their neighbors or adopting a self-righteous demeanor for themselves. For over three hundred years, Ursulines in Europe and North America had succeeded during eras of intense political unrest and social upheaval because in the midst of chaos and brutality their leadership emphasized respect-based service. Uproarious Miles City would not be treated differently.

At the same time, the religious part of their own lives was crucial, and Amadeus saw to it that the sisters quickly conveyed this element to the residents of Miles City. On their first Sunday in town, the sisters rose from their barren earthen floor resting places at an early hour, took neither food nor drink, and walked along winter streets to the Catholic church, which they scrubbed thoroughly before the eight o'clock service. The nuns, having readied the altar, participated in the early liturgy, as well as one at eleven o'clock. At the latter, they supplied the organ music and choral pieces for a high mass, the first celebrated in Miles City.[19] Now, in an uncommon moment, the lay attendees watched as nuns took the communion of their faith and listened as the bishop lavished praise on the six women for accepting the privations of a Montana mission.

Following the conclusion of the church worship and the sisters' return to their house, a flurry of guests descended on the recently acquired convent. Visitors came and went for several hours, unaware that their presence prevented the sisters from breaking their eucharistic fast. The nuns, who had labored since before dawn, had no chance for nourishment until late in the afternoon. Yet as they finally took food and drink, the sisters could look back on a day in which public expectations had asked new things of long-held cloister identities. For nearly twelve hours, under a secular scrutiny foreign to their earlier convent life, the nuns facilitated and shared a range of rituals for people only slightly acquainted with the religious rule of Catholic nuns.

Under the guidance of Amadeus, the nuns had passed their first Sunday turning minds toward worship and its power on the human spirit, underscoring in that message the essence of why the sisters had ventured into Miles City. Whether Catholic or non-Catholic, friend or foe, or neutral observer, all recognized the symbols of religious life and perhaps remembered faith-based habits of their childhood homes. The nuns' distinctive garb, their genteel manner, their sacred music, their appearance at a public church service, and their convent reception all focused on ideals the Miles City populace had little time to cultivate. In a remote western community dominated by wrenching isolation, commercial competition, harsh cultural conflicts, and environmental destruction, the Ursuline nuns suggested a counterpoise in formal religion.

At the same time, Mother Amadeus restored the prayer routines of an Ursuline house, adding another dimension to the impression she was making on the local community. Although Miles City residents, where Catholics numbered few, might not witness the Ursulines prostrate before the chapel altar or engaged in spiritual reading, they knew nuns conducted a religious life beyond the view of outsiders. Matins, lauds, vespers, compline, the daily sounds of Latin prayer, the melodic rhythms of rosary recitation, and the harmonies of song floated from the little convent.[20]

Thus, Amadeus called on the private prescripts of a monastic house to make yet another public statement. It reminded laypeople that the nuns, servants to both religious and secular clocks, juggled the obligations of dual worlds. Further, they were dual worlds in which the nuns determined the borders, deciding when, where, and by whom they would be crossed.[21] Overall, citizens of Miles City could expect that personal conduct guided by spirituality and social service through education would be the double hallmarks of the Ursuline Convent of the Sacred Heart.

While the West was learning about these improbable pioneers, they were learning about the West. Some of the intense exchange with laypeople was alien to their long-held convent traditions, but some they sought intentionally. Although no one could predict the outcome of this convent venture, the Ursuline nuns, following the lead of Amadeus, assumed an active role in shaping their western lives. By design and some chance, these nouveau frontier women and their rough-edged neighbors exchanged cultural information, a linchpin in the reorganization of society in western environments.

For example, before the end of January, Amadeus had visited the public school, making the acquaintance of the principal and assessing the educational competition he, as a graduate of Harvard University, might represent.[22] She had conversed with Catholics and non-Catholics, businessmen and military personnel, white citizens and Native people, men and women. She worked her way into the nooks and crannies of Miles City life. The totality with which Amadeus embraced Miles City seemed to indicate that Bishop Brondel's advice to "go everywhere for a few weeks and after that to keep [your] enclosure as strictly as possible," rested on a faulty hope.[23]

Despite the bishop's words, the American West did not lend itself to the enclosure of nuns.[24] Amadeus was among an increasing number of American sisters who saw how this European convent device, rarely absolute, produced considerable tension between religious women and church authorities.[25] Masculine control over all temporal and spiritual matters implicit in the rule of enclosure did not always rest easily with religious women, and less so as the nineteenth century moved forward and sisters in the West spent weeks and months functioning in highly public forums.

Further, once the sisters loosened the yoke of enclosure, they seemed loathe to return to its strictest forms. It was, in its extremes, a procedure that made cloistered women dependent on the regular assistance—in both monetary and mundane ways—of outsiders. The most ordinary business of life had to be managed through a third party, who came and went on behalf of those behind the grates. Small wonder that Mother Amadeus had angled to find the sisters' quarters on her own, without the tedium of waiting for another person to do so.

As Amadeus had seen, a fundamental contradiction existed between expecting women to shun society, while pressing on them lengthy uncloisterlike travels to serve the Catholic poor. At the same time, nuns, regardless of their public work in a community, came from a long heritage of domestic privacy. Amadeus no doubt appreciated that sisters used convent seclusion to their advantage, finding in it the freedom to mold congregational goals away from the watchful eyes of men and according to the vision of women. Enclosure, especially in America, proved to be the sort of regulation that religious women preferred to define for themselves.

Most importantly, a life of enforced habitation did not integrate well with the economic realities of western living. The West was fueled and shaped by work—paid and unpaid labor performed by women, men, and children of every culture and ethnicity. In this place of work, monastic enclosure was impractical, and nuns, like other western residents, needed to support themselves through paid labor. A rule of strict enclosure threatened economic disaster for nuns cut off from available work in a surrounding frontier community.[26] Across the West, religious women took advantage of the vacuum in social services, establishing critically needed schools, hospitals, orphanages, women's boardinghouses, nursing homes, and child care centers as means for convent support.

Amadeus needed to do the same to assure her community became part of this western workforce. First and foremost, her thin purse required it. She left Toledo with slight funding, for Richard Gilmour, the Ohio bishop, had rather airily dismissed her inquiry about finances, chiding her to display no concern for such earthly matters, but to look for supernatural care.[27] The cost of travel, the price of the convent stoves, and the high tariff on food in Miles City—a barrel of flour cost $10—had depleted her cash.

Although Bishop Brondel gave a $1,000 stipend to the convent, the gift would not even begin to cover its many expenses. Most of his money had been allocated for land purchase or construction costs, the latter so inflated it was evident his donation would not stretch very far.[28] Mother Amadeus, while guided by spiritual conviction, was much too practical a woman to wait quietly for divine intervention.

Educators that they were, Amadeus and the sisters drew on their Ursuline mission to teach. Amadeus thought the sisters might be able to give French lessons to some public schoolteachers or that needlework classes would draw students, for she noted, "They are wild out here about fancy work. I wish we had someone to teach embroidery." She began plans for the opening of a school, and the first of February saw the Ursulines engaged with their teaching duties. They had gathered thirty-seven pupils for a Sunday school and thought this number reflected positive prospects for establishing a boarding academy, "if we had a house large enough."[29]

Not only would they secure income from the families of the residential students, but Amadeus, like teaching sisters everywhere, knew that offering the always popular music lessons promised a solid source of revenue. A boarding scholar could be charged $20 a month without music, but $25 if the student took vocal or instrumental instruction.[30] A music curriculum was critical to the success of the sisters' school.

With this in mind, Mother Amadeus directed her energies toward renting a piano, but Miles City had none. She made an appeal to the Toledo convent, which kept a steady supply of food, household goods, and school materials directed toward the Montana Ursulines. Amadeus poured all the Ohio donations into starting the school, but fretted about the arrival in Miles City of a German professor of music, feeling that "his coming is bad for us."[31] The importance of music instruction at the Ursuline school remained paramount in her planning, and its implementation demanded Amadeus secure a piano.

These difficulties aside, within a month after their arrival in Montana, the Ursulines had opened their classrooms, despite some displeasure from the public school principal, watching his students enroll with the nuns. Seventeen children signed on at the primary level and another eight began in the secondary class. Sister Sacred Heart took on vocal and instrumental music, a task made lighter when the much-desired piano arrived from Toledo at the end of March. Amadeus fairly glowed with pleasure, declaring, "Now I hope we will be able to get some good music students," for she added, "You ought to have seen the embraces the piano received!!!"[32] Although the convent treasury remained negligible, Amadeus, with the support of her companion nuns, had called on the fundamental ministry of her religious congregation, activating the source for income that would sustain the Ursulines in Miles City—education.[33]

Within a brief period of time, Mother Amadeus had exercised multi-layered authority. While her actions fell within the parameters of necessary decision making for a new mission, they quite exceeded the daily influence of most post-bellum, educated, white women. Miles City was not replete with women who engaged the business community, conversed with citizens from every class and culture, and established financial credit. Mother Amadeus Dunne had quickly and efficiently done all three.

In Montana, Amadeus enjoyed the freedom to make choices without a major superior or ever-watchful priestly advisor present to endorse or criticize her actions. No more were a senior mother superior and her board of councillors close at hand to supervise each move. If the Toledo bishop or Ursuline convent expressed displeasure or distress about something in Montana, it took the mail days or weeks to deliver the word to Miles City. By the time a cautionary suggestion or pointed question arrived from the East, the pioneer sisters, in the common pattern of frontier colonists, often had resolved the issue and moved on to other concerns.

Bishop Brondel, to whom Amadeus answered most formally, had returned to Helena, busy with the cares of his enormous diocese. Father Eyler, cursed with a fragile constitution fated to make him a less than sturdy missionary, was soon off to the Cheyenne reservation. Father Lindesmith, chaplain at Fort Keogh, while an attentive friend, was occupied with wide-ranging pastoral duties that kept him moving about the countryside. In the West, Mother Amadeus discovered weakened links in the patriarchal chain of command, which presented opportunities for greater personal agency, an advantage enhanced when distant superiors could not monitor the outpost convent with ease.

Inside the Miles City convent, the nuns appeared united in their support for the Mother Amadeus administration. If there were grievances, the sisters had few avenues by which to complain. Amadeus was the highest-ranking Ursuline in Montana, so the other sisters really had no easy way to murmur in distress to a more senior nun.

Given the intimacy in the tiny convent, secret messages to Toledo would have been extremely difficult to post. Of course, the recipients in Toledo might have deciphered veiled criticisms by virtue of their previous acquaintance with all the sisters in Montana. Their return epistles, however, were shared among the six mission sisters and read aloud during recreation. Responses to individual protests would have been awkward and not much in keeping with the general precept that sisters refrain from even the appearance of disobedience to a mother superior.

Regardless of these possibilities, the five nuns in the Miles City convent, at least in their letters to Toledo, endorsed the decisions and guidance of Mother Amadeus and wrote of her with admiration and affection. For example, Sister Holy Angels drew inspiration from Amadeus's refusal to yield to illness or infirmity, the more so because, "as rigid as she is with herself, as kind she is to us." The youthful Sister Francis hoped for more nuns to ease the burdens of Mother Amadeus, whom she observed, "has not as yet had any rest, as she went right into school and teaches 7 hours a day."[34] This loyalty added to the growing Montana authority of Mother Amadeus, an authority legitimated by her position as a superior in the Ursuline congregation, but one that also overrode secular gender roles.

The capable administrator now looked to push the Ursuline name deeper into the Montana frontier, sending the sisters into regions beyond Anglo settlements and the usual haunts of white women. Amadeus directed her attention to the establishment of a mission among the Northern Cheyenne, in the southeast corner of the territory. The plan to open a school for Native people had, in fact, constituted the original purpose for coming to Montana. Once she saw the Miles City convent and school operative, Amadeus began to press for a date to leave for the Cheyenne reservation.

With Father Lindesmith's help, she negotiated for government wagons to transport the sisters into the Indian country. This facilitated everything about the trek and meant the hefty price of the trip did not come from the convent coffers. Still, it was a frustration to wait day after day for the order to start forth.

The departure from Miles City for the reservation, however, depended more on the fickle weather than on human design. The lingering Montana winter competed with the burgeoning spring in a duel that kept the residents around the Tongue River ever alert for sudden snowstorms followed by a series of floods. The vexing cycle continued over several weeks, requiring the sisters to continually pack and unpack their few possessions, as they kept themselves poised to leave at a moment's notice.

Repeatedly, the military escort from Fort Keogh canceled its travel dates, determining the floodwaters too risky for the wagons. Finally, at the end of March, Mother Amadeus received a call that the caravan was ready; she quickly separated three sisters from the Miles City convent and accompanied them to the Cheyenne reservation, where their priest friend, Father Eyler, had gone ahead to ready the mission. Here in the Tongue River Valley, the Ursulines entered into another arena of Montana life, and Mother Amadeus explored a new level of personal adventure.

Forewarned that the passage from Miles City to the reservation would cross extremely dangerous roads, Amadeus accepted some easements for the trip from the military chaplain, Father Lindesmith. First, he dispensed the sisters from their daily obligation of group prayer. Second, on his advice, the four nuns suspended their usual fast as well. In a sharp departure from Catholic dietary requirements, he recommended eating meat three times a day and whenever it was served on Friday.[35] Typically, the governing rule for religious life could be physically exacting in the best of conditions. Lindesmith's advice showed that in frontier circumstances certain regulations should and could be circumvented. Another western message was not lost on Amadeus.

On this journey, Mother Amadeus observed a rugged environment far beyond the urban setting that once had delineated the boundaries of her existence. Early on, she had expressed her good feelings for the West, writing to Toledo about the purity of the air and the lack of cold.[36] Now, seated in a military wagon drawn by four mules, Amadeus chanced having the last vestiges of her circumspect eastern upbringing slip away. "Rough riding ... over steep gullies that descend 8 feet in a distance of 12 feet and ascend in the same proportion ... pitched from one corner of the ambulance to the opposite one ... shaken and jarred till we ... think there is no life left in us," Amadeus could say of Montana "there is sacrifice of some kind awaiting you every step you take."[37] At the same time, this distinctly western travel introduced her to a unique space, set apart by its non-traditional beauty and significant physical risk.

Mother Amadeus followed in the footprints of other pioneer nuns who had learned firsthand about the West's scenic outdoor muscle. In many western locations, missionary sisters encountered the raw force of nature.[38] Like the others, no doubt, Amadeus told herself she had two choices—retreat or stay the course. However she felt in perilous moments, she held her ground, allowing her inner boldness to blossom in the Montana wilderness.

In addition, the cultural landscape also rearranged itself, bringing this white Midwesterner directly into communities of Native people. It had

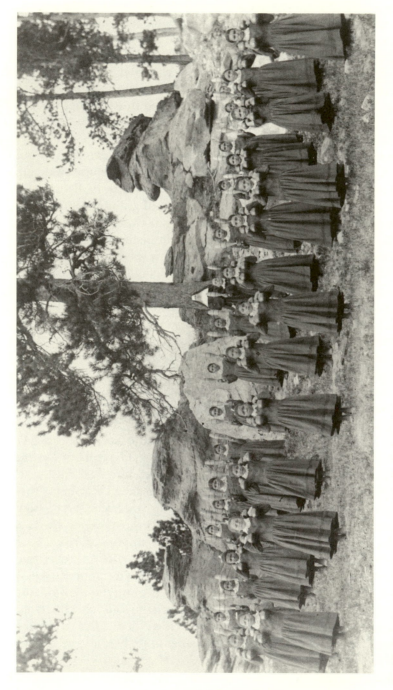

Fig. 4.2 Sister Ignatius oversees a group of identically dressed Cheyenne students doing exercises for gym class on the grounds of the St. Labre's Mission. Reprinted by permission of the Archives of the Ursuline Convent of the Sacred Heart, Toledo, Ohio.

been one thing, seated in a convent parlor in Toledo, to talk about bringing Catholicism to Indians. It had been yet another to meet and greet Native people in Miles City. Now, however, the balance of cultural power had shifted and, though white missionaries, traders, and soldiers passed back and forth through Indian country, Native identity defined the atmosphere. After a few months at the new mission, where Cheyenne language, music, work, medicine, religion, and recreation guided her daily life, Sister St. Ignatius predicted only military force would alter the reservation's demographics, for she said of these Indian families, "they love the Tongue Valley with its beautiful hills and verdant fields."[39]

The Crow and the Northern Cheyenne, squeezed together as unwilling neighbors, hunkered down on their government reserves, from whence they watched each other and the ever encroaching whites, with a cool eye and perhaps opinions that differed from the view of Sister St. Ignatius. The Cheyenne, buffeted by a series of horrific clashes with whites, had been removed to the southeastern Montana reservation only five years earlier. Their numbers decimated, their health broken, and their culture battered, they were, nonetheless, sophisticated in their perceptions of politics and economics.[40] Weakened though they might be, they dug in against further relocation, including efforts to drive them onto the land of the Crow.[41]

The Ursulines, commenting on "a rivalry between the 'Rosebud' and the Otter Creek Indians," perceived there were mixed sentiments swirling about them, although the nuns may not have fully understood the deep nature of these tensions.[42] The Cheyenne may have hoped a mission station, for which they had lobbied vigorously at the Miles City convent, would help solidify their claim to the reservation, as well as guarantee them food, medicine, and schools. In the nineteenth-century worldview of Mother Amadeus, without these basic improvements in Native life, the nuns would never be able to convince the Cheyenne or the Crow to try Christianity.

These cultural challenges and clashes lay ahead, but first Amadeus had to see the sisters to the Indian mission. As Mother Amadeus accompanied the nuns to their new assignment, other ingredients of western life overtook the superior. Father Lindesmith had spoken on the spiritual obligations, relaxing them to more sensible levels. Now the military escort directed the sisters' daily schedule. For the first time in many weeks, Mother Amadeus enjoyed a lull in her Montana responsibilities. For once, she could entertain the sights and sounds of the West, without the nearly constant day-to-day duties that had occupied her for three months. The release permitted Amadeus to engage, in a more personal way, the power of this Montana land.

The environment seemed to strike her almost immediately, surprising as it could be with its panoramic stretches of scenery. The expansive horizon allowed Amadeus to look far ahead to soldiers preparing the evening camp. Something about the shifting visuals as the convoy closed the gap between the two groups appeared to stir her. The impact of the surreal tableau reinforced an earlier comment from Amadeus to the Toledo convent: "everything out here is far different from what we imagined it."[43]

Once at the site, the nuns were instructed to rest in the ambulance, while the men laid out the evening fare. Following a bracing military supper of bacon and potatoes, the women headed for their tent, comfortably equipped with a stove and cots. Amadeus must have chuckled over the drastic difference between these orderly arrangements and the tumultuous evening at Bridget McCanna's house in Miles City.

Despite the possible vulnerability of women alone on the plains with a detachment of soldiers, Mother Amadeus expressed no worries and slept soundly until reveille. Even the nagging ache of persistent arthritis did not disturb her rest. A full night of sleep, undisturbed by the call for early prayer or the rollicking of urban neighbors, refreshed the somewhat overextended nun.

Amadeus and her companions pushed back the tent flap to find a fresh snowfall. Charmed by the surprise of the "beautiful snow," the four decided to amble a ways and "enjoyed a little walk," out onto the plains. This vast and silent weather-swept scene reminded them, "of a picture in one of our old geographies," and showed the novice campers a spacious Montana, where they had never walked or slept before.[44]

It was only the beginning of travel destined to include more than exquisite winter scenes. That day took the group over an even more stunning, as well as treacherous, route. Early in the trek the nuns, no longer strolling for pleasure, picked their way along the rough terrain, for the road had turned to a steep and narrow pathway, precarious at every twist and bend. Two vehicles navigated past a nasty danger spot without a problem, but a third broke loose, sliding haphazardly down an embankment. The soldiers set about to haul it back to the so-called road, after which it took hours to repair the broken parts. The men had hardly started forward when quicksand snared one of the wagons. Wearied by the first mishap, the soldiers again put their shoulders to an arduous task, agreeing among themselves that the entire wagon must be unloaded, freed from the quagmire, and loaded again.

On the second night out from Miles City, a passing group of Native people materialized out of the dusk and joined the camp. From their wagon, the silent nuns from Toledo watched as silent women of another society—one they hoped to understand—engaged in the work of their domestic lives. On a nearby hill their seated men kept a cautionary gaze on the white soldiers. In this place of physical uncertainty and cultural variances, one sister wrote, "we felt danger but resolved to show no signs of fear, so sat quietly in our places."[45]

With each hour, the American West revealed more of itself and its dangers. Again and again, the same swollen rivers required fording; the ubiquitous quicksand set its traps, portage undercut each day's mileage, inclement weather destroyed meals, underbrush blocked the way, muddy slush meant hasty construction of a corduroy bridge. The sisters climbed into the wagon, out of the wagon, rode for an hour, walked for three. Inching their way toward their mission destination, the Ursuline nuns learned about the exacting and unpredictable demands the American West could and would make on its immigrants.

The station, approximately eighty miles from Miles City, was close to Otter Creek, at a place known as the St. Labre Mission. Here Father Eyler, already in failing health after only a few weeks, awaited their arrival. The very day the soldiers delivered the travelers into the care of the sickly priest, the military men turned back to Fort Keogh. Nor did Amadeus tarry long at the new Ursuline mission. She named Sister Sacred Heart superior, confident the three nuns would live and work according to the Ursuline rule and teaching philosophy, as much as their limited number and conditions at Otter Creek would allow.[46] Two days after the sisters moved into their convent, little more than an unappealing shack, Mother Amadeus headed for the Ursuline house in Miles City.

Once again she noticed western life often adjusted traditional convent practices. Extraordinary enough that on an American frontier, European expectations of enclosure for nuns collapsed. Amadeus had seen how unsuitable such a policy could be in Miles City and on the Montana plains. On her return trip, she further bent conventions for nuns, traveling for days without a companion, thus breeching a rule found in virtually all congregations—sisters abroad in the secular world went in pairs and only during daylight hours.[47] With such a meager number of sisters, the pragmatic Amadeus had no way to comply. Without hesitation, she carried out her responsibilities as she saw them, and in so doing, moved herself deeper into the mission West and the lives of Native people. Later, when questioned about her several days of travel as a lone Anglo nun in the wagon of a Cheyenne family, she would only comment cryptically, "God knows."[48]

Still she never shied from arduous trips across Montana. Rather, she embraced excursions in all hours of the day and seasons of the year.

For example, preparing for an unexpected visit to the St. Labre sisters, Amadeus dashed off a short note about the possibly dangerous drive ahead, commenting, "We expect a grand time."[49] Her character did not yield to intimidation, and for the rest of her life she remained undaunted by hazardous travels and life-threatening situations.[50] Clearly, that first rocky ambulance ride to St. Labre's Mission had shown the once-cloistered nun her own penchant for adventure and made her an eager wilderness traveler.

Typical of the western sojourner, Amadeus had begun to feel the subtle invasion of western space and place into her spirit. By the fall of 1884, as she was on her way to open another Ursuline mission, she stopped with the Sisters of Charity of Leavenworth at St. John's Hospital in Helena. Taking a moment to pen a quick letter to Mother Stanislaus in Toledo, she enthused "Here we are in the heart of the Great Rocky Mountains. On every side we see them towering around us with their snow-capped tops."[51] Three days later found her again plunged into the Montana wilderness, as she arrived at the Jesuit mission of St. Peter's, a distance of seventy miles from Helena. Delighted to be warmly received by the Jesuits, whose congregation she greatly admired, Amadeus decided to establish a school and an Ursuline novitiate at this location and undertook their organization immediately.[52]

By this time, the third ingredient of Mother Amadeus's first year in the West—the pursuit of congregational autonomy—had emerged. Amadeus came to Miles City invested with a legitimate authority assigned by her religious superiors in Ohio; in Montana she inflated that authority by increasing the number of Ursuline missions and consequently her own governing role as mother superior. As a result, the original administrative separation from Toledo widened.

Before the departure of the six nuns from Toledo, Bishop Richard Gilmour, Mother Stanislaus, and Mother Amadeus had drawn a formal statement about the present and future status of the mission band. Such covenants were commonly undertaken, intended to keep an order's congregational structure sound and to avoid misunderstandings, easily fueled by great distance and poor communication. As guides for harmony, these documents rarely succeeded totally, as it was impossible to anticipate the various pressures, rivalries, or circumstances that could arise in the mission fields.

The six-point contract between Mother Stanislaus and Mother Amadeus established the Montana colony as an independent Ursuline house, one that could not expect support or direction from Toledo. Yet the agreement also included the provision that the nuns in Toledo would, as possible, assist Miles City with "advice and material help." In the event that the Montana mission failed, either as a whole or for an individual sister, the Toledo convent promised to readmit any or all of those in the West.[53]

Thus, Mother Amadeus arrived in Montana wearing a somewhat complicated mantle of authority, one woven of a porous fabric. The weft of independence, outlined in item one of the agreement, and the warp of attachment, stated in item six, rubbed against one another. While the Miles City convent was freestanding from Toledo and Amadeus its superior, the Montana nuns were still tethered by a possible return to Mother Stanislaus.[54]

At the same time, the missioned nuns retained close emotional and spiritual connections to the sisters at the mother-house. Amadeus had lived in the Toledo convent for twenty years; her relationships with those nuns were, for good or ill, familial. Even the young sisters in Montana, with shorter cloister memories, looked to the East with longing for the older nuns who had led them in their religious formation. The pain of separation often weighted the letters to Ohio.[55]

These letters between the two convents constituted the primary avenue for communication, but the intent of the messages sprang from differing goals. Mother Stanislaus looked for regular reports from all the sisters, presumably for assurances they retained something of their Ohio Ursuline identity and loyalty.[56] The letters, long or short, from Mother Amadeus contained direction and purpose. She filled her Toledo correspondence with imaginative descriptions of the West, sketching out pictures with which distant nuns might envision the work of the missionaries. Perhaps the rich images of mission life would strengthen her persistent requests for additional staff and entice other Toledo Ursulines to service in Montana.

If not, she still cared about demonstrating that her small group adhered to the principles of Ursuline community life. She inquired about sisters she had left behind—their health, their projects, their feast days. She acknowledged each gift with gratitude, explaining precisely how it made a critical difference in their world of want. She kept prayer, recited in Montana and requested of Ohio, prominent in her language.[57] Throughout 1884, Mother Amadeus juggled the obligations to her past with the duties of the present.

Nonetheless, Amadeus kept her Ursuline commitment concentrated on the West. She operated from a well-formed definition of her responsibility, one that drove her to promote the Ursulines in Montana. A decisive thinker, she trusted her own judgment, as she made choices designed to give her sisters greater visibility in the territory.

As early as April 1884, two young women wishing to become lay sisters, requested admission to the Ursuline convent in Miles City, and Amadeus welcomed them warmly.[58] Nothing strengthened pioneer religious congregations more than a local novitiate, where hometown daughters could take their convent training. Mother Amadeus, with her earlier tenure as the mistress of novices in Toledo, understood the benefits of recruiting young women from nearby families. Parents felt an instant concern and affection for the religious institute that became home to their child. The order's roots in the community deepened, and with increased staffing, the ability to accept new fields of endeavor broadened.

Alert to those possibilities, before the end of 1884, Amadeus had opened an Ursuline mother-house and novitiate at the St. Peter's mission, fulfilling a vision she had on the first day she arrived at the reservation, located near Fort Shaw, north of Helena.[59] The substantial building deep in the recesses of Montana gave visual affirmation to the stability of the Ursuline presence in the Rocky Mountain West. From St. Peter's, Mother Amadeus sent Ursulines to other missions, eventually placing her teacher nuns among the Blackfeet, Assiniboine and Gros Ventres, Cheyenne and Crow people.[60]

As her numbers of sister workers rose, Amadeus did not desist in her entreaties that Toledo release more nuns for the Montana initiative. She argued that the Ursulines would never be able to manage the St. Peter's mission without at least two more sisters from Ohio. When Mother Stanislaus denied the petitions, Amadeus funneled her request through Bishop Gilmour, flattering him that she told her Montana bishop the Ohio prelate was "almost all powerful," in the city of Toledo. It was Gilmour who in 1883 strongly encouraged Mother Stanislaus to send missionaries to Montana, and Amadeus must have believed he could be convinced to do so again.

She knew, of course, that her letter bypassed Mother Stanislaus, risking the ire of the Toledo superior, who emphatically had rejected the idea of more nuns for Montana. Stanislaus would hardly be pleased that her former colleague continued a long-distance "raid" attempt on the Toledo convent by courting the higher authority of the bishop. In an effort to deflect a clash, Amadeus explained her action as acquiescence to instruction from Bishop Brondel that she write his Toledo counterpart.[61] Her explanation did not appease Stanislaus, whose apparent rebuke Amadeus answered in direct language.

In a letter with lists of items she wanted immediately from the mother-house, Amadeus overlooked the contradictions of being a supplicant and a rebel, and again defended herself for writing to Bishop

Gilmour. She declared, "You mistake, Mother, when you suppose … I thought episcopal authority would be necessary to wrest assistance from our Toledo Nuns." Again, she insisted she only followed "the injunctions of our present bishop who ordered me to proceed in the manner in which I made the application."[62] Where once she had pushed for personal autonomy with Bishop Brondel on her first days in Miles City, now she adopted the role of the compliant nun, required to obey. She saw her action as one taken on behalf of her original mother-house, rather than as a rejection of its authority. She spoke about the "glorious labor for the Toledo Ursulines" and resisted a solution that would send sisters from convents in Youngstown or Tiffin, Ohio, protesting that she could not believe the Toledo nuns would "let strange Ursulines come in to help us."[63]

As she flexed her independence, Amadeus increasingly chaffed under some points made in the letters she received from Toledo. Flickers of annoyance, perhaps based on disagreements of the past, darted in and out of her correspondence. Like other western settlers, she considered life in the West beyond the scope of comprehension for those who remained in the East. She told Mother Stanislaus, "you cannot conceive how we are placed out here *sometimes*." In a second letter of the same date she continued her lament, saying, "I do not dare offer any excuse, for I am sure I will not be understood."[64]

Whatever old tensions fueled these comments, they mingled with her growing Montana-centered life, one where she was the most senior Ursuline for several hundred miles. She dismissed a suggestion from Toledo that the sisters at St. Labre's be recalled if the reservation had become unsafe. Amadeus declined to bring the nuns back to Miles City, insisted such a move would "not be prudent," and promised to send reports as she gathered news. Apparently she failed to send the missives, brushing off her silence as based on an assumption the mission "correspondents" supplied Toledo with detailed accounts.[65]

Although the attachments between the two houses buckled, they remained in place. Mother Amadeus never hesitated to ask for various kinds of support, even as she charted her own course in Montana. Ultimately, Bishop Richard Gilmour closed off the connections, chiding the Toledo Ursulines that some had a "spirit of restlessness" and a "feverish desire" to join the Amadeus group. He announced to the Toledo nuns he would no longer permit conversations about their longing to teach among the Indians for, "hereafter, Montana must depend on itself."[66] His pronouncement actually paralleled the trajectory of Mother Amadeus's mission life since her first day in Miles City, when she had declared, "we had no help from anyone—happier to do it alone."

The year of 1884 seasoned Mother Amadeus to the West. It placed on her physical and emotional demands that transformed her into a resident of the Rocky Mountain frontier and, in general, deepened the contours of western womanhood. She devoted herself to spreading Ursuline missions through Montana, providing education for Anglo children and Native people, accepting young women into the congregation and, from time to time, welcoming nuns from Toledo, Cleveland, and Tiffin.[67] Sixteen years after she stepped from a train in Miles City, Montana, Mother Amadeus was more than ready for a Vatican conference expected to bring all the Ursuline houses together into an affiliated international union.

As an advocate of union, Amadeus developed a network of contacts within the European clergy, and she assumed a prominent position in the fall 1900 discussions in Rome.[68] Ultimately, she guided the sisters under her supervision into the union. Mother Amadeus returned to America as the first provincial of the northern United States, bearing the title of congregational autonomy she appeared to seek many years earlier. Curiously, in her new role, the mission nun who so loved the West administered her province from New York.

Over the next several years, illnesses and a near crippling train accident eroded Amadeus' already bad health. Burdened with chronic pain, she moved about with great difficulty. Still in 1910, fired by her old zeal for new adventures, she left New York and joined a small convent of Ursulines she had missioned in Alaska five years earlier.

The last decade of her life brought increasingly sorrowful days. She quarreled with her old friends, the Jesuits, tangled with the bishop of Seattle, and suffered a final indignity when several young Ursulines refused to live with her as their superior.[69] She took refuge in her congregation, trying to bolster the Alaska missionaries with her visits and enthusiasm. By now, however, her intellectual and physical resources had faded. She could not indefinitely ward off the agonies of the bitterly cold Alaskan mission life or the infirmities of age. Finally, no longer able to stand on her frostbitten feet and fatigued by illness, Amadeus, the intrepid missionary, returned to Seattle, Washington. There, at the age of seventy-three, she died on 10 November 1919. Eventually, her body was returned to the St. Ignatius mission in Montana, for burial.

Mother Amadeus Dunne of the Ursulines did not fit neatly into a nineteenth-century mold. As a woman, she rejected marriage and family, choosing instead a career as an educator inside a Catholic cloister. As a nun, she built a life of secure patterns, framed by academic and religious calendars. Within that context, she accumulated considerable stature and had every reason to expect she would conclude her life among the ranking teacher/administrators of the Ursuline congregation in Toledo, Ohio. On the cusp of middle age, however, she tried herself in a pioneer world about which she knew very little, but where she created a legacy as a leader of women.

This new western world, with its ferocious hardship and great diversity, quickly overtook Mother Amadeus—invigorated her and shaped the remainder of her life, as well as that of the nuns for whom she was mother superior. Seemingly without fear or hesitation, Amadeus used her early convent experience and her own quick mind to build Ursuline identity in the West. She held tenaciously to the tenets of her faith, comfortable with nineteenth-century attitudes that produced a mixed narrative of joy and sorrow in the Catholic West. Yet under her direction, other unmarried women living by a religious rule successfully planted institutions of learning and religion in a region dominated by family groups, both immigrant and indigenous. Amadeus provided these Ursulines with unusual gender opportunities, linked them to Euro-America families and Native American people, brokered intercultural relationships, extended the reach of education, pushed back the boundaries of female accomplishment, and advanced the interests of her religious congregation in the American West.

Mother Amadeus, inspiring to some and distressing to others, melded into a Rocky Mountain West associated with pioneers of boldness and independence, but her frontier account also resonated with personal spirituality and professional ambition. Great energy, administrative vision, and physical stamina, reinforced by her willingness to exercise power, both temporal and spiritual, set the tone for her western life.

Although Amadeus would never have thought in these terms, the concept of the New Womanhood as a western phenomenon is broadened by the various components of her richly patterned life. Through her western experience, Mother Amadeus stamped into her various frontier worlds a gendered religious legacy that contributed to the building of community and the forming of western Catholicism. In mission environments, Mother Amadeus of the Ursulines worked tirelessly for others, expanded her own agency, lived out her sense of adventure, and pursued congregational autonomy for herself as a governing superior.

ACKNOWLEDGMENTS

The author thanks Louis L. Renner S. J.; Heather Block Lawton; and the archivists of the Ursuline Convent of the Sacred Heart of Toledo, Ohio, Sister Kathleen Padden O.S.U., and Sister Mary Rose Krupp O.S.U.

NOTES

1. For an uncritical narrative of the life of Mother Amadeus, see, Joseph B. Code, "Mother Mary Amadeus of the Heart of Jesus of the Ursulines of Montana and Alaska," in *Great American Foundresses* (New York: Macmillan, 1929), 437–71.
2. Amadeus suffered from rheumatism/arthritis, but the nature of her other medical difficulties remains unclear, though her health was a frequent subject in the Ursuline letters to Toledo. For example, see Sister St. Angela to My very dear Mother, 27 January 1884; Your Montana Francis to My dear Mother, 28 January 1884; Sister Holy Angels to My dear Mother, 24 February 1884; Sister Francis to My ever dear Mother, 27 April 1884, Miles City, Letters, January 1884–May 1884, Folder 8, Archives, Ursuline Convent, Toledo, Ohio. Hereafter, AUC, Toledo.
3. This territory had been the mission arena of the Jesuits since the legendary priest Pierre Jean de Smet, S. J. had come to Montana forty years earlier. For a history of the Rocky Mountain missions, see Gerald McKevitt, S. J., "The Art of Conversion: Jesuits and Flatheads in Nineteenth-Century Montana," *U. S. Catholic Historian* 12, no. 4 (fall 1994): 49–64. For background on the Ursulines, see Jo Ann Kay McNamara, *Sisters in Arms: Catholic Nuns through Two Millennia* (Cambridge: Harvard University Press, 1996), 459–61, and Elinor Tong Dehey, *Religious Orders of Women in the United States: Accounts of Their Origin, Works and Most Important Institutions*, rev. ed., (Cleveland, OH: W. B. Conkey, 1930), offprint copy by St. Athanasius Press, Dickeyville, Wisconsin, 1–42.
4. Granville Stuart, *Pioneering in Montana: The Making of a State, 1864–1887*, II, Paul C. Phillips, ed. (Lincoln: University of Nebraska Press, 1977, Bison Books), 195–226. The disastrous winter of 1886 to 1887 also had an impact on grazing in the area. See, H. Duane Hampton, ed. "Promise in the West: The Letters of Isaac Schultz, 1884–1887," *Montana the Magazine of Western History* 36 no. 4 (autumn 1986): 52–63.
5. Sister M. Amadeus to My dear Mother, 18 January 1884, Miles City, Letters, January 1884–May 1884, Folder 8, AUC, Toledo. Also see, Samuel Gordon, *Recollections of Old Milestown* (Samuel Gordon: 1918, Miles City, Montana), <http://www.milescity.com/history/books/room>. Some dates on the Ursuline letters from Montana do not match with events. Several sources say the nuns arrived on 18 January 1884; Mother Amadeus, on the very day she came to Miles City, could not have written a letter that discussed events that occurred after 18 January.
6. John Lancaster Spalding, *The Religious Mission of the Irish People and Catholic Colonization*, 3rd ed. (New York: n. p., 1880), 106, 141–7, 160–74, Pamphlets in American History: Catholicism and Anti-Catholicism, microfiche, Theodore M. Hesburgh Library, University of Notre Dame, South Bend, IN; Kathleen O'Brien, R. S. M., *Journeys: A Pre-Amalgamation of the Sisters of Mercy, Omaha Province* (Omaha, NE: n. p., 1987), 104–6; Marvin R. O'Connell, *John Ireland and the American Catholic Church* (St. Paul: Minnesota Historical Society Press, 1988), 148–55; Charles R. Morris, *American Catholic: The Saints and Sinners who Built America's most Powerful Church* (New York: Vintage Books, 1997), 39–40.
7. Sister M. Amadeus to My dear Mother, 18 January 1884, and Your Montana Francis to My dear Mother, 28 January 1884, Miles City, Letters, January 1884–May 1884, Folder 8, AUC, Toledo.
8. Sister M. Amadeus to My dear Mother, 18 January 1884, ibid. Another account of the events is in the extended memoir of Sister St. Angela Louise Abair, "A Mustard Seed in Montana." See Orlan J. Svingen's edited article in *Montana the Magazine of Western History* 34, no. 2 (spring 1984): 16–31.
9. In general, nuns belong to contemplative institutes, take solemn vows, and follow the rule of enclosure; sisters belong to service congregations, take simple vows, and undertake ministries outside their cloister, as in a school or a hospital. The Ursulines followed

a rule that mixed the styles; their experiences in the United States showed how the distinctions between these two categories blurred in North America. For purposes of literary variety, the terms *nun* and *sister* are used interchangeably in this essay.

10. Brondel, from his residence in Helena, may have relied on Father Lindesmith to find accommodations for the Ursulines. Lindesmith ministered to the Catholics at Fort Keogh and those living in the Miles City area. He had known the Bridget McCanna family for at least four years. See E. W. S. Lindesmith Diary, Sick Calls, first book, Miles City, Montana, 1880–3, file folder 21, E. W. S. Lindesmith Papers, File folder 21, Archives of the Catholic University of America, Washington, D. C.

11. Sister M. Amadeus to My dear Mother, 18 January 1884, Miles City, Letters, January 1884–May 1884, Folder 8, AUC, Toledo.

12. Many religious women collided with the autocratic manner of unbending priests and bishops, whose power over women's congregations was broad. For examples of the often arbitrary and competing authority male clergy exercised over nuns see, Mary Richard Boo, O. S. B., *House of Stone: The Duluth Benedictines* (Duluth, MN: Saint Scholastica Priory Books, 1991), iv; the account of Benedicta Riepp, O. S. B. in Sister Grace McDonald, O. S. B., *With Lamps Burning* (St. Joseph, MN: St. Benedict's Priory Press, 1957), 1–49, and the Franciscan Sisters of the Immaculate Conception at Belle Prairie, Minnesota, in Sister Mary Assumpta Ahles, O. S. F., *In the Shadow of His Wings* (St. Paul, MN: North Central Publishing, 1977), 165–248.

13. Sister M. Amadeus to My dear Mother, 18 January 1884, Miles City, Letters, January 1884–May 1884, Folder 8, AUC, Toledo.

14. Sister M. Amadeus to My dear Mother, 18 January 1884; S. S. H. to My dear Mother, 2 February 1884, ibid.

15. Sister St. Angela to My very dear Mother, 27 January 1884, ibid.

16. Sister M. Amadeus to My dear Mother, 18 January 1884, ibid.

17. Ibid.

18. S. S. H. to My dear Mother, 2 February 1884, ibid. At the same time, nobody expected the nuns would openly endorse behaviors they considered inappropriate. See Sister St. Rose of Lima to Dear Mother, 14 May 1885, Miles City, Letters, June 1884–December 1885, Folder 8B, AUC, Toledo.

19. Sister M. Amadeus to My dear Mother, 18 January 1884, Sister St. Angela to My very dear Mother, 27 January 1884, Miles City, Letters, January 1884–May 1884, Folder 8, AUC, Toledo.

20. Sister St. Angela to My very dear Mother, 27 January 1884; Sister St. Ignatius to Dear Mother, 28 January 1884; Your Montana Francis to My dear Mother, 29 January 1884; Sister of the Sacred Heart of Jesus to My dear Mother, 2 February 1884, ibid.

21. Native people, however, often ignored these boundaries, as noted by one nun who wrote, "They were at the convent incessantly, sometimes fifteen or twenty together … where they would sit for hours." Sister Sacred Heart to Dear Mother, 27 April 1884, ibid.

22. At least one of the other nuns thought the teacher, Mr. Logan, to be "rather hostile," and a graduate of Hartford, not Harvard, University. Sister St. Ignatius to Dear Mother, 17 February 1884, ibid.

23. Sister M. Amadeus to My dear Mother, 29 January 1884, ibid.

24. European monastic enclosure evolved over several hundred years. By the thirteenth century, the rule required professed women to remain inside a particular convent for life, forbidden to leave, except for the most extreme reasons. This cumbersome regulation gave rise to auxiliary groups that conducted secular business for enclosed nuns. See, Dismas W. Bonner, O. F. M., *Extern Sisters in Monasteries of Nuns*, Catholic University of America Canon Law Series, No. 430 (Washington, DC: Catholic University of America, 1963), esp. 15–6, and James R. Cain, *The Influence of Cloister on the Apostolate of Congregations of Religious Women* (Rome: Pontifical Lateran University, 1965), 28–37.

25. See David F. Noble, *A World without Women: The Christian Clerical Culture of Western Science* (New York: Oxford University Press, 1992), esp. 83–107; Chester Gillis, *Roman Catholicism in America* (New York: Columbia University Press, 1999), 58.

26. In the 1850s and 1860s, Benedictine nuns in Minnesota particularly struggled over the rules of enclosure, efforts to support themselves, and directives from male clergy. See Sister Grace M. McDonald, O. S. B., *With Lamps Burning* (St. Joseph, MN: Saint Benedict's Priory Press, 1957), 17–8, 43–4, 54, 60–1.

27. Joseph B. Code, *Great American Foundresses* (New York: Macmillan, 1929), 440.

28. Sister M. Amadeus to My very dear Mother, 18 January 1884; Sister M. Amadeus to My dear Mother, 29 January 1884, Miles City, Letters, January 1884–May 1884, Folder 8; Sister Sacred Heart to My dear Mother, 14 July 1884, Miles City, Letters, June 1884–December 1885, Folder 8B, AUC, Toledo.

29. Sister M. Amadeus to My dear Mother, 18 January 1884; Sister M. Amadeus to My dear Mother, 29 January 1884, Miles City, Letters, January 1884–May 1884, Folder 8, AUC, Toledo.

30. This resulted in complaints to the Ursulines because in Bismarck, Dakota, sisters of another congregation had charged only $12 and $15 at their boarding school, and the difference rankled some families with children at the Miles City school. Your Sister Mr. Amadeus to My dear Mother, Mothers and Sisters!, 29 May 1884, ibid.

31. Sister M. Amadeus to My dear Mother, 29 January 1884, ibid.

32. Sister Mary Amadeus to My dear Mother, 29 March 1884, ibid.

33. Sister St. Ignatius to Dear Mother, 17 February 1884; Sister Holy Angels to My dear Mother, 24 February 1884; Sister of the Sacred Heart of Jesus to Dear Mother, 25 February 1884, ibid.

34. Sister Holy Angels to My dear Mother, 24 February 1884; Sister Francis to My ever dear Mother, 27 April 1884, Miles City, Letters, January 1884–May 1884, Folder 8. See also, Your Montana Francis to My dear Mother, 28 January 1884; Sisters Holy Angels, St. Angela, and Ignatius, 23 December 1884; Your Ignatius to My dear Mother, 10 January 1885; St. Labre's Mission, Letters, 1884–1885, Folder 7, AUC, Toledo.

35. Sister Sacred Heart to Dear Mother, 27 April 1884, Miles City, Letters, January 1884–May 1884, Folder 8, AUC, Toledo. Many pioneer nuns endured deprivation while traveling; for examples, see "The Presentation Sisters in North Dakota," *Annals, 1880–1938*, 1–5, Archives, Sisters of the Presentation, Fargo, North Dakota; *Annals, Sisters of St. Dominic of the Congregation of the Holy Cross, 1890–1923*, 46–8, Archives, Dominicans of Edmonds, Edmonds, Washington; Sister Grace M. McDonald, O. S. B., *With Lamps Burning* (St. Joseph, MN: St. Benedict's Priory Press, 1957), 24.

36. Sister M. Amadeus to My dear Mother, 18 January 1884, Miles City, Letters, January 1884–May 1884, Folder 8, AUC, Toledo.

37. Sister Mary Amadeus to My dear Mother, 29 March 1884, ibid.

38. For examples, *Chronicles, St. Mary's Academy, Portland, Oregon*, v. 2, 1859–1885, 1–21, Archives, Sisters of the Holy Names of Jesus and Mary, Portland, Oregon; for description of an 1867 hurricane, *Annals of the First Monastery of the Incarnate Word and Blessed Sacrament in America*, 25–8, Religious Orders, Women, Catholic Archives of Texas, Diocese of Austin Chancery, Austin, Texas. For the impact of the 1900 Galveston hurricane on Dominican and Ursuline nuns, Sheila Hackett, O. P., *Dominican Women in Texas: From Ohio to Galveston and Beyond* (Houston, TX: D. Armstrong, 1986), 106–14, and James Talmadge Moore, *Acts of Faith: The Catholic Church in Texas, 1900–1950* (College Station: Texas A&M University Press, 2002), 21–7.

39. Sister St. Ignatius to Dear Mother, 27 April 1884, Miles City, Letters, January 1884–May 1884, Folder 8; Sisters Holy Angels, St. Angela, and Ignatia to My dear Mother, Mothers, and Sisters, 23 December 1884; Ignatius to My dear Mother, 10 January 1885, St. Labre's Mission, Letters, 1884–1885, Folder 7, AUC, Toledo.

40. Elliott West, *The Contested Plains: Indians, Goldseekers, and the Rush to Colorado*, (Lawrence: University Press of Kansas, 1997), as well as an essay, "Called Out People: The Cheyennes and the Central Plains," *Montana the Magazine of Western History* 48, no. 2 (summer 1998): 2–15.
41. Sister Saint Ignatius to Dear Mother, 27 April 1884, Miles City, Letters, January 1884–May 1884, Folder 8, AUC, Toledo.
42. Sister Sacred Heart to Dear Mother, 27 April 1884, ibid.
43. Sister Mary Amadeus to My dear Mother, 29 March 1884, ibid.
44. Sister Sacred Heart to Dear Mother, 27 April 1884, ibid.
45. Ibid. Details of this trip are also found in L. B. Palladino, S. J., *Indian and White in the Northwest: Or a History of Catholicity in Montana* (Baltimore, MD: John Murphy, 1894), 206–7; Sister St. Angela Louise Abair, Orlan J. Svingen, ed., "A Mustard Seed in Montana," *Montana the Magazine of Western History*: 20–1.
46. Sister St. Ignatius to Dear Mother, 27 April 1884, Miles City, Letters, January 1884–May 1884, Folder 8; Sister St. Ignatius and Companions to My dear Mother, 4 January 1885, St. Labre's Mission, Letters, 1884–1885, Folder 7, AUC, Toledo.
47. For an example, see N. A., *Regulations for the Society of the Sisters of Charity of the United States of America for the Motherhouse of Nazareth, Kentucky* (Cincinnati, OH: Benzinger Bros., 1877), and N. A., *A Brief Historical Sketch of the Sisters of Charity* (n. p., n. p., 1908), Sisters of Charity of Nazareth, Box 2, Folder 1 and Folder 2, Printed Materials Religious Orders of Women, Archives of Notre Dame University, South Bend, Indiana.
48. Typescript, no author, "The First Trip to St. Labre's (complete)," n.p., St. Labre's Mission, Letters, 1884–1885, Folder 7, AUC, Toledo. This typescript is part of "A Mustard Seed in Montana," ed. Orlan J. Svingen, ed., *Montana the Magazine of Western History* 34 no.2 (Spring 1984), 21.
49. Sister M. Amadeus to My dear Mother, 27 August 1884, Miles City, Letters, January 1884–December 1885, Folder 8B, AUC, Toledo.
50. 22–3 October, 30 November, 13–6 December 1897, *Annals, St. Peter's Mission, 10 July 1897–30 December 1897*, Ursuline Archives, Ursuline Center, Great Falls, Montana. Hereafter, UA, Great Falls; Sister Genevieve McBride O. S. U., *The Bird Tail* (New York: Vantage Press, 1974), 124–5.
51. Sister Mary Amadeus to My dear Mother, 29 October 1884, St. Peter's Mission, Letters, 1884–1906, Folder 12B, AUC, Toledo.
52. Your Sister Mary Amadeus to My beloved Mother and Sisters, 1 November 1884; Sister Mary Amadeus to My very dear Mother, 8 December 1884; Your Sister Mary Amadeus to My very dear Mother, 14 December 1884; Sister M. Amadeus to My very dear Mother, 19 December 1884, St. Peter's Mission, Letters, 1884–1906, ibid.
53. "To Whom It May Concern," mss. document, "Original Agreement," Miles City, Folder 1, AUC, Toledo.
54. Apparently, a newspaper article that identified the Miles City Ursulines as part of the New Orleans mother house offended Mother Stanislaus. Sister of the Sacred Heart of Jesus to My ever dear Mother, 2 February 1885; Sister Francis to My ever dear Mother, 8 February 1885, Miles City, Letters, June 1884–December 1885, Folder 8B, AUC, Toledo.
55. Your Montana Francis to My dear Mother, 28 January 1884; Sisters Holy Angels, St. Angela, and Ignatius to My dear Mother, Mothers, and Sisters, 23 December 1884; Sister St. Angela to My beloved Mother, 11 January 1885; Sister of the Holy Angels to My dear Mother, 11 January 1885; Sister Amadeus to My dearest Mother and Sisters, 8 October 1885, St. Labre's Mission, Letters, 1884–1885, Folder 7, AUC, Toledo.
56. Srs. Holy Angels, St. Angela, and Ignatius to My dear Mother, Mothers, and Sisters, 23 December 1884; Sister St. Ignatius and Companions to My dear Mother, 23 December

1884; Your Ignatius to My dear Mother, 10 January 1885; Sister of the Holy Angels to My dear Mother, 11 January 1885, St. Labre's Mission, Letters, 1884–1885, Folder 7, AUC, Toledo. Also, in 1886, Mother Stanislaus traveled to St. Peter's mission when Mother Amadeus was ill with pneumonia, suggesting the Toledo superior still felt some oversight for and attachment to the Montana sisters. "A Sort of 'Diary,' May 1884–October 1892," UA, Great Falls.

57. See especially, Sister Mary Amadeus to My dear Mother, 29 January 1884; Sister Mary Amadeus to My dear Mother, 29 March 1884, Miles City, Letters, January 1884–May 1884, Folder 8; and Sister M. Amadeus to My very dear Mother, 29 May 1884; Sister Mary Amadeus to My dear Mother, 29 July 1884, Miles City, Letters, June 1884–December 1885, Folder 8B, AUC, Toledo.

58. Your Sister Mary Amadeus to My dear Mother, Mothers, and Sisters, 29 May 1884, Miles City, Letters, June 1884–December 1885, Folder 8B, AUC, Toledo.

59. Your Sister Mary Amadeus to My beloved Mother and Sisters, 1 November 1884; Sister M. Amadeus to My very dear Mother, 19 December 1884, St. Peter's Mission, Letters, 1884–1906, Folder 12B, AUC, Toledo. L. B. Palladino, S. J., *Indian and White in the Northwest: Or a History of Catholicity in Montana* (Baltimore, MD: John Murphy, 1894), 195.

60. Sister Genevieve McBride, O. S. U, *The Bird Tail* (New York: Vantage Press, 1974), 74.

61. Sister Mary Amadeus to Rt. Rev. R. Gilmour, D. D., My Lord, dearest Father and Bishop, 22 July 1884; Sister Mary Amadeus to My dear Mother, 29 July 1884, Miles City Letters, June 1884–December 1885, Folder 8B, AUC, Toledo.

62. Sister Mary Amadeus to My dear Mother, 31 August 1884, ibid. Mother Stanislaus and Bishop Gilmour exchanged several letters about the staffing for the Montana mission. Mother Stanislaus apparently preferred that Mother Amadeus stay out of these negotiations. See R. Gilmour to Dear Child, 17 June 1884; R. Gilmour to Dear Child, 28 July 1884; R. Gilmour to Mother St. Stanislaus, 14 February 1885; R. Gilmour to Dear Child, 19 February 1885; R. Gilmour to Dear Child, 28 February 1885; R. Gilmour to Dear Child, 5 March 1885, Bishop Richard Gilmour, Letters, 1884–1890, Folder 17B, AUC, Toledo.

63. Sister Mary Amadeus to My Lord dearest Father and Bishop, 22 July 1884; Sister Mary Amadeus to My dear Mother, 29 July 1884, Miles City, Letters, June 1884–December 1885, Folder 8B, AUC, Toledo.

64. Sister M. Amadeus to My very dear Mother, 29 May 1884; Your Sister Mary Amadeus to My dear Mother, Mothers, and Sisters, 29 May 1884, Miles City, Letters, January 1884–May 1884, Folder 8, AUC. Toledo.

65. Sister Amadeus (?) to My dear Mother, 19 June 1884; Sister Mary Amadeus to My dear Mother, 18 August 1884, Miles City, Letters, June 1884–December 1885, Folder 8B, AUC, Toledo.

66. R. Gilmour to the Religious of the Ursuline Convent, 28 February 1886, Bishop Richard Gilmour, Letters, 1884–1890, Folder 17B, AUC, Toledo.

67. "A Sort of 'Diary', May 1884–October 1892," and *Annals, St. Peter's Mission, 10 July 1897–30 December 1897*, UA, Great Falls.

68. The decision to join the Ursuline Roman congregation or to remain a diocesan institute cast a long shadow across some religious houses for several years. For example, see the 1916 through 1926 correspondence between and among Sister M. Carmel, Sister Agatha, Sister Monica, and Archbishop Edward J. Hanna, Ursuline Sisters, Religious Orders of Women, Archdiocese of San Francisco, Chancery Archives, Menlo Park, California.

69. Sister Mary Amadeus of the Heart of Jesus to Rt. Rev. Edward O'Dea, 24 October 1912; J. Vander Pol, S. J. to Bishop of Seattle, 12 November 1912; Bishop of Seattle to Mother

Amadeus, 2 January 1913; Mother Angela to Right Reverend Bishop, 27 September 1915; The Novices, per Sister Evangelist to Right Reverend Edward J. O'Dea, 11 August 1917, Record Group 900, Religious Women, Ursulines Nuns of the Roman Union, Correspondence (1912–31), vol. 1, Archives, Archdiocese of Seattle, Seattle, Washington.

Fig. 5.1 Mary Fields, studio portrait. Reprinted by permission of the Ursuline Archives Northwest, Great Falls, Montana.

5

FINDING MARY FIELDS: RACE, GENDER, AND THE CONSTRUCTION OF MEMORY

Dee Garceau-Hagen

"She was big, about six feet tall and 200 pounds with the tenacity of a bulldog" and "the temperament of a grizzly bear." A legend in her own time, Mary Fields' notoriety increased after her death when Montanans claimed Fields as one of their most colorful pioneers. Some said she "could pick up a quarter of beef like [it was] a potato." Others bragged that she "could shoot the eye of a squirrel at fifty paces."[1] Journalists nationwide picked up her story, trading on lore that reached mythic proportions. "Black Mary could whip any two men in the territory." Her reputation for "ferocity" went hand in hand with "a fondness for liquor matched only by her capacity to put it away."[2] Everything about Fields appeared in superlatives. She was the biggest, the toughest, and the blackest woman ever to walk the Montana plains. One writer dramatized her place in frontier history by comparing her to the western landscape itself: "Mary Fields was black as burnt-over prairie."[3]

The storied Mary Fields invites us to reflect on the construction of memory. One wonders about the actual woman, who she was, how she made her way in Montana, and why her life story took on such exaggerated proportions. Some facts of her life are known without exaggeration. Mary Fields was born into slavery somewhere in the American South during the early 1830s. After the Civil War, Fields moved to Toledo, Ohio, where she took a job as groundskeeper for an Ursuline convent. She migrated West late in life, at fifty-odd years old, in 1885. In Montana, Fields worked for an Ursuline mission near Great Falls, established by nuns from a Toledo convent. In 1895, she left the mission to live in the nearby town of Cascade. From 1895 until 1903, Fields drove the mail wagon between Cascade and the mission. By 1904, the now elderly woman had quit the mail wagon and supported herself by working as a laundress, janitor, and babysitter. Mary Fields died in 1914.[4] Such are the bare outlines of Fields' life. Scratch the surface, and word about her becomes contradictory and full of distortion.

Talk with residents of Cascade, Montana, and it becomes clear that the journalists who wrote about Fields drew upon local oral tradition.[5] In doing so, they mirrored informal processes of social control that defined the boundaries of race and gender in turn-of-the-century Montana. That is, Mary Fields' legend began during her own lifetime, as the local community of Cascade framed her place in their lives. Cascade residents would assign Mary Fields separate status as a notorious figure, an adopted eccentric whom they kept on the margins. The record will show how one African-American woman navigated the dubious path of "mascot" status in a white ranching community.

THE LEGENDS

If oral tradition exposes the relationship between Mary Fields and the town of Cascade during her lifetime, the myths surrounding Mary Fields after her death reveal more about the writers' agendas than about Fields herself. White, African-American, and Catholic journalists each created different versions of the Fields legend. White journalists gave her a masculine, Wild West persona, African-American journalists made her a feminine race heroine, and Catholic journalists presented her as a model of sin and redemption.

Consider the myth created by white journalists. One cannot help but notice the way Fields is masculinized and the ways her race is emphasized. A *Great Falls Tribune* reporter, writing in 1939, printed the following story, based on oral tradition, about Fields: "A priest, ... arrive[ed] at the Mission earlier than expected, [and] the nuns asked how he came. He replied, 'Oh, that big colored man met me at Cascade and drove me out.' He was quite shocked when he learned that the man was a woman, Mary Fields."[6] Confirming Fields' alleged masculine appearance, WPA writer Edith Maxwell claimed "she wore a man's coat and shoes ... and an apron under which was strapped a holster carrying a 38 Smith and Wesson ... She was seldom seen without an enormous cigar in her mouth."[7] Mary Fields' legendary manliness was faithfully portrayed in local pageantry, and duly noted by the *Cascade Courier* in 1951: "Lester Monroe will act as the cigar-smoking, whiskey-drinking ... character 'Nigger' Mary Fields."[8] If Mary Fields could be mistaken for a man, or role-played by a man, the better to cast her in the mythic image of gunfighter in the old Wild West. Perhaps to add drama to their portrayals of central Montana in American history, white journalists painted Fields as a gunslinging brawler, worthy of any Hollywood western. Susan Dwyer, writing for the *Blade* in 1981, called "Stagecoach Mary" the "terror of the countryside." Marjorie Drew echoed this theme for a Wedsworth Library publication when she wrote, "Mary was a crack shot and would settle for nothing less than a showdown in the dusty street."[9] Her image as a two-fisted brawler has been resurrected every decade since then.[10]

So, too, race is a consistent marker in the Fields legend written by white journalists. Phrases like "her face was black as coal," exaggerated her color. They dubbed her "Black Mary," "Colored Mary," and in the racist vernacular of the mid-twentieth century, "Nigger Mary." These monikers affirmed a caste system based on race, even as they celebrated Fields' notoriety. Racial categories surfaced in subtler forms as well. A *Tribune* reporter in 1939, for example, mentioned that "*Mary was not managed easily*" [emphasis mine] by the nuns at the Ursuline mission.[11] The implication here is that Fields belonged to a servant class, to be "managed" by the Sisters. In 1940, a WPA historian echoed this theme when she wrote that Mary Fields "loved [the] Mother [Superior] with the devotion of her race."[12] The role of loyal servitude was thus linked to Fields' race, affirming a hierarchy of white over black. Racial stereotyping reappeared in a 1948 magazine feature on Mary Fields that described a comic episode involving Fields and a skunk: "A skunk invaded the chicken house, killed sixty-two of Mary's choice baby chicks." Fields killed the skunk with a hoe, and carried it to the sisters to report the loss of the chickens. A visiting priest looked at the dead skunk and inquired, "'Mary, didn't you receive the odor of his wrath when you killed him?' 'No suh,' replied Mary, 'Ah killed him from de front, not de rear.'"[13] Intended to amuse, this anecdote depicted Fields as a comic figure speaking in dialect, reinforcing the "Stepin Fetchit" trope of the black servant. As late as 1963, Montana journalists still referred to Fields as "Nigger Mary."[14]

Popular illustrators contributed to Mary Fields' image as a racial subordinate in the local community. Charlie Russell, an up-and-coming artist at the turn of the century, spent time in the small ranching town of Cascade. One of his sketches, titled, "A Quiet Day in Cascade," features Mary Fields as a slapstick figure. The scene Russell sketched was anything but quiet; unruliness prevailed. In the background, two men on bucking broncs scatter alarmed pedestrians and bicyclists. In the foreground, Mary Fields has fallen flat upon her backside, arms and legs akimbo, her basket overturned. Pigs and chickens root around her; it looks as though they tripped her in flight from the broncs. Clumsy and undignified, Mary Fields is immortalized in a pratfall, down with the pigs and chickens, a bit of minstrelsy, good for a laugh.[15] In short, white journalists and illustrators depicted Mary Fields in terms that reinforced race hierarchy. Either they placed her outside respectable society by virtue of her status as a masculinized fighter, or they cast her in a subordinate role as servant, speaking in dialect and committing comic blunders.

In contrast, African-American journalists found in Mary Fields a heroine neither masculine nor laughable. Instead, they made her a paragon of feminine virtue and a symbol of freedom for African Americans. The feminine virtues in these stories centered on Fields' role as a selfless caregiver or as a charitable cook who fed the poor. One legend casts Fields in the role of capable nurse who saved the life of Mother Amadeus, director of the Ursuline missions in Montana. In 1950, *Negro Digest* reported that Fields "became a close friend to Mother Amadeus" in Toledo at the mother convent. When Amadeus left Toledo to start a mission in Montana, Fields initially stayed behind. However, when word came that Mother Amadeus lay on her deathbed with pneumonia, Fields hurried to her aid. Fields traveled to Montana "alone, despite the triple obstacles of vast distance, unsettled and wild country … to nurse Mother Amadeus."[16] Similarly, in 1974 *Essence* magazine heralded Fields as lifesaving nurse to the Mother Superior: "Mother Amadeus … soon recovered with the help of Mary's expert care."[17] Another apocryphal story illustrating Fields' selflessness appeared in *Ebony* in 1959: When Mary Fields left the mission in 1895, the mother superior helped her start a restaurant in Cascade. But the restaurant failed because "Mary was too goodhearted and carried too much credit on her books. She would feed sheepherders during the winter and they would promise to pay her when they worked in the summer."[18] The legend of Fields' generosity toward the cash-poor reappeared in African-American publications from the 1970s, 1980s, and 1990s. A biographical essay in *Notable Black American Women*, for example, said that "Fields demonstrated benevolence toward those who needed help," and retold the restaurant story.[19]

As well as celebrating Fields' charity and nursing skills, black jour-nalists drew her as a freedom-loving spirit, a woman who transcended the oppression of slavery. In the 1950 *Negro Digest* feature, the author created a story about her escape from slavery: "When she was old enough to think about the matter at all, she decided slavery wasn't for her. So she took off … [and] worked her way northward." The *Ebony* article referred to Fields' escape metaphorically, calling her "one of the freest souls ever to draw a breath." *Essence* underscored this image, describing Fields as "proud" and "independent." Similarly, a black essayist in 1987 termed Fields "an adventuresome and free spirit … able to surmount the system of human bondage imposed upon her."[20] Black writers, then, claimed Fields for their own usable past, rewriting her as a brave soul who rose above the burden of slavery, whether through physical escape or liberation of the spirit.

In another take on Fields as a model of triumph over oppression, one black journalist imagined a kind of race solidarity between African-American and Native American women in the West. Mark Harris, writing for *Negro Digest* in 1950, implied that Fields was critical of white mis-sions among the Indians. Harris remarked on Fields' decision to remain behind when Mother Amadeus first set out for Montana: "Possibly she [Fields] was loath to participate in any way in a program sponsored by whites, however idealistic, the end-goal of which was to impose white cultural patterns upon colored peoples."[21] Regarding the challenges faced by Ursulines converting the Indians, Harris added an acerbic note: "these tribes had already had a taste of white civilization, and didn't like it."[22] Most telling, though, was the illustration that accompanied the *Negro Digest* piece. Mary Fields appeared as a tall, shapely woman in a cowgirl skirt, cowboy boots, and a battered Stetson, gun belt slung around her hips and pistol pulled, shielding a frightened Native American girl from three white ruffians. Two of the ruffians are poised to draw their guns, while the third holds a horse. The horse has a remarkably human expres-sion of shock and disapproval at the men's action. In this illustration it appears that Fields is protecting a young Indian woman from harass-ment by the white men (see figure 5.2).[23] There is nothing in the written record or oral tradition to suggest that Fields defended the honor of Native American women against rapacious white men. What is striking is that this illustration in *Negro Digest* hinted that women of color could make common cause against white oppression, with Mary Fields in the imagined lead role. In a later version of Fields' mythic alignment with Native Americans, a fictional, book-length biography has her wearing buckskins, burning sage, and carrying a live eagle on her arm.[24]

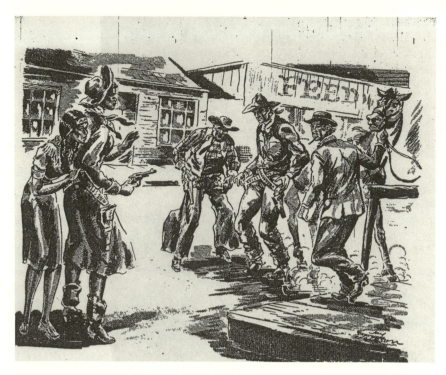

Fig. 5.2 Illustration from *Negro Digest* (1950).

If black journalists recast Fields as a race heroine who defied white hegemony, Catholic writers shifted focus even further. They wove Fields into a nun's tale of triumph over adversity, a victory of faith. In 1891, an Ursuline press release stated, "today … [the sisters in Montana] are trained to be true Spouses of the crucified and the spiritual parents of His disinherited children, burying themselves in a mysterious north in mission work among the Indians."[25] A memoir by Sister Angela Abair detailed the challenges of a harsh climate, geographic isolation, and constant poverty.[26] Through faith and perseverance, the Ursuline mission in central Montana, St. Peter's, had made "the desert bloom as a rose."[27] Mary Fields was one of the stalwarts in this tale. During the building of St. Peter's massive school buildings, Fields hauled stone and mortar by wagon from Great Falls to the mission site. The Ursulines credited her as "a beloved helping hand" whose work had been "invaluable."[28]

More dramatic were Catholic journalists' stories of sin and redemption, with Mary Fields as the prodigal daughter. In these accounts, a hard-drinking, swearing, and combative Fields is stricken with remorse and returns to the church in time to save her soul. Indeed, Mary Fields' role as lay helper to the mission took on new luster in a story written by Sister Genevieve McBride, Ursuline historian: In 1898, when Fields was in her mid-sixties, "she was thrown from the mail coach and arrived at the Mission in a pitiful condition. The Sisters used the occasion to remind her that she must return to the sacraments for she was not so fervent ... Mary went to confession and the next morning the penitent appeared ... High Mass was sung to commemorate Mary's return to God."[29] The *Catholic Digest* retold this story in 1959. In this version, the author added that when Fields returned to worship, "she was not wearing her usual men's clothes but a beautiful dress and long white veil the nuns had made for her during the night."[30] Gender-appropriate clothing was part of her salvation. Catholic writers, then, celebrated Mary Fields' contributions to the success of the mission, and placed her iconoclastic behavior within a narrative of waywardness and salvation.

Whether they created the masculinized figure of white legend, the selfless caregiver of black history, or the prodigal of Catholic lore, all of Fields' biographers claimed that she was well liked among her contemporaries. This, too, took mythic proportions. According to journalists, Mary Fields was not only "much beloved by the people of Cascade," she also became "one of the most respected and loved pioneer women of the West."[31] But as we shall see from the evidence of her life, Mary Fields' place in the community was far more complex than legend allowed.

THE EVIDENCE

Mary Fields left no written memoir, no diary, no journal of her days. We have only scattered eyewitness testimony, volumes of hearsay, a few official documents, and a handful of vivid photographs. To the careful reader, even this patchy evidence can yield new insights into Fields' life. In recent years, historians of gender and race have developed useful strategies for piecing together the lives of those who left no record in their own voice. One is "reading against the grain"; another is "controlled speculation;" and still another is interpreting photographs as a form of self-representation.

Reading against the grain involves interpreting the observations about one's subject made by contemporaries, in light of their cultural biases.[32] In this study, the records left by Ursuline nuns who worked with Mary Fields offer tantalizing clues to her behavior, as do the narratives of Cascade residents. Weighed in light of the Ursuline agenda, and in light of white attitudes regarding race in turn-of-the-century Montana, such clues reveal some of the choices that Mary Fields made.

"Controlled speculation" is another way to fill in information in the absence of a personal narrative. Controlled speculation requires building the historical context within which one's subject lived. In other words, if one understands the geography and settlement of a region, one can infer some of the conditions that shaped an individual's life. As one historian advised, "find the contours of [the] woman by painting around her, by marking out the natural and historical setting in which she ... lived. Then, ... step inside, inhabit the silhouette and give it form by building with insight on the few known facts of her life."[33] In the case of Mary Fields, we can assess the "few known facts of her life" within the contexts of recent historical research on African-Americans in Toledo, Ohio; on African-American women in the West; and on race relations in Montana. Finally, photography offers yet another route into the identity of those who left no memoir. By the late nineteenth century, photography had become a widely accessible medium for self-representation.[34] Photographs of Mary Fields, some candid and others posed, offer images of her without the filter of legend. Indeed, the ways that Fields presented herself in everyday photographs leaven the myths that envelop her.

In sorting the written and photographic evidence from Fields' life, three questions come to mind. The first addresses her legend: What parts of the Mary Fields myth collapse under scrutiny? The second is an inquiry into the woman herself: What circumstances did she face, and given those circumstances, what choices did she make? The third asks: What do her legend and her actual life suggest about race and gender in turn-of-the-century Montana?

Every story about Fields says she was born into slavery on a farm in Hickman County, Tennessee, during the early 1830s.[35] But nonnarrative sources show no trace of Fields in Hickman County between 1840 and 1860, the years she presumably grew up under slavery. The 1840 federal census for Tennessee did not identify slaves by name; it only listed the number of slaves owned by each head of household. No free blacks or whites with the surname Field or Fields appear in Hickman County in 1840. Similarly, the federal census "Slave Schedules" for 1850 and 1860 show no slave families with the surname Field or Fields in Hickman County.[36] Thus the story of Mary Fields' beginnings as a slave in Hickman County, Tennessee cannot be confirmed, and her origins remain mysterious. What we do know is that sometime during the antebellum years, Fields became a slave in the Warner household of West Virginia. When the Warners moved to Cleveland, Ohio, Fields remained with them as a house servant. Oral histories with descendants of the Warner family confirm this.[37]

Contrary to the myth of her escape from slavery, Fields either was freed by emancipation in 1863, or emancipated by the Warner family before the Civil War.[38] For a time during the 1860s, Fields worked as chambermaid aboard a paddleboat on the Mississippi. By 1870, Fields had returned to the Warner family, where she earned wages as a free domestic servant.[39] That same year, one of the Warner daughters, Mary, chose to become a nun. When Mary Warner entered the Ursuline Convent of the Sacred Heart in Toledo, Mary Fields went with her. There, Fields hired on as a groundskeeper for the Ursulines.[40]

By all accounts from the convent in Toledo, Mary Fields was quarrelsome. Though she worked hard and capably, Fields reportedly had "a temper." Sister Mary Grace Connelly, a Toledo Ursuline, remembered stories passed down by nuns at the convent about Fields' irascible personality. "God help anyone who walked on the lawn after Mary had cut it," she said.[41] Sister Mary Rose Krupp, Ursuline archivist in Toledo, corroborated these stories. Krupp said the Toledo nuns were glad when Mary Fields left for Montana, because she had been so "difficult."[42] The nuns in 1870s Toledo had no investment in mythologizing Fields as a frontier gunfighter. Their characterization of her as "difficult" predates the western lore. Free from the distortions of frontier myth, the narratives of Fields' Toledo contemporaries gain credence. If oral tradition from the Toledo convent holds that Fields was a contentious person, perhaps that was the mundane truth behind her exaggerated reputation as a brawler and gunfighter.

Reinforcing the Toledo stories is a financial statement signed by Mary Fields that indicates an argument over wages. At first glance it appears to be a receipt for $100.00 paid to Fields by the Toledo convent on January 3, 1884. But this is no simple accounting, with employee name, wages earned, and balance due. Rather, it is a statement aimed at resolving a protracted dispute between Fields and the convent over her pay:

> I do hereby acknowledge the receipt of One hundred Dollars to my full satisfaction from the Ursuline Convent of the Sacred Heart of Toledo, of all pay and compensation due me for any and all services heretofore rendered by me to said Institution, Order, and Community and I do further hereby release and discharge said Community from any and all claims or demands I may have against them, hereby declaring that all my claims and demands against them have been fully paid, satisfied, and discharged up to and including this date. [signed] Mary Fields[43]

The language of "demands" and "claims" made "against" the convent suggests that Fields had wrangled with the nuns over what they owed her.

And the statement that "all my claims and demands against them" had been resolved "up to and including this date" indicates a conflict that had been ongoing. Significantly, later records of Fields' wages included no such language about "demands" or "claims" made "against" the convent.[44] One can infer that this particular $100 had been disputed, moving the nuns to secure in legal terms a resolution of the conflict. If Fields disputed her wages, she probably did not conform to racial codes of deferential behavior. Perhaps this earned her the reputation for being difficult at the convent in Toledo.

Fields worked on salary at the convent from the 1870s through the mid-1880s. A record of wages dated May 19, 1885 shows that she earned $50 per month, and that she roomed and boarded in the convent at no extra charge.[45] Occasionally, Fields borrowed against her wages. Between February 1884 and May 1885, she borrowed a total of $15.40 for medicines and a traveling bag. Fields also borrowed $5.00 to buy a banjo, $9.00 for a harmonica, and $9.76 for sheet music. Fields signed her name to the account in a careful, cursive script.[46]

Consider, for a moment, the fact that Fields lived with the Ursulines in Toledo. She had her own room on the first floor of the convent, a significant choice for a literate, free black woman in Ohio after the Civil War. When Mary Fields arrived in Toledo in 1870, race relations there had a charged history. Despite Ohio's reputation as a sanctuary for escaped slaves, Toledo's antebellum years had seen overt hostility toward blacks. Ohio Black Codes had denied employment and residency to any Negro who lacked "freedom papers," prohibited blacks from testifying against whites or serving on juries, and denied free black men the vote.[47] In 1850, Toledo whites had endorsed fugitive slave law by a large majority, and the city had maintained segregated churches, housing, and schools.[48] In 1862, race prejudice broke out into open violence when white dockworkers attacked black stevedores during a strike for higher wages. Striking whites stoned the black workers, starting a melee that inflicted injuries on both sides. Mob violence followed, as whites roamed the city attacking black pedestrians.[49] The Toledo Riot of 1862 exposed the racist underbelly of the free state of Ohio. After the Civil War, the Toledo Board of Education opened city schools to black pupils, but segregation persisted in housing, worship, and employment.[50]

In an urban environment segregated by race, why did Mary Fields choose to live with a white, female, religious community? Fields herself was not particularly devout, and an African-American neighborhood thrived in "the near downtown area of Erie Street,"[51] within walking distance of the convent. Why had not Fields lived there? The record offers no answers to this conundrum. Perhaps Fields weighed Toledo's recent history and saw the convent as a refuge from race-related violence.[52]

Legend holds that Mary Fields lived at the convent out of devotion to Mother Amadeus. Sarah Dunne, or Mother Amadeus, spent her formative years at the Toledo convent, coinciding with Mary Fields' years there. Amadeus left Toledo in 1884 to establish Ursuline missions in Montana. Recall the lore about Fields' migration West, in which she rushes to Montana in 1885 to nurse the ailing Mother Amadeus. To what extent can we confirm the mythic bonds of friendship between Fields and Amadeus? The evidence begins circumstantially, with Fields' ties to the Warner family, who became related by marriage to the Dunne family. At the Toledo convent, novitiates Mary Warner (Sister Annunciation) and Sarah Dunne (Sister Amadeus) became good friends. In 1874, Sarah Dunne was elected mother superior, and became Mother Amadeus Dunne. Meanwhile, Amadeus's brother, Edmund Dunne, married Mary Warner's sister, Josephine. Thus Mother Amadeus Dunne and Sister Annunciation Warner became in-laws. The Warner/Dunne family ties, and Mother Amadeus's governance of the Toledo convent, brought Mary Fields within her orbit.[53] Mother Amadeus was an effective leader who generally inspired respect and affection from novices and peers. Perhaps Mary Fields, too, came to trust and like Mother Amadeus as she worked at the Toledo convent.

The record of Fields' relationship with Mother Amadeus becomes clearer once both parties left Toledo. Put simply, Fields was *not* the one who nursed Mother Amadeus back to health. In January 1884, Amadeus and a small cadre of nuns left the Toledo convent to answer the call for missionaries in the West. They established a base for mission work in Miles City, Montana. Nearly a year later, Amadeus pushed farther West into central Montana, where she set up a girls' school and convent at St. Peter's Mission, thirteen miles south of Great Falls. "I am overtaxed with *all* kinds of work," Amadeus wrote from Montana, "I need at least two nuns more."[54] In a second letter, Amadeus sent greetings to the Toledo convent. Her mention of Mary Fields in this correspondence is revealing:

December 19, 1884. I will try to answer the dear letters received ... of my beloved Sisters Annunciation, Mary Conception, and St. Agnes and Mother Aloysius. ... Mary Fields may expect a New Year's present—I must send her some little remembrance at least. There are twenty-one letters to Toledo and dozens to other places to be answered, what am I to do with 'old Father Time'?[55]

While Amadeus referred to her closest friends as "beloved" sisters and planned to answer their "dear letters," her reference to Mary Fields was less intimate. Amadeus mentioned that she "must send" a small present to Mary Fields because she may "expect" it. This remark sounds more like a sincere gesture of goodwill from manager to employee, than an expression of deep friendship. In this letter, Mary Fields appears as another long-distance consideration in Amadeus' crowded days.

The evidence becomes more telling as Mother Amadeus fell ill. "Have pity on me … I am for the first time *really* overtaxed," she wrote in another plea to Toledo for more nuns.[56] As winter dragged on with no response from Toledo, Mother Amadeus succumbed to pneumonia. When her illness grew worse, the nuns notified a bishop in Great Falls. He telegraphed Mother St. Francis in Miles City to "hasten to St. Peter's" and do all in her power "to save the precious life."[57] Mother St. Francis was the first to arrive at Amadeus' bedside. In March of 1885, a nun at St. Peter's wrote, "Mother Amadeus got pneumonia very bad, a Jesuite sent a despatch to Toledo. In a short time we had helpe, Reverend Mother Stanislaus of Toledo and Mother Mary of the Angels Carroll and black Mary Fields from Toledo [and] Mother St. Thomas of Cleveland."[58] According to the Ursuline annals, Mother Stanislaus took over care of the ailing Amadeus: "This devoted friend stood at Mother Amadeus' bedside … and nursed her back to health."[59] Ursuline historian Genivieve McBride clarified Mary Fields' role in this episode. "When Mother Amadeus was near death," she explained, "Mary [Fields] came to Montana *to help the missionaries* [emphasis mine].[60] Thus it was Mother St. Francis followed by Mother Stanislaus who nursed Mother Amadeus, while Mary Fields and two more nuns from Ohio represented Toledo's response to the request for more staff to keep the mission going. From March through December 1885, the nuns reported on Amadeus's long convalescence in letters to the Toledo convent. In all of this correspondence, not one letter identified Mary Fields as Mother Amadeus's nurse.[61] In short, Fields' mythic role as devoted nurse to the Mother Superior is not borne out by the evidence.

If Mary Fields was not the lifesaving nurse, she was, nonetheless, a much needed worker at the mission. As the Catholic school grew, a handful of nuns taught, fed, clothed, and housed anywhere from twenty to seventy students, plus staff.[62] From 1885 to 1895, Fields helped shoulder this burden, but on her own terms. That is, Fields accepted room and board, but refused wages.[63] Why? In the absence of a contract or salary, Fields was not bound by obligation. Instead, she felt free to come and go as she chose. After nine years with Fields at the mission, an Ursuline diarist summarized their arrangement: "She [Fields] has labored pretty much as she pleased, refusing wages. ... Several times did Mother [Amadeus] wish to have her accept wages and sign a contract, both of which she stoutly refused to do."[64] The Ursuline explained that Fields alternated work at the mission with outside jobs, at will: "For a time she directed the washing [at the mission] which was done by half-breed [mixed-blood Native American] women, she herself doing the sacristy wash—and for a time she also freighted for her own amusement."[65]

This is not to say Fields abandoned work at the mission. Eyewitnesses wrote that Mary Fields kept four hundred chickens and raised a large vegetable garden to feed mission staff and students.[66] She hunted game birds, and planted potatoes. The nuns adjusted to Fields' self-imposed work rhythms, filling in on chores during her occasional absences. In July 1892, for example, an Ursuline wrote, "Our evenings are spent weeding and bugging in the potato patches."[67] On October 7, 1892, she wrote, "Mary Fields gone freighting," and mentioned that the nuns cleaned Fields' laundry room. About two weeks later, Fields returned.[68] Work at the mission without contract or wages allowed Fields to control her own labor. Clearly, she valued her autonomy, but lest we recreate the free spirit of lore, let us avoid hyperbole. The evidence does not indicate independence of legendary proportions. Rather, Mary Fields' work rhythms outline a woman who shaped an occupational niche for herself in which her labor was needed but never dictated. For an African-American woman raised in slavery, work under one's own initiative had the pungency of freedom.

Mary Fields probably would have lived and worked at St. Peter's until she died, had it not been for Bishop Brondel in Great Falls. When the bishop heard rumors of Fields' uncouth behavior, he wanted her off the premises. Fields drank alcohol and sometimes cursed, transgressions of acceptable female behavior on church grounds. The nuns overlooked these lapses, for they relied on Fields to provide most of the mission's food. And so the bishop demurred. Eventually, though, a disturbing rumor tipped the scales against her.

Recall that in legend, Mary Fields was a volatile gunslinger who staged a shootout. There is no evidence to support this story. The tale of Fields' shootout probably began as an exaggerated version of one incident at the mission. On September 9, 1892, "John Mosney and Mary Fields touched rifles at each other, but there was no firing."[69] John Mosney, a white hired hand, worked at the mission for $1.25 per day. If there was tension between them, perhaps it was because they held similar positions, but Fields worked when she pleased while Mosney was under contract. Perhaps Mosney resented holding a position similar to that held by a black woman; perhaps he felt that his gender and race should place him above her. Or perhaps she did not defer to him. We can only speculate. What we do know is that Mosney and Fields disagreed over something, pointed guns at each other, and then both backed down. This was the extent of Fields' legendary shootout. Fields may have been cantankerous, but she was not a killer. Indeed, she and Mosney had worked together before, without incident. For example, two months earlier, when "soot took fire in the pipes, ... Mr. Mosney, our hired man, and Mary Fields arrived on the scene of action and by throwing salt on the fire and turning the hose on the chimney and heated wall, saved this beautiful house."[70] But Mosney and Fields' cooperative work never made its way into rumor. Instead, the armed confrontation between Mosney and Fields fueled gossip that echoed all the way to Great Falls, prompting Bishop Brondel to order Fields' eviction from St. Peter's Mission.[71]

Dismayed, the nuns struggled with their duty to obey church authority. "It is hard for Mother [Amadeus] to dismiss this faithful servant in her old age ... but the Bishop's orders are peremptory," wrote one of the nuns. In an eloquent statement of their dilemma she added, "The darkness of obedience will be light in the next world."[72] The bishop's orders went against the nuns' every instinct, for they saw Fields as a permanent member of their community.[73] As one nun expressed it, "She had been overbearing and troublesome but it was our intention to keep her till death."[74] Fields shared their conviction that the mission was her home. Another nun reported that Fields felt "determined to come back here to die."[75] If the nuns were troubled by Fields' ouster, Fields herself was distraught, and "at first refused to go but was at length persuaded. Sister Philomena sat up all night to make her dress."[76] Without sentimentalizing the ties between Mary Fields and the Ursulines at St. Peter's, it is clear they had developed a strong bond of care and interdependence.

Thus daily records from St. Peter's Mission in Montana, as well as from the convent in Toledo, offer new insights into Fields' life. We find that she was neither the devoted nurse nor the violent gunslinger of legend. Instead, a more human portrait emerges. Mary Fields surfaced in Toledo in 1870, a literate, free woman of color who chose to live with white, Catholic nuns. Mary Warner, Sister Annunciation, was her connection to that post. At the Toledo convent, Fields protected her own interests, at one point contesting her wages. In the mid-1880s, the Ohio Ursulines sent her West with two nuns to assist Mother Amadeus' mission near Great Falls. There, Fields worked on her own terms, farming, freighting, or laundering when she chose. For better or worse, Mary Fields shared a bond of mutuality with the sisters in Montana, forged by the demands of survival on the northern plains.

Following her eviction from St. Peter's, Fields moved to the small ranching town of Cascade, Montana. The town sat on a plain adjacent to the foothills of the Rocky Mountains, several miles from the mission. Records from Mary Fields' life in Cascade add further dimension to her portrait. Without the forbearance of the nuns, Fields quickly became the subject of local gossip. Townsfolk nattered that she wore men's clothes, drank whiskey, and carried a gun. Or, with a show of magnanimity, they characterized her as a "mascot." Indeed, the mythic personas of beloved mascot and masculine gunslinger began in Cascade during Fields' lifetime, as the white community defined her place in their lives. Both images call for analysis in terms of race and gender systems in late-nineteenth- and early-twentieth-century Montana.

But first, consider the outlines of Fields' life after leaving St. Peter's. Twice Mother Amadeus helped Fields set up a restaurant in Cascade. Twice it failed. In 1896, Fields took in laundry, but it yielded too little income to make a living. Finally, Mother Amadeus arranged with the U.S. Postal Service to hire Fields for mail delivery between Cascade and the mission. Amadeus' persistence in finding work for Mary Fields testifies to the nuns' commitment to her welfare. In the ensuing years, Fields continued to visit the mission and the nuns tracked her progress. From 1896 to 1903, Fields drove the mail wagon and occasionally carried passengers as well.[77] From 1904 until 1913, Fields did laundry out of her home in Cascade, and did janitorial work in local saloons.[78] During the last few years of her life, Fields also babysat children.[79] In 1914, in her early eighties, Mary Fields passed away.[80]

Place this chronology within the frame of race relations in turn-of-the-century Montana, and a troubled picture emerges. Historians concur that African Americans who migrated west did not escape race prejudice and discrimination. Racial stratification in the wage workforce, segregated housing, truncated legal rights, and harassment of black settlers plagued western states and territories after the Civil War and into the twentieth century.[81] Montana was no exception. During the 1860s, "a large, vigorous element of Southerners" traded up the Missouri River or tried their luck in Montana gold camps. The territorial legislature reflected their values, mandating separate schools for students of color, prohibiting the black vote on school issues, and barring blacks from testimony against whites in court.[82] Violence reinforced white hegemony in Montana. For example, when the city of Helena experimented with black suffrage in 1867, an African-American man was shot dead as he approached the polls. A mob gathered to shield the perpetrator, shouting "Let him go—he only killed a nigger!" One arrest and a jailbreak later, the killer was never held accountable.[83]

But if black Americans found injustice in Montana, they also resisted it through community-building, journalistic protests, and political activism. Westering blacks settled primarily in urban areas where they formed mutual aid societies, fraternal organizations, women's clubs, and churches. These institutions supported black enterprise, social life, and Progressive reforms aimed at black advancement.[84] Black-owned newspapers like the *Montana Plaindealer* of Helena and the *Butte New Age* editorialized against racism and exhorted readers to vote in state and local elections. Black activism paid off in 1883 when the Montana legislature desegregated the school system.[85] Still, African-Americans comprised a tiny minority in the northern Rockies, about 1.1 percent of the population.[86] In central Montana, where Fields lived, Great Falls was the nearest city, roughly thirteen miles from both the mission and the town of Cascade. Great Falls in 1900 had 128 black residents, only .8 percent of its total population.[87] Despite their enterprise and community-building, blacks in Montana remained a vulnerable minority.

From the 1880s through the early 1900s, racism erupted sporadically in Montana, through a thin veneer of civility. In 1882, for example, white residents of Helena loudly opposed integration of city schools, for fear it would lead to miscegenation. An editorial in the *Helena Daily Independent* said, "We believe that the Caucasian race is superior to the African, and that such amalgamation would have a tendency to degrade our nation."[88] In Glendive, Montana, in 1893, an interracial marriage provoked mob violence. When John Orr, a white man, married Emma Wall, a black woman, a crowd surrounded the couple and stripped off their clothing. The mob then painted Mr. Orr black, using lampblack, and painted Mrs. Orr white, using alabastine. Next, the mob gave the terrified couple twenty-four hours to "pack up and leave town."[89] The *Glendive Independent* reported the whole incident in a jocular tone. Blacks who read this news, however, took it seriously. If whites used such violence to maintain racial boundaries, then African-Americans held a precarious position in Montana.

Sometimes the rift took subtler form. When blues musician W. C. Handy played Helena in 1897, he described an attitude of "friendly contempt" toward blacks.[90] According to Montana historian William Lang, Helena's racism "consisted of what W. E. B. DuBois called 'those petty little meannesses,'" the patronizing behaviors that could not be legislated away.[91] In Great Falls, closer to Mary Fields' home, racist attitudes surfaced as well. A large ad in the *Great Falls Tribune* in 1904 announced a "Thanksgiving Sale of Table Linen," and illustrated the holiday theme with a turkey chasing an African-American boy. The child was rendered in exaggerated blackface, with rolling white eyes and oversized lips. He was shown running in terror from the harmless turkey, appearing as a dim-witted object of mockery.[92] Such ads bespoke the casual bigotry of white culture in turn-of-the-century Montana.

From 1886 to 1914, Mary Fields was the only black resident of Cascade, Montana. There, the record suggests a tacit struggle between Fields and townsfolk over her social identity and position. To the whites of Cascade, Fields would refuse to fit neatly into familiar racial stereotypes such as mammy or servant. Unsure how to categorize her, townsfolk would subject her to rumor and speculation. Fields, in turn, would carve out a social life that bypassed conventional restrictions on race and gender. That is, she would go where black men and white women were forbidden, into the leisured social spaces of white men. At the same time, she would enter the dubious role of *mascot* to the Cascade baseball team. By accepting Fields as a mascot, white residents of Cascade would create a narrative of themselves as openhearted. For her part as a mascot, Fields would gain direct access to men of influence—the town fathers of Cascade.

Recall the lore that Fields won the hearts of everyone in town. The implication of these narratives is that race was never an issue; that the people of Cascade transcended color prejudice and welcomed Mary Fields into their midst. In this way, Cascade residents created a collective memory about their town as a sheltering place. But the myth of community embrace is too simple, for the evidence suggests a profoundly ambivalent relationship between Fields and her white contemporaries in Cascade.

On the one hand, the town accepted Fields' presence and partially supported her as she aged. When her two-room cabin burned in 1912, the townspeople built her another one. When Fields became too frail to drive the mail wagon and lost income as a result, the New Cascade Hotel gave her hot meals, gratis.[93] And when, in her last days, Fields grew seriously ill, Cascade Mayor D.W. Monroe brought her to a hospital in Great Falls. There she received medical attention for several days before she died.[94] Townsfolk donated their energies to her funeral as well. A priest from St. Peter's Mission led the service, the mayor and the proprietor of the New Cascade Hotel marched as pallbearers, two Cascade matrons "rendered several vocal selections," and "floral contributions were especially in evidence."[95] In these ways, the people of Cascade took care of Mary Fields as one of their own.

On the other hand, while she was alive, Fields also encountered open hostility and disrespect from locals. In one incident, Fields loaded a wagon bound from St. Peter's to Cascade, when one of the horses broke loose and cracked a singletree. Fields' passengers, a priest and two nuns, alighted while Fields examined the harness. The mission foreman, Mr. Burns, walked over to investigate, but he showed little respect for Fields. An eyewitness said Burns "made a grimace" at Fields. Fields grew irate in response, and chucked a stone in his direction. The priest intervened to prevent an argument.[96] Cascade resident Edgar Tilton described another incident of hostility toward Fields: "Once when Mary was driving the stage, it tipped over. Several men were sitting nearby, and they started laughing at her."[97] Whatever chivalry may have been present for white women was not forthcoming for Mary Fields. Instead, her wagon accident became the object of derisive humor. In other cases, townspeople simply judged Fields a class below themselves. White matrons of Cascade avoided her because she "talked rough." In one school essay, a Cascade student referred to Fields as "a low, foul creature," a phrase the child probably heard at home.[98]

Other clues to her marginal status surface in innocuous details, mentioned in passing. One Cascade informant said that early in the morning Fields "would walk down the streets of Cascade picking up cigar snipes" to smoke later.[99] If Fields resorted to scavenging discarded stogies, she probably lived on the edge of solvency. The town that rebuilt her cabin after it burned was content to maintain her at poverty level. In many ways, then, evidence from Cascade does not support the sentimental myth that townsfolk warmly embraced this lone black woman. Instead the record shows a checkered mix of social distance, petty hostility, and limited benevolence on the part of locals toward Mary Fields. Given the context of episodic violence against blacks in Montana, as well as the mix of charity and condescension in Cascade, it is no wonder Fields sometimes got testy.

If it was bigotry that provoked Fields' surliness, local reporters carefully avoided the issue. Instead, they focused cheerily on what became another linchpin in the Fields myth, that of mascot status. The 1939 *Great Falls Tribune* retrospective on Mary Fields included a photograph of the Cascade baseball team, circa 1913, with the original caption. In the photo, five men in baseball uniforms sit cross-legged on the ground, and four more uniformed teammates stand behind them. An umpire in shirtsleeves, and the team manager in suit and tie, flank the players on the left. Mary Fields, wearing skirts and holding a pennant, flanks the players on the right. The caption described Fields as "the official mascot."[100] Similarly, a photograph from the *Cascade Courier* presented the team, umpire, manager, and Mary Fields. That caption identified Fields as "negress mascot."[101] According to the *Tribune*, Fields traveled with the team and "took care of the bats and other paraphernalia." Local histories say baseball was a "very popular sport" in central Montana;

"fans would travel miles to watch their team play."[102] Fields shared their enthusiasm for the game.

Oral tradition from Cascade drew on Fields' position as mascot to amplify her mythic qualities. Some storytellers milked the scenario for details to build her masculinized persona, and journalists would repeat these tales: Fields "would punch any man in the mouth who talked against the team," claimed one reporter. If an opposing fan insulted the Cascade team, "he was roughly handled by the capable mascot," wrote another.[103] Others portrayed Fields as a gentle, nonpartisan fan: "She would fix a buttonhole bouquet for the members of each team and five large bouquets for each of those who made home runs."[104] According to local mythmakers, then, Fields was either the pugnacious defender of team honor or the generous fan whose pansies delighted batters. Probably there was more truth to the flowers story. A photograph bears this out, in which the aging Mary Fields stands amid her flower garden in long skirts, smiling with pride at a proliferation of blossoms nearly waist high.[105]

Townspeople referred to Fields as a mascot without critical reflection. With the benefits of hindsight, however, the term *mascot* comes into focus. A team mascot is typically dressed in a playful costume and entertains spectators in a clownish way. Fields did not take the costumed, clownish role. She merely supported the team as a kind of batboy, tendered with enthusiasm and flowers. Still, the word mascot suggests a pet or favored child, and a mascot is not an equal. The role of mascot placed Fields in a separate category from her white peers, lower on the social hierarchy. In defining Fields as a mascot, Cascade residents defined the limits of their tolerance for racial integration. They could express goodwill toward Fields and the team welcomed her, as long as she remained socially subordinate.

Evidence suggests that Mary Fields was not unique in this regard. Elsewhere in Montana, black women who entered a white community as the only person of their race met similar attitudes. Near Lewistown, Montana, white ranchers dubbed a black woman "Aunt Adeline," and cast her in the role of devoted servant. In 1939, the *Bainville Democrat* featured Adeline, as she neared age one hundred, in a story highlighting her faithful service to the Skaggs family. Born into slavery, Adeline remained with the Skaggs family after emancipation. A reporter wrote, "Hers has been a slavery of mutual devotion," and remarked, "You read stories about faithful old family retainers of the deep south, but you don't often encounter them in the foothills of the Rockies."[106] Similarly, Tish Nevins became "Aunt Tish" to white residents of Hamilton, Montana, celebrated for her devotion as nursemaid to the Smithey family, and hailed for her good cooking.[107] Such women were celebrated in their old age, and in memory, within a subtext of social subordination.

Historians have documented other instances where a white settlement drew careful boundaries around a woman of color, through a process of community objectification. In a study of Native American women in late-nineteenth-century western Canada, Sarah Carter found that white communities marginalized women of color through both institutionalized and informal segregation. Her discussion of informal modes of segregation was revealing. By the turn of the century many western Canadian settlements "had their 'local Indian' who was tolerated on the margins or fringes of society and whose behavior and appearance was the subject of local anecdotes."[108] In Virden, Manitoba, for example, an elderly Indian woman named "Liza" survived on the edge of town life. White residents of Virden were charitable enough to feed her, shovel her out when she was snowed in, and allow her to warm herself during the winter inside a storefront. Carter observed that "the presence of Liza, and the stories told about her, served to sharpen the boundaries of community membership ... Liza was the object of both fascination and repugnance as she violated norms of conventional behavior [and] dress."[109] The white community maintained Liza on its margins because she served their need to define racial difference. Her persona as a marginal figure supported their beliefs about the superiority of white society and the necessity of racial segregation.

Similarly, in a study of the Wabanaki people in northern New England, Bunny McBride documented elderly Indian women who took on legendary proportions in their community while living on its margins. Molly Ockett, for example, survived on the fringes of white society in Rumford and Andover, Maine during the early nineteenth century by trading Indian crafts and doctoring Anglo settlers with herbal remedies. To the white community, Ockett became an object of rumor and innuendo; stories circulated that she could level a fatal curse upon anyone who insulted her. Like "Liza," Ockett was supported at poverty level in her old age, but when Ockett wandered off course during a snowstorm, families in the nearby village of Snow Falls turned her away when she asked for shelter.[110] White charity toward a woman of color had its limits. McBride also investigated Molly Belassie, a Wabanaki woman whose position resembled that of Ockett. Belassie lived out her old age in Bangor, Maine, during the late nineteenth century. Walking the streets of Bangor, Belassie played on white notions of "Indian magic" by glaring at pedestrians until they gave her money. Legend held that she would call down a curse upon those who did not give.[111] In Virden, Rumford, Andover, and Bangor, respectively, "Liza," Ockett, and Belassie's positions resembled that of Mary Fields in the town of Cascade, Montana. In each case, the town accepted a woman of color, treated her charitably, objectified her with rumor and exaggeration, and used her notoriety to sharpen the boundaries of race and gender.

As the only African-American woman in Cascade, to whom could Mary Fields turn for companionship? After leaving the convent, she no longer sought the company of women. Though freighting periodically drew Fields to Great Falls, she did not seek the companionship of black matrons there. Unlike many black women in the West, Fields was not involved in building black community institutions, such as church societies and women's clubs.[112] Membership rolls of the Great Falls African Methodist Episcopal Church did not list her; neither did membership lists from the Great Falls branch of the Confederated Colored Women's Clubs. Nor does Fields' name appear with the white matrons of Cascade who formed a chapter of the Eastern Star, or a service group for the Catholic Church, the Sacred Heart Altar Society.[113] Following her eviction from St. Peter's, Fields did not participate in the female culture of either black Great Falls or white Cascade.

Instead, she created a new niche for herself in Cascade. There she associated with white men in the social spaces created by male leisure pursuits. That is, Mary Fields joined white men at the baseball diamond, the billiards hall, and the saloon. In these space the men she joined were not marginal figures. They were successful businessmen and skilled workers, their lives securely woven into the social fabric of Cascade. A photograph of Mary Fields in downtown Cascade shows her standing outside Krause's Sample Room, a clapboard saloon on Front Street. She wears a long, dark dress, a small brimmed hat, and a bandanna tied loosely around her neck.[114] Just in front of her sits a dog on a beer barrel. Standing with Fields, in casual attitudes, are white residents Fred Lentz, Jim Cornell, George Donaldson, and the saloon proprietor, Herman Krause. Next to Krause are his sons, two little boys on horseback. The men sport moustaches, cowboy hats, and denims with tucked-in shirts; Cornell and Krause also wear vests. All look like respectable, middling citizens of a ranch town, as indeed they were. Krause owned his own saloon, Lentz was a skilled boot maker, and Cornell a horse wrangler who took over ownership of the Sample Room in 1910. Similarly, Fields' companions in the baseball dugout were respected citizens. The team during Fields' tenure as mascot included Bruce Glover, A. P. Murphy, Bill Berger, George Hall, Julius Hilgard, Dan DeCoix, Elmer Cardell, Happy Hogan, and Charles Riley. Glover owned and managed the New Cascade Hotel, where DeCoix clerked and Cardell worked as a porter. Murphy owned and ran the Briscoe & Murphy Dray Company, while Hall sold real estate and insurance. Berger managed the Cascade Mercantile Company and published the *Cascade Courier*. Hilgard kept accounts for the First State Bank of Cascade and served as Deputy Clerk for the district court. Hilgard, Murphy, Berger, and Happy Hogan were volunteer firemen together.[115] These town fathers accepted Mary Fields' presence in their off hours.

Cascade resident Lester Monroe remembered seeing Fields banter with the men at the saloon within the New Cascade Hotel. "She was standing at one end of the bar, and the men were lined out along the bar. She took part in their conversation and jokes."[116] On the one hand, Fields' position with these white men reinforced her marginal status. That is, the town fathers of Cascade encouraged Fields toward behaviors that placed her outside the boundaries of respectable womanhood. For example, D. W. Monroe, mayor of Cascade, promoted Fields' drinking habit by suspending—for Fields only—a town ordinance that barred women from saloons.[117] As the only woman who drank publicly at saloons, Fields violated the norms of mainstream society. Like Liza, Molly Ockett, and Molly Belassie, she was well known, but her notoriety placed her on the margins.

On the other hand, Cascade was such a small town that the margins were not too far from the center. Fields' marginal behavior as a drinking woman brought her into contact with white men who routinely claimed masculine privileges at the social center of town life. As members of the baseball team and the volunteer fire department, these men were embraced by the town; they belonged. In their leisure time, they could retire to saloons for a smoke and a drink at no cost to their reputation. If we consider Fields' own agency, perhaps her choice of white men as social companions was a deliberate attempt to share in that license. Perhaps she cultivated her niche as an anomalous figure because it allowed her access to social privileges enjoyed by the town fathers, the most advantaged class she knew. Within these recreational venues, Fields claimed an entree that neither men of color nor white women had in Cascade. Moreover, the town fathers were influential men who could extend useful favors to Fields in her old age. It was Bruce Glover, manager of the baseball team, who extended free, hot meals to Fields at the New Cascade Hotel after she quit the mail route.[118] For their part, perhaps the town fathers were not threatened by Fields because she had become too old to represent a sexual temptation to them.[119] In any case, Mary Fields and the white men of Cascade enjoyed a curious symbiosis. The Cascade baseball team and saloon habitués defined themselves as charitable and tolerant, while Fields appropriated some of their social privilege.

For women, the flip side of masculine privilege was notoriety. Townspeople gossiped about Mary Fields not only because she drank in public, but because she did men's work, that of freighting and mail delivery. Historians of women in the American West have documented instances where communities mythologized women whose behavior undermined gender norms. Susan Johnson and Sally Zanjani each found that women miners who claimed "the trappings of male privilege," such as "men's work," drew criticism from contemporaries and became objects of legend after their death.[120] Sometimes the lore exaggerated their feminine qualities, as in the case of Nellie Cashman, a miner known as "the frontier angel" for her mythic nursing abilities.[121] In other cases, as with Mary Fields, white communities masculinized women who crossed gender boundaries. One study of ranchers, for example, found that work with cattle was defined as a male preserve at the turn of the century. Women who herded cattle were accepted only as "fellers" or "one of the boys," but not as women.[122] Whether they masculinized such women or mythologized them as feminine saints, western communities avoided coming to terms with the challenge to gender hierarchy posed by women who did men's work.

Local lore about Mary Fields followed a similar trajectory. As a female wagon master who freighted mail, Fields implicitly challenged gender norms, which held that women were too frail for such work. To defuse this challenge, townsfolk exaggerated her masculine traits, thereby marginalizing her as atypical. Presumably, an atypical woman would not threaten gender norms; rather, the exception proved the rule. In 1910, the *Cascade Courier* featured Mary Fields as a local "character." The newspaper reported that Fields was "the second woman to drive a mail stage," and then proceeded to masculinize her. Described as "hearty," engaged in "hard labor," a "crack shot," a "familiar figure on the streets of town … smoking her cigar,"[123] Mary Fields appears in masculine terms. Cascade resident Earl Monroe, over fifty years later, disagreed with this description. He amended it to say, "Mary Fields smoked in private, not in public."[124]

Photographs add sobriety to the giddy rhetoric about Fields' alleged masculine ways. Firsthand images of Fields speak more convincingly than rumor. While Cascade residents gossiped about her wearing men's clothes, every photograph of Fields, whether driving a wagon, walking in town, gardening, or posing with the Cascade baseball team, shows her wearing skirts.[125] Fields wore the unadorned long skirts, wool or cotton dresses, and aprons typical of rural western women at the turn of century. During the cold Montana winters, Fields sometimes added men's wool trousers under her skirts, to keep warm while driving the mail route. And Fields wore a man's wool overcoat in winter because women's overcoats were too small to fit her large frame. Fields also wore a man's wool cap during the winter, probably the most snug protection from icy winds. A nun conveyed the severity of a central Montana winter when she reported that Fields' wagon overturned "in a snowdrift about halfway between the mission and Cascade...[Fields] walked all night to keep from freezing."[126] A photograph, circa 1893 (see figure 5.3), shows Fields in winter, in front of St. Peter's, wearing the man's coat and hat, with her skirts. The winter landscape shows miles of stark white snow-fields, forbidding even across the lenses of time.[127] Given that temperatures dropped as low as thirty-nine degrees below zero in January, such clothing was necessary for work outdoors.[128] But the practical need for winter clothing was lost on Cascade's rumor mill. Local gossip about Fields highlighted her male attire as an eccentricity, rather than a necessity for survival.[129]

Fig. 5.3 Mary Fields in front of St. Peter's Mission. Reprinted by permission of the Ursuline Archives Northwest, Great Falls, Montana.

If Cascade residents talked about Fields' "masculine" clothing, they also remarked on her carrying a firearm as another marker of masculinity. The Ursuline Annals from St. Peter's report that Fields hunted for the convent during her tenure there. Once she began working the mail route, Fields continued to carry a rifle, to protect herself from wild animals on the lonely road between Cascade and the mission.[130] Like her winter clothes, a gun was necessary to survival. Still, only two out of eleven photographs of Fields show her carrying a gun. The first is the winter scene at St. Peter's, described above. The second shows her indoors, in a carefully posed photograph taken at a photographer's studio (see figure 5.1). Behind her is an artificial backdrop intended to create a genteel interior setting. The backdrop includes a painted balustrade, framed picture on the wall, paneled wood molding on the wall, and a patterned carpet, emblems of propriety.

Fields wears a fitted, dark cloth dress with a rounded white collar and a short jacket. She holds a rifle pointing downward, her arms relaxed, and she gazes off toward the right. A black and white dog lays at her feet.[131] Her expression is calm and a bit sad, her persona neither violent nor threatening. This image blends emblems of femininity—the fitted dress, rounded collar, relaxed arms, and indirect gaze—with emblems of masculine recreation, the dog and the rifle. Assuming that Fields staged this portrait according to her own wishes, it communicates the identity she forged in central Montana: her clothing is distinctively feminine, and thus we might surmise that Fields herself had no intention of adopting a masculine persona. The rifle represents either her role as game hunter for the mission or her means of protection on the mail route. And perhaps in the uncertain racial climate of Montana, the gun discouraged harassment of a lone black woman. The dog is an emblem of white male leisure time, associated with hunting for pleasure and with social groups of men. This is significant, given that Fields cultivated social ties with white men in Cascade. In short, Fields' self-representation in this photograph suggests a person who affirmed her womanhood but expanded its boundaries to include elements of male social privilege.

In her old age, Fields left the male trade of wagon master. Now, instead of masculinizing her, townsfolk made Fields a monument to her own history. A *Cascade Courier* article from 1913 marked Fields' eighty-third birthday with the statement that she "has become to Cascade what the 'Cradle of Liberty' has to Philadelphia or Fanueil Hall has to Boston. She is a sort of landmark."[132] One local went so far as to refer to Fields as a tourist attraction: "Tourists from all parts of the United States and Canada stop in Cascade to get a real 'touch of western atmosphere' and a glimpse of Negro Mary."[133] These tributes were not expressions of

Fig. 5.4 Mary Fields driving the mail wagon. Reprinted by permission of the Ursuline Archives Northwest, Great Falls, Montana.

personal friendship, rich with individual detail. Rather, Fields had become a showpiece that put Cascade on the map. One stops to ponder the difference between friendship and notoriety; townsfolk endorsed Fields' legend, but they did not bond with her as a personal friend. Perhaps the most telling challenge to the myth that Fields rested in the bosom of the town is that in the end, Mary Fields chose to die alone. In 1914, in her early eighties, Fields suffered from *dropsy*, or cardiovascular disease. Significantly, she did not feel comfortable calling upon her saloon contemporaries or members of the baseball team for help when she fell ill. Only when Mayor D. W. Monroe heard from a grade-school boy that she was close to death, did he bring Fields to a hospital in Great Falls where she died within a few days.[134] Without irony, townsfolk held Fields' funeral at the Pastime Theater in Cascade.[135] Even in death she was spectacle.

CONCLUSIONS

Mary Fields' roles as a living legend and her actual place in Cascade reveal informal processes by which white residents reinforced familiar categories of gender and race. White residents cast her as an aberrant woman or a lovable mascot. Both constructions of her identity placed her in a social category apart from her white peers. Thus whites maintained social distance, even as they accepted her presence and built her legend. As a masculinized woman, she might drink with white men but she was not invited to their homes.[136] Domestic social circles, those of middling, white society, excluded her. Similarly, Fields might root for the Cascade baseball team and even join them in the dugout, but as a mascot, she remained their social inferior. When confronted with integrating an African-American woman into their midst, whites in Cascade did not welcome her as a peer. Instead, they defined her as a social outcast or a social subordinate. This observation is not to indict Cascade residents as racists. They were decent people who did not examine their own privilege or question the banal ways they maintained that privilege. Indeed, white enthusiasm about Fields' notoriety can lead one to believe the legend of her beloved status. But notoriety is a form of isolation; to be a "landmark" is not the same as to be befriended. To be a character is not the same as to belong, and to be a mascot is not the same as to be an equal. Thus white residents of Cascade maintained the separation and subordination of blacks as they defined Fields' place in the community.

Just as Mary Fields' legend within her lifetime reveals racial boundaries, so too it exposes the assertion of gender norms. On the central Montana frontier, occupational roles flexed to allow a woman to do a man's job. Fields worked capably as a wagoner and freighter, but the implications of such flexibility would not be entertained. Cascade residents were not ready to debate "the woman question." If gender-based divisions of labor collapsed under the weight of necessity, what would happen to the gendered social order? They sidestepped the issue by calling Fields "masculine," thus keeping intact familiar gendered divisions of labor. The unspoken assumption was that ordinary women, feminine women, would not or could not do what she did. Thus Fields' reputation as a manly woman held conventional wisdom in place as much as it set her apart.

After Fields' death, writers embellished local oral tradition and her legend grew more dramatic. Mary Fields became the gunfighter of the old Wild West; the model caregiver who loved freedom, and the prodigal daughter who returned to the fold. Against the background of these exaggerations, Fields' actual choices create a poignant human portrait, more complex and more revealing of the social landscape. In the tense, postbellum racial climate of Toledo, Ohio, Fields chose the sanctuary of an Ursuline convent, a place so safe she could contest her wages without fear of reprisal. On the Montana frontier, at St. Peter's Mission, Fields and the nuns developed a mutually sustaining relationship. They provided room and board, while she provided vital labor. Without a contract, Fields worked on her own terms at St. Peter's, perhaps the greatest freedom she would know. Once she left the protection of the nuns, Fields chose the town fathers of Cascade as social companions, and they admitted her to the male worlds of the saloon and the baseball dugout. Still, in the racially divided world of central Montana, Fields endured petty bigotry from townspeople. Perhaps her choice of the town fathers as associates represented a hedge against more severe forms of racism. In any case, while the town fathers defined themselves as benevolent, she partook in elements of their social privilege, another reciprocal arrangement. Mary Fields' actual history thus suggests how one woman navigated the constraints of gender and race in turn-of-the-century Montana. At the same time, local constructions of memory reveal the vulnerability of minority women in the West to subtle processes of separation and marginalization, processes obscured by the patina of charity and celebration.

ACKNOWLEDGMENTS

The author would like to thank Jennifer Brady, Michael Drompp, Jeff Jackson, Gail Murray, and Dwain Pruitt for their thoughtful reading of this essay in earlier drafts.

NOTES

1. For "bulldog/grizzly bear" see Eunice Boeve, "Mary Fields: The Tough, Tender Legend of Cascade," *Montana Magazine* 165 (January–February 2001): 70–4; 70. For "potatoe" see "Nigger Mary Fields, Early Cascade Resident, Noted Character in State," *Cascade Courier* (May 31, 1939): 1. For "squirrel shoot" see Boeve, "Mary Fields," 70.

2. For "whip two men," see Gary Cooper, as told to Marc Crawford, "Stagecoach Mary," *Ebony* 14:12 (October 1, 1959): 97–100; 100. For "ferocity," see Tanya Bolden, "Mary Fields," *And Not Afraid to Dare: The Stories of Ten African-American Women* (New York: Scholastic Press, 1998): 35–43; 38. For "liquor," see "Stagecoach Mary," *Catholic Digest* (Chicago: Johnson Publishing Co., December 1959): 40–2; 40.

3. Dan Miller, "Mary Fields," *True West* (August1982): 52–55; 52. See also "'Nigger Mary' Fields, Early Day Resident of Cascade, One of State's Noted Characters," *Great Falls Tribune*, May 22, 1939, 10; and Edith Maxwell, *Great Falls Yesterday* (Works Progress Administration, 1940), 376.

4. Sister Genevieve McBride, "Mary Fields," *Mountains and Meadows; A Pioneer History of Cascade, Chestnut Valley, Hardy, St. Peter's Mission, and Castner Falls, 1805–1925*, ed. Mrs. Clarence Rowe (Great Falls, MT: Blue Print and Letter Co., 1971), 157–8.

5. Many of the magazine and newspaper articles used the phrase, "It is said that," referring to oral tradition. Cascade resident Earl Monroe confirmed that much of the written lore reflects local oral tradition. Monroe, born in 1908, grew up in Cascade knowing Mary Fields and hearing stories about her repeated by townspeople. Interview, Earl Monroe by Dee Garceau, August 31, 2001, Cascade, Montana. Transcript in author's possession.

6. "'Nigger Mary' Fields," 10.

7. Maxwell, *Great Falls Yesterday*, 376.

8. Newspaper article of *Cascade Courier*, August 2, 1951, quoted in "Twelve Years Ago This Week," *Cascade Courier*, August 8, 1963, 8.

9. Susan Dwyer, "The Legend of Stagecoach Mary," *Blade*, (Toledo, Ohio) June 7, 1981, 11. Marjorie Drew, "Mary Fields, Survivor in a Rough Land" unpublished manuscript (Cascade County Archives), 1. William Loren Katz repeated the gunfight story in *Black People Who Made the Old West* (New York: Crowell Publishers, 1977), 80–3; 81. Miller, in "Mary Fields," added, "She was tough enough to take on any two men," *True West*, 52.

10. "Nuns' Servant Brawled Her Way into Local Legend," *Great Falls Tribune*, November 19, 1995, 2; Boeve, "Mary Fields," *Montana Magazine*, 2001, 70–4.

11. "'Nigger Mary' Fields," *Great Falls Tribune*, May 22, 1939, 10.

12. Ibid. See also Maxwell, *Great Falls Yesterday*, 376; and McBride, "Mary Fields," 158. McBride writes that Mother Amadeus was "unable to control Mary."

13. M. McBride, "Black Mary at Old St. Peter's," *Calumet* 35 no. 4 (November 1948): 8.

14. "Twelve Years Ago This Week," *Cascade Courier*, August 8, 1963, 8.

15. Charlie Russell, *A Quiet Day in Cascade*, (1897). Original hung in the Stockmen's Bank of Cascade until 1970, when it was loaned to the Montana Historical Society. The original now hangs in the Charlie Russell Gallery in Helena, Montana, but the city clerk of Cascade makes print copies of the sketch available to tourists.

16. Mark Harris, "The Legend of Black Mary," *Negro Digest* (August 1950): 84–7; 85.

17. Anita King, "The Legend of Black Mary: A Westerner with Style," *Essence* 4 (January 1974): 23, 91; 23. See also Crawford, "Stagecoach Mary," *Ebony*, 98.

18. Crawford, "Stagecoach Mary," *Ebony*, 99.

19. Xeroxed excerpt, Jessie Carney Smith, "Mary Fields, 'Stagecoach Mary'" *Notable Black American Women*, 34 (Cascade County Archives). Katz, "Mary Fields," 81. Ardenia Jones Terry, "Mary Fields, aka. Stagecoach Mary," *In Search of Our Past; Women of Northwest Ohio* Vol. I (YWCA Women Alive! Coalition, 1987), 21–2; 22. Jones writes, "Mary, who was kind and affectionate, had a practice of giving food away instead of selling it."

20. Harris, "Legend of 'Black Mary,'" 84. Crawford, "Stagecoach Mary," 97. King, "Black Mary," 23. Terry, "Mary Fields," 21. Bolden reiterated this theme in 1996, in "Mary Fields," *Not Afraid to Dare*, 39.
21. Harris, "Legend of Black Mary," 85.
22. Ibid.
23. Ibid., 87.
24. James Franks, *Mary Fields: The Story of Black Mary* (Santa Cruz, CA: Wild Goose Press, 2000), 39–42, 132.
25. Press release in the *Toledo Commercial*, reprinted without date or author in *The Chronicles of the Ursuline Convent of the Sacred Heart*, unpublished manuscript dated 1891 (Archives, Ursuline Convent, Toledo, Ohio; hereafter AUC, Toledo).
26. Sister Angela Abair, "A Mustard Seed in Montana: Recollections," ed. Orlin Svingen, *The Magazine of Western History* 34 no. 2 (spring 1984): 16–31.
27. "In the Heart of the Rocky Mountains; Glimpses of St. Peter's Mission," *Ave Maria; A Catholic Magazine Devoted to the Honor of the Blessed Virgin* 33 no. 2 (July 11, 1891): 37–41.
28. Ursuline Sisters of Toledo, *A Tree in the Valley*, no date (AUC, Toledo): 48. See also "St. Peter's," *Ursulines of the West*, by an Ursuline of the Roman Union, 1936 (AUC, Toledo), 38–45.
29. Sister Genevieve McBride, "A Black Face among the Blackfeet," in unpublished draft of *The Bird Tail* (Ursline Archives, Ursuline Center, Great Falls, MT; hereafter UA, Great Falls), 8–9. See also Genevieve McBride, O.S.U., *The Bird Tail* (New York: Vantage Press, 1974).
30. "Mary Fields," *Catholic Digest* (1959): 42.
31. Miller, "Mary Fields," 55; "Nuns' Servant Brawled Her Way into Legend," *Great Falls Tribune*, November 19, 1995, 2E. For additional quotes about her beloved status, see "'Nigger Mary' Fields, Early Cascade Resident," *Cascade Courier*, May 31, 1939, 1; Terry, "Mary Fields," 21–22; Crawford, "Stagecoach Mary," 100; Smith, "Mary Fields," *Notable Black American Women*, 344;
32. For discussion of reading against the grain, see Bunny McBride, *Women of the Dawn* (Lincoln: University of Nebraska Press, 1999), 136. For examples of reading against the grain, see Lillian Ackerman, "Complementary but Equal: Gender Status on the Plateau," *Women and Power in Native North America* (Norman: University of Oklahoma Press, 1995), 75–100, 77; and Kathleen Brown, "The Anglo-Algonquian Gender Frontier," *Negotiators of Change: Historical Perspectives on Native American Women*, ed. Nancy Shoemaker (New York: Routledge, 1995), 26–48. Ackerman reads clues to Salish women's roles through the filter of a Jesuit priest; Brown reads clues to Algonquian women's roles through the filter of British settlers' observations about Powhatan Indians.
33. For discussion of controlled speculation, see McBride, *Women of the Dawn*, 3. For another example of controlled speculation, see Natalie Zemon Davis, *The Return of Martin Guerre* (Cambridge, MA: Harvard University Press, 1983). Zemon Davis explored the life of an unlettered sixteenth-century peasant.
34. For discussion of reading photographs as self-representation, see Nell Irvin Painter, "Representing Truth: Sojourner Truth's Knowing and Becoming Known," *Journal of American History* 81, no. 2 (September 1994): 461–92, 482–88; and Nell Irvin Painter, *Sojourner Truth: A Life, A Symbol* (New York: W. W. Norton, 1996). For discussion of self-representation in postcards created for private use, see Patricia Albers and William James, "Illusion and Illumination: Visual Images of American Indian Women in the West," *The Women's West*, ed. Susan Armitage and Elizabeth Jameson (Norman: University of Oklahoma Press, 1987), 35–50; 39.

35. Terry, "Mary Fields," 21; Crawford, "Stagecoach Mary," 97; Boeve, "Mary Fields," 70; Katz, "Mary Fields," 80; Miller, "Mary Fields," 52; King, "Legend of Black Mary," 23; Harris, "Black Mary," 84–5.

36. Barbara and Byron Sistler, eds., *1840 Census, Tennessee* (Nashville: Byron Sistler and Associates, 1986), 174–75. Ronald Vern Jackson, ed., *Federal Census Index: Tennessee, 1850 Slave Schedules* (West Jordan, UT: Genealogical Services, Inc., 1989), pages are unnumbered, but "Field" and "Fields" appear alphabetically. Ronald Vern Jackson, ed., *Tennessee 1860 Slave Schedule* (Salt Lake City, UT: Accelerated Indexing Systems International, 1990), 197.

37. Interview, Mother Amata Warner, 1974, unpublished transcript (AUC, Toledo), 1–3. Mother Amata Warner is a descendant of the same Warner family that employed Mary Fields, niece to Sister Annunciation (Mary Warner), whom Fields accompanied to the Toledo convent. These ties lend credence to Mother Amata Warner's information. Telephone interview, Sister Mary Rose Krupp in Toledo, Ohio, by Dee Garceau, October 16, 1994; transcript in author's possession.

38. Ibid. See also Lillian Carroll, "Mary Fields," *Ohio Cues* (January 1977): 3.

39. Interview, Mother Amata Warner.

40. Ibid.

41. Interview, Krupp. Connelly is quoted in Dwyer, "The Legend of Stagecoach Mary," 11.

42. Interview, Krupp.

43. Handwritten receipt dated January 3, 1884 and signed by Mary Fields (AUC, Toledo).

44. Wages and account balance for Mary Fields, Ursuline Convent of the Sacred Heart, May 19, 1885 (AUC, Toledo).

45. Ibid.

46. Ibid.

47. Leroy T. Williams, "Black Toledo: African-Americans in Toledo, Ohio, 1890–1930," (Ph.D. Dissertation, University of Toledo, 1977), 5–10.

48. Ibid., 14.

49. Ibid., 22.

50. Ibid, 19, 34–39.

51. Ibid., 46.

52. Perhaps Fields had been sexually abused as a young woman under slavery, and saw the convent as a refuge from sexual assault. Without evidence, however, this remains pure speculation.

53. Ursuline Sisters, *A Tree in the Valley*, 47. Terry, "Mary Fields," 21.

54. Ursuline Sisters, *A Tree in the Valley*, 39; Interview, Mother Amata Warner; Letter, Mother Amadeus at St. Peter's Mission, Montana, to the Reverend Mother Superior in Toledo, December 14, 1884 (UA, Great Falls).

55. Letter from Mother Amadeus at St. Peter's Mission to the Rev. Mother Superior in Toledo, December 19, 1884 (UA, Great Falls).

56. Ibid.

57. *Life of the Reverend Mother Amadeus of the Heart of Jesus; Sketch Compiled from Convent Annals* by an Ursuline of Alaska (New York: Paulist Press, 1923), 94.

58. Letter from an unidentified Ursuline at St. Peter's Mission, March 1885 (UA, Great Falls). The original letter is without punctuation. I have added minimal punctuation for clarity.

59. *Life of the Reverend Mother Amadeus*, 94.

60. McBride, *The Bird Tail*, 172.

61. During the spring, summer, and winter of 1885, letters to Toledo from Montana described Mother Amadeus's slow recovery. See letter, Mother Amadeus at St. Peter's to Rev. Mother Superior in Toledo, March 29, April 2, and April 20, 1885. Letters, Sister Mary of the Angels at St. Peter's to Rev. Mother Superior in Toledo, July 13 and

December 26, 1885. Letter, Sister St. Francis at St. Peter's to Rev. Mother Superior in Toledo, December 18, 1885 (UA, Great Falls).

62. In 1886, St. Peter's Mission boarded 22 children. By 1887, 54 children lived at the mission. By 1892, about 70 students, Indian and white, boarded at the mission, while the mission staff had grown to 12 in residence. Letter, Sister Mary of the Angels at St. Peter's to Rev. Mother Superior in Toledo, October 28, 1886 (UA, Great Falls). For 1887, see McBride, *The Bird Tail*, 71–73. *Annals of the Ursuline Mission at St. Peter's*, October 7, 1892 (UA, Great Falls). "Quarterly Report of the Indian Schools. Report of ... St. Peter's Mission, Montana for the Quarter Ending December 31, 1892," and "Quarterly Report," March 31, 1893 and "Quarterly Report," June 30, 1893 (Foley Library Special Collections, Gonzaga University, Spokane, WA): Box 861, Folder 7.

63. McBride, *The Bird Tail*, 173.

64. *Annals of the Ursuline Mission*, July 27, 1894 (UA, Great Falls).

65. Ibid.

66. McBride, *The Bird Tail*, 75.

67. Ibid., 93.

68. Ibid.

69. *Annals of the Ursuline Mission*, September 9, 1892 (UA, Great Falls). See also McBride, *The Bird Tail*, 95.

70. Ibid., July 7, 1892. See also McBride, *The Bird Tail*, 92.

71. Bishop Brondel "heard aspersions of the woman's [Fields] character which noone has ever yet been able to prove," wrote an Ursuline. *Annals of the Ursuline Mission*, July 27, 1894 (UA, Great Falls).

72. Ibid., July 27, 1894. The Ursuline diarist commented that the nuns were "determined to support her [Fields] wherever she goes."

73. Ibid., July 28, 1894.

74. Ibid.

75. Ibid., July 28, 1894.

76. Ibid., July 26, 1894.

77. W. T. Ridgley, *Cascade County Directory and Gazeteer, 1896–97* (Great Falls, MT: Press of W. T. Ridgley, 1896), 210. W. T. Ridgley and R. L. Polk, *Great Falls City Directory* (Helena, MT: R. L. Polk & Co., 1903): 381. Cascade County listings were included in this volume. The directory wrote "Exp." after Fields' name. Their abbreviations index (p. 79) said "Exp." = Express (i.e., mail delivery).

78. Ridgeley & Polk, *Great Falls and Cascade County Directory*, 357; (1906): 380; (1909): 383; (1911): 447; (1913): 467. Within the caption inserted into a glass frame holding a photograph of Mary Fields, a Cascade County Historical Society curator wrote that Fields was a janitor at local saloons (Cascade County Archives).

79. Interview, Monroe. Monroe remembers being babysat by Fields when he was about five years old.

80. Ibid.

81. Quintard Taylor, "From Esteban to Rodney King: Five Centuries of African-American History in the West," *Montana: The Magazine of Western History* 46, no. 4 (winter 1996): 2–23; 10–12. Quintard Taylor, *In Search of the Racial Frontier: African Americans in the American West, 1528–1990* (New York: W. W. Norton, 1998), 134–63, 192–221; and Glenda Riley, "American Daughters: Black Women in the West," *African Americans on the Western Frontier*, ed., Monroe Lee Billington and Roger D. Hardaway (Niwot, CO: University Press of Colorado, 1998), 160–80.

82. J. W. Smurr, "Jim Crow Out West," *Historical Essays on Montana and the Northwest*, ed., J. W. Smurr and K. Ross Toole (Helena, MT: Historical Society of Montana, 1957), 149–203; Stanley Davison and Dale Tash, "Confederate Backwash in Montana Territory," *MMWH* 17, no. 4 (fall 1967): 50–8.

83. Davison & Tash, "Confederate Backwash", 54.
84. Quintard Taylor, "The Emergence of Black Communities in the Pacific Northwest: 1865–1910," *Journal of Negro History* 64 (1979): 342–54. William Lang, "The Nearly Forgotten Blacks on Last Chance Gulch, 1900–1912," *Pacific Northwest Quarterly* 70, no. 2 (April 1979): 50–7. Lang defines black Progressivism as "the effort to acquire rights, opportunities, and rewards that America seemed to offer" (53). Lawrence DeGraaf, "Race, Sex, and Region: Black Women in the American West, 1850–1920," *Pacific Historical Review* 49 (1980): 285–313. Roger Hardaway, "African-American Women on the Western Frontier," *Negro History Bulletin* 60, no. 1 (1997): 8–13.
85. Taylor, "The Emergence of Black Communities," 344–48.
86. Smurr, "Jim Crow Out West," 163. In 1880, the black population in Montana territory totaled 346. In 1890 it reached 1,490, and in 1910 it remained low at 1,834. See Billington and Hardaway, *African Americans on the Western Frontier*, Appendix: 259.
87. Taylor, "The Emergence of Black Communities," 352, Table I.
88. *Helena Daily Independent*, February 4, 1882, quoted in Smurr, "Jim Crow Out West," 182.
89. *Glendive Independent*, August 12, 1893, Archives of the Montana Historical Society, Helena, MT.
90. Smurr, "Jim Crow Out West," 163.
91. Lang, "The Nearly Forgotten Blacks," 51.
92. *Great Falls Tribune*, November 19, 1904, (Helena, MT: Archives of the Montana Historical Society).
93. "'Nigger Mary' Fields," 10.
94. "Well-Known Negro Woman of Cascade Brought to Hospital in Critical Condition," *Great Falls Tribune*, December 9, 1914, 12.
95. "Old Timer Passes Away," *Cascade Courier*, December 11, 1914.
96. McBride, *The Bird Tail*, 173.
97. Typed transcript, interview, Edgar Tilton, June 30, 1983 (Cascade County Archives).
98. Interview, Monroe; Gayle Shirley, "Mary Fields," *More Than Petticoats* (Helena, MT: Falcon Press Publishing Co., 1995), 56–61, 59.
99. Unpublished transcript of radio broadcast, undated (Great Falls Chamber of Commerce and Soroptimist Club), 29, Cascade County Archives.
100. "'Nigger Mary' Fields," 10.
101. "'Nigger Mary' Fields, Early Cascade Resident, Noted Character in State," *Cascade Courier*, May 31, 1939.
102. Mrs. Clarence Rowe, Ed., *Mountains and Meadows*, 55.
103. Crawford, "Stagecoach Mary," 100; Maxwell, *Great Falls Yesterday*, 376.
104. Drew, "Mary Fields," 77; King, "Mary Fields: A Westerner with Style," 91.
105. Photograph of Mary Fields in her flower garden (UA, Great Falls).
106. Chadburne Wallin, "Aunt Adeline, Near 100," *Bainville Democrat*, August 7, 1939, 1. Montana Newspaper Association Inserts (Helena, MT: Montana Historical Society).
107. Glenn Chaffin, "Aunt Tish: Beloved Gourmet of the Bitter Root," *MMWH* 21, no. 4 (October 1971): 67–9. The exception to this pattern was Mattie Castner, a black woman who married the white founder of Belt, Montana. Local historians plainly said that her husband's status as a wealthy mining magnate and town father elevated her status: "Mattie commanded the respect of the people of Belt ... to some extent, because she was the wife of John K. Castner, the highly regarded founder of Belt." Ethel Kennedy & Eva Stober, *Belt Valley History, 1877–1979* (Belt, MT: Advanced Litho Printing, 1979, 22.
108. Sarah Carter, "Categories and Terrains of Exclusion: Constructing the 'Indian Woman' in the Early Settlement Era in Western Canada," *Great Plains Quarterly* 13 no. 3 (summer 1993): 147–61; 158.
109. Ibid., 159.
110. McBride, *Women of the Dawn*, 54–66.

111. Ibid., 75–94.
112. Shirley Ann Wilson Moore and Quintard Taylor describe black women's community-building activities in "The West of African American Women, 1600–2000," *African American Women Confront the West, 1600–2000*, ed., Quintard Taylor and Shirley Ann Wilson Moore (Norman: University of Oklahoma press, 2003), 3–21; 10–12.
113. Rowe, *Mountains and Meadows*, 47, 51, 54. In Maxwell's *Great Falls Yesterday*, the biographies of women typically list the women's clubs and service organizations to which they belonged, such as Eastern Star or Altar Society. Mary Fields' biography lists no such affiliations (Maxwell, 376).
114. Ibid., 43.
115. Ridgeley and Polk, *Cascade County Directory*, (1896): 210, 211; (1911): 444, 447–9; (1913): 464–8. Rowe, *Mountains and Meadows*, 35, 38, 39, 43, 45, 53, 55.
116. Interview, Monroe.
117. Ibid. Though women did consume alcohol, they typically did so at home, in the form of patent medicines. It is possible that Fields suffered from alcoholism. All sources concur that she was a frequent patron of the local saloons.
118. "Mary Fields," *Catholic Digest* (1959): 42.
119. Interview, Monroe. Monroe made it clear that the men did not view Fields as "fair game" sexually.
120. Susan Johnson, "Sharing Bed and Board: Cohabitation and Cultural Difference in Central Arizona Mining Towns, 1863–1873," *The Women's West*, 77–91; 85–6.
121. Sally Zanjani, *A Mine of Her Own: Women Prospectors in the American West, 1850–1950* (Lincoln: University of Nebraska Press, 1997), 46–8.
122. Dee Garceau, "Nomads, Bunkies, Cross-Dressers and Family Men: Cowboy Identity and the Gendering of Ranch Work," *Across the Great Divide: Cultures of Manhood in the American West*, ed., Matthew Basso, Laura McCall, and Dee Garceau (New York: Routledge, 2001), 149–68.
123. Article from *Cascade Courier*, 1910, quoted at length in an obituary for Mary Fields, "Old Timer Passes Away," *Cascade Courier*, December 11, 1914, 1.
124. Interview, Monroe.
125. Photographs: Mary Fields outdoors on snow-covered ground, with St.Peter's Mission in the background, wearing overcoat, hat, and skirts, 1893 (UA, Great Falls). Front view, Fields driving wagon with white horse, next to storefront (UA, Great Falls). Side view, Fields driving wagon pulled by white horse (UA, Great Falls). Fields standing in flower garden (UA, Great Falls). Fields indoors, seated with dog at her feet (AUC, Toledo). Fields in front of her home in Cascade (Cascade County Archives). Fields wearing belted jacket and long skirt, holding two flags (Cascade County Archives). Side view, Fields walking down street in long skirts and white apron (Cascade County Archives). Fields standing in front of the Mint Saloon, Cascade, wearing skirts and white apron (Cascade County Archives). Fields flanking Cascade Baseball team, 1913, in "'Nigger Mary' Fields," *Great Falls Tribune*, May 22, 1939, 10. Fields with Cascade baseball team, with Fields identified in caption as "negress mascot," *Cascade Courier*, May 31, 1939.
126. *Annals of the Ursuline Mission*, November 27, 1893 (UA, Great Falls).
127. Photograph, Mary Fields in winter landscape at St. Peter's, 1893 (UA, Great Falls).
128. McBride, *The Bird Tail*, 102.
129. Interview, Monroe.
130. McBride, *The Bird Tail*, 100. *Annals of the Ursuline Mission*, April 26, 1894 (UA, Great Falls).
131. Photograph of Mary Fields indoors, with dog and rifle (AUC, Toledo).
132. "Mary Fields Celebrates Her 83rd Birthday at Her Home in Cascade," *Cascade Courier*, March 15, 1913 (Cascade County Archives).

133. Unpublished transcript of radio broadcast, undated (Great Falls Chamber of Commerce and Soroptimist Club), Cascade County Archives.
134. Interview, Monroe.
135. "Mary Fields Passes Away," *Great Falls Tribune*, December 11, 1914 (Cascade County Archives).
136. The exception to this would be that in her old age, Fields was invited into white homes as a babysitter, which placed her in the familiar racial category of black nanny.

Fig. 6.1 Polly Bemis, born Lalu Nathoy, for whom the River of No Return became home. Reprinted by permission of the Idaho State Historical Society.

6

RECLAIMING POLLY BEMIS: CHINA'S DAUGHTER, IDAHO'S LEGENDARY PIONEER

Ruthanne Lum McCunn

The life of Polly Bemis, born Lalu Nathoy, formed the basis for *Thousand Pieces of Gold*, a biographical novel that was first published in 1981 and has since been translated into six languages and adapted for a feature-length film.[1] This essay explores the challenges I faced reconstructing her life for the novel and it examines subsequent discoveries. Polly Bemis, a woman of legendary status in Idaho frontier history, already had been featured in numerous magazine and newspaper articles. References to her also appeared in regional histories, a master's thesis, and a pioneer's unpublished memoir. But conflicting claims and gaps of information, especially about her life in China, made piecing together an accurate biography for the novel difficult. Moreover, while books on Chinese history and culture yielded a wealth of information about village life, bandits, and the flora and fauna of nineteenth-century northern China; histories of Idaho, even those sympathetic to the Chinese, failed to include the Chinese viewpoint. And although interviews with white people who had known Polly were possible, one of the many long-range effects of the intense anti-Chinese violence and legislation that prevailed in nineteenth-century America was the complete absence of

Chinese pioneers or their descendants in the Salmon River canyon and Warrens, Idaho. For *Thousand Pieces of Gold*, then, the life of Lalu Nathoy/Polly Bemis had to be reconstructed within these limitations.

THE BASIS FOR *THOUSAND PIECES OF GOLD*

Most of what we know about Lalu/Polly's early life can be traced to an interview she gave Countess Eleanor Gizycka in 1922 and three newspaper articles published in the next decade.[2] From these accounts, it would seem Lalu Nathoy was born on September 11, 1853 in northern China, near one of the upper rivers, in an area frequently ravaged by bandits.[3] Although Lalu's parents were impoverished farmers, her feet had been bound, and later unbound. When Lalu was eighteen, there was a prolonged drought during which her father was forced to sell her to bandits in exchange for enough seed to plant another crop that would, he hoped, save the rest of their family from starvation. Lalu said she had been in Shanghai, and that may have been her port of departure for the United States. Certainly it seems more probable than the *Statesman's* wild claim that Lalu was one of three Chinese girls lured to Idaho via Hong Kong by an American woman, or Gizycka's contention that Polly told her, "My folluks in Hong-Kong."[4]

As to how Lalu came to Warrens, the *Oregonian* claims, "The bandit leader took Polly down the river to one of the big seaport cities, whence he sailed to San Francisco. Soon afterwards the gold rush around Idaho City lured him to Warrens, where he either died or deserted Polly, who operated a restaurant for several years." But Gizycka quotes Polly as saying, "Old woman smuggle me into Portland. I cost $2,500 ... Old Chinee-man he took me to Warrens in a pack train."[5] In any case, Polly arrived in Warrens, Idaho, during the early 1870s.

Idaho's gold rush had begun in 1861, and Warrens was one of many rip-roaring camps that had sprung up in the territory. As in most camps, Chinese were initially prohibited from holding claims or working as hired men. It was 1869 before the white miners, believing most of the gold gone, decided by majority vote to allow Chinese into Warrens, fully eight years after James Warrens found gold in the district now known as Warren.[6]

Mining was then an almost exclusively male activity that involved moving from place to place in search of the most productive site. Few men of any race or nationality brought their families with them, and among the earliest female arrivals were those who hired themselves out for dances or sex or both. Some of these women were Chinese. Of the Chinese women who labored as prostitutes, however, almost none were free agents. Indeed, the majority worked as chattel for masters who had bought them. Beginning in 1861, California passed a series of codes aimed at restricting the importation of Chinese women for prostitution. As a result, the enslaved had to be smuggled in, sometimes "disguised as boys, hidden in buckets of coal, or concealed in padded crates labeled as dishware." Losses through discovery or death and the need to bribe officials raised the prices for the women, with the sum paid for Lalu on the high side of the $1,000 to $3,000 range.[7]

Historian Lucie Cheng is clear that "[i]n the organization of the trade, importation was a separate activity from that of procurement. Importers received the women from recruiting agents, arranged for their passage, and handed them over to the brothel owners upon arrival in the United States." It is therefore very unlikely that Lalu was brought to America by the bandit leader who had purchased her from her father. Furthermore, when she told Countess Gizycka she'd been smuggled into Portland, Polly did not necessarily mean that had been her point of entry to America. Most Chinese at that time were landing in San Francisco, and its Chinatown had barracoons where enslaved Chinese women were either held while awaiting distribution or auctioned off to the highest bidder. So Lalu might well have been smuggled into Portland *after* being smuggled into San Francisco and taken to a barracoon for sale or distribution. Regardless of where she landed initially, she would likely have traveled by boat from Portland to Lewiston, then by pack train to Warrens.[8]

Warrens, northeast of McCall, has an elevation of 6,000 feet, and the snow is so deep in winter that it is sometimes completely inaccessible. Not surprisingly, the population has always been greater in summer than winter. The population also fluctuated depending on the amount of gold being recovered. Shortly after Chinese were allowed into the camp they became the majority. Yet they did not live in the "town proper" but just below in tiny, windowless cabins "not much larger than doghouses."[9]

The town proper had a single crooked street parallel to the gold-bearing gulch. Each side of this street was lined with saloons, dance halls, bunkhouses, hotels, and stores. All the buildings were built of logs. Even the floors were hewn logs. Hong King, who had purchased Lalu, was an old man who ran a dance hall/saloon/gambling house in the town. Charles Bemis, the man she would marry, also ran a saloon in Warrens. According to pioneer George Bancroft, this is where the pack train must have brought Lalu on July 8, 1872, because "she was greeted by a stranger who said, 'Here's Polly,' as he helped her from the saddle." Then somebody called for Charles Bemis to come outside and "introduced the slave girl to him in this way, 'Charlie, this is Polly.'" Thereafter Lalu was called Polly.[10]

When recalling Polly's arrival in Warrens, pioneer A. W. Talkington added, "Polly was a good woman and entitled to a good deal of consideration because of her upright conduct in rather difficult circumstances." Perhaps as part of that consideration, he did not elaborate on those circumstances. Similarly, the articles published in Polly's lifetime did not delve into her first decade in Warrens. George Bancroft is the only pioneer who has ever claimed Polly "got money from women's time-honored methods." He did not condemn her for it. Indeed, he described her as having "shy, modest ways;" he thought highly of her and considered himself a good friend. But he did not meet her until the early 1900s, and all other Idaho pioneers insisted that Polly had never worked as a prostitute, though they acknowledged that she may have been purchased by Hong King for that purpose. As the daughter of Polly's longtime friend, Bertha Long, put it, "Polly Nathoy was brought from China to Warrens for the world's oldest profession. When taken to [Hong King's] saloon, she was terrified! Charlie Bemis was present and protected her from unwanted advances."[11]

How was Bemis able to accomplish this? Born in Connecticut in 1848, Bemis had come to Warrens in the mid-1860s with his father. For a while, father and son had labored together at placer mining. But the son, frail and averse to physical labor, preferred card playing to mining. He must have been good at cards, too, because he soon had enough money to buy a saloon. A skilled violinist, Bemis played at all the dances, yet he was not particularly popular. He was, however, widely respected for his scrupulous honesty. More importantly for subduing the men in Hong King's saloon, Bemis's "fearless personality, coupled with his skill at shooting, enabled him to maintain order without getting into trouble."[12]

Just the fact that Bemis was a white man would probably have been sufficient for him to enforce his will on Hong King. During the ten years Chinese had been migrating to the Idaho Territory, they had not only been prohibited from working rich claims, but forced to pay a miner's tax of four dollars a month regardless of their occupations. They had also been subjected to random and orchestrated violence throughout the territory. In one camp, children were not allowed out of the house on Saturdays for fear of being accidentally shot by white miners using Chinese for target practice. In Warrens, Chinese did interact with whites, freighting supplies for both, and working in mines operated by whites. News articles over the years indicate there was limited mingling in some activities, such as July 4th celebrations, but a Chinese man accused of stealing a pair of boots was lynched.[13]

Slavery was then against the law, but Bemis apparently did not challenge Polly's status as Hong King's slave. And because she did remain chattel, Polly most likely had to grant Hong King sexual favors as well as do any necessary cooking and cleaning. She must have served drinks to his customers in the saloon, and she may have danced with them, too, despite her peculiar rolling gait, a result of her childhood experience with foot binding. Polly's tiny feet were often remarked upon, as was her height—variously given as "no taller than a broom," between four and five feet, or that of an eight- to ten-year-old. All the descriptions of Polly in her youth are those of a beauty, and a reporter noted that she had "a broad understanding of the mountains and mountain folk." On those occasions when Polly's wit was not enough to keep her out of trouble or "things got too rough" in Hong King's saloon, she would call for Bemis. Or she would fly out the back door of the saloon and into Bemis's back door, and "he never failed her." The back door of Bemis's saloon opened into his bedroom. Polly, "always industrious and noting the untidiness of her neighbor's bedroom, used to slip over during the early afternoon to tidy up. This of course pleased Bemis."[14]

At what point the two became lovers is not known, but by the 1880s they were living together. Polly was not financially dependent on Bemis, however. She took in laundry from miners and ran a boardinghouse that Bemis had built for her beside his own, a short distance from his saloon. While Bemis's house was a single room, Polly's boardinghouse had a small kitchen and combination sitting/dining room downstairs, and a bedroom upstairs. She had taught herself how to cook western food by watching the white women in Warrens, and young people liked to eat at her place, especially after a dance. Some of Polly's boarders and their families became her lifelong friends, and their reminiscences offer snapshots of her personality. When doing laundry, she would mend before she washed. And once she silenced boarders' complaints about her coffee by waving a butcher knife while asking, "Who no like my coffee?"[15]

Theodore Swarts, the government mail carrier, always stayed overnight at Polly's when he brought in the mail. There, he would talk about his family; and back home he would tell his family about Polly. When his sister, Bertha, came to live with her husband, John Long, at the Little Giant Mine in the late 1880s, the two women became good friends. While living within a mile of each other, they visited frequently, even in the winter when Bertha would have to walk over deep snow on homemade skis. But after Bertha and John Long settled on a farm outside Grangeville, she and Polly rarely saw each other. Still, they remained close friends until Polly's death, and according to Bertha, "When Bemis took [Polly] from the Chinese and gave her a home she was very happy."[16]

It is not clear whether Bertha intended "the Chinese" to refer to Hong King alone or to the Chinese community as well. Certainly Polly would have been happy to be free of a master, but was her separation from the other Chinese simply unavoidable given her relationship with Bemis and the divisions, geographic and otherwise, in Warrens between Chinese and whites? Or was she happy to live and work outside of Chinatown because her northern origins alienated her by language and custom from most of the Chinese in Warrens, who would have been from southern China?

A. W. Talkington, who had been in Warrens when Lalu arrived and in the years since, was emphatic that "(Bemis) did actually take Polly away from her Chinese owner." Legend has it that Bemis and Hong King were playing poker together. Bemis was having a run of good luck, Hong King bad. Finally, Hong King had nothing left to stake except Polly, which he did, only to lose her as well. Because both Bemis and Hong King were dedicated gamblers who sometimes played poker together, this tale seems plausible. Besides, if there was no poker game, how did Polly get free of Hong King? Bringing Chinese women into the country had become so difficult that men with women already in their possession were refusing to sell them. It does not seem likely, then, that Hong King would have allowed Polly, an asset to his saloon, to buy her freedom, let alone give it to her.[17]

Nevertheless, there are many who insist that the poker game between Bemis and Hong King is nothing more than a myth or even a deliberate hoax, and that Polly herself denied she was a "poker bride." Of the naysayers, C. J. Czizek, a former boarder of Polly's and a good friend, was the most vociferous. As if to augment his claim, he invariably would add that Molly Smead, a Lemhi Shoshone from the Sheepeater Band, was the true poker bride. Nor was he alone. But John Carrey, a personal friend of Molly and her husband, A. D. (Pony) Smead, dismissed this, and since Polly and Charlie Bemis lived together for many years before they married, she was, in fact, not a poker bride.[18]

There are some who suggest Polly and Bemis married as the result of a poker game in 1890, in which Bemis won $250 from John Cox, a known troublemaker. According to several sources, the next morning, Cox demanded his money back. Bemis refused. Cox said he'd give Bemis the time it took to roll a cigarette to hand over the cash. If Bemis failed to comply, Cox would shoot his right eye out. When Bemis did not return the money, Cox fired. Luckily, the shot missed Bemis's eye, but it tore into his cheek, shattering the bone, and a doctor was quickly sent for.

Dr. Bibby, who came 87 miles by horseback from Grangeville, enjoyed a reputation for being dedicated and inventive: "One time when he had to perform an operation at an isolated ranch and needed a special instrument, he went to the ranch's blacksmith shop and made it from a piece of iron using forge and anvil." In Bemis's case, however, Dr. Bibby was less successful. There are even accusations that he refused to treat Bemis yet charged $500. In fact, the bullet, on striking Bemis's cheekbone, had split, and although Dr. Bibby was able to find and extract one half of the ball and fourteen pieces of bone, he feared the wound would prove fatal from blood poisoning unless Bemis's system proved strong enough to expel the remaining fragment of the ball.[19]

While there was no Western doctor in Warrens, there were two Chinese, Ah Kan and Lee Dick, who were credited as healers by whites as well as Chinese, and "one of their unusual methods of treatment was the use of mold for the curing of infection." Whether Polly used this mold or a concoction of her own devising is not known, but she did clean out Bemis's wound with her crochet hook, then packed it with an "extract of herbs." Within a month, her patient was sitting up, dressed, able to talk and smoke, although "looking ghastly." Still the wound continued to discharge pus, and Polly, despite the help of a Mr. Troll, never left Bemis's side. Finally, she found the remaining piece of bullet embedded in the back of Bemis's neck and cut it out with a razor.[20] At least one account of this incident ends with "Afterward Bemis married her," as if he did not recognize Polly's value until she saved his life, or married her out of gratitude or a sense of obligation. But Bemis and Polly already had been living together for several years, and they did not marry for another four years, in 1894.[21]

More likely, the true impetus for legalizing their relationship came as a result of the 1892 Geary Act which required Chinese legally in the United States to carry a certificate of residence at all times. Polly, by her own admission, was in the country illegally, and there was very real fear that she would be deported. According to several local informants, "to prevent Polly from being sent back to China as an alien, Bemis was married to her August 13, 1894 at Warrens." And, as a result of "continued efforts by her husband," Polly received her Certificate of Residence in 1896. There are no details as to these efforts, but the photograph on Polly's certificate appears cropped from the full-length portrait that she said was her "wedding photograph." And since Sister Mary Alfreda Elsensohn, who interviewed many pioneers, places her in Florence in 1896 and the *Free Press* claimed Polly was once in Slate Creek, she perhaps had to leave Warrens at some point as part of the process for getting her certificate. Ironically, Idaho law at the time prohibited whites from marrying those who were not, but then Justice of the Peace A. D. Smead, who performed the ceremony for Polly and Bemis, had himself broken the law with his marriage to a Native American.[22]

Some time after their wedding, Polly and Bemis left for the Salmon River, popularly known as the River of No Return because it could only be navigated in one direction. There, Bemis had a two-story house built directly across from the river's Crooked Creek, seventeen or so miles by trail from Warrens. Bemis is said to have bought this land, but my own search for a record of purchase yielded none, and Bob J. Waite, county recorder for Idaho County in 1980, suggested Bemis may have simply squatted on the property.[23]

Periodically Bemis would return to Warrens to sell the produce they raised, check on his saloon, or play at a dance. Polly remained at the ranch to care for their cows, horses, chickens, ducks, extensive garden, and orchard. The canyon, thousands of feet deep, was mostly too steep for farming. For years, however, Chinese had been raising vegetables on terraced slopes near the south fork of the Salmon River for sale to mining camps in the vicinity. At the base of the canyon, Polly grew herbs for Lee Dick and Ah Kan in Warrens. Most of the tillable land was given over to cherries, pears, plums, grapes, blackberries, raspberries, chestnuts, mulberry, watermelons, clover, and a variety of root vegetables including purple potatoes, corn and other garden truck, some of which the couple sold, and some of which they gave away or fed to strangers or friends passing through.

Bemis, refusing money for ferrying people across the river, would invite them to enjoy Polly's cooking and spend the night. Guests leaving would be offered pies, cakes, fruit, or vegetables to be delivered to old friends, or given delicacies for the sick and injured. Captain Harry Guleke, when shooting the rapids with boatloads of adventurers, usually stopped at the ranch. And in the winter, when the river was frozen over, "people would come down from Warrens to gamble and stay a few days because Polly's cooking was so good and her company too."[24] The couple became known for their generous hospitality, but it was Polly's warmth and humor that people talked about most; it was Polly who would take in those who were injured or ill and nurse them back to health. As pioneer John Carrey put it, "There was nobody in my day who carried the respect Polly earned through her kindness to everybody." Not surprisingly, the Bemis ranch soon became known as Polly Place, and a government survey party named the creek running through the property for Polly in 1911.[25]

There are many stories of how Polly hoed while her husband fiddled, how she would come upon Bemis playing cribbage and order him to go fill her wood box, how he would call her over to watch ants at work and she would tell him he would do better to emulate them. Her own hands were occupied with chores, making silk scarves, knitting, crocheting, even goldsmithing. While working in her garden, though, Polly would pick up worms and slip them into her apron pocket so that, without fail, she would be ready at three o'clock to go fishing. Much as Bemis avoided physical labor, he filed a mining claim in February of 1899 in which he noted he had "opened new ground to the extent or depth of ten feet as required by the laws of Idaho."[26]

Assays from claims located at Buffalo Hump the previous summer had been rich, and the huge vein of ore ran straight through the Salmon River. By the late fall of 1899, hundreds were coming on foot and horseback to try their luck, and the fires at night resembled those of an encamped army. Many of these prospectors would have traveled into Buffalo Hump through Polly Place, and because of the timing of Bemis's claim, it is likely that he filed it to ensure he and Polly would not lose their ranch to those pouring in. Homesteading would, of course, have entitled Bemis to the property, but not Polly. Chinese by law could not become naturalized citizens, and only U.S. citizens were permitted to homestead. Chinese could hold mining claims, though, and even after the rush was over, Bemis and Polly would placer every spring, keeping the claim valid.[27]

In 1909, Charlie Shepp purchased the ranch across the river. Later that year, his partner, Pete Klinkhamer, joined him from Buffalo Hump, where the two had met. Shepp was the gardener and carpenter, and he built a fine two-story house for them. Pete, who was much younger, took care of the stock and brought in cash by doing assessment work on mines for companies and individuals who wanted to keep their claims valid. He also made the six-day roundtrip to Grangeville once a year to pick up necessities such as sugar, coffee, tea, flour, and lamp oil for himself and his partner and for Polly and Bemis.[28]

From Shepp's diary we know that Bemis's health, never great, continued to deteriorate. By 1919, Bemis was bedridden, most likely with tuberculosis. Countess Gizyka, stopping at the ranch in July 1921, asked Polly where Bemis was, "and she said, 'Abed. He bin abed most two year now. He pletty closs, too. I gotta pack grub all time—all a time.'" But Polly clearly had not lost her sense of humor, for when Gizycka said, "'You'd better get another husband,'" Polly responded with a laugh and, "'Yas, I tink so, too.'"[29]

Polly was not literate. "When school come to Warren, I can't go," she explained. I got to make money." So Shepp helped by writing away for seeds Polly wanted, glasses she needed, and he measured her for a new dress that he sent for from Montgomery Ward. Shepp, Pete, and Polly also arranged a signal for when she and Bemis needed them: a dishtowel spread on a bush facing the river. Then Shepp and Pete strung a telephone line between the two ranches, and the neighbors spoke daily. "How many eggs you get today?" Polly would ask. "Six? I got ten." Or, "How many fish you catch? None? You no good. You fella come over Sunday. I cook great big fish I catch today."[30]

At least one pioneer claimed, "No one, but no one, could fry fish and make biscuits like Polly," and she would boil squaw fish in a salted bag so that "the flesh just fell off the bones." Her favorite fishing spot was at Crooked Creek on the Shepp Ranch side of the river. After Bemis was no longer strong enough to row Polly over, Shepp or Pete would come for her. And when the Bemis house caught fire the summer of 1922, it was Shepp who helped Polly drag Bemis out to safety. With Pete away in Dixie, Polly and Shepp were unable to save the house or her dog, Teddy. Shepp noted in his diary that "everybody's feet burned." After Pete returned from Dixie, he was able to round up thirty of Polly's chickens; the rest had been destroyed. But Polly did save the gold buttons that Bemis had made her and which she changed from dress to dress; as well as her certificate of residence, marriage certificate, and the mining claim. Since the survival of these documents by chance was unlikely, their existence indicates that the couple recognized their importance for Polly.[31]

For the next two months, Polly and Bemis lived at Shepp Ranch. On October 29, 1922, Shepp wrote in his diary: "Bemis passed in at 3 A.M. I went up to War Eagle camp at 5 A.M. to get Schultz and Holmes. We buried the old man right after dinner. Fine day." A few days later, he noted: "Polly going to Warrens. Took her stuff over river. Pete went to Warrens with Polly. Took 4 horses." As was typical of Shepp's diary entries, only facts were recorded, but according to Czizek, Polly took her husband's death very hard. Pete later explained that he had taken Polly to Warrens because he and Shepp thought she would be happier among other Chinese. Whether Polly herself had expressed a desire to return to Warrens or to be among Chinese is unknown, as is the number of Chinese, if any, she had seen or spoken to during almost three decades in the canyon.[32]

Warrens, completely rebuilt after a devastating fire in 1904, would have been unrecognizable to Polly. But Bemis and Polly, while living in Warrens, had been "like father and mother" to at least one child, Taylor Smith, who had come to Warrens as a twelve-year-old. Now Polly took in six-year-old Gay Carrey to live with her.[33] Like other children from outlying ranches, Gay and her brother Johnny had to board out while attending school in Warrens, and the two were staying with the teacher.

"She was a drag," recalled Johnny and Gay Carrey, "She couldn't boil water, and we got on her nerves." Gay had to share a bed with the woman, who had garlic breath. Desperately homesick, Gay wet the bed, and the teacher would beat her. "I tried to stay awake, but I couldn't," Gay recalled, her misery still palpable after almost sixty years. "Polly took good care of me. I loved her." Since Polly's cabin was "tiny," Johnny went to stay with Ethel Roden, who ran a hotel. But he visited his sister and Polly frequently. "I'd borrow a fiddle and walk up to Polly's house. She was very appreciative, more so than anybody else in town. She would stop [whatever she was doing], sit down, and listen," her favorite tunes being "You've got to quit kicking my dog around," "Where has my little dog gone," and "The Chinese Breakdown."[34]

The only time Johnny Carrey saw Polly angry was when he suggested they go visit the few Chinese still living in Warrens. What precisely caused her anger, he never knew. That he and his sister never wanted for Polly's attention or affection, however, is clear. But Polly must have been homesick for the Salmon River Canyon because Pete and Shepp woke one morning to see smoke rising above her chicken house. Rowing across to investigate, they found Polly had walked the seventeen miles from Warrens to offer them her property in exchange for their making it possible for her to come back and live in the canyon. Both men agreed, and Shepp began building a cabin immediately, but it would be 1924 before he finished. Meanwhile, Polly remained in Warrens.[35]

Friends, striving to ease her grief and to repay her kindnesses, twice took Polly out of Warrens for needed dental work and visits with old-time residents of Warrens who had moved on. Going to Grangeville, Polly experienced her first automobile ride. During her stay, she saw her first picture show and her first locomotive. In Boise, she rode in her first elevator, saw her first street car, watched her second picture show, and went "to pay a visit to some members of the local [Chinese] colony." Who initiated this visit is not known, and the phrasing in the *Statesman* makes it unclear whether Polly was hoping to see an old friend or to meet somebody for the first time. Leaving Grangeville, Polly declared, "I have best time in fifty year. Maybe I come back next year." About Boise, however, she said, "Lots of people, I like it, but it makes me tired to look so much."[36]

The cabin Shepp built for her, a single room with a sleeping loft, was on the site of the house Polly had shared with Bemis, where sunlight touched earliest in the morning and lingered longest in the evenings. Shepp installed a cookstove and furnished it with a bed, table, and chairs that he had crafted. He and Pete reconnected the telephone line between the two homes, and the men did heavy work for Polly, such as chopping wood and bringing her game. Foster Morgan, while working for the county tax collector in 1929 or 1930, recalled stopping in at Polly's and not finding anything to tax. He also noted that she was not at home but "off visiting." How often she left home, how far afield she went, whether she walked or traveled by horse, we do not know, but adventurers going down the Salmon River in 1931 and 1932 observed that she was "active and cheerful," "full of energy and pep."[37]

In her old age, Polly and her neighbors exchanged daily telephone calls. When she failed to answer the phone on August 6, 1933, they rowed across the river and found her ill. Unable to care for her themselves, Shepp and Pete took her on horseback to the War Eagle Mine where they were met by an ambulance that drove Polly to the Idaho County Nursing Home in Grangeville. She was said to be unconscious during the grueling, nine-hour journey.[38] As described by the daughter of Polly's nurse, the County Nursing Home was for the indigent, mostly the elderly, those who were dying. There was one big room for men and two small rooms for women. Polly, who stayed in a room by herself, arrived wearing tennis shoes, a dress of quilted percale, and one copper earring. "The other was lost. Her toes were completely curled over, and she was bedridden, so she had bedsores."[39]

At the County Nursing Home, Polly had frequent visitors. There were good friends like Bertha Long, who brought her grandson, and acquaintances such as Frank McGrane who had eaten at Polly's boardinghouse just once after a dance. Polly recognized that she was "too tired, too old" to get well, yet she remained interested in life, especially in children. "Her wrinkled face lights up with a lovely smile when she hears the little folk," her nurse wrote Lament Johnson, adding, "She had a keen interest in an expectant mother at the hospital, and was anxious to see the baby when it was born."[40]

On November 6 at 3:30 in the afternoon, Polly died. She had wanted to be buried in the canyon she loved, but winter had set in, and neither Shepp nor Pete could be located. So, with the members of the city council of Grangeville acting as pallbearers, Polly was buried in the Prairie View Cemetery. Before Shepp died in 1936, he signed everything over to his partner, and on December 8, 1936, Pete filed a U.S. Patent (No. 210249) for Polly's land. A devout Catholic, Pete donated what he had of Polly's belongings to St. Gertrude's Museum. He also shared what he knew of Polly with Sister Mary Alfreda and with Paul and Mary Filer with whom he lived on Shepp Ranch for many years. After he died in 1970, his sister, who inherited his estate, purchased a stone for Polly's grave. The marker reads: Polly Bemis September 11, 1853–November 6, 1933.[41]

SUBSEQUENT DISCOVERIES

After *Thousand Pieces of Gold* was published, readers who had known Polly shared their personal or family memories. There also were readers like Cheryl Helmers, Joyce Justice, and Tsoi Nuliang, who suggested additional sources and undertook new avenues of research themselves, leading to fresh discoveries that require examination. Figures from census summaries were used for the novel, but a search of the 1880 manuscript census for Warrens revealed Polly's place of birth as Peking and her age as twenty-seven. She was listed as "widowed" and sharing a household with Bemis, thirty-two, who was "single" and owned a saloon. Her occupation was "housekeeping." While she might have been born in Peking [Beijing], this attribution more likely reflects the limitations of Polly, Bemis, and Victor Hexter [the census taker] in stating her precise place of birth in English. The designation of Polly as "widowed" was a surprise. Long before she and Bemis were married, however, Polly was referred to as Mrs. Bemis in an 1881 news item; thus the census taker, in making her a widow, was perhaps not unlike the reporter who made her a wife.[42]

Warren Times, a compilation by Cheryl Helmers of information about Warrens from two dozen Idaho newspapers, interviews with local residents, collections of letters and memoirs, national and county records, and regional magazines and books, offers myriad confirming details for life in Idaho County as depicted in *Thousand Pieces of Gold*, as well as pertinent new information. For example, Bemis's father, Alfred, was still in the Warrens area when Lalu arrived, and he died of consumption four years later. By the mid-1880s, Bemis not only monopolized the saloon business in Warrens, he also worked as deputy sheriff. A reporter noted, "[Bemis] knows how to treat his friends," but he also knew now to do business. In the early 1890s, Bemis initiated a foreclosure on a loan he had made to three men. He also forced the sale of the old Washington Hotel. The fire he and Polly suffered at their ranch was not their first. On May 18, 1887, their home in Warrens burned to the ground but was rebuilt in a matter of months.

Of particular significance are articles in Grangeville's *Idaho News Press* about the 1892 Geary Act, which required Chinese nationals to register with the federal government or face deportation. On January 25, 1894, the paper noted the intention of Chinese in the county to register; "the failure of the government official to put in an appearance as advertised"; and the resulting "hardship, annoyance, inconvenience and expense" to those Chinese living in the mining camps. On May 4, "the last day of grace" for Chinese to register, "Photographer Hanson" was in Warrens "shooting celestials for registration purposes." At least one Chinese in an outlying spot, Ah Jack, had made two trips to Grangeville in hopes of registering. Thwarted both times by the absence of the government official, "he concluded it was no longer safe to wait, as he has too many property interests to risk being sent back to China," so he went "clear to Portland" to comply with the law.[43]

Polly would surely have been as fearful of deportation as Ah Jack, albeit for different reasons. Had she, too, made failed attempts to register? Was this when she and Bemis decided to marry and move to the Salmon River? Was that why she called the picture on her certificate of residence her wedding photograph? Did Hanson take that photo? According to case files discovered by archivist Joyce Justice in the National Archives in Seattle, Polly was just one of fifty Chinese in Warrens who pleaded not guilty to "the alleged violation of Section 6 of Act November 3rd, 1893 of the Statutes of the United States." All fifty blamed their failure to register on the government official's inability to come to Warrens as promised because "the roads were impassible owing to the snows and rains," and were represented by the same attorney, D. Worth.[44]

On May 13, 1896, the case of "The United States vs. Polly Bemiss [sic] in the matter of the arrest and deportation of said defendant" was heard in Moscow, Idaho. As required by law, Polly had a white witness who testified she had already been living in the United States when the Geary Act passed, that she was a "peaceable law abiding Chinaman, inoffensive, and has been continuously engaged in laundrying for ten years in Idaho County." Her witness was a resident of Grangeville, and his testimony was given on May 7, 1896 before W. A. Hall, U.S. Circuit Court commissioner for the District of Idaho. Polly also presented testimony before W. A. Hall that same day. Was Polly actually arrested and taken to Moscow? Since the judge made his decision to grant her and the other Chinese certificates of residence "after reading the testimony," arrest was doubtful, but she may well have traveled to Grangeville to give her testimony. And if Polly was still laundering in 1896, as her witness testified, then she and Bemis did not move to their ranch in the Salmon River directly after they married in 1894 but at least two years later.[45]

Questions about the couple's Salmon River ranch remain unresolved. In "Charlie Bemis: Idaho's Most 'Significant Other,'" Priscilla Wegars reveals Bemis had purchased property on the south fork of the Salmon River from three Chinese men in 1888. In addition to the land, $500 bought him "improvements ditches waterrights, crop and apurtenances also 6 Horses with rigging & all the farming [equipment]." As already known, however, Bemis and Polly did not settle there but on the main Salmon, on land for which he did not seem to have a deed. Why?[46]

No answers came in letters from people who had known Polly and been moved by *Thousand Pieces of Gold* to write to me. Some simply expressed their pleasure in revisiting Polly through the novel. Of these, the most surprising was from William Drysdale, my deceased father's brother, who told me that he and my father, Robert, met Polly while working for the U.S. Forest Service in the Salmon River Canyon during the 1920s. Others, like Lucille Moss, whose mother had been a friend of Polly's, confirmed what I'd written: "[Mom] used to tell me the story of how Charlie looked after he was shot, her gold buttons, and how clean her house was." But a letter from August Hoene, deputy sheriff of Idaho County in 1933, provided a more detailed and somewhat different picture of Polly's departure from the Salmon: "In late summer of 1933 we [Hoene and Sheriff Walter Altman] were notified by Pete Klinkhammer that Mrs. Bemis was ill and needed care that he and his partner Shepp could not give." The sheriff made arrangements for Hoene and a registered nurse, Bernice Naser, to pick Polly up at the deserted War Eagle Mine. When Hoene and Naser arrived, Shepp, Klinkhammer, and Polly were waiting. "Not much talk was necessary or expected with these mountain men so we introduced ourselves to Polly and put her and her suitcase into the [sheriff's] car." Far from unconscious, Polly "talked a leg off the nurse" on the long drive into town and "did not seem to be very sick either physically or mentally."[47]

More startling than any discovery about Polly in Idaho were revelations about her origins. The name Lalu Nathoy had been puzzling because it does not sound Chinese, but many a Chinese name has been changed beyond recognition when transliterated from characters. Wondering whether there might be a different explanation, the translator for *Thousand Pieces of Gold* in Guangzhou, Tsoi Nuliang, wrote to a contact at Beijing University's Research Institute of Chinese Nationalities, who forwarded the inquiry to Huang Youfu in the Research Department on Northeastern and Inner Mongolian Nationalities. Huang recognized the name immediately: In Mongolian, Lalu means "Islam" and Nathoy, pronounced Nasoi, "Long Life". Based on her name, her northern China origins, and a photograph of Lalu, Huang determined she was not Chinese but Mongolian, quite likely a Daur, a minority in Mongolia that is related culturally and linguistically to the Mongols and Tungus—Manchu speaking peoples.

In the mid-nineteenth century, Huang explained, many Mongolians, previously nomadic, settled in Han areas to farm. Some of the settlers adopted Han customs such as footbinding. When living among people who professed Islam, some even gave up the Mongolian faith, Lamaism, and became followers of Islam. This, Huang speculated, had been the case for Lalu's family. Regrettably, too many years had passed for him to find a precise location for Lalu's family; nor could he ascertain how much, if any, of the Daur culture Lalu's family might have retained.[48]

The Daur wore buckskin tunics with pants and underclothes made of cotton. Their winter clothing included leather gloves, boots, and leggings. Their houses, sturdy, rectangular, one-story log structures, were considered ideally situated when there was a mountain rising behind them and a river flowing in front. They farmed grains, vegetables, and tobacco. They also fished and hunted bear and deer. A generous people, they would ostracize any hunter who did not share his kill, and strangers were always welcome.[49] Familiarity with even a few of these characteristics would explain the ease with which Lalu seemed to have adapted to living in Idaho, her apparent alienation from most of the Chinese in Warrens, and her affection for her home in the Salmon River canyon. But was she, in fact, Lalu Nathoy?

In Polly's testimony for her deportation case is space for her signature, and it has two characters, difficult to decipher because the ink blotted, yet written with a sure hand, 恭享, Gung Heung. Below the characters Gung Heung is the signature of W.A. Hall, U.S. Circuit Court commissioner for the District of Idaho, and it seems doubtful he would have permitted somebody else to sign on Polly's behalf. Besides, the calligraphy for Gung Heung does not match that of any other Chinese who gave testimony before W. A. Hall or A. Kavanaugh, the justice of the peace in Warrens, at the same time as Polly.[50]

Given her background and the absence of any evidence to the contrary, one could assume Polly was illiterate in Chinese as well as English. But was she? When I revisited Polly's cabin in June 2001, I noticed two Chinese characters, 觀迎 (welcome), carved on a piece of wood above her door. The area, under an overhang, is dark, and I may have missed them during my visit in 1980, or they may have been added later. In any case, the first character, 觀 gwoon, should be 歡 foon. Despite this error, the calligraphy is well rendered. Adding to the puzzle, Terrie Havis, who showed me around the restored cabin, pointed out nine notches on a windowsill that were said to have been made by Polly, one for each year she lived there. I had not noticed these during my 1980 visit. If Polly was illiterate, she might well have made them. If she was literate, however, why would she have used such a crude method for marking time?

Regardless of who wrote the two characters on Polly's testimony, why don't they sound out as any of her known names? A Mongolian living among Han Chinese might well have had both a Mongolian and a Chinese name, in which case Gung Heung could have been Lalu Nathoy's Chinese name. Or Gung Heung might have been the name under which she was smuggled into America. According to professor Marlon Hom, Gung Heung is a man's name, not a woman's. Does that mean she was smuggled in as a man? Translator Tsoi Nuliang contends the characters were written by a man as a deliberate act of malice. "'Heung' means 'enjoy' (and) the sound 'Gung' can mean 'public' or 'provide.'" Acknowledging the character on the form is for a name, Tsoi maintains it was chosen for its sound, so "'Gung Heung' would mean the woman is 'provided for public enjoyment,' in other words, a prostitute."[51]

AN ASSESSMENT

With imperfect records and memories and the virtual absence of her own voice, it seems unlikely that the facts of Lalu/Polly/Gung Heung's life will ever be completely recovered or without contradictions. But her unique character, resilience, and generosity of spirit, which made her noteworthy in life and memorable in death, have never been contested, even by the new discoveries. It was these attributes that I wanted to honor and attempted to convey in *Thousand Pieces of Gold*. It also was these attributes that inspired Jim Campbell, then owner of the Polly Bemis Ranch, to bring her remains back to the canyon, restore her cabin, turn it into a museum, and nominate it for entry into the National Register of Historic Places. In 1987 the Department of the Interior deemed the cabin significant in Idaho's heritage, and at the museum's dedication ceremonies, Governor Cecil Andrus declared, "The history of Polly Bemis is a great part of the legacy of central Idaho. She is the foremost pioneer on the rugged Salmon River."[52] Although the Polly Bemis Ranch is now privately owned, the seventy-one owner/members are committed to maintaining the cabin museum and keeping it open to the public. And Polly's spirit seems to linger—with characteristic good humor—in her cabin. In 1999 Kathy Schatz was struggling to reach a high shelf when she distinctly heard Polly say, "Ha ha, you short like me too."[53]

ACKNOWLEDGMENTS

I would like to reiterate my thanks to all those acknowledged in *Thousand Pieces of Gold*. I'm also indebted to Terrie Havis for encouraging me to return to the Polly Bemis Ranch in 2001, for making my visit possible, and—together with Steve Havis, Mike Sohrakoff, and Dixie Weber—for making available opportunities for further research during my stay.

Valerie Matsumoto has encouraged me to write this essay since she first suggested it many years ago, and her guidance—together with sound advice from Sue Armitage, Patricia Hart, Tsoi Nuliang, and Judy Yung—

helped me complete it. Katie Gilmartin, Yvette Huginnie, Don McCunn, Peggy Pascoe, and Jan Venolia provided useful suggestions as well. Dee Garceau-Hagen's direction was indispensable for the adaptation in this anthology. I am deeply grateful to them, to all those named in the footnotes, and to Lalu Nathoy/Polly Bemis/Gung Heung, who continues to inspire me.

NOTES

1. In print since its publication in 1981, *Thousand Pieces of Gold* has been available from Boston's Beacon Press in trade paperback since 1988. The 1991 film adaptation was produced by American Playhouse Theatrical Films and Maverick Films International, Ltd. in association with Kelly/Yamamoto Productions and Film Four International. *Thousand pieces of gold* is a Chinese term of endearment for daughters.

2. Countess Eleanor Gizycka, "Diary on the Salmon River, Part II," *Field and Stream,* June 1923 (hereafter cited as "Diary"); "Woman of 70 Sees Railway First Time," *Idaho County Free Press*, August 16, 1923 (hereafter cited as *Free Press*); *Idaho Statesman,* August 8, 1924, reprinted in August 8, 1954 (hereafter cited as *Statesman*); Lament Johnson, "Old China Woman of Idaho Famous," *Oregonian*, November 5, 1933 (hereafter cited as *Oregonian*).

   Note: Because I was writing a novel, I did not copy down page numbers when taking notes, and my notes from Sister Mary Alfreda Elsensohn's letters, articles, and books sometimes simply reference "Elsensohn." These decisions, made over 20 years ago, now make for incomplete footnotes, and for this I apologize.

3. This is the date on Polly's tombstone. If Lalu did arrive in Warrens in 1872 and was 18 when sold and 19 when landed, she would indeed have been born in 1853. On Polly's 1896 Certificate of Residence, however, her age is 47, making her year of birth 1849.

4. Sister M. Alfreda Elsensohn, "Memories of Polly Bemis," *Spokesman-Review*, May 12, 1957 (hereafter cited as "Memories"); *Statesman;* Gizycka, "Diary".

5. Johnson, *Oregonian;* Gizycka, "Diary".

6. Sister M. Alfreda Elsensohn, *Pioneer Days in Idaho County*, Vol. I (Cottonwood, ID: The Idaho Corporation of Benedictine sisters, 1947) (hereafter cited as *Pioneer)* and *Idaho Chinese Lore* (Cottonwood: The Idaho Corporation of Benedictine Sisters, 1970) (hereafter cited as *Chinese Lore*); Eileen Hubbell Macdonald, "A Study of Chinese Migrants in Certain Idaho Settlements and of Selected Families in Transition" (master's thesis, University of Idaho, 1966) (hereafter cited as "Study"); Johnson, *Oregonian.*

7. Lucie Cheng Hirata, "Free, Indentured, Enslaved: Chinese Prostitutes in Nineteenth-Century America," *Signs: Journal of Women in Culture and Society* 5, no. 1 (1979) (hereafter cited as "Free, Indentured") and "Chinese Immigrant Women in Nineteenth-Century California" in C. R. Berkin and M. B. Norton, Women of America (Boston: Houghton Mifflin, 1979).

8. Hirata, "Free, Indentured"; Alexander McLeod, *Pigtails & Golddust* (Caxton Printers, 1947); Charles Frederick Holder, "Chinese Slavery in America," *North American Review.*

9. Iris Anderson, "Life at Warren Today Is Shared with Ghost of Her Colorful Mining Days," *Lewiston Morning Tribune*, September 4, 1960 (hereafter cited as "Life at Warren"); G. M. Campbell, "A Chinese Slave Girl Charmed An Idaho Town," Salt Lake Tribune, July 9, 1972 (hereafter cited as *Tribune*); Elsensohn.

10. George J. Bancroft, "China Polly (Lalu Nathoy) a Reminiscence" (unpublished typescript, Denver Public Library) (hereafter cited as "Reminiscence"); Louise Cheney, "China Polly Was a Pioneer" (Idaho Historical Society) (hereafter cited as "China

Polly"); Grace Roffey Pratt, "Charlie Bemis' Highest Prize," *Frontier Times* 36, no. l, (winter 1961) (hereafter I cited as *Frontier);* Campbell, *Tribune;* Elsensohn; *Free Press.*

Note: Gizycka's claim that Polly said an old Chinese man brought her to Warrens seems implausible because running a pack train that carried supplies was physically demanding work performed by young men. For this and other reasons I created the packer Jim in my novel. (See my article "Reclaiming Chinese America: One Woman's Journey," *Amerasia Journal* 26, no. 1, 167).

Although all sources of Lalu's arrival in Warrens seem to stem from the eyewitness account of pioneer A. W. Talkington, one of Elsensohn's several reconstructions has Lalu arriving with two other Chinese girls, a claim also made by Otis Morris and George Bancroft, neither of whom were present. Since the one Chinese woman in the 1870 census might have been gone by the time Lalu arrived, I opted in my novel for Lalu to arrive alone and be the only Chinese woman in Warrens.

All sources using the name with which Polly arrived, Lalu, and the name of her owner, Hong King, seem to originate from Elsensohn. Having failed to ask for her source while she was living, I can only speculate that she got this information from Talkington as well. The name Nathoy appears on Polly's marriage certificate.

11. Elsensohn, *Pioneer;* Bancroft, "Reminiscence"; letter from Mary Long Eisenhaver to author October 8, 1980.

12. Elsensohn; Bancroft, "Reminiscence"; Preface by Taylor Smith, November 2, 1961, to Peter Beemer "Original Music Manuscript" (Idaho Historical Society); author interview with John Carrey, July 18, 1980; letter from John Carrey to author, September 15, 1980.

    Note: In *Thousand Pieces of Gold,* Bemis's background only comes up during an exchange about freedom on p. 144, where Polly refers to Bemis as being the son of a doctor and having worked as a deckhand. The former came from Fern Cable Trull, "The History of the Chinese in Idaho from 1864–1910" (master's thesis, University of Oregon, 1946) (hereafter cited as "History"); the latter from Robert G. Bailey, *River of No Return* (Lewiston, ID: Bailey-Blake Printing Co., 1935) (hereafter cited as *River*).

13. Betty Derig, "Celestials in the Diggings," *Idaho Yesterdays* (fall, 1972) (hereafter cited as "Celestials"); Macdonald, "Study"; Trull, "History"; Elsensohn.

14. Elsensohn; Cheney; "China Polly," Gizycka, "Diary"; Pratt, *Frontier;* author interview with Vera Weaver Waite, July 15, 1980; letter from Verna McGrane to author, August 24, 1980; author interviews with John Carrey and Gay Carrey Robie, July 18, 1980; Johnson, *Oregonian;* Polly's dresses in the Polly Bemis Collection, Historical Museum at St. Gertrude, Cottonwood, Idaho; *Free Press;* Bancroft, "Reminiscence."

15. Bertha Long, "Polly Bemis—My Friend" (typescript written for Clara Landrus, a niece in late 1930s, in possession of the author) (hereafter cited as "Friend"); *Statesman;* Elsensohn; Campbell, *Tribune; Free Press;* interviews with John Carrey and Gay Carrey Robie, July 18, 1980; author interview with Vera McGrane, July 20, 1980; author interview with Vera Weaver Waite, July 15, 1980; letter from Denis Long to author September 18, 1980.

16. Letters from Denis Long to author September 18, 1980, August 31, 1980, October 13, 1980; Long, "Friend"; letters from Mary Long Eisenhaver to author October 8, 1980, December 3, 1980.

    Note: John Long also boarded with Polly, but it was from Theodore that Bertha first heard about her. Since Theodore was carrying mail in the 1870s, that would mean Polly and Bemis were living together by the mid 1870s. This is consistent with Johnson's article in the *Oregonian,* which states Polly and Bemis lived together for twenty years before they married.

17. Elsensohn; Trull, "History"; "Polly Bemis, 'Poker Bride' of Salmon River County, Expires," *Lewiston Tribune,* November 7, 1933 (hereafter cited as "Expires"); Pratt, *Fron-*

tier; Cheney, "China Polly"; Trull, "History"; Hirata, "Free, Indentured"; Campbell, *Tribune.*

18. "Golden Past of Warren Adds Spice of History to Fishermen's Jaunts," *Evening States-man*, July 22, 1965; "Czizek Explodes Myth of Chinese Poker Bride," newspaper clipping; Johnson, *Oregonian.*

   Note: Examining the claims and counterclaims regarding the validity of the poker game story, it seems to me that naysayers like Czizek found it insulting for Polly to be called a "poker bride." Since she clearly was not, I agree. But that does not mean she did not win her freedom through a poker game, and the attempts to foist the "poker bride" label onto Molly Smead are, to me, dishonorable.

   In my research, all sources identified Molly Smead as a Sheepeater Indian, and I followed suit in earlier versions of this essay. I am grateful to Kevin Marsh, Laura Woodworth-Ney, and John Mann for their assistance in arriving at the identification "Lemhi Shoshone from the Sheepeater Band" used here. Any error is mine.

19. Elsensohn; Johnson, *Oregonian;* Bancroft, "Reminiscence"; *Free Press; Idaho County Free Press*, August 16, 1923 and September 26, 1890; Campbell, *Tribune;* letter from Denis Long to author, September 18, 1980.

20. Letter from John Carrey to author, December 9, 1980; Anderson, "Life at Warren"; Elsensohn; Bancroft, "Reminiscence"; "Mountain Notes," *Idaho County Free Press*, October 24, 1890; Johnson, *Oregonian;* Campbell, *Tribune.*

21. *Free Press;* Marriage Certificate for Polly Nathoy and C. A. Bemis, August 13, 1894, Historical Museum at St. Gertrude, Cottonwood, Idaho.

22. Author interview with Gay Carrey Robie, July 18, 1980; Ann Adams, "The Legend of Polly Bemis Retold," an undated, unattributed article that quotes extensively from the *Idaho County Free* Press and may actually be from that newspaper; John Carrey, "Moccasin Tracks of the Sheepeater" in *Sheepeater Indian Campaign* (Grangeville: Idaho County Free Press, 1968); 1896 Certificate of Residence, Polly Bemis, Historical Museum at St. Gertrude; Johnson, *Oregonian;* Campbell, *Tribune*, Elsensohn.

23. Johnny Carrey and Cort Conley, *River of No Return* (Cambridge, Idaho: Backeddy Books, 1978) (hereafter cited as *No Return*); Elsensohn, *Polly Bemis;* letter from Bob J. Waite to author, May 29, 1980.

24. Letters from John Carrey to author, September 15, 1980 and December 9, 1980; Trull, "History"; *Free Press;* Johnson, *Oregonian;* Carrey and Conley, *No Return;* Bailey, *River;* Bancroft, "Reminiscence"; Elsensohn; author interview with Mary and Paul Filer, July 20, 1980.

25. Letters from John Carrey to author, September 15, 1980, November 21, 1980, December 9, 1980; Bailey, *River;* Bancroft, "Reminiscence."

26. Letter from John Carrey to author, December 9, 1980; letter from Mary Long Eisenhaver to author, October 8, 1980; Carrey and Conley, *No Return;* Trull, "History"; Elsensohn; Bancroft, "Reminiscence"; Placer Location #522, Idaho County Records.

27. Elsensohn, *Pioneer;* letter from John Carrey to author, November 21, 1980.

28. Author interview with John Carrey, July 18, 1980; author interview with John Carrey, Paul Filer, and Mary Filer, July 20, 1980; Carrey and Conley, *No Return.*

29. Elsensohn; Gizycka, "Diary".

30. *Free Press;* Elsensohn; letter from Inez Wildman to author, September 16, 1980.

31. Letter from Inez Wildman to author September 16, 1980; author interview with Mary and Paul Filer, July 20, 1980; Carrey and Conley, *No Return;* Elsensohn.

32. Elsensohn, *Chinese Lore;* Johnson, *Oregonian;* interview with Mary and Paul Filer, July 20, 1980.

33. Elsensohn, *Polly Bemis; Free Press.*

34. Author interview with John Carrey and Gay Carrey Robie, July 18, 1980; letter from John Carrey to author, November 21, 1980.

35. Author interview with John Carrey, July 18, 1980; author interview with Mary and Paul Filer, July 20, 1980; Frances Zaunmiller Wisner, "Simply River Women," *Incredible Idaho* 3, no. 4 (spring 1972) (Boise: Idaho Department of Commerce and Development); Elsensohn; Carrey & Conley, *No Return.*
36. Johnson, *Oregonian;* Long, "Friend"; *Free Press; Statesman.*
37. Author interview with Jim Campbell at Polly's cabin, July 18, 1980; Elsensohn; letter from Verna McGrane to author, August 24, 1980; Bailey, *River;* Charles Kelly, "He Won His Wife in a Poker Game," *Pony Express,* February 1970, Sonora, CA.
38. Author interview with John Carrey, July 18, 1980; Johnson, *Oregonian;* Elsensohn, *Polly Bemis;* "Expires."
39. Interview with Vera Weaver Waite, July 15, 1980.
40. Long, "Friend"; Johnson, *Oregonian;* Elsensohn; letter from Mary Long Eisenhaver, December 8, 1980.
41. "Expires"; author interview with John Carrey, July 18, 1980; Elsensohn; letter from Mary Long Eisenhaver to author, December 8, 1980; author interview with Paul and Mary Filer, July 20, 1980.
42. *Nez Perce News,* August 11, 1881.
43. Cheryl Helmers, *Warren Times, a Collection of News About Warren, Idaho* (Odessa, Texas: The Author, 1988), specifically *Idaho Tristate Weekly,* March 30, 1876; *Nez Perce News,* August 13, 1885, September 2, 1886; *Idaho County Free Press,* March 18, 1892, June 19, 1891, June 3, 1887, January 25, 1894, May 4, 1894, May 11, 1894.
44. United States District Court for the District of Idaho, May 13, 1896, No. 132, the *United States vs. Lee Ping,* Hon. Jas H. Beatty, Judge (hereafter cited as "Lee Ping").
45. In the District Court of the United States for the District of Idaho, Judgment roll No. 181, the *United States vs. Polly Bemiss* [sic], Register No. 1, filed May 14, 1896 (hereafter cited as "JR181"); "Lee Ping."
46. Priscilla Wegars, "Charlie Bemis: Idaho's Most 'Significant Other,'" *Idaho Yesterdays* 44, no.3 (fall 2000): 6.
47. Letter from Lucille Moss to author, May 7, 1992; letter from August Hoene to author, August 26, 1991.
48. Letter from Tsoi Nuliang to author, June 27, 1984; translation of letter from Huang Youfu to Tsoi Nuliang by Tsoi Nuliang, October 1, 1984.
49. Mark Bender and Su Huana (translators), *Daur Folk Tales: Selected Myths of the Daur Nationality* (Beijing: New World Press, 1984).
50. "JR181"
    Note: Because I am illiterate in Chinese, I could not read the characters myself and I am indebted to Marlon Hom, Wei Chi Poon, You Shan Tang, Tsoi Nuliang, Ellen Laishan Yeung, and Judy Yung for their help. Because of the blotted ink, the characters were read differently by the individuals listed here. *Gung Heung* was the most frequent reading.
51. E-mail from Tsoi Nuliang to author, October 16, 2001.
52. "Old Cabin Becomes Museum," Associated Press, June 6, 1987; Alice Koskela, "Polly Bemis Finally Rests at Homestead," *Star-News,* June 10, 1987, l; Bill Loftus, "Salmon River Museum Dedicated to Pioneer Polly Bemis," *Lewiston Tribune,* June 6, 1987, 6A.
53. Conversation with author, June 28, 2001.

Fig. 7.1 Emma Sansaver, seated front right, and her teammates from the 1904 Fort Shaw squad. Other members of the team include (standing, left to right) Nettie Wirth, Katie Snell, Minnie Burton, Sarah Mitchell, and (seated left to right) Genie Butch and Belle Johnson. Reprinted by permission of Terry Bender. Reprinted by permission of Terry Bender.

7

UNLIKELY CHAMPION: EMMA ROSE SANSAVER, 1884–1925

Linda Peavy and Ursula Smith

On an evening in mid-June of 1903, eighteen-year-old Emma Rose Sansaver and her teammates from the Fort Shaw Indian Boarding School engaged in a hard-fought exhibition game of "basket ball" that gave residents of Havre, Montana, their first glimpse of the fledgling sport. "Fort Shaw Indian Girls Play a Good Fast Game before a Large Audience," the *Havre Plaindealer* reported. Yet whatever pleasure Emma might have taken from seeing that article in her hometown paper must have been overshadowed by the pain and chagrin triggered by news that her uncle had ridden in from Maple Creek, Alberta, the day before. He had come to organize a new search for the body of her mother, "Mary Sansavere, a half-breed Cree Indian," who had disappeared some five years earlier. By the end of the week a front-page article in the *Plaindealer* confirmed rumors that the murdered woman was indeed "the mother of Miss Sansseuver, a member of the Fort Shaw Indian girls' basketball team, which gave so creditable an exhibition here Wednesday evening."[1]

Weathering that storm, Emma returned to the Fort Shaw campus in the Sun River Valley, glad to be "home" with her teammates, the girls who had replaced the shattered unit that had once been her family.

There they would begin training in earnest for their eagerly anticipated trip to St. Louis, where they were to spend five months the following summer as students at the Model Indian School on the fairgrounds of the Louisiana Purchase Exposition, playing exhibition and challenge games and giving afternoon concerts and recitations. That St. Louis summer turned out to be one of the most empowering interludes in Emma Sansaver's life. She and the other members of the Fort Shaw team not only drew praise for their excellence in recitation, dance, and music, they also introduced an international audience to the excitement and intensity of women's team sports. And they returned to Montana with a trophy declaring them "basket ball" champions of the World's Fair of 1904, in effect, champions of the world.[2]

Champion—a lofty title for a young woman born in a "breed camp" south of Havre, Montana Territory, sometime around 1884. Like many other details of Emma Sansaver's early life, the exact date, place, and circumstances of her birth remain unconfirmed. According to one of her granddaughters, Emma, "like most mixed-blood kids, was just born 'out there' somewhere." Indeed, the kinds of statistics we term vital were of relatively little concern to parents descended from peoples who marked the passage of time in terms of seasonal migrations. Yet Emma Sansaver's date and place of birth, her tribal affiliation, and her nationality would soon become a major concern of those who were to assume the task of educating her for an adult life in a world far different from the one her parents and grandparents had known.[3]

Even so, her elders found it difficult to reduce Emma's life experiences to a concise and accurate list of names and numbers that corresponded with blanks on the enrollment forms that the Office of Indian Affairs provided to government Indian schools. Many of the requested "facts" of Emma's young life depended on the best guesses of relatives. The primary concern of school administrators was determining whether Emma and her siblings were legitimate wards of the United States Government or Canadian-born offspring of the wandering "British Indians" Canada had nudged into exile and Uncle Sam was determined not to support or educate. If ascertaining the national heritage, and thereby the entitlement, of Indian peoples was a relatively new concern for government officials, consider how irrelevant such concepts must have seemed to Native American families caught up in a paper chase after proof of things they marked by other means. Emma Sansaver's parents and grandparents before them had paid scant attention to what they called "the Medicine Line." Moving freely back and forth across that invisible 49th parallel during their seasonal migrations, they had little concern for whether a baby was born on lands claimed by the Queen Mother or on those claimed by the Great White Father.[4]

If there were questions about Emma Sansaver's nationality, there was no question as to her heritage. Government boarding school records list her as 3/4 Chippewa, though her parents and her grandparents on both sides were, more precisely, Metis. The Metis were members of a proud mixed-blood nation whose skin was said to be the color of *bois brule*—scorched wood—and whose lives blended Native American and European traditions. Their settlements along Canadian rivers featured small homes and garden plots; while out on the plains during the buffalo hunts of June and September they lived in skin tipis or canvas tents. They conversed in a language as mixed as their bloodline, a potpourri of Chippewa, Cree, and French with a sprinkling of English words and phrases. And in place of rituals overseen by medicine men, Metis hunters relied upon blessings bestowed by the French Black Robes, Jesuit missionaries who had come to the area to minister to the Indians.[5]

Emma's parents had both been born at a time when mixed-blood people still outnumbered whites ten to one in the area known as Rupert's Land, the thousand-mile stretch of prairie that bordered Lake Superior on the east, the Rockies on the west, and the 49th parallel to the south. Her father, Edward Sansaver, was born near Fort Pitt, Alberta, in 1859 to parents of Chippewa-Cree and French heritage. Her mother, Marie Rose LaFromboise Sansaver, was born near Prince Albert, Saskatchewan, around 1858, to parents of the Little Shell Band of the Red River peoples. During the early 1870s, Marie Rose LaFromboise met Edward Sansaver, and the two sixteen-year-olds married in Edmonton, Alberta, around 1875. Within a couple of years they had crossed the 49th parallel, following family and tribal kin south onto the Blackfeet Reserve, a vast area stretching from the Rockies to the western Dakota border. They were bound for Fort Benton, the farthest navigable port on the Missouri. A rough-and-tumble river town and a supply depot for the miners, ranchers, and homesteaders of Montana Territory, Fort Benton was a good place for Edward Sansaver to look for work, if not a good place to bring a wife heavy with her first child. The couple settled a few miles north of Fort Benton in a Metis camp near present-day Loma, Montana. There, in July of 1877, Marie Sansaver birthed her first child, a daughter she named Mary. It is doubtful her husband was on hand for the birth, for by that time he was herding cattle over the open range between the upper reaches of the Missouri and the Canadian border.[6]

It was a job for which Edward Sansaver was particularly well suited. As more and more cattle were driven up from the southern plains, ranchers looking for wranglers were glad to hire Metis. After years of hunting buffalo on horseback, young men like Edward Sansaver were considered superb cowboys, and the wages were good for a man with a growing family. But in the late 1870s a drought on the northern plains stressed the economy for settlers and Natives alike. Even the Blackfeet, Assiniboine, and Gros Ventre, all of whom were receiving rations from the federal government, found themselves in dire circumstances during this period. Conditions were much more severe among the mixed-blood peoples for whom no agency had been established. Edward Sansaver, dependent on the wages he earned herding cattle, spent more and more time on the open range. At one point, Marie and their little girl, Mary, followed Edward to a camp at Medicine Lodge, near the site of present-day Malta, Montana. It was there, in March of 1882, that she gave birth to their second surviving child, a son they named Isadore.[7]

By the early 1880s, the construction of Fort Assiniboine fifty miles south of Havre offered employment opportunities for brick makers and carpenters, drawing the Sansavers to a newly established Metis settlement at the northern edge of the fort. Initially about one-half-mile long and one-third-mile wide, the post continued to expand in size and amenities, with each expansion providing sporadic but welcome work for the area's Native peoples. Known as "the breed camp," the Metis settlement in which Edward and Marie Sansaver and other "British Cree refugees" lived consisted of numerous tipis and a few log structures. In the midst of the camp seven-year-old Mary and little Isadore played under the watchful eye of elders. Marie, pregnant with her third child, cooked her family's meals over an open fire, washed their clothes in water from the creek, and fought the dust and grime of prairie living. Meanwhile, her husband spent his days building a fort designed to protect the area's ranchers and other settlers from "Indian depredations."[8]

The birth of the Sansavers' second daughter, Emma Rose—she who would one day be hailed as champion—was met with joy, though not, as yet, with fanfare. The date was sometime in mid-August of 1884 or 1886, depending upon which family and public records are relied upon. Two years later, the family welcomed yet another baby girl, Flora. By this time, major changes were underway that would have direct impact on many of the Native peoples living on the Blackfeet Reserve. In 1888 Congress ratified an agreement in which three-quarters of the reserve, 17.5 million of the 23.5 million acres set aside for the Indians, had been ceded to the United States Government. In return, the government was to convert the remaining quarter, about 6 million acres that were, by design, not contiguous, into three separate reservations. The Blackfeet would have their own reservation located just east of the Rockies. The Gros Ventre and a portion of the Assiniboine would be assigned to Fort

Belknap Reservation east of Havre; and the remainder of the Assiniboine would share Fort Peck Reservation, located in the northeastern corner of the territory, with the Lakota Sioux. Within a reasonable time all members of those tribes were to relocate accordingly. As long as they remained within the boundaries of their designated reservations, they were promised increasing support from the government. That support included improved rations and better health care, education and training for their children, and land allotments that would allow families to farm and ranch after the manner of white settlers.[9]

While members of these tribes were leaving what had been government land set aside as a pan-Indian hunting reserve and moving to their assigned reservations, day-to-day life in the Metis settlement into which Emma Rose Sansaver had been born remained relatively unchanged. True to their vow not to support British Indians, the government further disenfranchised the Metis/Chippewa-Cree by once again leaving them landless and obliged to fend for themselves. Since that was essentially what the Sansavers had been doing all along, little Emma and her siblings continued to take for granted the relative security of everyday life.

That security was abruptly shattered in June of 1890 when their father contracted pneumonia while moving cattle from the open range to Fort Assinnibione in a driving rainstorm. Already weakened by tuberculosis, he died at the age of thirty-two, leaving his widow and four children in less than ideal circumstances. It soon became evident that Marie Rose Sansaver had neither the stability nor the means to provide adequately for her children. When she subsequently entered into a stormy relationship with Joseph Rondo, another Metis, conditions at home rapidly deteriorated. Marie enrolled all four of the children at St. Paul's, an Ursuline mission school under government contract on the Fort Belknap Reservation.[10]

Until this time it is doubtful that Emma and her siblings had received any formal schooling. Moving from the relative chaos of life with their mother and Joseph Rondo to the regimentation of mission school life, they were first exposed to the course of study prescribed for government-funded mission schools. Such schools, like the government's own day and boarding schools, were part of the movement afoot to assimilate America's Indians by stripping their children of their language and culture, and teaching them English, academic subjects, and vocational trades. Thus from the day of their enrollment at St. Paul's, the Sansavers and their classmates were required to leave their own language behind and speak only English.[11]

Distanced from her mother, Emma now formed an attachment to the nuns who were charged with her care and education and who buffered her from the abusive situation at home. For their part, the Ursuline sisters marveled at how quickly this petite child picked up English, how obedient she was to them, and how cordial she was to her classmates. Eminently teachable, Emma became an ideal pupil, spending her mornings in the study of English, reading, spelling, grammar, arithmetic, and geography, plus calisthenics, music, and art. In the afternoons Emma and her classmates did laundry, housekeeping, and kitchen chores prescribed by the gendered industrial training that came with government-funded Indian education. In addition to such mandated instructional activities, Emma also took required classes in religious education and attended mass on Sundays and Holy Days.[12]

In 1895, the year she turned eighteen, Emma's older sister Mary ended her schooling at St. Paul's and married Frank Dubois, a Metis well known as a builder in Havre. Though Mary's marriage effectively removed her from the increasingly volatile situation at home, Isadore, Emma, and Flora were obliged to return to their mother's home anytime St. Paul's was not in session. With the passage of time, the school came to symbolize a place of safety and support for Emma. It was therefore with mixed feelings in the fall of 1897 that Emma learned she and Flora were to be taken from the mission and enrolled at Fort Shaw Government Indian Boarding School. Fort Shaw must have seemed a world away from St. Paul's, for it was located about 200 miles distant, on the grounds of a recently abandoned military post in the Sun River Valley.[13]

Established in the late 1860s to protect the vital Fort Benton-Helena overland freight route and the valley's early Euro-American settlers from "marauding Indians," Fort Shaw had also been instrumental in discouraging intertribal warfare between the Blackfeet and other nations, notably the Assiniboine and the Lakota Sioux who contested their hunting grounds. In 1892, as the Indian wars subsided, Fort Shaw was deactivated as a military post, transferred from the War Department to the Department of the Interior, and reactivated as an off-reservation boarding school.[14]

Influenced by the successes of Col. Richard Henry Pratt, founder of Carlisle Indian School in Pennsylvania, the government had become fully committed to the idea that Indian children educated in off-reservation boarding schools far from the influence of their families were more likely to master the English language, as well as the academic and industrial skills they were taught. In Pratt's view, mission and reservation schools were "the merest stepping-stones," institutions where students would, ideally, come to realize the importance of continuing their education at an off-reservation school. Indeed, even the off-reservation schools themselves were, in a sense, stepping-stones, since the ultimate goal was to give Indian students "the capacity and the courage to go out from ... *all these* [Indian] *schools*" into the white world.[15]

The recently abandoned fort in the Sun River Valley seemed to the government the perfect location for a school that would serve the needs of children ages 5 to 18 from various tribes in Montana, Idaho, and Wyoming. The campus provided some ready-made facilities. The administrators and faculty could be housed in the old officers' quarters, the children in the soldiers' barracks. The large building that had served military personnel as a dance hall and theater could be put to good use as a gymnasium and drill hall. The school would have its own chapel, mess hall, post office, store, laundry, and hospital. Once considered "the Queen of Montana's Forts," Fort Shaw would now become "the Queen of Montana's Indian Schools."[16]

By June of 1892, Dr. William Winslow, a veteran of the Indian Service and a physician, had been named Fort Shaw School's first superintendent. Shortly thereafter he moved into his quarters and plunged into the task of turning a fort into a school. In addition to supervising the retrofitting of the buildings, Winslow corresponded with Indian agents and visited reservation and mission schools across the states of Montana, Idaho, and Wyoming. His commission was to seek out and enroll the region's most promising children in a program designed to give them the training they needed to take their place in the white world.[17]

By 1897, after four years of exemplary work at St. Paul's, thirteen-year-old Emma and eleven-year-old Flora Sansaver were obvious choices for transfer to the school at Fort Shaw. Thus it is not surprising that in September of that year, when Joseph Rondo loaded the girls and their belongings into his wagon for their annual trip to boarding school he headed west, bound for the Fort Shaw campus. Isadore, who at fifteen was well aware of the mistreatment his mother suffered at the hands of Joseph Rondo, did not accompany his sisters to Fort Shaw, convinced that he should stay closer to home.[18]

The abrupt severance of Emma's ties with the Ursuline nuns, in whose presence she had felt such security, could not have been easy for her. She could hardly imagine attending classes that were not presided over by the sisters. And as Joseph Rondo's wagon passed through the gates of Fort Shaw, the difference between that post and what she had known at St. Paul's would have been immediately evident. Fort Shaw's main structures—the officers' quarters that now housed faculty and staff, the barracks that were home to the students, and the administrative buildings in which classes were held—all faced inward on a 400-square-foot green. Tree-shaded boardwalks, flower beds, and manicured lawns graced the compound. And in place of the ever-present soldiers at Fort

Assiniboine, there were scores of boys and girls, plus a scattering of teachers and staffers, some of whom looked younger than Emma's sister Mary.[19]

The assistant matron who welcomed the Sansaver sisters to the campus and introduced them to the school's routines was Josephine Langley, a twenty-year-old Piegan (Blackfeet) who had come to Fort Shaw in the fall of 1893. Among Emma's roommates in the "big girls' dorm" were Katie Snell from Fort Belknap Reservation, and Nettie Wirth and Sarah Mitchell from Fort Peck Reservation. Katie, Nettie, and Sarah were all born of Assiniboine mothers, and all three were transfers from other government day or boarding schools. Over the course of the next few years these four young women—Josie, Nettie, Sarah, and Katie—would be among Emma's closest friends. Despite their different tribal affiliations, the girls had much in common, not the least of which was their mixed-blood heritage. Emma, officially listed as Chippewa, was the only Metis in the group, but the other four girls all had non-Indian fathers who looked with favor on the educational opportunities offered at Fort Shaw.[20]

Emma's experiences that first year on campus probably mirrored those of other students attending Indian boarding schools in the last years of the nineteenth century, at least the experiences of those students for whom school was refuge rather than prison. The curriculum at Fort Shaw was set by government fiat, with each weekday morning featuring academic work in the classroom and each afternoon given to gender-specific vocational training. Both girls and boys participated in calisthenics during "physical culture" classes, and all students engaged in precision drills, accompanied by the highly acclaimed school band. Pursuing an interest in music first fostered at St. Paul's, Emma joined the mandolin club and resumed her study of piano. An apt and ready student in the classroom, an adept seamstress and cook, and a talented musician, Emma Rose Sansaver would have been a striking example of the effectiveness of the government's Indian education program. Even so, there is little likelihood that her story would be known to us a century later were it not for her prowess at the fledgling game of basketball.[21]

James Naismith's new sport was barely five years old when Emma saw her first scrimmage in the huge dance hall that served as Fort Shaw's gymnasium. Developed to keep the boys at the Springfield, Massachusetts, YMCA active during the long New England winters, basketball had gained instant popularity, spreading to YMCA facilities and then to high school and college campuses across the country. By 1897, this new game had been introduced to Native American students at a remote boarding school in Montana's Sun River Valley. No other high school or college team in the state was playing the game at that time, and yet Fort Shaw's closing exercises that June featured an exhibition game of girls' basketball. Though the school had, early on, fostered competitive athletics for boys, fielding baseball, football, and track teams that engaged in contests with area high schools, the first athletic competition for girls was the intrasquad game of basketball in June 1897.[22]

The school's prior lack of team sports for its female students is hardly surprising, given the fact that the white women these Indian girls were being trained to emulate had, until recently, been forbidden to engage in any physical activities that might appear less than "ladylike." Indeed there had been no team sports for white women until Senda Berenson visited Naismith's gymnasium in Massachusetts and decided his new game would be an excellent addition to the physical culture classes she taught at Smith College. Though other college and high school instructors soon followed her example, competitiveness and physicality were frowned upon, and males were barred from attending practices and games. Despite this accommodation to Victorian sensibilities, many at Smith College remained strongly opposed to the very idea of young women in bloomers running around a field or court in pursuit of a ball.[23]

In contrast, Emma Rose Sansaver and her friends at Fort Shaw would have grown up hearing stories about the fiercely competitive games of lacrosse, shinny, and double ball engaged in by their grandmothers and great-grandmothers before missionaries and Indian agents discouraged such pastimes. From such stories they would also have known that those games had been an integral part of the spiritual as well as the physical development of Plains Indian women. Thus while the rules and regulations of basketball were new to Emma and her friends, the introduction of the game at Fort Shaw sanctioned a return to the kind of competitive play their foremothers had known. But this is a retrospective analysis, hardly the sort of thing the girls themselves would have remarked upon as they learned to shoot, pass, and dribble the heavy leather ball.[24]

Engrossed as she was in her school activities and given the fact that her sister Flora was close at hand, it is doubtful Emma experienced the kind of homesickness that plagued many Indian children sent away to boarding schools far from home and family. She might, at first, have been lonely for the companionship of the Ursuline sisters who had been so central to her life at St. Paul's, but in due time she was to find sisterhood of another sort in the companionship of her friends at Fort Shaw. And though her separation from Isadore would have been difficult, it is unlikely that she or Flora harbored any desire to return to their mother's camp at Fort Assiniboine, for the news from home was increasingly discouraging. Marie Sansaver had become hopelessly addicted to alcohol, and Joseph Rondo was more belligerent and abusive than ever. Indeed, when Isadore had attempted to defend his mother from one of Rondo's beatings, the man had buried a knife in the boy's arm.[25]

Thus as Emma and Flora started home at the close of their first year at Fort Shaw, they did not know what to expect. They spent that summer with their sister Mary in Havre, where they learned that their mother, with Isadore's help, had finally escaped from Rondo. However, she had soon thereafter taken up with a Canadian Cree named Hunting Dog, a fiercely jealous man rumored to be more abusive than Rondo. Then came foreboding news: Marie Sansaver, last seen in the company of her new lover, had simply disappeared. Despite persistent rumors that she had been murdered by Hunting Dog, who allegedly disposed of her body and fled to Canada, local police were reluctant to investigate north of the border. There was no corpse and therefore no proof of a crime. And given Marie's problems with alcohol, perhaps she had simply wandered off and would turn up again in due time.[26]

When his mother's disappearance left him with no further reason to stay at home, Isadore Sansaver, now sixteen, packed up his few belongings and joined his sisters on their return to Fort Shaw. From that point in mid-September of 1898, school records show Mary Sansaver DuBois as the guardian of her younger siblings, and from that point onward Fort Shaw was home as well as haven for Emma, Flora, and Isadore.[27]

Isadore Sansaver's arrival at Fort Shaw coincided with that of the school's newly assigned superintendent, Fred C. Campbell. A native of Kansas, Campbell, a big, broad-shouldered redhead, was thirty-four years old that fall of 1898 when he arrived with his wife and three children to become the superintendent of Fort Shaw. He had begun his career in the Indian Service after graduating from the University of Kansas, where he had been hailed as the best catcher ever to play for the college team. Indeed, Campbell had earned his way through school playing semipro baseball. It was only natural that he would bring a lively interest in athletics to Fort Shaw. As proud as Campbell was of the school's academic standing, he knew from experience the self-esteem that sports could impart to young people. Superintendent Campbell thus set about increasing the opportunities for his students to participate in competitive games. He also increased their exposure to the larger world. Like Dr. Winslow before him, he invited the public to visit the school and see the progress being made there. In the spring of 1901, he managed to entice U.S. Senator Paris Gibson of Great Falls to come inspect the government boarding school that was practically in his own backyard, knowing Gibson's visit would likely bring important publicity and perhaps increased federal monies.[28]

Campbell's instincts were right. In honor of the visit by Senator Gibson, the *Great Falls Daily Tribune* devoted front-page coverage to what its feature editor hailed as "one of the largest and best of the Indian boarding schools." The visitors were impressed with the discipline evident among the ranks of the Fort Shaw students, and it could not have passed their notice that close bonds between classmates seemed to have replaced tribal loyalties. This was no small shift, given that the student population was drawn from at least nine different tribes, some of whom, historically, had been enemies.[29]

The reporter was equally impressed by the academic achievement of Fort Shaw students, declaring that "for the number of hours of study and not [even] taking into consideration the difficulties consequent upon a poor understanding of the English language," the Indian children at Fort Shaw seemed "much further advanced than [the state's] … white children of the same age." This was a striking assertion, given that most Fort Shaw students spent the first two years of their school life "mainly in acquiring the English language" and that only half of each school day was spent in the study of academic subjects. But there was more at work here than academic achievement. Essays on display in the schoolrooms showed the extent to which students had not only mastered the language of their conquerors, but had also begun to internalize the mores of white society. Consider Emma Sansaver's essay titled "Farming."

> When I leave school, I shall be a housekeeper. I will live on a ranch out in the country. I will prepare a garden and plant all kinds of vegetables, grain and any kind of fruit that will grow in this country. In summer I will go out picking berries and make my own jelly and preserves. … I shall have some flower beds and vines running up the porch and windows.

Written in an elegant hand and without a single spelling error, the essay goes on to describe Emma's plans for chickens that will lay "lots of eggs" so she can bake "cake, tarts, pies" and for cows that will provide her with "lots of milk butter cheese and cream." Her closing lines are particularly poignant, given her changing perspectives on the life she had left behind: "Above all I will keep this house looking nice and clean. So when any of my friends come to visit me I will not be ashamed to bring them in."[30]

Friends she had in great numbers, having established herself as a favorite among her classmates and the school staff. Emma also formed a close attachment to the superintendent's family, often looking after the two Campbell boys and their little sister while their mother, Ella, went about her duties as the school's assistant matron and postmistress. Though described as small in stature and "ladylike" in manner, Emma nevertheless exuded energy and enthusiasm that seemed contagious. Beyond that, her quickness and leadership skills soon made her a natural on the basketball court at Fort Shaw—the hard-packed dirt floor of the gymnasium. By 1901 Fred Campbell was promoting the girls' interest in the game, realizing that their skill at this new sport could lead to statewide publicity for Fort Shaw and its mission. Toward that end, he studied the latest rule books and began to spend time with the girls in the gym. Superintendent Campbell became Coach Campbell.[31]

From the simple rules coined in its infancy ten years earlier, the game of basketball had evolved into a rather sophisticated sport. Where once there had been nine, or as many as twenty players on each team, now there were five. The peach basket had become a net strung on an iron hoop, though the net still trapped each ball that entered the basket and had to be released after every score. The height of the basket was set at 10 feet, the size of the ball at 32 inches in circumference, and the size of the court at 50 by 94 feet. Two points were earned for every basket made from the field, one point for every successful foul shot. Scores were low by today's standards—13 to 11 or 9 to 6, for example. This was in large measure because of the running clock, which counted off the 20-minute halves with no pause, not even for an errant ball to be retrieved from out of bounds or for the ball to be released from the basket after a score and returned to center court for the mandatory "jump ball".[32]

Coach Campbell soon had the Fort Shaw girls working seriously on their game, running up and down the dirt court, practicing the dribble, the pass, the field throw, and the free throw. Teamwork was the essence of the game to Campbell, and he drilled that concept into the girls, their tribal differences notwithstanding. The team he assembled in the fall of 1902 included Minnie Burton, Lemhi Shoshone; Nettie Wirth and Genie Butch, Assiniboine; Delia Geboe, Spokane; Belle Johnson and Josie Langley, Piegan; and Emma Sansaver, Chippewa-Cree. The girls ranged in age from fifteen to twenty-four. Josie was the oldest, Genie the youngest, Minnie the tallest, and Emma the shortest. Different as their backgrounds, attributes, and personalities were, the girls were proud of the spirit that brought them together. They also were proud of their uniforms, middies and bloomers of navy blue wool serge with collars and cuffs piped in white. These uniforms were modeled on those worn by other female basketball players of the day and fashioned by the girls themselves in the sewing room at the school. Their gym shoes were made in the campus cobbler shop by boys being trained in the shoemaker's craft.[33]

In the course of their practices under Coach Campbell, the girls adapted to each other's strengths. Josie captained the team and played center. Belle and Emma played the forward positions, designated in those early years as right forward and left forward. Minnie played left guard, Nettie right guard. In time, those positions would shift as the girls' abilities became more apparent and better developed. But Emma, despite being the shortest, was the quickest of hand and foot, and Campbell kept his sparkplug at forward, though in today's game her leadership and ball-handling abilities would put her at point guard. Genie Butch and Delia Geboe, the youngest girls, were the alternates.[34]

As their talents developed, Campbell looked around for an opportunity to schedule some competition so he could see if the Fort Shaw girls were truly as good as he thought they were. By late fall of 1902, the high schools in Butte and Helena were fielding girls' basketball teams. Campbell contacted the coaches and arranged for a pair of games. In late November of 1902, the girls rode the train to Butte, where they defeated the home team 15 to 9. Early the next morning they boarded the train again, this time bound for Helena. There, despite "superb passing on the part of the forwards from the Indian school," they lost by a score of 13 to 6. Somewhat chagrined, they returned home to make adjustments in the lineup. Minnie Burton and Belle Johnson exchanged positions at forward and guard. And Nettie Wirth, whose prodigious leaping ability had become apparent that season, took over the center position while Josie Langley moved to right guard.[35]

Now Campbell set about making arrangements for what was to be "the first basketball game ever played in Great Falls," matching the girls from Butte Parochial against the girls from Fort Shaw. On Thursday evening, January 15, 1903, Luther Hall was "crowded to its limit with spectators." The hometown crowd had little knowledge of the game of basketball, but there was no question as to their enthusiasm for the new sport, even though the Fort Shaw team lost by a score of 15 to 6. It was the last loss this team would ever suffer.[36]

Two weeks later, "numbers of persons who desired admission to the hall" to see Fort Shaw play the team from Montana State University in Missoula had to be "sent away, it being impossible to accommodate them." In a journalistic turning point, "the Indian girls" began to be seen as individuals. Newspapers began to print the team's photo, reporters began to cite the players by name and tribal affiliation, and columnists mentioned the Fort Shaw girls' achievements beyond the basketball court. Emma Sansaver, described in the *Great Falls Tribune* as "the little one," was said to be "just as quick about her school room and detail work as she is in getting after the ball." The journalistic prejudice against Native people that abounded during that era in Montana melted before the skills and charms of the girls from Fort Shaw. Though reporters continued to use stereotyped phrases such as "dusky maidens" or "on the warpath" in their articles, their growing respect and admiration for the Fort Shaw team was obvious—and with good reason. In a few short months the mesmerizing play of this Indian basketball team had transformed an activity once seen as mere exercise for high school and college women into a standing-room-only spectator sport.[37]

During the rest of that 1902–1903 season, the girls played and won at least six more games. Twice they humbled the "Farmerettes" from Montana Agricultural College in Bozeman, where well over eight hundred people, "probably the largest crowd that ever attended a college game," squeezed into a downtown hall for their first glimpse of "the Indian girls." Perhaps the team's sweetest victories that season were gained over the girls of Helena High and Butte Parochial, victories that avenged their earlier defeats. Having run up a record of nine wins and two losses, the Fort Shaw team concluded its first year of interscholastic basketball as the sport's undisputed, if unofficial, state champions. In the process they became the acknowledged favorites of fans across Montana. In effect, they became "Montana's team."[38]

Moreover, the young women from Fort Shaw earned an entree into social as well as athletic circles in the non-Indian world. When the team traveled to Bozeman to play the Farmerettes in late March 1903, the girls were special guests at a schoolwide assembly followed by a luncheon where "each Indian was seated beside the white girl who was to be her opponent [that] evening." And during a postgame dance held that night, the victorious "dusky bell[e]s had no cause to complain of a lack of partners among the college boys."[39]

From the standpoint of Superintendent Campbell and his colleagues, the fact that the girls on the Fort Shaw team could move gracefully in the white world provided ample evidence that Fort Shaw was meeting or even exceeding the goals of the government's Indian education system. Other educators in that system took notice. In March of 1903 Campbell received an invitation from S. M. McCowan, superintendent of Oklahoma's Chilocco Indian School. McCowan was the newly appointed director of the Model Indian School that would be constructed in St. Louis for the great Louisiana Purchase Exposition, the World's Fair of 1904. The Model Indian School was to house 150 students selected from among the Indian boarding schools located within the boundaries of the original Louisiana Purchase territory. McCowan wanted Campbell to send a cadre of Fort Shaw's best students to reside at the Model Indian

School from opening day on April 30 through closing ceremonies on December 1, 1904.[40]

Choosing those students was a relatively simple matter, for Superintendent Campbell immediately turned to the girls on the basketball team. If they met all their classroom and workroom requirements, he told them, and if they played as well in the upcoming season as they had in the season just concluded, then they could represent Fort Shaw at the St. Louis Exposition the next year. Emma and her teammates responded with "the greatest enthusiasm, unanimously determined to make themselves worthy of the honor." With this new goal in mind, Coach Campbell expanded the roster to ten players so that when there was no competition to take the floor against them, a situation that was to become increasingly common, Fort Shaw could field two teams and engage in scrimmages against each other.[41]

The front line of the first team, the Blues, remained in place: Nettie at center, Emma and Minnie at the forward positions. The back court, however, underwent a major change. Josephine Langley was engaged to be married and left the team. Genie Butch, the substitute who had seen the most playing time in the recently concluded season, took Josie's place at right guard. Belle Johnson, who remained the starting left guard for the Blue team, took Josie's place as captain. The newly formed Red team would be made up of new recruits, anchored by Delia Gebeau, the other substitute from the 1902–1903 season.[42]

So it was that these veterans welcomed their new teammates that spring as they began preparing for the adventure to come. The recruits were, of course, already their classmates and friends. Indeed they had likely participated in earlier team practices. Fifteen-year-old Genevieve Healy, a Gros Ventre, and seventeen-year-old Katie Snell, an Assiniboine, both from Fort Belknap Reservation, took over the two guard positions. Fifteen-year-old Sarah Mitchell, an Assiniboine from Fort Peck Reservation, and Flora Lucero, a Chippewa-Cree from Choteau, Montana, joined Gebeau in rounding out the Red team.[43]

With schoolwork done for the year, the girls, now ten strong, traveled to Havre in mid-June of 1903 for an exhibition game played before "a large audience, many of whom had never seen a basketball game" and most of whom "[had never] seen the Indian girls [who] exemplify the sport." Though the citizens of Havre might never have seen the Fort Shaw girls in action, one of those girls, Emma Rose Sansaver, had certainly seen the town of Havre. With the exception of the four school terms she had spent at St. Paul's, Emma had lived most of her first thirteen years in the Metis camp south of town. Even after her mother's disappearance, she had spent many of her Fort Shaw summers in the Havre home of her married sister, Mary Sansaver DuBois. Surely Emma's thoughts were on her mother that evening as she played for the first time before the hometown crowd. Though Marie Sansaver had, in a sense, disappeared from her children's lives some years before she had been murdered, the finality of her absence must have been heavy that evening, given Emma's knowledge that her uncle had come from Canada to search for her mother's body.

Fortunately Emma was back at Fort Shaw when Sunday's edition of the *Havre Plaindealer* carried a front-page article describing new leads in the disappearance of Marie Sansaver. According to the missing woman's brother, her murderer had thrown her body into the well behind Devlin's slaughterhouse. On the basis of that report, the sheriff was planning to excavate the abandoned well in hopes of turning up the dead woman, "the mother of Miss Sansseuver," a member of the team that had played in Havre the Wednesday evening before.[44]

Spared this public blow to her pride, "Miss Sansseuver" coped by getting on with her life at Fort Shaw. Reluctant to return to the town still caught up in the tawdry details of her mother's death, Emma spent the summer of 1903 in the Campbell household, taking care of the three youngsters, keeping house for Ella Campbell, and practicing her field throws as she waited for the return of her friends in the fall. Reunited on September 1 with Nettie, Minnie, and her other teammates, Emma joined them in working as diligently in the classroom as on the gym floor, determined to meet Superintendent Campbell's requirements for the team's participation in the World's Fair.[45]

When the basketball season opened that winter, Campbell could find few opponents willing to play against the Fort Shaw girls. In the words of one reporter, there was "no girls' team in the state that [could] give them ... a tussel [*sic*]. They stand alone and unrivaled." Thus Campbell was reduced to scheduling a series of exhibition games around Montana that allowed fans to see the Fort Shaw girls play each other. These games also gave his second team, the Reds, a chance to gain experience before large crowds. Through February and March of 1904 the girls not only impressed sellout crowds with their athletic skills, they also entertained them with a postgame program that included exercises with Indian clubs, a mandolin concert, and a literary recitation performed in native dress. This program was a preview of the entertainments the girls were to provide for visitors at the St. Louis fairgrounds. Though they had been selected to go to the World's Fair on the basis of their basketball prowess, they had also been scheduled to present weekly literary programs, musical concerts, and gymnastics demonstrations. Each of their Montana appearances that spring was billed in the local press as the "last chance to see the Fort Shaw girls in action before they leave for the World's Fair."[46]

While the Louisiana Purchase Exposition officially opened on April 30, 1904, the Model Indian School did not open until June 1. And it opened without the delegation from Fort Shaw, for school commitments kept the girls in Montana until the end of May. Finally, on the first day of June, Emma, her teammates, and their faculty chaperones were given a festive send-off. As their Northern Pacific coach car rolled across eastern Montana, North Dakota, and Minnesota, the girls played whistle-stop exhibition and challenge games in various towns along the way, earning money to help with trip expenses and honing their performance for the big stage that awaited them.[47]

By the time the train pulled into Union Station at St. Louis two weeks later, the girls' exhilaration had reached a fever pitch. For the next five months their enthusiasm did not slacken. When the girls were not playing exhibition games on the plaza in front of the Model Indian School or giving weekly mandolin concerts and literary recitations, they were engrossed in the daily schedule required of all students at the school. In their time off, they enjoyed taking in the marvels offered by the fair, including all the curiosities of the fabled midway called the Pike.[48]

Emma and her friends were well aware, of course, that as residents at the Model Indian School, they were themselves "curiosities" on exhibit. For in celebrating the centennial of the Louisiana Purchase, the exposition focused on displaying the marvelous advances made in the century since Jefferson signed the treaty with France that doubled the size of the United States. Advances in technology, science, agriculture, and the arts were on display, and in line with the forward "march of mankind" theme there were also "living exhibits" of the country's indigenous peoples. At the Native encampments on "Indian Hill," members of several western tribes carried out their daily activities under the gaze of fairgoers. Within the Model Indian School itself, "blanket Indians" demonstrated their "primitive" crafts across the corridor from students who demonstrated modern homemaking, woodworking, and blacksmithing. It could hardly have escaped Emma Sansaver's attention, or that of her teammates, that these juxtapositions, plus the daily demonstrations of academic, athletic, artistic, and industrial accomplishments of the school's 150 students, were intended to prove the success of the government's Indian education program.[49]

Ironic as they knew their position to be, Emma and her friends had worked long and hard to earn their right to be a part of the Model Indian School program, and they made the most of their World's Fair experience.

Fig. 7.2 Emma Sansaver, front row, left, pictured with her Fort Shaw teammates in traditional dress. Standing, left to right: Nettie Wirth, Genevieve Healy, Josephine Langley, Belle Johnson, Minnie Burton, and Sarah Mitchell. Kneeling with Emma are team mascot, Gertrude LaRance, and player Rose LaRose. Courtesy, Barbara Winters.

They reveled in the heady atmosphere of the World's Fair even as they fulfilled their part of the bargain. They were there to demonstrate their aptitude at the game of basketball and that they did, playing twice a week in the mid-afternoon heat and humidity of a St. Louis summer in their wool bloomers and middies. Often these exhibition games were played on the plaza in front of the Model Indian School, though the girls sometimes left the fairgrounds to accept challenges from teams in nearby Missouri and Illinois towns. Then, as fall approached, having beaten every team they had played, the Fort Shaw girls agreed to a best-two-out-of-three series against an all-star team made up of young women from St. Louis Central High, the perennial basketball champions of Missouri and Illinois. Local papers as well as papers back home in Montana reported the games in detail, for the idea of a World's Fair championship had captured the imagination of all who followed the achievements of the girls from St. Louis and the team from Fort Shaw.[50]

With press coverage generating widespread interest, a large crowd gathered at St. Louis's Kulage Park on Saturday afternoon, September 3, 1904, to watch a battle of the titans. Though Emma Sansaver played that first game on a sprained ankle, she "nonplussed her opponents … by dodging here and there with the rapidity of a streak of lightning." Her teammates were no less brilliant, and the Fort Shaw girls won the game, 24 to 2. Their second match with the St. Louis Central High All-Stars, played on the plaza in front of the Model Indian School a month later, was so widely anticipated that the Jefferson Guard, the fair's security police, had to be called out for crowd control. Again, the Fort Shaw girls were unstoppable, and again the All-Stars went down in defeat, this time by a score of 17 to 6. Newspapers and officials declared the girls from Fort Shaw the official basketball champions of the St. Louis World's Fair. The papers back home took their triumph to another level, declaring the Fort Shaw team "the undisputed … world's champions" at the game of basketball.[51]

With the coming of fall there was a certain melancholy in the air. It was apparent that the exposition was drawing to a close. Anticipating the day she must say goodbye to her friends at the Model Indian School, Emma Rose Sansaver passed around an autograph book that was soon filled with nostalgic passages promising to treasure forever the times shared that summer. "Remember the fun we used to have in St. Louis," urged Lucy. "Dear Friend Emma," wrote Simon, a member of the Indian School Band, "only remember. …" And on the evening the "band boys went away," Etta admonished, "It is sad but cheer up little girl."[52]

Welcomed home in mid-November by jubilant Fort Shaw classmates, Emma and her teammates settled back into campus routine. They had rich memories of their time in St. Louis, and the promise of still more challenges. In 1905 Emma was elected captain of the team that played yet another series of exhibition and challenge games, this time on their way to the Lewis and Clark Exposition in Portland. Though the girls had hoped to take on all comers there, as they had in St. Louis, their reputation preceded them and the competition was thin. In fact, they picked up only one contest in all of Oregon, a game against Chemawa Indian School outside Salem. That match ended as had all the others, in a clear victory for the girls from Fort Shaw.[53]

The world champions played as a unit only one more year, going undefeated through the 1906 season. By 1907, among the girls who had gone to St. Louis only Emma Sansaver, Katie Snell, and Genevieve Healy were still playing basketball for Fort Shaw. The others had, one by one, left school to begin their adult lives. Even Emma's younger sister Flora was no longer on campus, having married a Canadian citizen in 1906 and settled in Medicine Hat, Alberta. Isadore also left the school, marrying a Fort Shaw classmate and taking a job as a conductor for the Great Northern Railway.[54]

With the end of the 1907 season, it seemed time for Emma to move on too. She had long since satisfied the requirements for her diploma, and no matter how reluctant she was to leave Fort Shaw, there was really no further reason for her to stay. Influenced perhaps by her sister Mary DuBois, Emma answered an ad for a housekeeping position posted by a rancher who lived roughly forty miles north of Havre. A native of Ontario, Canada, Ernest Simpson had immigrated to Montana with his brother Barney in 1892, and the two had done well raising sheep on the open range between the Milk River and the Canadian border. In 1898, with much of that range now open to permanent settlement, Ernie had taken American citizenship and filed a homestead claim at Oldham, a settlement just south of the 49th parallel. It was there at Oldham that Emma took up housekeeping duties for Ernie Simpson. Six months later she accepted her employer's proposal of marriage. On January 8, 1908, in a Catholic service in Helena, Montana, twenty-three-year-old Emma Sansaver married thirty-two-year-old Ernest Simpson. Long accustomed to moving between the Indian and the white worlds, Emma made a telling concession—or choice—as she began her new life, indicating on her marriage license that she, like her husband, was white.[55]

Not long after their marriage, Emma and Ernie filed on a larger homestead at Spring Coulee, between Oldham and present-day Simpson, a settlement named for Ernie and his brother Barney. On the new claim, the Simpsons built a one-room log cabin, 12 by 24 feet. In October of 1908, Emma delivered her first child, a son named for his father. Over the next three years, two more boys were born. These were prosperous years for the Simpsons, and as their family grew they enlarged and improved their home. In March of 1914, they welcomed their first baby girl. Knowing how eagerly Emma had looked forward to the arrival of a daughter, and how much she had missed having access to a piano, Ernie surprised her by ordering a solid mahogany upright grand, a Beckwith, the best the Sears catalog had to offer.[56]

By 1918, the care of two more little boys added to Emma's daily routine, yet she did not neglect her muses. She seized what free moments she had to fill the house with music and to write and illustrate poetry. Then, during the dry autumn of 1919, the log home in which she had taken such pride burned to the ground. The loss was major, but as Emma set up housekeeping in a small bunkhouse saved from the flames, she felt blessed that all her children and her prized piano had been saved. Saved from the flames as well was a box of memorabilia from her days at Fort Shaw and her summer at the St. Louis World's Fair.[57]

As the family continued to grow, a second little girl, named Ella Campbell Simpson for the wife of Fort Shaw's superintendent, and a sixth boy were born in the bunkhouse home. But hard times followed prosperous ones. In the face of drought and increasing debts, Ernie Simpson lost the homestead and moved the family to a ranch near Monarch in the mountains southeast of Great Falls. Then, in 1922, he gave up ranching altogether and moved his family into Great Falls, where he took a job with the Great Northern Railway.[58]

In October of 1924, Emma birthed a third daughter, Kathleen, her ninth and last child. When that infant was just over three months old, Emma underwent emergency surgery to staunch hemorrhaging from a gastric ulcer. Three days after that operation, on February 5, 1925, Emma Rose Sansaver Simpson died of "streptococcic septicaemia." The death certificate listed her as "about 39" and "Indian." Two days later, with her husband and nine children at her graveside, Emma was buried in Calvary Cemetery in Great Falls. After the burial, Emma's sister, Mary Sansaver DuBois, took baby Kathleen to Havre to raise as her own. Soon thereafter, Ernie's sister, May Simpson Wellacher, came from San Francisco to take the two older girls, ages eleven and five, home with her. The six Simpson boys, ranging in age from three to sixteen, remained in Great Falls with their father.[59]

Over the years, Ernie kept the story of Emma's days at Fort Shaw alive for his children, taking them several times to the State Historical Society in Helena to see the trophy that the team brought home from St. Louis. And though Emma Sansaver Simpson's untimely death meant that her children were left with only fragments of the story surrounding her experience as a member of a world championship basketball team, they knew enough of it to cherish that part of their legacy even as they, like their mother, moved between two worlds. Traces of Emma's own vacillations concerning her cultural identity can be seen in the diverse views of her many descendants: There are those who have thought of themselves as white and those who have claimed their Indian heritage. Their differences aside, all of Emma's descendants have embraced as their own "the little one," whose achievements on the court and off continue to intrigue and inspire them.[60]

But the impact of Emma Sansaver's life extends far beyond her direct descendants. Indeed, her story has influenced a far wider circle of Native Americans, most notably the young athletes, male and female, for whom basketball today is a passion. It is easy to connect turn-of-the-century media coverage of the Fort Shaw team to interest generated by the modern version of this sport across the state of Montana, particularly within the Indian community. The exhilarating game introduced to Montanans by the girls who wore the Fort Shaw uniform has evolved today into the phenomenon known as *Indian ball.* And Emma Sansaver embodied the skills and competitiveness that have come to be associated with that brand of basketball.[61]

Emma embraced the success she achieved through basketball, both as an individual and as a member of a team. Why would she not? Basketball took her from the narrow confines of an Indian boarding school in rural Montana to exposure to the larger world within the state and in the end, to the wonders of a world's fair where, she was both an object on display and a full participant in a grand adventure. In the course of this journey Emma both reshaped expectations and broadened opportunities for her gender and her race. Through her talents on court, she moved into an emerging world of women's athletics. Those same talents gave her an entree to other worlds traditionally closed to women of color.

Emma Sansaver would never again enjoy the fame that had been hers as she played before capacity crowds throughout the state of Montana and on the grounds of the St. Louis World's Fair. Yet a photograph taken on the Simpson ranch in northern Montana, suggests the extent to which her experiences on the basketball court shaped her identity. That photo shows Emma, five years out of school and already a wife and mother, sitting confidently astride a chestnut mare. Her face framed by a cowboy hat, she is wearing dark bloomers and a middy blouse whose collar bears the "F" and "S" of Fort Shaw.

NOTES

1. The uncle who rode into Havre was the older sister of Marie LaFromboise. (*Havre (MT) Plaindealer*, June 13, 1903; Fort Benton (MT) *River Press*, June 17, 1903.) Though direct descendants have standardized the spelling of "Sansaver," Emma's surname alternately appears in surviving records as "St. Sauveur," "St. Sevier," "Sansavior," and "Sansavere."

2. For an overview of the experiences of the Fort Shaw team as a whole, see the authors' "World Champions: The 1904 Girls' Basketball Team from Fort Shaw Indian Boarding School," *Montana The Magazine of Western History* (winter 2001): 2–25. See also their forthcoming book on the Fort Shaw team.

3. Barbara Winters, Emma Sansaver's granddaughter, telephone interview with Linda Peavy, February 22, 2003. School records consistently give Emma Sansaver's birth year as 1884, a date supported by her marriage certificate, which lists her as twenty-three years old as of January 8, 1908, but contradicted by her death certificate, which lists her as "about 39" as of February 5, 1925, and by the 1886 birth date carved on her tombstone. (*Register of Pupils, 1892–1901*, vol. 1, Record of Fort Shaw Indian School, Field Office Records of Non-Reservation Schools, entry 1358, PI-163, Records of the Office of Indian Affairs, Record Group 75, National Archives and Records Service, Region 8, Denver [hereafter RG 75, NAD]; copies of Emma Sansaver Simpson's marriage and death certificates are attached to the Family Group Record derived and held by Barbara Winters; Calvary Cemetery, Great Falls, Montana.) The 1886 date was likely derived from the August 15, 1886, birth date given for Emma in a handwritten, unattributed, undated partial genealogy of the Sansaver-Simpson family signed by Emma's husband, Ernest Simpson, and completed sometime after her death in 1925. (Sansaver-Simpson genealogy provided by Barbara Winters.)

4. The Office of Indian Affairs (OIA) became the Bureau of Indian Affairs sometime after 1905. For more on Native Americans and the 49th parallel, see Beth LaDow's comprehensive study, *The Medicine Line* (New York: Routledge, 2001).

5. Further details concerning Emma Sansaver's Metis heritage are available in Barbara Winters' Family Group Record; the Sansaver-Simpson genealogy; Sansaver genealogical papers provided by Donna Sansaver Wimmer, Emma's second cousin. Ogden Tanner, *The Canadians* (Alexandria, VA: Time-Life Books, 1977), 133; Verne Dusenberry, "Waiting for a Day That Never Comes," *Montana The Magazine of Western History* (spring 1958): 37–38.

6. Family Group Record; Wimmer's Sansaver Genealogical Papers; letter from Lillian DuBois Baker, Emma Sansaver's niece, to Betty Simpson Bisnett, Emma's daughter, January 11, 1974, in the possession of Barbara Winters; *Grit, Guts, and Gusto: A History of Hill County* (Havre, MT: Hill County Bicentennial Commission, 1976), 35. For more on the Blackfeet Reserve, designated in the Fort Laramie Treaty of 1851, see Joel Barker's "Preliminary Inventory of the Records of the Blackfeet Agency, Bureau of Indian Affairs, Record Group 75," RG 75, NAD.

7. Baker's letter to Bisnett mentions another son, William, who "died young." (Baker to Bisnett, January 11, 1974). Mary Sansaver DuBois obituary, *Havre Daily News*, February 19, 1935; Fred C. Campbell letter to the commissioner of Indian Affairs [hereafter CIA], October 24, 1901, Records of the Bureau of Indian Affairs, Letters Received, 1901, entry 61154, Record Group 75, National Archives Washington, DC [hereafter RG 75, NAW].

8. Strategically sited to keep Sitting Bull and his Lakota Sioux, who had fled to the Cypress Hills of Canada after the battle of the Little Bighorn, from entertaining thoughts of moving south of the Medicine Line, Fort Assiniboine was located on Beaver Creek, a mountain stream flowing from headwaters in the Bears Paw range to a confluence with the Milk River some five miles north of the fort. After 1884, Fort Assiniboine was

spelled with a double "n," as opposed to the spelling of the name given the Assiniboine tribe. Ultimately a million-dollar installation, Fort Assiniboine boasted over one hundred buildings by the turn of the twentieth century. *Grit, Guts, and Gusto*, 21–24; Michael Malone, Richard Roeder, and William Lang, eds., *Montana: A History of Two Centuries*, rev. ed. (Seattle: University of Washington Press, 1991), 138–39, 141.

9. Family Group Record; Baker to Bisnett, January 11, 1974; *Register of Pupils*, RG 75, NAD; Malone, Roeder, and Lang, *Montana*, 143; Barker's "Preliminary Inventory," 2.

10. Notice of the death of "Edwin St. Sevier, a halfbreed native of Winnipeg, Canada," appeared in the June 19, 1890, edition of the *Chinook (MT) Opinion*, a paper that rarely provided obituaries for nonwhites. Family Group Record; Baker to Bisnett, January 11, 1974; Campbell to CIA, October 24, 1901. St. Paul's Mission was established by Frederick Eberschweiler, S.J., around 1887, just prior to the establishment of the Fort Belknap Reservation in 1888. Genevieve McBride, O.S.U., *The Bird Tail* (New York: Vantage Press, 1974), 76–77.

11. For a better understanding of the government's goals for Indian education and of the impact boarding school education had on the lives of Native American students, see, among others, David Wallace Adams, *Education for Extinction: American Indians and the Boarding School Experience, 1875–1928* (Lawrence: University Press of Kansas, 1995); K. Tsianina Lomawaima, *They Called It Prairie Light: The Story of Chilocco Indian School* (Lincoln: University of Nebraska Press, 1994); Brenda Child, *Boarding School Seasons: American Families, 1900–1940* (Lincoln: University of Nebraska Press, 1995); and Margaret Archuleta, Brenda Child, and Tsianina Lomawaima, eds., *Away from Home: American Indian Boarding School Experiences, 1879–2000* (Phoenix, AZ: Heard Museum, 2000).

12. Afternoon duties for Emma's brother, Isadore, and the other boys at St. Paul's centered on farming and ranching activities similar to those they would presumably pursue upon completion of their schooling. McBride, *Bird Tail*, 161–62.

13. Family Record Group; *Grit, Guts, and Gusto*, 277; Campbell to CIA, October 24, 1901. Fort Shaw was located twenty-five miles west of Great Falls.

14. John Greer, "A Brief History of Indian Education at Fort Shaw Industrial School" (master's thesis, Montana State University, 1958), 1; John Bye, "'Shoot, Minnie, Shoot': Lusty Cry of the Unbeaten Indian Girls," *Montana Post* (Montana Historical Society newsletter), August 1965, 1–2.

15. Adams, *Education for Extinction*, 54–55.

16. Greer, "Brief History," 1; Bye, "'Shoot, Minnie, Shoot,'" 3–4; Don Miller and Stan Cohen, *Military and Trading Posts of Montana* (Missoula, MT: Pictorial Histories Publishing, 1978), 76–79; Dorothy Baldwin, "History of Fort Shaw," 5, Fort Shaw Vertical File, Montana Historical Society Library, Helena; *Great Falls (MT) Tribune*, July 11, 1999.

17. Baldwin, "History of Fort Shaw," 7–8; Report of the Secretary of the Interior, *Indian Affairs*, vol. II, 1892 (Washington, DC: Government Printing Office, 1893), 36.

18. Campbell to CIA, October 24, 1901; Baker to Bisnett, January 11, 1974.

19. Miller and Cohen, *Military and Trading Posts*, 77; *Great Falls (MT) Tribune*, July 11, 1999.

20. William Winslow to CIA, no date, 1896, RG 75, NAW, Letters Received, 1896, entry 31783; Catherine Snell Wiegand, application for enrollment on the Fort Belknap Reservation, 1921, copy in possession of Thelma Warren James, Weigand's granddaughter; Bill Thomas, "Early Life and Times of the Montana Smith Family: A Biography of Tom Smith," 1995, manuscript copy in possession of the authors, 74; Sarah Mitchell Courchene obituary, *Wolf Point Herald*, February 1933. Josephine Langley's father had been a soldier stationed at Fort Shaw. (Joseph Tatsey genealogy in Blackfeet records, Browning, Montana). Nettie Wirth's father was a German immigrant who had come west as a soldier in the U.S. Army in 1866. (Smith, "Early Life and Times," 27) And

Sarah Mitchell's father was David Mitchell, a son of the Indian fighter who had brought most of the Plains tribes together to sign the Fort Laramie Treaty of 1851. (Dorothy Courchene Smith, Sarah Mitchell Courchene's daughter, letter to authors, June 8, 2000).

21. Fort Shaw had its share of homesickness and runaways. See Peavy and Smith, "World Champions," 7–8, and *Discharged from School,* Record of Fort Shaw Indian School, RG 75, NAD; Greer, "History of Fort Shaw," 46.

22. James Naismith, "Basket Ball," (YMCA) *Triangle* (January 1892): 145–46; Joanne Lannin, *A History of Basketball for Girls and Women: From Bloomers to Big Leagues* (Minneapolis, MN: Lerner Sports, 2000), 10; Betty Spears, "Senda Berenson Abbott: New Woman, New Sport," in *A Century of Women's Basketball: From Frailty to Final Four,* ed. Joan Hult and Marianna Trekell (Reston, VA: National Association for Girls and Women in Sport, 1991), 24; *Great Falls (MT) Leader,* June 12, 1897. College basketball came to Montana in 1898 when the women of Montana Agricultural College (today, Montana State University) in Bozeman began practicing the game twice a week in the drill hall on campus and "urg[ed] the men to form a team too." (*The Exponent,* campus newspaper, November 1898);*Rising Sun* (Sun River Valley weekly), June 26, 1895. For an excellent overview of athletics at government Indian boarding schools, see John Bloom, *To Show What an Indian Can Do: Sports at Native American Boarding Schools* (Minneapolis: University of Minnesota Press, 2000).

23. Spears, "Senda Berenson Abbott," 24–25.

24. Stewart Culin, "Games of North American Indians," in *Twenty-Fourth Annual Report of the Bureau of American Ethnology* (Washington, DC, 1907), 647–Traditional Indian sports have enjoyed a revival in modern tribal games staged across the West.

25. Campbell to CIA, October 24, 1901.

26. Ibid.; *Havre (MT) Plaindealer,* June 13, 1903; Fort Benton (MT) *River Press,* June 17, 1903.

27. Campbell to CIA, October 24, 1901; *Register,* Fort Shaw School, RG 75, NAD. Though Emma's paternal grandparents were living in Sweet Grass County in south-central Montana, they were evidently never a presence in her life, nor in the lives of Isadore and Flora. Wimmer genealogical records.

28. Fred DesRosier, Campbell's grandson, to authors, February 5, 2000; LaRue Smith, "Campbell Mountain in Glacier National Park: The Story of a Sigma Nu and His Huge Namesake," *The Delta,* March 1943, 164; *Great Falls (MT) Daily Tribune,* May 26, 1901.

29. *Great Falls (MT) Daily Tribune,* May 26, 1901. The 1901 "statistical report" filed by Fort Shaw listed ninety children from the various Sioux tribes, sixty-two Piegans [Blackfeet], twenty-one Assiniboines, eighty Chippewa, nine Shoshone, five Bannock, seventeen Cheyenne, twenty-one Flathead, and eleven Gros Ventre, five Crow, one Pend O'Reille, one Snake, three Colville, one Cree, and five Nez Perce. *Fort Shaw Statistical Report,* June 1, 1901, RG 75, NAW.

30. *Great Falls (MT) Daily Tribune,* May 26, 1901; Emma Sansaver, "Farming," classroom essay, ca. 1900, provided by Barbara Winters. Though Fort Shaw offered no classes above the eighth-grade level and officially limited its enrollment to students aged five to eighteen, many students, including Emma Sansaver, stayed on beyond the official age. (Greer, "Short History," 56.) The Great Falls reporter's assertion deserves a closer look. Considering the catch-as-catch-can educational opportunities available to non-Indian students living on isolated ranches across the state, and given the relative lack of motivation among students whose parents considered labor at home more essential to the family's survival than studies in school, students in Montana's public schools might well have been lagging behind those attending Fort Shaw. In addition, the discipline and structure of nine full months of compulsory education at Fort Shaw, coupled with the staff's constant reminders that success in school would open doors in the world beyond, might well have tipped the balance in favor of the Indian school.

31. Transcript of Barbara Winters' interview of Gertrude LaRance Parker, November 1994; Barbara Winters to authors, January 3, 2000;*Official Register of the United States, Containing a List of Officers and Employees in the Civil, Military, and Naval Service*, 1899. Campbell would have had access to such publications as the *Spalding Official Basketball Guide, 1901–1902* (New York, 1901).

32. Dave Anderson, *The Story of Basketball* (New York: William Morrow, 1988), 9; Zander Hollander, ed., *The Modern Encyclopedia of Basketball* (New York: Four Winds Press, 1969), 3–5; *New York Times*, October 10, 1900; Naismith, "Basket Ball."

33. "Three Survivors in This Area of Famous Indian Girls' Team," undated *Phillips County (MT) News* clipping in family scrapbook in the possession of Donita Nordlund, granddaughter of Genevieve Healy Adams. For more details concerning the backgrounds and achievements of the new team members, see Peavy and Smith's "World Champions," 15. Information concerning the anonymous student who made the girls' basketball shoes was relayed to Linda Peavy on October 18, 1998, by his daughter-in-law.

34. The relative sizes of the girls and their assigned positions have been established through news accounts of the early games and descendants' memories of the heights of their mothers and grandmothers. See, for instance, *Great Falls (MT) Daily Tribune*, January 30, 1903; "Indian Girls Win Out," undated news clipping in Nettie Wirth Mail's scrapbook in the possession of Terry Bender, Mail's great-niece; "Fort Shaw Wins Again," undated [circa late March 1903] news clipping in Mail's scrapbook; and *Bozeman (MT) Avant Courier*, April 3, 1903.

35. *Butte (MT) Inter Mountain*, November 28, 1902; *Helena Daily Record*, November 29, 1902.

36. *Great Falls Weekly Tribune*, January 22, 1903. The team that played under the colors of "Butte Parochial" was likely a group of girls enrolled in the city's St. Patrick's High School.

37. "Indian Girls Win Out," undated news clipping in Mail's scrapbook; *Great Falls (MT) Daily Tribune*, January 30, 1903. See also *Missoula (MT) Missoulian*, January 31, 1903.

38. "Fort Shaw Wins Again," undated news clipping in Mail's scrapbook; *Bozeman (MT) Avant Courier*, April 3, 1903; *Exponent*, April 1903; *Kaimin*, college paper of Montana State University in Missoula, April 1903.

39. *Exponent*, April 1903.

40. *Anaconda (MT) Standard*, March 25, 1904.

41. Ibid.; *Helena (MT) Daily Record*, February 29, 1904.

42. Non-Reservation Schools, Field Office Records, *Roster of Employees, 1892–1901*, Fiscal Year 1903, vol. 1, OIA, RG 75, NAD.

43. Lineups have been extrapolated from news reports of the exhibition games played through the spring of 1904 and from newspaper accounts listing the ten girls who made the trip to St. Louis.

44. *Havre (MT) Plaindealer*, June 13, 1903; Fort Benton (MT) *River Press*, June 17, 1903.

45. Barbara Winters to authors, January 3, 2000.

46. *Anaconda (MT) Standard*, March 20 and 25, 1904; *Great Falls (MT) Daily Tribune*, May 31, 1904; *Helena (MT) Daily Record*, May 6, 1904.

47. *Great Falls (MT) Daily Leader*, June 2, 1904; *Great Falls (MT) Daily Tribune*, June 11, 1904; *Mandan Pioneer*, June 10, 1904.

48. *St. Louis Republic*, June 15, 1904; *Great Falls (MT) Daily Tribune*, June 21, 1904; W. J. McGee, "Universal Exposition of 1904, Division of Exhibits: Report of the Anthropological Department," Box 30, Missouri Historical Society, St. Louis.

49. *Daily Reports of the Department of Anthropology* (St. Louis, 1904), 33; "Indian Exhibits at the St. Louis Exhibition," in *Department of Interior Report to Congress, Part I* (Washington, DC: Government Printing Office, 1905) 51–56. The Fort Shaw team's experiences at the World's Fair of 1904 provide a particularly vivid example of the ways

in which Indian students like Emma Sansaver were able to turn boarding school experiences to their own use. For a fuller delineation of the idea that students took advantage of the opportunities offered by boarding school education, all the while "retaining their tribal values," see Lomawaima 's *Prairie Light.*

50. *St. Louis Republic,* June 16, and August 24, 1904. In September of 1904 the Anthropology Department of the fair staged an "anthropological athletic meet" in which "natives from the four quarters of the globe" engaged in track and field events. Won by the American Indian contingent, this meet—rightly described decades later as "the low point of the entire summer"—was, at the time, hailed by Dr. W. J. McGee, head of the fair's Anthropology Department, as having demonstrated "what [scientists] have long known, that the white man leads the races of the world, both physically and mentally" and that the Native American more closely models the white man's achievements than does any other aboriginal. The Fort Shaw girls' basketball team did not participate in these "anthropological games."("A Novel Athletic Contest," *World's Fair Bulletin,* 5, no. 11, September, 1904, 50.) For an in-depth analysis of the infamous anthropological meet, see Nancy J. Parezo and Don Fowler's "Anthropology Days or the Special Olympics: Testing Racial Strength and Endurance at the 1904 Louisiana Purchase Exposition," a 2001 paper presented at the American Society for Ethnohistory meeting, October 17–21, 2001, Tucson, Arizona. An expanded version of this paper can be seen in their forthcoming book *Anthropology Goes to the Fair: Anthropology at the 1904 Louisiana Purchase Exposition.* See also Allen Guttmann's *The Games Must Go On* (New York: Columbia University Press, 1984), 19–20.

51. *St. Louis Post-Dispatch,* September 4, 1904; *Great Falls (MT) Daily Tribune,* September 9, and October 14, 1904; "Basketball Champions," undated *Great Falls (MT) Daily Tribune* news clipping in Mail's scrapbook.

52. Inscriptions by Lucy Collins of White Eagle, Oklahoma, Simon Marquez, a student at Chilocco, and Etta, whose last name and place of origin are unknown are from Emma Sansaver's autograph book, in the possession of Barbara Winters.

53. *Great Falls (MT) Daily Tribune,* September 5, 1905; *Portland Oregon Journal,* August 21, 1905; *Chemawa American,* September 8, 1905.

54. Campbell to CIA, May 22, 1905, *Letters Received 1905,* entry 40232, RG 75, NAW; Winters to authors, March 27, 2002; Baker to Bisnett, January 11, 1974; Winters interview with Parker, November 1994.

55. Winters to authors, April 8, 2002; "History of Simpson" as published by the Cottonwood Home Demonstration Club, ca. 1979, 180–82; Betty Simpson Bisnett, "Autobiography," 1998, unpublished manuscript in possession of authors; marriage license and marriage certificate, Lewis and Clark County, Montana, January 7 and 8, 1908. Nearly a century later there is no way to know whether Emma's designation as "white" on the marriage license was a carefully considered, mutually agreed upon decision or a unilateral action on the part of her husband-to-be.

56. "History of Simpson," 181; Bisnett, "Autobiography." Ernest Patrick Simpson was born on October 25, 1908, Eugene Michael on April 19, 1910, Elmer Francis on April 16, 1912, and Betty Marie on March 5, 1914. Betty Simpson Bisnett letter to authors, January 5, 2000; Bisnett, "Autobiography."

57. Emmett Weir Simpson was born on April 20, 1916, Edward Joseph on May 1, 1918. Bisnett letter to authors, January 5, 2000; Bisnett, "Autobiography." The Beckwith piano stands today in the home of Barbara Winters. Winters, "Letter to Grandmother Emma Rose Sansaver," *News from Indian Country,* November, 2000.

58. Ella Campbell Simpson was born on November 3, 1919; John Brennan on January 22, 1922. 1924. Bisnett letter to authors, January 5, 2000; Bisnett, "Autobiography."

59. Kathleen Virginia Simpson was born on October 24, 1924. Bisnett letter to authors, January 5, 2000; Bisnett, "Autobiography"; Emma Simpson's death certificate, Cascade

County, Montana, #9473, February 6, 1925; Bisnett to authors, January 5, 2000. The baby died in Havre before her first birthday, and the older girls came home to their father after having spent five years in San Francisco. Bisnett to authors, January 14, 2000.

60. Bisnett to authors, January 5, 2000.

61. In 1904 a reporter for the *Anaconda Standard* observed that the "entertaining" style of the Fort Shaw girls had "much to do with making the game [of basketball] so popular in Montana." *Anaconda (MT) Standard*, March 25, 1904. For more on "Indian ball" and its impact on reservations over the past quarter century, see Larry Colton's *Counting Coup: A True Story of Basketball and Honor on the Little Big Horn* (New York: Warner Books, 2000) and Ian Frazier's *On the Rez* (New York: Farrar, Straus, Giroux, 2000). For an analysis of the presence and power of reservation basketball as depicted in the fiction of Native American authors, see Peter Donahue's "New Warriors, New Legends: Basketball in Three Native American Works of Fiction" in *American Indian Culture and Research Journal* 21, no. 2 (1997): 43–60.

Fig. 8.1 "The Woman Homesteader" by N. C. Wyeth, from *Letters of a woman Homesteader* by Elinore Pruitt Stewart (1913). Courtesy, Houghton Mifflin Publishers, Boston.

8

THE CURATIVE SPACE OF THE AMERICAN WEST IN THE LIFE AND LETTERS OF ELINORE PRUITT STEWART

Natalie A. Dykstra

In 1913, four years after she had settled on her Wyoming homestead, Elinore Pruitt Stewart wrote of wanting

> to bring the West and its people to others who could not otherwise enjoy them. If I could only take them from whatever is worrying them and give them this bracing mountain air, glimpses of the scenery, a smell of the pines and the sage, ... I am sure their worries would diminish and my happiness would be complete.[1]

She had moved to the rural West in late March 1909 to remedy her own despair. Uneducated, orphaned early in life, and a single mother, Stewart had supported herself and her daughter Jerrine in Denver working as a furnace tender, housekeeper, and laundress. But the work did not satisfy and did nothing to improve her lot. By the time she was in her mid-thirties, she felt a baffling combination of captivity and homelessness. Homesteading in Wyoming offered her the alternative of a home of her own, adequate food, and as she said, the "blue veil of distance." To that end, she hired herself out to housekeep for Clyde Stewart, a Scottish widower who owned a ranch near Burnt Fork, Wyoming.

When she arrived, she filed her homestead claim on land that adjoined Mr. Stewart's quarter section, and they married shortly thereafter.

Elinore Pruitt Stewart's vision of the West drew its power from the agrarian myth of previous generations of immigrants to America's frontier. In a region still culturally endowed with the ability to renew those who ventured into its ample spaces, Stewart redefined her domestic space by including the physical space of the West within the borders of what she considered her home. Stewart's letters to her former employer Mrs. Juliet Coney depicted both her ranch work and the West's "blue veil of distance" as key elements of her own renewal. The letters also conveyed stories of female empowerment at a time when conventional gender roles were being modified and reconfigured. Like the New Woman in more urban areas back east, Stewart desired autonomy outside the requirements of Victorian womanhood. She found such autonomy by homesteading in the open spaces of Wyoming, and in her writing joined the nineteenth-century promise of a curative American West to the early twentieth-century promise of New Womanhood for herself and for her female readers.

Most of what is known about Elinore Pruitt Stewart comes from her own published correspondence. Mrs. Coney, her correspondent in the published letters, had arranged through her Boston connections for sixteen letters to be printed serially by the *Atlantic Monthly* during the fall and early winter of 1913. The following year, Houghton Mifflin published the series, with illustrations by N.C. Wyeth, as *Letters of a Woman Homesteader,* and they commissioned another collection the next year that was entitled *Letters on an Elk Hunt.*[2] What is known outside of these publications has been gleaned from county records and family interviews by Susanne K. George in her 1992 biography, *The Adventures of the Woman Homesteader: The Life and Letters of Elinore Pruitt Stewart.*

Elinore Pruitt was born on June 3, 1876 in the Chickasaw Nation, Indian Territory in what is now south-central Oklahoma.[3] The Chickasaw Nation census, according to George, indicates that Elinore's maternal grandmother, Mary Ann Courtney, may have been one-half Chickasaw. Elinore's father was killed while serving in the military on the Mexican border, and her mother, Josephine, married her husband's brother, Thomas Isaac Pruitt, a millwright with whom she bore eight more children.[4]

The family was poor, and Elinore taught herself to read and write after a brief schooling. Her mother, Josephine, died in childbirth when Elinore was seventeen and her stepfather died the next year in a work accident, leaving her, the oldest, to shift both for herself and her siblings. In an early letter to Mrs. Coney, Elinore confided that her relatives "offered to take one here and there among them until we should all have a place, but we refused to be raised on the halves and so arranged to stay at Grandmother's and keep together" (15–16). Instead, she worked at a variety of jobs, including laundering for railroad crews. At twenty-six, she married Harry Cramer Rupert, a man twenty-two years her senior. Together, they filed a homestead claim in Grand, Oklahoma, and four years later Elinore gave birth to her daughter Jerrine.[5] Details about their marriage remain obscure, though her biographer postulates a divorce because Harry Rupert eventually did remarry, as did Elinore.[6]

After separating from Harry Rupert, Elinore lived in Oklahoma City, then eventually moved to Denver to find work in early 1907. Her poverty, lack of education or parental support, as well as her status as a single mother conspired to make her feel both trapped and unsettled. She had few options for employment except manual work: "cooking, cleaning, ironing, scrubbing floors, and stoking coal furnaces."[7] Eventually, Elinore found work with Mrs. Coney, where she was nurse and housekeeper for the weekly wage of two dollars. Disheartened and worn-out, Elinore remained far from the dreams she had for herself. Many years later, she confessed her adventurousness to Mrs. Coney, acknowledging that she

> had planned to see the old missions and to go to Alaska; to hunt in Canada. I even dreamed of Honolulu. Life stretched out before me one long, happy jaunt. I aimed to see all the world I could, but to travel unknown bypaths to do it (188).

Elinore concluded the above list of ambitions with this caveat: "But first I wanted to try homesteading." The Homestead Act of 1862 offered a solution to economic problems, promising land ownership, self-employment, and agrarian subsistence. In addition, the law allowed women to apply, requiring only that they be "twenty-one years old, single, widowed, divorced, or head of a household."[8] The Expanded Homestead Act of 1909 extended the amount of land for each filing to 320 acres.[9] Promising both independence and freedom from want, the West was thus attractive for unmarried white women otherwise held back by more emotionally and economically claustrophobic jobs in urban areas. Sherry L. Smith cites a study revealing that "nearly twelve percent of homestead patents issued in five Wyoming counties between 1888 and 1943 went to women."[10]

To that end, when Elinore read an ad in the *Denver Post* in the early winter of 1909 announcing that a Wyoming rancher wanted a housekeeper, she had little difficulty deciding what to do.[11] Clyde Stewart had placed the ad two years after his wife, Cynthia Hurst, had died of cancer in 1907. An immigrant from Scotland, Stewart and his first wife had no children, and at forty-one he found himself alone on his 260-acre homestead. That winter Elinore had been studying for the civil service exam, but afflicted with the grippe, she was "in pain" and desperately "blue" (226). The Reverend Father Corrigan, a Catholic priest and her tutor for the civil service exam, recommended that she look for a position as housekeeper for a rancher who might advise her on how to homestead.[12]

Elinore answered Clyde's ad, and by the end of April 1909, Elinore and Jerrine met up with Clyde in Boulder, Colorado where his mother lived, and the three took a train from Boulder to Carter, Wyoming. From there, they traveled on a spring wagon to Burnt Fork, a small settlement fifty miles southwest of Rock Springs. They arrived at Clyde's ranch a few miles southeast of Burnt Fork during early March. Elinore filed her homestead claim five weeks later, and shortly after that she married Clyde Stewart. However, in her published letters she would hide her marriage for more than a year, recognizing that the fact of her marriage might conflict with or discredit her claims of adventure and independence in the West. She did not want to highlight romance in her narrative, but rather, emphasize the space of the West as a cure for women who suffered from anomie or bleak prospects.

The Stewart ranch is located in southwestern Wyoming, a windy stretch of open plateaus and buttes. The elevation is high plains desert, over 6,000 feet above sea level. Vegetation is primarily "sage, greasewood, prickly pear, and alkali spike grass."[13] At the turn of the century, "there were an estimated 861,000 head of cattle in the state and 6,091,000 sheep,"[14] and supporting cattle on such land required vastly more acreage than in the more lush regions at lower elevations with higher rainfalls. When the 1914 census declared that a population density of two people per square mile gave a region the status of "frontier," southwestern Wyoming still qualified.[15]

The Stewart homestead itself is still standing, though parts of the roof are missing and the central stone chimney is partially broken (see Figure 8.2). Built of rough-hewn logs with double-square notching, the structure is located near the center of Burnt Fork valley, on a sloping hillside facing east. The Uinta Mountains lie to the south, Cedar Mountain to the northwest, and Burnt Fork Creek to the west. The house itself is relatively large, with a high-gabled center cabin built by Clyde Stewart in 1898, which is flanked by smaller additions to the north and south built by Elinore and Clyde in 1909. Elinore considered the south wing with its two 15-by-15 foot rooms her "'really room,'" a place of her own with space enough for all her "treasures" (137).

Fig. 8.2 The Stewart homestead in Burnt Fork, Wyoming. Reprinted by permission of Richard Collier, Wyoming State Historic Preservation Office, Cheyenne, Wyoming.

Elinore was deeply proud of the home she established for herself and her daughter Jerrine, as is evident in a letter dated early December 1911, inviting Mrs. Coney over for an imaginary visit: "I feel just like visiting to-night, so I am going to 'play like' you have come. It is so good to have you to chat with. Please be seated in this low rocker." (137). She proceeds to paint a word picture of her home, detailing how it was built and how she has decorated the rooms. "Every log in my house is as straight as a pine can grow. ... The logs are unhewed outside because I like the rough finish, but inside the walls are perfectly square and smooth" (138). Elinore covered the walls with gray building paper, stained the woodwork, oil-finished the wooden floor, and arranged two goatskins for the rug. In her cabinet bookcase were "my few books, some odds and ends of china, all gifts, and a few fossil curios" (140–141). She includes in her descriptive tour the many gifts she received, "showing off" the teapot Mrs. Coney had once given to her: "Now I feel that you have a fairly good idea of what my house looks like, on the inside anyway" (142).

Elinore joined her cabin to Clyde's, "though at first I did not want it that way" (77). She felt conflicted about marrying again, mindful of lost opportunities: "Jerrine was always such a dear little pal, and I wanted to just knock about foot-loose and free to see life as a gypsy sees it" (188).[16] Because her own ambivalence about marriage combined with a fear of appearing inconsistent, she sidelined Clyde in her letters, still signing a letter as late as December 1911 with "Your sincere friend, Elinore Rupert" (142).[17]

Yet if marriage posed a potential conflict with her declared desires for economic self-sufficiency and emotional independence, Elinore also recognized the real advantages of marrying Clyde. It was difficult to sustain a homestead with just 160 acres in the dry climate of Wyoming. In fact, despite all rhetoric to the contrary, failure at homesteading was more common than success.[18] Elinore saw her chance in marrying Clyde to have both a "home of her own" and the possibility of proving up on her homestead claim. To be sure, she was not homesteading on her own, as she would have her readers believe. Yet to understand her marriage as any kind of defeat is too simplistic, implying that independence was possible for women *only* outside of marriage.

Instead, Elinore seems to have enjoyed a large measure of independence within the context of her relatively egalitarian marriage, as when she declares: "I am at liberty to go where I please." (66). What started out as an obvious marriage of convenience, by all accounts, turned into a loving relationship. The tenor of their bond is captured in a photograph showing Clyde standing in front, with Elinore leaning and peaking around him, her face at his elbow. Both are laughing at a shared joke: Clyde had bet Elinore he could find a weed in her one-acre garden, then tried to produce the weed he was keeping in his pocket but Elinore beat her "mon" to it.[19]

Elinore and Clyde would raise three boys together, all born between 1911 and 1913: Clyde Jr., Calvin, and Robert. They already had buried two children in 1910, their first-born son James who had lived ten months and died of erysipelas, and a daughter born prematurely, probably earlier that fall. On nearing the second anniversary of Jamie's death, Elinore wrote to Mrs. Coney, assuring her that grief had not capsized her in part because of her relationship with Clyde. Describing the funeral service of their son in which Clyde made the coffin and she said the homily to a gathered group of neighbors, Elinore wrote, "So you see, our union is sealed by love and welded by a great sorrow" (191).

In this same letter, dated December 2, 1912, Stewart summarized the key elements of her domestic scene:

> When you think of me, you must think of me as one who is truly happy. It is true, I want a great many things I haven't got, but I don't want them enough to be discontented and not enjoy the blessings that are mine. I have my home among the blue mountains, my healthy, well-formed children, my clean honest husband, my kind, gentle milk cows, my garden which I make myself. I have loads and loads of flowers which I tend myself. There are chickens, turkeys, and pigs which are my own special care. I have some slow old gentle horses and an old wagon. I can load up the kiddies and go where I please any time. I have the best, kindest neighbors and I have my dear absent friends. Do you wonder I am so happy? When I think of it all, I wonder how I can crowd all my joy into one short life (192).

Clyde, her children, her neighbors, and her distant friends give Stewart a place within which to locate herself. Balanced against these relationships is work that is deeply connected to home, but work that she nonetheless performs on her own and outside the home's parameters where she can see out to that inviting "blue distance." She has her garden which "I make myself," the flowers which "I tend myself," the animals which are "my own special care." She expresses not a simple inversion of confinement into freedom, but rather a complex accommodation that allows her to affirm her home even as she modifies its expectations by way of work that connects her to the wide-open spaces of the Wyoming landscape.

When the editors of the *Atlantic Monthly* announced the publication of Stewart's letters in the back section of the magazine, they highlighted Stewart's abundant humor, even now the most noted quality of the letters: "These letters fall naturally into a series of complete stories, humorous, touching and exciting." The *Atlantic* ad, however, ignores a central theme of her letters: the work of the ranch. Instead they presented her opportunity in a frontier West as a respite from her wage-work in Denver: "The contrast they [the letters] present between the freedom of glorious opportunity and days of sweated labor in Denver give the reader an exhilarated sense of holiday."[20] In her editors' view, Stewart could not be working because she represented a western escape from urban work.

But such a tactic obscures the intent of the letters even as it tries to sell them. Unlike what the *Atlantic Monthly* would have had its readers believe, Stewart did not picture herself as escaping work. Instead, homesteading delivered Stewart simultaneously from the fate of urban wage work and from the pejorative stereotype of a frivolous woman. She escaped not *from work* itself but from the containment of conventional domestic codes *through the work* she performed.

Elinore's pleasure in her work, so evident in the passage cited above, is present in the letters from her first summer on the ranch. Homesteading for Elinore is a verb. Cooking for Clyde and the ranch hands, milking seven cows twice a day, cutting all the hay: she recites this list of chores with a breezy tone, declaring that "[t]his has been for me the busiest, happiest summer I can remember. I have worked very hard, but it has been work that I really enjoy" (15). Homesteading required many skills Elinore had acquired after her parents' deaths that other women, more fortunately situated, would never have had to learn. When recalling the outside work at her grandmother's home in Oklahoma, where there had been no money to hire men to do it, Stewart remembers running the mowing machine and how "my hands were hard, rough, and stained with machine oil, and I used to wonder how any Prince Charming could overlook all that in any girl he came to" (16). Such outside work traversed conventional gender codes for women, leaving a record literally on the body: "my hands were hard, rough, and stained with machine oil."

Yet the blurring of gender roles for ranch women was more the rule than exception, where "the world of work bounded women's everyday lives."[21] Homesteading often required that women plant crops, mow hay, fix fences, butcher and cure meat, and take care of chickens and other livestock. The work was conducted outside, crossing over into the physical arena of men's work. Elizabeth Jameson concludes: "the spheres, if separate, were permeable," allowing women to recast their domestic role.[22]

Ranch women themselves understood their work by distinguishing between two kinds of labor.[23] Washing, housecleaning, and cooking were considered maintenance work, which women, like Elinore, rarely mentioned in their letters and diaries except as a source of frustration. In contrast, sustenance work, or work that produced consumable goods, was often a source of enormous pride, as when Elinore declares to Mrs. Coney that "I milked ten cows twice a day all summer; have sold enough butter to pay for a year's supply of flour and gasoline" (281). Such productive work proved a source of pleasure and personal esteem, giving women control over resources and extending the scope of their decision making and responsibility.[24]

Of course, not all women found ranch work either pleasurable or an increase of their power, and there is much in the written evidence to indicate that women on the frontier were limited precisely because of the amount of work that needed to be done.[25] Even so, homestead laws promised women the possibility of financial and personal independence by granting them the legal right to own their own land and the liberty to manage their claims however they wished prior to ownership.[26] Such benefits inspired Stewart to want to share her good fortune with other women, particularly as a shield from the risks and degradations of urban wage labor:

> I am very enthusiastic about women homesteading. It really requires less strength and labor to raise plenty to satisfy a large family than it does to go out to wash, with the added satisfaction of knowing that their job will not be lost to them if they care to keep it (214).

In Stewart's vision, the work required to succeed at homesteading would not defeat the spirit, as did the drudgery of wage labor. Instead, such work could sustain and satisfy women.

> I am only thinking of the troops of *tired*, worried women, sometimes even cold and hungry, scared to death of losing their places to work, who could have plenty to eat, who could have good fires by gathering the wood, and comfortable homes of their own, if they but had the courage and determination to get them (216–217).

In a letter entitled "How It Happened" and dated June 12, 1913, Elinore recounts to Mrs. Coney how she first decided to homestead in Wyoming, remembering that she was "so blue" that she could "hardly speak without weeping." She was tired of her life in Denver, wearied by "the rattle and bang, of the glare and the soot, the smells and the hurry" of city life. Instead, what she "longed for was the sweet, free open" that homesteading promised (226). Indeed, she would construct the outdoor West as a curative space for women.

Following her move from Denver to southwest Wyoming, Stewart celebrated the solace and inspiration she discovered in the expanse of the high plains.[27] A praise of nature in the letters often follows a change in her domestic routine. On October 8, 1913, she writes that she finally found a woman to help her with her work, and regales her reader with the trip she took to fetch her employee. "The mountains were so majestic ... the larks were trying to outdo each other and the robins were so saucy ... while the purple asters and great pink thistles lent their charm" (231). Her description of western space sometimes possessed a human face, as when she describes a chain of buttes "looking like old men of the mountains,—so old they had lost all their hair, beard, and teeth" (58). She also considered the beauties found in the West as compensation for discomfort and pain. Taking a wagon trip to a more distant neighbor for a Christmas dinner, Stewart and her traveling companions struggled to make it over a large rise. She regretted the trip, fearing that her youngest son would not keep warm. When reassured that he "kept warm as toast," Stewart exclaimed: "The day was beautiful, and the views many times repaid us for any hardship we had suffered" (196).

Stewart's emphasis on what she saw, the views in the West, is not surprising, given the visual intensity of western landscapes. John Dorst observes that the American West is "conceived precisely in visual terms. Both literally and metaphorically the open vistas and lucid, magnifying air of this West have made the act of looking a defining feature of how we experience it as an actual place."[28] When Stewart recounts a day-trip to a neighbor's ranch, she lists all that is within her view:

> the warm red sand of the desert; the Wind River Mountains wrapped in the blue veil of distance; the sparse gray-green sage, ugly in itself but making complete a beautiful picture; the occasional glimpse we had of shy, beautiful wild creatures. So much happiness can be crowded into so short a time" (123).

Here Stewart joins the visual expanse of Wyoming to a sense of personal abundance. It is as if the West's expanse—its physical wideness—enables Stewart to reimagine horizons within which she might thrive.[29] Susan

Stewart (no relation), in her investigation of how we visualize and experience our world in relation to the miniature and the gigantic, contends that the gigantic resists our attempts to know it in its entirety.

> Our most fundamental relation to the gigantic is articulated in our relation to the landscape, our immediate and lived relation to nature as it "surrounds" us. ... [W]e are enveloped by the gigantic, surrounded by it, enclosed within its shadow. ... [B]oth the miniature and the gigantic may be described through metaphors of containment—the miniature as contained, the gigantic as container.[30]

The landscape thus allows perspective on what might be made smaller by comparison. In Elinore's case, the Wyoming landscape miniaturizes the home against a far larger canvas, sapping the power of traditional domestic borders to define and contain her.

While Stewart envisioned the West as a space that freed women from drudgery, poverty, and illness, she was not the first to ascribe such rejuvenating power to the spaces of the West. She drew on a long-standing tradition that began as early as the 1840s, when health seekers had moved to the mountains and deserts in the West to cure their ailments. For consumptive patients after the Civil War, the West became such a popular destination that, according to Sheila Rothman, "the biographies of health seekers are integral to the history of the westward movement."[31] Likewise, when Dr. S. Weir Mitchell advocated that women take his rest cure, he also prescribed that neurasthenic men "go West."[32] While contending that radically decreased physical and mental activity in the sickroom would protect women's overtaxed nervous systems and restore their equilibrium, Mitchell believed that the fresh air and increased physical activity in the vast spaces of West would heal men's jangled nerves. In this way, the West was figured literally as a cure.[33]

In her article, "The Nervous Origins of the American Western," Barbara Will details the complex relationship between nervous ailments and narratives of the West in her examination of Owen Wister's best-selling western, *The Virginian* (1902). Wister, originally from Philadelphia, had been diagnosed by Mitchell himself after complaining of "nervousness." Mitchell's immediate advice was to "head West *and write* about the experience" [my emphasis] because such writing functioned "as part of a cure for neurasthenia."[34] Owen Wister eagerly followed both aspects of the West cure, traveling to Wyoming in the summer of 1885 and then writing about his western adventures in his journals and later in his fiction.[35]

By contrast, Mitchell's rest cure strictly prohibited women from travel, reading, or writing. Within the web of seclusion provided by the rest cure, some patients recovered. Others, of course, did not. Charlotte Perkins Gilman famously worsened, emerging from the shadows of neurasthenia only after defying Mitchell's cure. Her short story "The Yellow Wallpaper" protested the infantalizing regime of the female sickroom.[36] Instead of staying in the sickroom, Gilman challenged the male bias of the West cure not only through her prodigious writing career, but also through her move to California, where she found the "health, freedom, and independence that [she] had been unable to find in the East."[37]

Like Gilman, Stewart crossed the gender divide and took up the male-identified West cure as her own. Not only did she move to the West, but she wrote of it as well, thereby recuperating and redefining the West as a remedy for ailing female readers. Mrs. Juliet Coney was, of course, Stewart's initial reader. A widowed and wealthy former schoolteacher originally from Boston, Mrs. Coney had become, by the time of her acquaintance with Stewart, a housebound invalid. Her correspondence with Stewart provided an outdoors to her otherwise inert indoor life, as when Stewart declares to Mrs. Coney that she is "so glad when I can bring a little of this big, clean, beautiful outdoors into your apartment for you to enjoy" (220). In the same letter, Stewart announces that she planned a "set of indoor outings for your invalid [friends]," women who had been enjoying the letters along with Mrs. Coney. Stewart thus extended the West's curative possibilities to her women readers by making the indoors (a place) into outings (an activity), in effect transposing the invalid's confined immobility into a shared and active liberty. Moreover, just as Stewart's productive labor transformed her homestead from a place into an activity that healed her, so Stewart intended her writing to connect her female readers to healing western landscapes.

The serial publication of the letters in the *Atlantic Monthly* expanded this initial circle of readers, bringing Stewart renown and appreciation.[38] She wrote to her editors at the conclusion of the series, expressing both her astonishment and pride at the response of readers, exclaiming that "you are right about my getting letters and cards from many people on account of my *Atlantic* articles." She goes on to relate how one "old lady eighty-four years old wrote me that she had always wanted to live the life I am living, but could not. ... She said she had only to shut her eyes to see it all, to smell the pines and the sage."[39]

The book versions of the letters only increased Stewart's success. The fact that the first edition of *Letters of a Woman Homesteader* was graced with seven original N.C. Wyeth illustrations indicates Houghton Mifflin's investment in her manuscript because Wyeth, after the publication of

Charles Scribner's Sons' 1911 illustrated edition of Robert Louis Stevenson's *Treasure Island*, had "established himself as the foremost book illustrator of his day."[40] Elinore received $500.00 up front for the collection of sixteen letters, and ten percent of all subsequent profits, terms typical for contracts with first-time authors. The book sold for $1.25 and sold 1,331 copies the first year and 650 the second year on the market. From 1915 to 1923 Stewart earned a total of $359.25 in royalties.[41]

Though the content of Stewart's letters was undoubtedly western in character, she was popular among the same readership that had made Owen Wister's *The Virginian* a national bestseller in 1902. Homesteading had by that time, as Dee Garceau notes, "functioned as an economic opportunity in the West alone, but as a social metaphor nationwide."[42] In turn-of-the-century America, there was an intense appetite for stories of life on an earlier, now mythologized frontier. Zane Grey, the writer of over fifty westerns, "made the best-seller list nine times between 1914 and 1928, a figure not matched by any other writer in the first half of the twentieth century."[43] Henry Nash Smith explains that the appeal of such stories resided in how they depicted the West as a safety valve, providing alternatives for those unable to thrive in an urban, industrialized economy.[44] Given the potency of this vision of the West, with its attendant hopes of regeneration and rescue, stories of success in the West appealed to largely white middle-class readers who were also, not incidentally, Stewart's readers.[45]

Tales of homesteading were also stories of female empowerment at a time when traditional notions of domesticity were giving way to a reconfiguration of female identity: New Womanhood. Many of these daughters of the late nineteenth century were urban, middle- to upper-middle-class women, often college educated and often single. Typically, the urban New Woman was engaged in work outside the home, whether in the professions of nursing, teaching or work in settlement houses, trade union associations, or suffrage organizations.[46] New Women had begun to imagine possibilities that Stewart was already enacting in her letters, an identity that did not deny the need for a home yet escaped the confinements of earlier generations. Hers was a distinctively western version of New Womanhood that remedied domestic drudgery with productive work outdoors, and that expanded the home to include the boundless spaces of the Wyoming landscape.[47]

Elinore Pruitt Stewart would spend the rest of her life on her Wyoming ranch. She and Clyde would enjoy the company of their four children and their many friends who would come for a visit and stay for weeks or even months at a time.[48] Clyde and her children would outlive her. During her last summer in 1933, she camped in the nearby mountains, tenting and hauling in a stove, trying to recover from persistent ailments that had afflicted her for several years. Even at the end of her life, Stewart was prescribing for herself the cure of the outdoor West. Her last letter is dated June 26, 1933,[51] and it expresses well her lifelong love of the Wyoming landscape as well as her desire to give something of its healing power to her readers. She wishes that her correspondent, her longtime friend Josephine Harrison, was with her looking out the window at her "beloved flowers."

> You could see the mountains and you would know that on their cool slopes columbines are nodding, that higher up, under the edge of the snow, anemones are still blooming. You would like the friendly little robins that are out in my garden pulling worms out of the wet soil. I have been camping up in the juniper hills where it is so high and dry that this irrigated spot looks beautiful to me.[49]

Stewart died on October 8, 1933 from a blood clot following a gallbladder operation in Rock Springs hospital. She was fifty-seven.

Stewart's letters do not always match up with her biography. She believed the promises inherent in the idealized vision of the curative West, and she offered herself up as proof, distorting some of the facts of her experience to protect the cultural fantasy. In addition to presenting herself as a widow and then hiding her subsequent marriage to Clyde, Stewart also deeded over the title to her homestead claim to her mother-in-law, Ruth Stewart, in June 1912. According to homestead law, a husband and wife could not "'maintain contemporaneous residences upon different tracts under the homestead law.'"[50] So even the basic fact of landownership was not as simple as Stewart would have her readers believe. While such discrepancies make the retelling of her story more complicated, they do not invalidate her self-representation. Instead, they add layers of complication and richness to her narrative. Though Stewart may not have technically homesteaded on her own, she presented herself in accord with an image that nonetheless suited her and was consistent with the autonomy she felt on the ranch—that of an independent woman homesteader.

Moreover, the fact that Stewart found ranch work and the literal space of the West liberating does not mean she completely dismantled conventional gender ideology.[51] Instead, Stewart repeatedly extended domestic space into western outdoor space on her "many enjoyable outings," always returning to "a household that does not hold her bound."[52] She was an independent figure who moved between two cherished spaces, in the process redefining the meaning and content of each respective space. N. C. Wyeth's cover illustration for the Houghton Mifflin first edition of the letters captures precisely how Stewart stood neither completely within nor completely outside of domestic ideology.[53] In his black-and-white watercolor wash, Stewart is standing in the doorway, half in and half out, her toes hanging over the ledge of the stoop. Her daughter, Jerrine, is standing to her left, cradling a doll in her own left arm. To the right are geraniums in a pot, and chickens pluck at the ground near Elinore's feet. A washtub and rag hang on the outside wall near the door and to her left. And yet behind the open door is darkness; the interior of the home is thus occluded from view. Against this backdrop, Stewart faces out, looking straight ahead to an imagined scene in front of her. Her right hand is lifted over her eyes to provide shade as if to help her see more easily into some far distance. Stewart stands, then, both pictorially and narratively in an in-between space, a position that combines the strengths and advantages of both the home and the western landscape beyond.

In an early letter dated September 28, 1909, Stewart tells of a trip she took with her daughter on horseback through the countryside during a week Clyde was away. Camping overnight on a tableland, Stewart felt jubilant about her surroundings: "The sun was just gilding the hilltops when we arose. Everything, even the barrenness, was beautiful" (28). The day of travel was made more difficult because of the thick forest, but again she ends with the refrain that the sights were worth it: "it was quite dusky among the trees long before night, but it was all so grand and awe-inspiring" (29). The trip intensified as the day proceeded. Stewart found herself both dwarfed by and contained within the views of sky and snowy peaks, and the account escalates to a reckoning where she sees her everyday life in a spatial relation to the infinite—a relation that was, admittedly, not entirely comfortable.

> Occasionally there was an opening through which we could see the snowy peaks seemingly just beyond us, toward which we were headed. But when you get among such grandeur you get to feel how little you are and how foolish is human endeavor, except that which reunites us with the mighty force called God. I was plumb uncomfortable, because all my own efforts have always been just to make the best of everything and to take things as they come (30).

The grandeur overwhelmed her, made her feel small. At the same time, this was exactly the effect she found so liberating. That same evening, Elinore and Jerrine made camp against a crevice of rock, near to a stand of "immense trees." She lit a fire, letting the heat "into as *snug a bedroom* as any one could wish" [my emphasis]. It is as if the immensity of the trees and the surrounding view allowed her to experience connectedness even more intensely, as if the two kinds of spaces, that of cozy domesticity and that of the vast outdoors, momentarily merge into one. In addition, such accommodations equalized Stewart's status in comparison to other women. Her next sentence reads: "The pine needles made as soft a carpet as the wealthiest could afford." It is as if all categories of value momentarily dissolve. Not surprisingly, that same night she kept thinking

> how superior I was since I dared to take such an outing when so many poor women down in Denver were bent on making their twenty cents per hour in order that they could spare a quarter to go to the "show." I went to sleep with a powerfully self-satisfied feeling (32).

The perspective afforded by her engagement with the space of the West allowed Stewart to claim equality in a home she enjoyed herself and that she extended to other women by way of her letters. In other words, through the productive work of the ranch and by joining western space to domestic space, Stewart took ownership of the West cure for herself and for her female readers. Her desire to escape poverty and to establish a life of her own, her new womanhood, was at last realized. Her home was indeed as comforting and capacious as the western sky itself.

NOTES

1. I first read Stewart's *Letters of a Woman Homesteader* in the weeks following my own move to Wyoming in the spring of 1989. I want to thank my mom, Harriett Dykstra, for her prescient gift of Stewart's book. I also want to thank the many readers who contributed their insight to this essay: Ann Schofield, Barry Shank, Dee Garceau-Hagen, Cotten Seiler, Uta Walter, Nadine Requardt, Helen Sheumaker, Leslie Tuttle, and Jeanne Petit. Thanks to Richard Collier for his beautiful photograph of the Stewart ranch. And finally, to Eric Sandeen, who first encouraged me to write about what I most read: American autobiography.

   This letter is dated May 5, 1913. Elinore Pruitt Stewart, *Letters of a Woman Homesteader* (Boston: Atlantic Monthly Co., 1913–1914; Boston: Houghton Mifflin, 1914; reprinted 1988), 220–221. This reprint of the original edition also reproduces the illustrations by N. C. Wyeth. All subsequent citations of *Letters* will be designated by the page number in the text.

2. Houghton Mifflin published a second collection of Stewart's's letters in 1915, entitled *Letters on an Elk Hunt*. This collection had been commissioned by the *Atlantic Monthly*, which published them in 1915 in the February through May issues. The letters were based on an elk hunt Elinore undertook with Clyde Stewart, Jerrine, and Clyde and Elinore's sons, Calvin and Robert, as well as another hunting party. This second collection does not enter directly into my discussion here, but the fact of their commission registers the popularity of the initial volume of letters. *Letters on an Elk Hunt by*

a Woman Homesteader (Lincoln: University of Nebraska Press, originally published in 1915; republished in 1979).

3. This biographical information comes from Susanne K. George's biography, *The Adventures of The Woman Homesteader: The Life and Letters of Elinore Pruitt Stewart* (Lincoln: University of Nebraska Press, 1992). Sherry L. Smith gives both a different birthplace and maternal name than George, stating that Elinore was "born in Fort Smith, Arkansas, to Elizabeth Courtney Pruitt." Smith, "Single Women Homesteaders: The Perplexing Case of Elinore Pruitt Stewart," *The Western Historical Quarterly* (May 1991): 166.

4. What has proved difficult to measure or understand is how Stewart's sense of herself may have been shaped by a possible Indian cultural and/or familial heritage. She nowhere indicates a self-consciousness of this cultural position, especially in relation to the West. She seems to have obscured this part of her history even in her own prodigious self-knowledge, ascribing her financial worries to both her gender and her class. This occlusion is also in the historiography—there is no mention of how her youth on the Oklahoma reservation may have shaped her understanding of either her life circumstances or the West. This study follows suit, with the unhappy result that the space of the West appears without reference to race. Indeed, the West is the space wherein America's racism found another bloody stage. Moreover, it was on this very stage that "whiteness" and masculinity were restaged again and again to recover their conquering vitality. See especially, Gail Bederman's introduction, "Remaking Manhood," in her *Manliness and Civilization: A Cultural History of Gender and Race in the United States, 1880–1917* (Chicago: University of Chicago Press, 1995), 1–44; Jennifer S. Tuttle, introduction to *The Crux: A Novel* by Charlotte Perkins Gilman (Newark: University of Delaware Press, 2002; originally published in 1911), 36–42.

5. Sherry L. Smith, "Single Women Homesteaders," 166.

6. George, *The Adventures*, 5–6. This personal history is further complicated because Stewart portrays herself in her letters as a widow. She may have been embarrassed by the failure of her first marriage or was protecting Jerrine. Perhaps she did not feel her first marriage legitimate in any case. But even Ellery Sedgewick, her editor at the *Atlantic Monthly*, thought she was a widow, writing in his autobiography that Stewart's "husband had been killed in a train wreck and she was left with a two-year-old." Ellery Sedgewick, *The Happy Profession* (Boston: Little, Brown and Company, 1946), 198.

7. George, *The Adventures*, 6. Thomas Dublin states that "wage labor, which appeared to increase women's independence in the first half of the nineteenth century, became a major constitutive element in the dependence of women ... by century's end." Dublin, *Transforming Women's Work: New England Lives in the Industrial Revolution* (Ithaca, NY: Cornell University Press, 1994), 27. Alice Kessler-Harris documents how, by the late nineteenth century, "[u]nskilled, largely unorganized, and crowded into few occupations, women found themselves subject to some of the worst conditions of any wage workers." *Out to Work: A History of Wage-Earning Women in the United States* (New York: Oxford University Press, 1982), 142. See also Ann Schofield, *"To do & to be": Portraits of Four Women Activists, 1893–1986* (Boston: Northeastern Press, 1997).

8. Smith, "Single Women Homesteaders," 163.

9. Acreage was restricted to "non-irrigable, non-mineral lands having no merchantable timber which were within the states of Colorado, Montana, Nevada, Oregon, Utah, Washington, Wyoming, and the territories of Arizona and New Mexico." In 1912 the act was amended to reduce the amount of years of residency from five to three years. For an expanded discussion, see Stanford J. Layton, *To No Privileged Class: The Rationalization of Homesteading and Rural Life in the Early Twentieth-Century American West* (Salt Lake City, UT: Brigham Young University, 1988), 21–35.

10. Smith, "Single Women Homesteaders," 164. Proving up on homestead claims posed challenges to even the most experienced, and "[s]tatistically, only one in three women

managed to remain long enough to get deeds to their farms." Paula Bauman, "Single Women Homesteaders in Wyoming, 1880–1930," *Annals of Wyoming*, 58 (1986): 42.

11. Although Elinore claims in the *Letters* that she herself had placed the want ad in the newspaper (227), her biographer states that it was Clyde who placed the ad in the Denver Post. George, *The Adventures*, 11–12.

12. Stewart had, of course, experience homesteading with her first husband in Oklahoma, but little is known about this time of her life, and more importantly, there is no way to determine if Father Corrigan knew of her earlier history of homesteading when he suggested that she make such inquiries.

13. Dee Garceau, *The Important Things in Life: Women, Work, and Family in Sweetwater Country, Wyoming, 1880–1929* (Lincoln: University of Nebraska Press, 1997), 16. Garceau's study is an excellent source for details about the landscape of southwestern Wyoming. See especially pp. 15–38.

14. Gretel Erlich, forward to Elinore Pruitt Stewart, *Letters of a Woman Homesteader* (Boston: Houghton Mifflin, 1988), xiii.

15. Garceau, *The Important Things*, 35.

16. The local justice of the peace came to the Stewart ranch to perform the ceremony. The morning of the wedding, Elinore was "hustling" to get the house in order and to make dinner for the guests. In her hurry, she neglected to change clothes for the ceremony, forgetting "all about the old shoes and the apron I wore" (187).

17. Sherry L. Smith rightly notes that Stewart "seems to set individualism at odds with marriage and family … [even as] she blended them quite effectively into her own life." Smith understands such an apparent contradiction in a larger historical frame, arguing that Stewart keeps with western women of the time who promoted a "proto-feminist" viewpoint though they "operated on a daily basis in the cultural context of domestic ideology." Smith, "Single Women Homesteaders," 181.

18. Families often had qualified members file on adjoining lands to increase total acreage. A homesteader would have to pay filing and surveyor fees, buy livestock, building supplies, and seed as well as equipment for digging a well, laying fence, and building an irrigation system—expenses that often proved too much for a single person, according to Garceau (*The Important Things*, 118). In her study of homesteading in the high desert region east of the Cascades in Oregon, Barbara Allen concludes that homesteading "was, in fact, a dismal failure, for only about half of the homesteaders stayed long enough to gain title to the lands they had claimed and fewer still managed to make a living from them afterwards." Allen, *Homesteading the High Desert* (Salt Lake City: University of Utah, 1987), xviii. For a powerful account of the generational legacy of homesteading failures, see Jonathon Raban's *Bad Land: An American Romance* (New York: Vintage Books, 1996.)

19. Suzanne K. George reproduces the photograph with the accompanying story that I relate here. But nowhere does she cite either where in the uncollected letters this remembrance appears or who might have this photograph. George, *The Adventures*, illustration section following p. 88.

20. "The Atlantic Monthly Advertiser," *The Atlantic Monthly*, June 1913, 97. The feature of Stewart's prose often noted has been her repeated flights of fancy and good humor. In a tone not unlike Mark Twain, Stewart is the raconteur, quick with a pungent line of description: "he grasped my hand and wrung it as if it were a chicken's neck" (244). Stewart was particularly apt to adopt a satiric tone when describing her domestic dilemmas. Nancy Walker suggests that such humor shares common elements: "[A] female persona or first-person narrator recounts, with some degree of self-deprecation, her chaotic attempts to achieve a level of ideality as a homemaker that is dictated by the culture. … While offering no solution to the problems of the homemaker, they have served as a relatively safe means of protest about those problems." Walker, *A Very Serious*

Thing: Women's Humor and American Culture (Minneapolis: University of Minnesota, 1988), 52. Sherry L. Smith convincingly argues, however, that "the cheery tone … does not completely mask the harsh realities," Smith, "Single Women Homesteaders," 176.

21. Garceau, *The Important Things*, 88.
22. Elizabeth Jameson, "Women as Workers, Women as Civilizers: True Womanhood in the American West" in *The Women's West* edited with introductions by Susan Armitage and Elizabeth Jameson (Norman: University of Oklahoma Press, 1987), 150. Joan Jensen, in her landmark study of mid-Atlantic farm women in the antebellum period describes how farm women transported their product to the marketplace to trade for supplies and labor. Through such production, Jensen argues, women "loosened the bonds" of their domestic role. Joan Jensen, *Loosening the Bonds: Mid-Atlantic Farm Women, 1750–1850* (New Haven: Yale University Press, 1986), see especially 79–113. Dee Garceau makes clear, however, that for ranch women "the meaning of 'outside work' is best understood in terms of their identity as contributors to a successful ranch," rather than "an individual accomplishment" that increased their power in relation to men. Instead, "even as their daily lives increasingly required crossing over into men's work, women minimized the import of such crossover by describing it as service to family—a familiar touchstone of female gender identity." Garceau, *The Important Things*, 101, 89.
23. Garceau, *The Important Things*, 94.
24. Garceau, *The Important Things*, 94–99. Garceau acknowledges Susan Armitage's earlier study of household work on Colorado homesteads, which first articulated the difference between maintenance and sustenance work. See Armitage, "Household Work and Childrearing on the Frontier," *Sociology and Social Research* 63 (April 1979): 467–74.
25. Lillian Schlissel maintains that "women did not greet the idea of going West with enthusiasm" because of the inordinate demands such an extended dislocation would impose. "The West to them meant the challenge of rearing a family and maintaining domestic order against the disordered life on the frontier." Schlissel, *Women's Diaries of the Westward Journey* (New York: Schocken Books, 1982), 155. For an excellent examination of this debate in the historiography, see Katherine Harris, *Long Vistas: Women and Families on Colorado Homesteads*, (Niwot: University Press of Colorado, 1993), 1–24.
26. Robert Cousins argues that "[b]y keeping her homesteading efforts constantly before us … Stewart strongly suggests that her remarkable freedom is a result of her status as an *independent* property owner" [author's emphasis]. Cousins, "Citizenship and Selfhood: Negotiating Narratives of National and Personal Identity, 1900–1920" (Ph.D. diss., Purdue University, 1997), 90.
27. What I want to denote is the physical distance and expanse of the western space, as compared to the spaces of more urban areas. I do not want to imply that the wide-openness of the Wyoming landscape means that the space was uninhabited. The West was not "virgin land," as Henry Nash Smith implies in his 1950 masterwork of the same title. Indeed, Nash Smith concedes in his 1986 essay that he had not accounted for "the tragic dimensions of the Westward Movement." Nash Smith, "Symbol and Idea in *Virgin Land*," *Ideology and Classic American Literature*, ed. Sacvan Bercovitch and Myra Jehlen (New York: Cambridge University Press, 1986), 21–35. For a discussion of how the West denoted freedom through its putative emptiness, see Eric Foner, *The Story of American Freedom* (New York: W. W. Norton, 1998), 50–52. In *The Legacy of Conquest*, Patricia Nelson Limerick argues, "the history of the West is a study of a place undergoing conquest and never fully escaping its consequences." Limerick, *Legacy of Conquest: The Unbroken Past of the American West* (New York: W. W. Norton, 1987), 26. For a historiography of the promise and brutality accompanying western expansion as articulated in women's writing, see Brigitte Georgi-Findlay, *The Frontiers of*

Women's Writing: Women's Narratives and the Rhetoric of Westward Expansion (Tucson: University of Arizona Press, 1996), 1–18.

28. John Dorst, *Looking West* (Philadelphia: University of Pennsylvania Press, 1999), 9. Wallace Stegner links western space with vision in this memorable formulation: "Distance, space, affects people as surely as it has bred keen eyesight into pronghorn antelope." Stegner, *The American West as Living Space* (Ann Arbor: University of Michigan Press, 1987), 27.

29. Women responded to open landscapes in richly various ways, from delight to revulsion and fear. Carol Fairbanks divides the response to the prairie landscape in fiction into four categories: prairie as garden, as wilderness, as real estate, and as wasteland. See Fairbanks, *Prairie Women: Images in American and Canadian Fiction* (New Haven: Yale University Press, 1986), 68–75. Some historians have argued that the potential erasure of the defining borders of the home inspired frontier women to adhere more rigorously to domestic ideals to protect their status within the home. See, for instance, Julie Roy Jeffrey, *Frontier Women: The Trans-Mississippi West, 1840–1880* (New York: Hill and Wang, 1979).

30. Susan Stewart, *On Longing: Narratives of the Miniature, the Gigantic, the Souvenir, the Collection* (Durham, NC: Duke University Press, 1993), 71.

31. Sheila M. Rothman, *Living in the Shadow of Death: Tuberculosis and the Social Experience of Illness in American History* (Baltimore, MD: The Johns Hopkins University Press, 1994), 132.

32. Neurasthenia confounded the afflicted individuals and their families, clergy, and doctors as to its exact causes or a sure-fire cure. Diagnosis was further complicated by the wide range of symptoms that sometimes mimicked those of older disease categories such as hysteria and hypochondriasis. Barbara Sicherman, "The Uses of a Diagnosis: Doctors, Patients, and Neurasthenia," *Journal of the History of Medicine and Allied Sciences* 32, no.2 (January 1977). By 1910, however, neurasthenia had fallen out of diagnostic fashion not only because a pathological basis for the disease had not been discovered, but also because the diagnosis could no longer interpret symptoms subsequent to the work of Freud. That is, the medical category was replaced by more satisfying and rigorous psychodynamic and psychoanalytical explanations for listlessness, weakness, tremors, fits, and other psychosomatic ailments once listed under the rubric of neurasthenia. See F. G. Gosling, *Before Freud: Neurasthenia and the American Medical Community, 1870–1910* (Champaign: University of Illinois Press, 1987). For a discussion of the dynamics of male neurasthenia and its connection to work and vocation, see Bederman, *Manliness and Civilization*, 84–92. For an explanation of how neurasthenia was construed as a form of woman's work, see Natalie A. Dysktra, "'Trying to Idle': Work and Illness in *The Diary of Alice James*" in *The New Disability History: American Perspectives*, ed. Paul Longmore and Laurie Umanski (New York: New York University Press, 2001), 107–130.

33. According to Jennifer Tuttle, "the rest cure and the West Cure were complementary parts of one process through which normative gender identities were constructed and reinforced." Tuttle, introduction to *The Crux: A Novel*, 45.

34. Barbara Will, "The Nervous Origins of the American Western," *American Literature* 70, no. 2 (June 1998): 303–304.

35. While traveling across the plains of Nebraska in 1885, Wister mused: "I don't wonder a man never comes back after he has once been here for a few years." Owen Wister Papers, Box 1, Folder 1, Typescript of Diary, American Heritage Center, University of Wyoming, Laramie, WY.

36. The scholarship on Charlotte Perkins Gilman's *The Yellow Wallpaper* is far-reaching and diverse, but critics agree that Gilman's fictive representation of one woman's experience in the sickroom was an indictment of nineteenth-century domesticity. See especially,

Diane Price Herndl, *Invalid Women: Figuring Feminine Illness in American Fiction and Culture, 1840–1940* (Chapel Hill: University of North Carolina Press, 1993), 129–133; Gillian Brown, *Domestic Individualism: Imagining Self in Nineteenth-Century America* (Berkeley: University of California Press, 1990); Gail Bederman, *Manliness & Civilization: A Cultural History of Gender and Race in the United States, 1880–1917* (Chicago: University of Chicago Press, 1995), 121–169. For a discussion of the rest cure, see Ellen L. Bassuk, "The Rest Cure: Repetition or Resolution of Victorian Women's Conflicts?" in *The Female Body in Western Culture: Contemporary Perspectives*, ed. Susan Rubin Suleiman (Cambridge, MA: Harvard University Press, 1986), 141–142. Nancy Theriot, "Women's Voices in Nineteenth-Century Medical Discourse: A Step toward Deconstructing Science," *Signs* 19, no. 1 (autumn 1993): 8; Charlotte Perkins Gilman, *The Living of Charlotte Perkins Gilman*, (Madison: University of Wisconsin Press, 1990; originally published in 1935), 100.

37. Tuttle, introduction to *The Crux: A Novel*, 42.
38. The *Atlantic Monthly* would publish Stewart's letters twice more: "The Return of the Woman Homesteader," *Atlantic Monthly*, May 1919, 590–96; and "Snow: An Adventure of the Woman Homesteader," *Atlantic Monthly*, December 1923, 780–785.
39. Elinore Pruitt Stewart, *Atlantic Monthly* April 1914, 532.
40. Unfortunately, the correspondence between N. C. Wyeth and Houghton Mifflin, now held at the Houghton Library, began in November 1918, several years after the publication of Stewart's book. I could find no reference to Stewart in Wyeth's letters to the publishers, nor does David Michaelis, his most recent biographer, mention her. David Michaelis, *N.C. Wyeth: A Biography* (New York: Alfred A. Knopf, 1998), 211.
41. These calculations were made on the basis of account books held in the Houghton Mifflin Papers. As late as 1930, a patron of the Atlantic Book Company bookstore inquired of Stewart's whereabouts: "Will you please write the address of Elinore P. Stewart, author of the Letters of a Woman Homesteader to the name on the front of the enclosed postcard. We have had this request from a customer of ours who evidently wishes to correspond with the author." Business correspondence between Atlantic Book Company and Houghton Mifflin, 27 February 1930, Houghton Mifflin Papers, Houghton Library, Harvard University.
42. Garceau, *The Important Things*, 127.
43. Jane Tompkins, *West of Everything: The Inner Life of Westerns* (New York: Oxford University Press, 1992), 164. More broadly, Roderick Nash notes that readers "seemed to have an insatiable appetite for nature novels in the first three decades of the twentieth century." Nash, *The Nervous Generation: American Thought, 1917–1930* (Chicago, IL: Rand McNally & Co., 1970), 141. Interestingly enough, however, Nash only implicitly connects this craving for representations of nature to any "neurasthenic world-view," even in a study entitled *The Nervous Generation*.
44. Nash Smith states that "[t]he doctrine of the safety valve was an imaginative construction which masked poverty and industrial strife with the pleasing suggestion that a beneficent nature stronger than any human agency, the ancient resource of Americans, the power that had made the country rich and great, would solve the new problems of industrialism." Henry Nash Smith, *Virgin Land: The American West as Symbol and Myth* (Cambridge: Harvard University Press, 1950), 206.
45. Smith, "Single Women Homesteaders," 177. This proclivity on the part of eastern readers no doubt in part accounts for Mrs. Coney's success in finding a publisher for the letters. As Smith says, "The publisher of *Atlantic Monthly* recognized her talent for expressing the perceptions, hopes, and aspirations of an American type: a woman homesteader. So, they published her letters" 180. Brigitte Georgi-Findlay, following J. Jackson Lears, argues that the popularity of western narratives of hardship with eastern readers at the turn of the century occurred "at a time when people ... felt that their

lives had become too soft, too civilized." Georgi-Findlay, *The Frontiers of Women's Writing*, 118.

46. For a fuller discussion of this complicated transition among middle-class white women between "true womanhood" and the "new womanhood" of the Progressive era, especially regarding issues of work, see Ann Schofield, *"To do & to be,"* 3–19; Alice Kessler-Harris, *Out to Work*, 142–179; Carroll Smith Rosenberg, *Disorderly Conduct: Visions of Gender in Victorian America* (New York: Oxford University Press, 1985), 244–296; Angel Kwolek-Folland, *Engendering Business: Men and Women in the Corporate Office, 1870–1930* (Baltimore, MD: Johns Hopkins University Press), 41–69; Anne Ruggles Gere, *Intimate Practices: Literacy and Cultural Work in U.S. Women's Clubs, 1880–1920* (Urbana: University of Illinois Press, 1997), 134–170.

47. Ironically, Stewart was living a daily life more in keeping with women homesteaders in the 1870s and 1880s. Rural Wyoming women in the opening decades of the twentieth century kept house like the generation before them, despite some household modernizations, such as manual washing machines. Garceau, *The Important Things*, 92.

48. In a letter dated February 19, 1925, Stewart aptly expresses her love for her many friends: "My only quarrel with life is that it will not be long enough for me to get my loving done up. I just love people, I just love to love them." George, *The Adventures*, 86–87.

49. George, *The Adventures*, 194.

50. Language from court decisions is quoted by Smith in "Single Women Homesteaders," 172.

51. To modify or dilute the power of a particular ideology to shape choices and behavior does not mean absolute or unilateral opposition to that same ideology. Lora Romero elegantly argues this point in her investigation of antebellum American literature, *Home Fronts: Domesticity and Its Critics in the Antebellum United States*. Domesticity, in her reading, was a popular and powerful ideology of gender, politics, and cultural production because it gave "people an expansive logic, a meaningful vocabulary, and rich symbols through which to *think* about their world." Domesticity, then, was not a uniform or static system. Likewise, resistance to domestic codes was not complete or unitary. For "[i]f one cannot stand entirely 'outside' of ideology, then one cannot stand entirely 'inside' of it either." Lora Romero, *Home Fronts: Domesticity and its Critics in the Antebellum United States* (Durham: Duke University Press, 1997), 19, 6. Gail Bederman contends that gender ideology hides the ways in which it is a historical process by appearing to be uniform. "Part of how gender functions is to hide these contradictions and to camouflage the fact that gender is dynamic and always changing." Bederman, *Manliness and Civilization*, 7.

52. Robert Cousins, "Citizenship and Selfhood," 88.

53. Wyeth himself had spent a sojourn in the West. In the summer of 1904, according to his recent biographer, David Michaelis, Wyeth found himself at a crossroads in his relationship with Carolyn Bockius, his future wife. An easterner, he went west. "Lighting out for the Territories, N.C. Wyeth donned the disguise that his heroes—Roosevelt, Wister, Remington—had adopted at moments of personal crisis. He became a cowboy." That October, from the eastern high plains of Colorado, Wyeth wrote to Carolyn: "Out of the north window, plains; out of the south window, plains; out of the east window, plains; out of the west window, plains." But, according to Michaelis, "[t]he exaggerated size and scale of the land suited him." David Michaelis, *N.C. Wyeth: A Biography* (New York: Alfred A. Knopf, 1998), 116, 117, and 121. For a discussion of how western women in the early twentieth century compare to earlier images of pioneer women, see Annette Stott, "Prairie Madonnas and Pioneer Women: Images of Emigrant Women in the Art of the Old West," *Prospects: An Annual of American Cultural Studies* 21 (1996): 299–325.

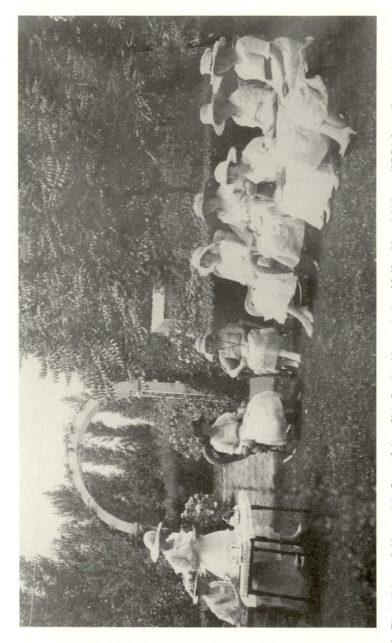

Fig. 9.1 Elizabeth Layton DeMary and the Rupert Culture Club. Reprinted by permission of DeMary Memorial Library, 417 7th Street, Rupert, Idaho.

9

ELIZABETH LAYTON DEMARY AND THE RUPERT CULTURE CLUB: NEW WOMANHOOD IN A RECLAMATION SETTLEMENT COMMUNITY

Laura Woodworth-Ney

A framed photograph of nine women, finely dressed in white and wearing fashionable hats, rests on a bookshelf in the now tattered reading room of the DeMary Memorial Library in Rupert, Idaho. The women sit on tasteful lawn chairs on a lush green surrounded by trees, shrubbery, and a white wooden arbor decorated with trailing vines. Most of the women face a lace-covered table, where two of the women preside. They drink from china teacups, and they gaze comfortably at the unknown photographer.[1] Who were these women, and what were they doing? How were they connected to the community in which they lived, an irrigated settlement town? Where was the sagebrush? The blowing dirt? How could this idyllic photograph, undated but probably taken around 1915, be reconciled with the dusty origins of the town of Rupert, founded only about ten years earlier?

The gendered implications of this incongruous find challenge the images associated with irrigated settlement and womanhood at the turn of the twentieth century. These women did not appear to be victims of heavy homestead work, although some of them certainly were; nor do they represent demure domesticity. Their confident gazes and purposeful demeanors suggest that they were engaged in serious business, all the while wearing fashionable dress, using good china, and sitting in a well-watered garden in the middle of a sagebrush desert. The women appear to have been interrupted in the course of their meeting by the photographer; thus, they probably did not dress for the photo, but rather for the meeting. This was not a diverse gathering. No ethnic faces, no colorful clothing, no abject poverty or extreme wealth appear in this framed moment. These women represent the white, middle-class, female settler of the irrigated plains. While Anglo pioneer women of the early settlement period in mining, homesteading, and ranching communities have received significant scholarly attention, women in irrigated settlement communities have been overlooked by historians.[2] And while their experiences reflect a only a narrow slice of Anglo pioneering, middle-class women pioneers in the late settlement period from 1870 to 1930 exercised considerable influence on the ideology of settlement, the formation of irrigated settlement towns, the elucidation of class and ethnic boundaries, and the culture of the arid West. Elizabeth Layton DeMary typified the middle-class, pioneer New Womanhood of the sagebrush plains. Her club work, literary practices, and creative writing contributed to the formation of a new western culture—a New West counter to the then popular Wild West—in her reclamation settlement community of Rupert, Idaho.[3]

Questions of class, place, and region are central to this study. Pioneers were attracted to sagebrush communities for many different reasons. The interior western United States held most of the so-called remaining uninhabited land, and those who sought economic freedom or stability took advantage of the new homesteading opportunities made available through irrigation legislation. Inherent in the irrigation settlement of the West was a racial, gendered ethic: the New West would be populated by white Euro-American families on land vacated by "savages" and formerly held by the corrupt Spanish and Mexican governments. By the end of the nineteenth century it was, of course, clear that the American continent had never been a virgin wilderness. The legislative impulse to push Euro-American settlers into the arid West was at once an extension of the mid-nineteenth-century notion of Manifest Destiny, a reach to a nostalgic agrarian past, and a Progressive attempt to mix industrialization with farming.

Woven in irrigation ideology was the role of a stereotyped, nostalgic figure: the white pioneer woman, who would populate the arid West with family farming communities. The text of the Newlands Act of 1902 (or Reclamation Act) identified American *families* as the target of irrigation projects, provided for an eight-hour workday, and banned

Asian labor. The bill limited homestead entries to the acreage "which, in the opinion of the Secretary, may be reasonably required for the support of a family upon the lands in question."[4] When this key irrigation legislation was passed, the female pioneer was already an icon in the popular memory of a white American public. As David M. Wrobel found in his examination of gender and pioneer reminiscences, white pioneer women "were described as more capable and self-reliant than contemporary women, who had not experienced the trials and tribulations of the frontier."[5] In memoirs written, edited, and read by women, white pioneer women were praised as essential to the process of settlement not only for their much-lauded civilizing tendencies but also for their diverse abilities. Typical was this memoir describing the pioneer woman's versatility:

> The fall and winter passed as quietly as could be expected. The boys taught me woodcraft; the compass, by reading rocks and trees. They taught me how to use firearms and I was an expert; and, old as I am, could take the head off of a gray squirrel in the tallest pine, in this day and generation.[6]

In the cultural memory that comprised Euro-American thinking about the settlement of the West, white pioneer women stepped out of the role of domestic submissive in order to harvest crops, kill rattlesnakes, dig ditches, put out prairie fires, keep the garden safe from squirrels, and cook over open fires. The cultural view of white frontierswomen does not lend itself to the "cult of true womanhood" analysis, since by the 1870s and 1880s, as David Wrobel points out, pioneer women were viewed as more "womanly" than the general population because of their more "manly" abilities.[7] Thus, middle-class white pioneers who came to the arid West between 1870 and 1930 were aware of, and somewhat wary of, their hardworking, innovative, white pioneer predecessors. In maintaining their class status and in seeking their own pioneer identities, middle-class white women in infant sagebrush communities repudiated what they saw as the distasteful characteristics of the Old West—lawlessness, liquor consumption, prostitution, violence, dusty streets, unkempt houses, and calico clothing—in both word and in action. They attempted to create a New West, where progress and irrigation combined with female activism to reclaim not only the arid land of the intermountain West, but also the arid culture of sagebrush settlements.

Educated, middle-class settlers were the town-builders, the civic leaders, and the entrepreneurs in irrigated Idaho, the epicenter of irrigated settlement. They built dams, founded civic societies, established churches, founded banks, and formed water users' associations. Theirs was not an integrated West; educated irrigation entrepreneurs created their own definition of what it meant to be middle class, a definition sometimes at odds with that of the East but racially, religiously, and ethnically exclusive. The ongoing significance of water management in the American West, and the remaining influence of middle-class pioneer ideology on the politics and social structure of the interior West, calls for a scholarly examination of the influence of these white settlers. Understanding them within the context of the complex social environment in which they lived illuminates class, racial, and ethnic identity in the arid West, and is thus essential for an integrated western history.

Elizabeth Layton DeMary interacted with the irrigated West on a number of different levels: she founded literary and civic organizations that tried to shape the cultural landscapes of Boise and Rupert, Idaho; she expressed female-gendered notions of the landscape through her poetry and speeches; and she participated in a broader effort, with other clubwomen and commercial clubmen, to consciously form and revise cultural perceptions of irrigation and western settlement. In dusty, irrigated Idaho communities between 1870 and 1920, Elizabeth Layton DeMary and others like her created a new sense of region—at once foreboding and utopian—at the confluence of place and culture.[8]

Elizabeth Layton DeMary founded the organization whose members appear in the photograph at the DeMary Memorial Library. The photographer captured the women as they held a meeting of the Rupert Culture Club in DeMary's lush, irrigated garden.[9] Elizabeth Layton was born in Jacksonville, Illinois, on September 6, 1875. At the time of her birth, Jacksonville was a vibrant agricultural community dependent on its central railroad location and on the wheat, pork, and cattle trades. Jacksonville boasted an active, progressive, middle-class group of citizens that included William Jennings Bryan, who practiced law there from 1883 to 1887. Jacksonville's emphasis on education resulted in the nineteenth-century founding of several colleges.[10] Layton attended the Illinois Female College, now MacMurray College, in Jacksonville, where she was honored as salutatorian of her class in 1893. Nineteenth-century women's colleges were at the forefront of the middle-class construction of New Womanhood.[11] New Women sought to self-consciously improve themselves and their surroundings. Layton's time at the private, Methodist women's college was characterized by a "rigorous educational program," which included "Latin, Greek, chemistry, natural and moral philosophy, and meteorology."[12] She may have experienced her first exposure to women's clubs at Illinois Female College, where students founded the literary societies Belles Lettres and Phi Nu as early as 1856.[13]

The college also offered a strong religious environment, and Layton continued to be a practicing Methodist for the rest of her life. While the social environment at the college was tightly controlled by curfews and chaperones, Layton must have found some time for socializing with a young male student, Albin Charles DeMary, at neighboring Illinois College. DeMary graduated from Whipple Academy in Jacksonville in 1892 and from Illinois College in 1896. Layton agreed to marry DeMary and the couple wed on November 8, 1900, in Denver, Colorado.[14]

Like many middle-class American families in the late nineteenth century, Albin Charles DeMary's family migrated west, first from Virginia to the old Northwest, and then to the far West. DeMary was born September 7, 1871 at Perkinsville, Virginia, the son of Amanda Adams and Newcomb Silas DeMary. DeMary moved with his parents to Jacksonville, Illinois, in 1877. After he graduated from college, DeMary took a job as a cub reporter for the *Idaho Statesman* in Boise, Idaho. He worked there from 1897 to 1898, when he became a clerk at the U.S. Assay Office in Boise. It is not clear if his parents accompanied him to Boise or whether it was a move by his parents that brought the young man to the frontier capital of Idaho, but his parents later joined him when he chose to move to a reclamation project in southern Idaho. The DeMarys made their first married home in Boise in 1900 and on September 12, 1901, Elizabeth gave birth to the couple's only child, a daughter. Dorothy DeMary followed in her mother's footsteps and attended Illinois Female College. Dorothy DeMary also majored in music at the University of Washington. The DeMary daughter's higher education choices suggest that her parents desired that she be educated outside of Idaho. Dorothy eventually taught school in Shoshone, Burley, and Blackfoot, Idaho, and finally in Kingman, Arizona. She died on February 7, 1937, from complications associated with intestinal flu. She was thirty-five years old and unmarried.[15]

Throughout her life, Elizabeth Layton DeMary focused on advancing middle-class culture through the establishment of organizations, education, and literary activities. In addition to her degree from Illinois Female College, DeMary pursued literary training at the University of California and the University of Chicago.[16] Throughout her life she published poetry, essays, and travel articles. Her work appeared in many local and national publications and anthologies, including *Times Magazine, The Reclamation Era, Seeing Idaho, Sunlit Peaks, Poems of the Northwest, Homespun,* and *The Book of American Verse.* When she moved to Boise, Idaho, as a new bride, DeMary organized the South Boise Improvement Society. The organization applied Progressive "city beautiful" principles to the section of town south of the Boise River, at that

238 • Laura Woodworth-Ney

time an unincorporated "sprawling village with few trees, bad roads, almost no sidewalks, a small church, and a new brick schoolhouse."[17] DeMary held the first meeting of the South Boise Improvement Society in her living room in March 1904; her child, Dorothy, was at that time about two and one-half years old. The club went on to found parks, plant trees, promote house-to-house mail delivery, build fences on school grounds, eliminate weeds in the neighborhood streets, and institute pedestrian walkways on busy bridges. The twenty-one young members of the club often brought their children to meetings, as evidenced by the frequent comment, "the usual number of babies were present" in the meeting minutes.[18]

DeMary continued her women's club activity after she moved with her husband to the desert of southern Idaho. In July 1904, thirty-three-year-old Albin C. DeMary traveled from the couple's home in Boise to the Reclamation Service's newly opened Minidoka tract. DeMary's duties as clerk of the U.S. Assay Office alerted him to the Reclamation Service's first Idaho irrigation project. DeMary returned with an enthusiastic vision for Minidoka's commercial future and with a steadfast commitment to reclamation. "The character of the soil is such that the establishment of a beet sugar factory upon the tract would prove an unbounded success," DeMary told a Boise newspaper reporter. He and his companions, DeMary emphasized, had been "struck" by "the absence of lava rock ... upon the entire 60,000 acres."[19] Within a year of his visit to the project, Albin and Elizabeth moved to the Minidoka Tract, where they established a homestead three miles northeast of present-day Rupert.[20]

A photograph from this period shows Elizabeth and Dorothy DeMary standing on the packed dirt outside of their one-room house, dressed in their finest clothes and hats, seemingly oblivious to the blowing dust and sagebrush surrounding them. Their ability to look beyond the dust to an agrarian paradise transcended economic development; the future held more than accessible water—it also possessed a Progressive culture.[21]

The land that the DeMarys chose to homestead represented a tiny portion of the Minidoka project, designed to encourage agricultural settlement in the arid regions of the Snake River Plain in southern Idaho. The sagebrush desert and lava fields of the south-central Snake had long intimidated potential homesteaders. Oregon Trail diarists told of the dust and heat of southern Idaho. For overlanders the trail through what would become Idaho's Magic Valley signified only hardship, an obstacle to bypass on the way to the Willamette Valley. Because of its lack of appeal to homesteaders, the area did not experience large-scale agricultural settlement until late in the nineteenth century. Much of this late-arriving settlement, moreover, came from the west, not the east. Homesteaders who reached Oregon and California too late to procure land in those regions turned back to try their luck in the arid interior regions. The first non-Indian settlement in the Minidoka area began in the 1880s and 1890s, when small numbers of farmers and ranchers came to the region and settled near the Snake River. Farmers like Henry Shodde constructed private irrigation systems, some under the homestead provisions of the Desert Land Act of 1877, using waterwheels in the river's flow to irrigate up to about two hundred acres. With its vast elevation variation, hot summers, and a yearly rainfall of between nine and twelve inches, the Snake River Plain defeated most individual and private irrigation enterprises.[22]

The failure of private and state irrigation projects provided federal reclamation adherents with the ammunition to lobby for a federal reclamation act. The national bill came in 1902 with congressional approval of the Newlands Act, a bold measure that created the United States Reclamation Service and authorized the federal government to finance and construct large-scale irrigation projects in the arid West.[23] After passage of the Reclamation Act, the Interior Department withdrew 130,000 acres of land from homestead filings north and south of the lower Snake River to create the Minidoka tract. Crews, including an all-female survey group, arrived to survey the Minidoka Dam site in March 1903. In April 1904 the interior secretary appropriated $2.6 million for the construction of a dam, spillway, canal system, powerhouse, and pumping mechanism at Minidoka, making it the seventh project funded under the Newlands Act. The Reclamation Service entered into a contract with Bates-Rogers Construction Company, Chicago, in August 1904, and within the year work on the dam commenced. Bates-Rogers completed the dam and its supporting structures in 1909; at that time the project's irrigation water impacted approximately 45,000 acres. It was during this initial phase of construction that Albin DeMary, along with his father and two other interested businessmen, visited the Minidoka project and became enthusiastic about the economic prospects of the region north of the Snake River—the territory that, through Albin DeMary's influence, became Minidoka County in 1912.[24]

Homesteaders appeared in the Minidoka area almost immediately after the Reclamation Service identified the site. Most of the early inhabitants of the project associated themselves with the Rupert town site, though the Reclamation Service also created the towns of Heyburn and Paul as part of the project. The *Rupert Pioneer* announced in November 1905 that, "Rupert is on the map, and is out for business, all she can get in a legitimate way." The boosters had their eye not only on the land north of the Snake River, at that time part of Lincoln County, but also on development opportunities south of the river in Cassia County. "No ordinary stream will be permitted to become a barrier in extending Rupert's commercialism," the Rupert paper warned the neighboring community of Burley in 1905. "Eight months ago a sagebrush plain, inhabited only by coyotes and long-eared jacks," the *Pioneer* continued, "now, at the close of eight months, a city of 400 inhabitants, a school of a hundred scholars, a business aggregation of 64 concerns, an opera house, two secret orders, a Methodist Church, a Sunday school, a lawyer to get people out of trouble ... a doctor to cure people of their ills, and a glorious future that no man can doubt."[25]

Albin and Elizabeth DeMary committed themselves to securing that glorious future. At first glance, the photograph of the Rupert Culture Club appeared to be the remnant of an unusual group of women who clearly wanted to distance themselves from what was already, by 1915, an image of the western frontier as a windblown, wild place inhabited by gun-slinging men and calico-clad women.[26] In fact, however, these women were not as much an anomaly as they appeared. The Culture Club women represented a larger female world of middle-class interaction, of literary endeavor, of civic participation, and of self-definition on the sagebrush plains. The associations of women like Elizabeth DeMary formed a self-styled Protestant elite during the irrigated settlement period. Dusty and desperate, irrigated settlement towns offered middle-class individuals a unique opportunity to shape business and social environments. While irrigation entrepreneurs reclaimed the desert, women's groups reclaimed the culture. Irrigated settlement and town development occurred in conjunction with the peak of the women's club movement.

By the end of the nineteenth century, women's clubs were an important component of American society and a mark of middle-class status.[27] The General Federation of Women's Clubs, founded in 1890, served as a national umbrella for women's organizations. Though wide-ranging in size, location, and membership, the federated clubs shared a commitment to education, literacy, political activism, and environmental beautification. The clubs enjoyed their greatest membership in urban environments, but may have had their greatest influence on the rural landscape. Isolation, blowing dust, unrelenting sun, and scarce water led many women on the reclamation frontier to seek female companionship through the club movement. Throughout the irrigated West, these groups supported public libraries, city parks, and restrictions on certain behaviors, including sidewalk spitting and alcohol consumption. The Culture Club and other federated clubs advocated a conservative political role for women, based on the moral exceptionality of women, rather than a more radical equal rights position. They also took the majority of their membership from the ranks of white, Protestant, and well-educated women. The General Federation of Women's Clubs' motto "Unity in Diversity" referred not to the diversity of the women but to the variety of clubs; few immigrant, African-American, American Indian, or Hispanic American women were invited to join the ranks.[28]

Women's clubs in the reclamation West were particularly lacking in diversity. In places like Rupert, where everyone started out in the same dusty shack, keeping up appearances meant associating with the "right people." By the early twentieth century, a certain level of consumption was required to maintain middle- or upper-class status—consumption that was often unattainable on the sagebrush flats.[29] The household manual *Our Home, Or Influences Emanating from the Hearthstone*, published in 1899, warned housewives that appropriate furnishings were essential for the proper rearing of children: "It is as much the duty of parents, then, to adorn and beautify their home as it is to keep the moral atmosphere of that home pure."[30] It was difficult to keep the home "pure," in both the figurative and literal sense, on the frontier, as nineteenth-century sentimental novels made clear in their representation of the degraded and "uncivilized" conditions of "frontier" life.[31] Dirt, dung, and dust were constant invaders of the frontier home. Making matters worse, pioneer women on irrigation settlements attempted Victorian and Progressive domesticity without gas lighting, indoor plumbing, or household help at a time when their urban peers experienced a revolution in home convenience.[32]

Middle-class women pioneers strove, nonetheless, to create proper homes in the sagebrush. Photographs from early irrigation projects often show well-dressed women and children in incongruous settings. "W. R. Pickle's original homestead dwelling on the North Platte Project," for example, reveals women in fine hats sitting on crates in the bare dirt in front of a sagging tarpaper shack.[33] Middle-class women viewed such conditions as all the more unseemly because unlike the more romantic Oregon Trail settlers, they engaged in pioneering efforts sixty or seventy years after the first Oregon Trail wagon train. To avoid the grim demise of female protagonists in Victorian sentimentality—to lose status, refined taste, and thus authority—middle-class women in irrigated settlement communities engaged in a variety of cultural practices: they created art and literature, they lobbied for civic improvements, they built and taught schools, they participated in the boosterism associated with settlement, and they founded literary societies.[34]

If their living conditions placed them among the laboring masses, their creative endeavors set them apart from both the irrigated landscape and from association with the working class. In this way, the practices of middle-class pioneer women defined not only their own status, but in their view at least, that of others, including Mexican migrant women, Asian immigrant women, and indigenous women. Cultural activities and institutions lifted the perceived status of frontier communities, allowing middle-class women to reconcile their presence in a place many viewed as uncivilized. This function was unique to the irrigated club movement because irrigated settlement women labored in new communities that lacked most of the basic accoutrements of middle-class status. Lori D. Ginzberg has argued that women's benevolent work and societies changed from a focus on the ideology of morality in the 1820s and 1830s to a focus on "business skills and on an unsentimental analysis of social ills" by the end of the nineteenth century. While this was certainly true of urban women's groups, the earlier emphasis on moral benevolence was resurrected in irrigated settlement communities, where "redemption" and "reclamation" formed the core ideology of middle-class women's cultural practices.[35] Moreover, middle-class women pioneers served as boosters, often in cooperation with men's commercial clubs, a service that civic-minded women in well-established urban centers did not perform. They were also relatively young, often in their twenties or early thirties, and therefore somewhat younger than the women who participated in cultural organizations in the Northeast. Northeastern women often waited until the time-consuming tasks of child care were out of the way before joining an organization; pioneer women did not share that luxury because there were no other women but young wives with children.[36]

In addition to defining class boundaries, women's club work and literary associations offered a gendered portrayal of the irrigated landscape. The literary and artistic expressions of women in irrigation towns reflected the unique circumstances of settling an arid land, and often provided a contrast to the progress narrative associated with booster reclamation literature.[37] Gilded Age fear of labor unrest, Eastern European and Asian immigration, and growing ambivalence about industrialization and corporate power contributed to an ideological reaffirmation of husbandry's counter to urban decadence. Late-nineteenth-century writers glorified the remaining western frontier as a safety valve for society's ills. A 1888 column in *North American Review* argued that "Once let the human race be cut off from personal contact with the soil, once let the conventionalities and artificial restrictions of so-called civilization interfere with the healthful simplicity of nature, the decay is certain."[38] Others, such as William E. Smythe in his influential *The Conquest of Arid America*, noted that irrigation's high yields represented unrivaled potential for utopian farm settlement. "As a factor in the social life of the civilization it creates," Smythe reasoned, "irrigation is no less influential and beneficent." Compared to what he called the "starvation of the soul" in rural areas in the East and central West, "the change which irrigation brings amounts to a revolution":

> Where settlement has been carried out upon the most enlightened lines irrigated farms range from five to twenty acres upon the average, rarely exceeding forty acres at the maximum. Each four or five thousand acres of cultivated land will sustain a thrifty and beautiful hamlet, where all the people may live close together and enjoy most of the social and educational advantages within the reach of the best eastern town.[39]

But the same women who participated in boosterism through an organized club also wrote poetry and fiction that contradicted the glowing image in the booster literature. This writing, supported and encouraged by the Culture Club and other women's associations that emerged with irrigated settlement, resided at the center of cultural construction in late-nineteenth- and early-twentieth-century frontier Idaho.[40] As Krista Comer has argued, the literary narratives of pioneer women "actually 'made history' to the extent that they profoundly influenced women's (and men's) self-perceptions, their sense of the new world around them, their attitudes toward the inhabitants of that new world, and the terms by which they would carry out their lives."[41] Women's clubs offered the means for literary practice, as the schedule of irrigated homestead work (five o'clock in the morning to seven o'clock in the evening) precluded creative work at home.[42] As women's associations created physical and intellectual space for literary work, they drew women away from children and domestic chores. In at least this sense, women's literary practices in the early irrigation settlement period represented a radical departure from the expectations of the homestead wife.

The life and writing of Idaho Territory's most celebrated literary woman, Mary Hallock Foote, contradicted both the image of the white female pioneer and the rhetoric of booster literature. Foote reluctantly moved to the Boise region in the 1880s when her husband launched the Idaho Irrigation and Mining Company.[43] Foote viewed the Idaho desert as a cultural wasteland, but her presence in the irrigated landscape helped to define its cultural boundaries. Between 1884 and the early 1890s, the Footes lived in the Boise River canyon. The arid landscape and her husband's dream of irrigation informed Foote's art. Her illustration of *An Irrigating Ditch*, published in *Century* magazine in 1889, depicted a pastoral setting with a woman and child standing in the forefront next to a slow-moving irrigation ditch. A backdrop of trees and the sense of verdant greenery betrayed the desert, which Foote described as a land "in which the principle of life, if it ever existed, is totally extinct."[44] The illustration placed women and children in the center of the irrigated landscape; the man toiled in the ditch in the background of the scene. In this depiction, Foote accomplished what her husband could not: she turned the desert into a garden.[45] Foote represented the desert landscape as a woman who gradually returned to her former beauty, and became civilized with the arrival of water: "Each freshly plowed field that encroaches upon the aboriginal sagebrush is a new stitch taken in the pattern of civilization which runs, a slender bright border, along the skirt of desert's dusty garment."[46]

If Foote's ideal irrigated garden was one that produced a female-gendered civilization, her portrayal of man's relationship with the desert landscape was much less optimistic. In this, too, she represented the origins of a self-conscious female literature reflecting and creating the irrigated landscape. Foote's 1892 novel *The Chosen Valley* depicted the defeat of the engineer at the hands of nature and of fickle eastern investors. The dam breaks with a swell of water that sweeps away the engineer, who was standing on the bridge at the moment of collapse. "Over the graves of the dead, and over the hearts of the living," the narrator intones, "presses the cruel expansion of our country's material progress: the prophets are confounded, the promise withdrawn, the people imagine a vain thing."[47] The disappointment and frustration that marked Mary Hallock Foote's life in the Boise Canyon emerged in this antipastoral novel, which reflected Foote's ambivalence between appreciation of the landscape's hard beauty and the desire for a western civilization.[48]

For some women, the cultural and social permission to write, as well as the solace of female company through women's clubs, were crucial to survival. Annie Pike Greenwood, who reluctantly accompanied her husband Charles to a remote Carey Act plot about twenty miles from Twin Falls, was a founding member of the tract's literary society and a participant in the area's first women's club, the Ladies Fancywork Improvement Club. This group did more than practice fine handwork; it attempted to meet the unique needs of the sagebrush community's female population. The club came to the aid of women like Mrs. Howe, whose experience on the sagebrush frontier defined the dangers of rural irrigated life for middle-class women. When she came to Idaho,

Greenwood recounted in her memoir, Mrs. Howe "was beautiful, with dark eyes, rosy cheeks, and a great rope of chestnut hair wound in a coronet around her head." She was "not well," but had been able to "get along" until her husband "had thrown up his good job and put their savings into sagebrush land, persuaded by speculators to that madness." Greenwood noted the harshness of the climate in contributing to Howe's circumstances, but she blamed the debased culture of the frontier for the woman's ultimate decline:

> She had come to a shack in the wilderness, tar-paper covered, like so many other shacks, cold in winter, broiling in summer. There were no conveniences. But these were only material hardships. The thing that killed Sally Howe was seeing the gradual degeneration of her family. They had come with books, and one of the most modern of phonographs, and good furniture. She lived to see them existing in a state lower than the farm animals, because when a human being no longer aspires, but simply lives to eat and sleep, he is lower than the beasts whose habits are the same as his.[49]

When Greenwood and two other members of the Improvement Club called on Sally Howe, they found her in a vermin-infested bed, with matted hair and deep bedsores. She had not been out of bed for several months, and her five children had been forced to fend for themselves in the filthy shack. Greenwood changed the sheets, fed the woman, and left food for the family. The club wrote to the Red Cross and secured funding for Howe to be placed in a sanitarium where she stayed until she died a few years later. "She recovered enough," Greenwood reported, "to enjoy sitting there, clean, well-fed, but she yearned not at all for the tar-paper shack, her five children, or her husband."[50]

Perhaps what is most striking about Greenwood's account of Sally Howe is the fact that she does not present this as an isolated case. Indeed, the Howe account is just one of many stories Greenwood told in a chapter that began with the sentence "I was recovering from the birth of one of my babies when the first insane woman of our sagebrush community was removed to the State Institution of Blackfoot."[51] Insanity, Greenwood emphasized, posed one of the greatest threats to farmwomen:

> But the life, in the end, gets a good many of them—that terrible forced labor, too much to do, and too little time to do it in, and no rest, and no money. So long as a woman can work, no matter how her mind may fail, she is still kept on the farm, a cog in the

machine, growing crazier and crazier, until she dies of it, or until she suddenly kills her children and herself. More farm women than city women kill themselves and their children.[52]

Greenwood's insurance against insanity, she explained in her book, was writing. She tried to write every day, no matter how tired she was from milking cows, churning butter, baking bread, washing clothes, or tending sick children: "I would sit down to my faithful old typewriter ... and gradually the ache would go out of my back, my feet would stop throbbing, I would no longer feel so tired I wanted to lie down and die."[53] Female associations, like the Improvement Club, provided Greenwood and others insurance against insanity by offering a combination of practical aid and an outlet for creative expression.

Like Foote and Greenwood, Elizabeth Layton DeMary's private literary practices challenged the imagery of homestead settlement, but her most significant contributions to the reclamation landscape came through her founding of the Culture Club. The Rupert Culture Club held its inaugural meeting at the home of Anna LaRue, the wife of one of Rupert's first homestead filers and businessmen, in October 1905. As DeMary explained in her 1907 presidential address at the club's annual banquet, seven young, educated women, mostly wives of irrigation entrepreneurs or professionals, "decided that the unspeakable quiet of the desert should be broken, that a woman's club should be organized and that it should be known as the Rupert Culture Club."[54] All of the women were recent transplants, and perhaps unwilling ones, to the new community on the sagebrush flats of southern Idaho. Idaho's first rural federated club limited its membership to eighteen, ostensibly because it planned to meet exclusively in private homes, and committed itself to the cultural and artistic advancement of Rupert. The club did not welcome immigrants or Catholics. The group held its second meeting in the DeMary home, but by the spring of 1906 moved some of its meetings to the (relatively) prestigious dining room of the Rupert Hotel, located on the town square. At the first meeting, club members signed a petition requesting that the State Traveling Library include Rupert on its schedule. The traveling library, founded by the Columbian Club of Boise in 1893, became the primary source of literary material for over two hundred Idaho communities by 1905. Hosted by women's clubs throughout the state, the traveling library illustrated the connection between literacy, education, class, and culture that infused rural women's groups. The Culture Club claimed the traveling library, which first visited Rupert in 1906, as an early victory in its perceived struggle against frontier illiteracy and degradation.[55]

The Culture Club funded a lyceum lecture series, sponsored an art exhibit, lobbied for women's public restrooms, and spawned a plethora of other women's clubs, including the Clionian Club, Fortnightly Club, Rupert Civic Club, and Merry-Go-Round Club.[56] In advocating the institution of public restrooms, the club supported more than a mere place for a lady to use private facilities. Public restrooms for women corresponded to a value system of domestic consumption. In order for women to shop in town, they needed to have access to a private place. Women's lounges offered an escape from street grime, and a place in which to gather, where literature and reading could be placed for the pleasure of the cultured woman. Restrooms also enabled farmwomen to come to town with the knowledge that there would be somewhere to rest and, perhaps, to read.[57] To further expand the minds of Rupert's populace, Culture Club women also lent their support to Rupert's Opera House and Dramatic Association, which hosted its first production in November 1905. The only such venue south of Boise, the opera house reflected the cultural idealism of Rupert's clubwomen. When it first opened, the town newspaper declared that the theater was "designed in such a manner that between acts out of town people can gaze upon it and be convinced that their wants can be supplied in our city."[58]

In spite of victories like the traveling library, women's lounges, and cultural institutions, organized womanhood did not create the kind of cultural agrarian paradise that Elizabeth DeMary envisioned. The Minidoka project remains one of the most successful in reclamation history, Rupert and the other project settlement towns are still surviving as viable communities with economies based on irrigated agriculture. But the DeMarys were not successful in fending off the "frontier image," or in preventing dangerous settler squabbles. Elizabeth DeMary's club activities could not, in the end, produce a permanent Protestant-controlled culture. In many ways, the idealism of Progressive settlers like the DeMarys stemmed not from actual successes, but from the desire to *appear to be succeeding* in their efforts to turn irrigation projects into Progressive garden oases. Observations by visitors to the project during the first decade illustrate the difficulty of this endeavor. Henry A. Wallace, who toured the Minidoka project in 1909 as part of his investigation of irrigated farmland for the family journal *Wallaces' Farmer*, found little to praise in Rupert and its surrounding landscape. Wallace attributed the slow development of irrigation and urban culture in the Minidoka area to the very fact that it was a federal project—as opposed to the more developed, private Carey Act project in Twin Falls. "Rupert is a government townsite, and shows the effects of it," Wallace wrote, "for it is one of the most dilapidated little towns which I have ever seen." The newspaperman's description must have horrified Rupert's boosters:

> All the buildings are little square frame affairs with just enough ambition to be painted. The ramshackle buildings are arranged on four sides of a square which has a fine stand of blue grass and white clover which the town hasn't had energy enough to mow. There are a few poplar and locust trees which may make some shade some day.

After observing the Rupert square, Wallace toured the countryside and interviewed individual homesteaders, many of whom expressed frustration with the landscape and with reclamation. "At first we didn't get water when the government promised it to us," a woman from Iowa told Wallace, "then when we did get water the wind was so strong that we could hardly get anything seeded down before the wind would come along and blow it out or cut it down." The owner of a three-year-old claim, a man from Montana, explained that Minidoka farms had a ramshackle appearance because "these people around here are not a very high class of irrigators." Most of the homesteaders came to the country without capital, and "for the first two years they had an awful hard time hanging on, for the water wasn't ready yet and on their own places there wasn't anything but sage brush ... then when the water did come they didn't have enough money to fix their land right, and they just stuck in their crops haphazard." Another settler complained of the wind, and to illustrate told Wallace the already mythic story of the Minidoka project. A man on one side of the project, the tale went, planted a garden. The wind came up and blew it fifteen miles across the river to another settler's claim, who then raised the garden himself.[59]

Still, Elizabeth DeMary and the women of the Culture Club clung to their vision of a refined, aesthetically pleasing town in which citizens might develop a culture to feed arid spirits, just as irrigation fed the arid lands. Indeed, the club boasted significant accomplishments between 1909 and 1917. Social redemption formed a core goal of the organization. The club discouraged alcohol consumption and participated in the elimination of Rupert's red light district. Village trustees and "a large number of citizens," the *Rupert Pioneer* reported in September 1906, met to discuss the town's "social evil." The group decided to inform red light district occupants that they had twenty-four hours to leave town or face arrest and fines; the "social evil" responded by leaving on the night train.[60] Saloons also became a target of the Progressive spirit in early Rupert. In November 1909, three of the original Minidoka reclamation towns—Rupert, Heyburn, and Acequia—passed legislation making the selling of alcoholic beverages illegal within town limits.[61]

Elizabeth Layton DeMary's club drew upon the irrigated landscape to portray Rupert as a uniquely progressive urban center. Yearly moonlit excursions to Minidoka Dam married the ideals of the Culture Club to the optimism of reclamation. The club had grown in membership "until a name upon our roll is a coveted possession," DeMary explained in her 1907 presidential speech, because "our aim is one of mutual helpfulness and a reaching out for those things which broaden and enrich life." "Our vision is not bounded by the endless sage brush and the encircling hills," DeMary continued, "[w]e have penetrated beyond." The 1907 banquet ended with a series of lecture presentations by Rupert's elite settlers. Topics included "A Little Journey in the World: A Contrast of Naples, Italy, and Minidoka, Idaho," "Reminiscences on Roast Turkey," and "Art in a Shack." The latter speech emphasized the need for culture even in a "humble shack" in a "bleak desert."[62] DeMary later described her cultural contribution in the *Reclamation Record*. Every reclamation woman, she emphasized, "had made a great sacrifice to come to this new land in order that she might help to create in the desert a new garden."[63]

The literary practices—reading, writing, and poetry—maintained by the Culture Club reflected and defined cultural perceptions of the irrigated landscape. DeMary's poem *Irrigation* appeared in *Reclamation Era* magazine, and illustrated the connection between women's literary work and the reclaiming of the desert:

> Oh, Mesa, with those wise clear eyes of old
> Could you have dreamed this vision to behold?
> Long aeons you have gazed across the plain
> And Man's control have held in high disdain
> But now where gone are deer and antelope
> The stubborn sage that clung to every slope
> The caravan that wound its weary way,
> The lurching stage that would not brook delay?
> Again where vanished tribes of warriors bold
> Who bravely fought these native trails to hold?
> Gone to oblivion, and through the land
> A magic wand is Irrigation's hand.
> From distant ports skilled birdmen
> wing their flights
> While desert dark gives way to myriad lights;

> Where once the drifting dunes of sand held sway
> The children gather flowers as they may,
> And tapestries are spread o'er all the fields
> Where yellow ripening grain abundance yields
> Oh, Mesa, with those wise clear eyes of old
> Could you have dreamed this vision to behold?[64]

Like DeMary, Irene Welch Grissom, a reclamation clubwoman appointed Idaho's Poet Laureate in 1923 "in response to the request of the State Federation of Women's Clubs," portrayed a gendered irrigated landscape in her work. DeMary's desert is transformed by "Man's control"; Grissom's desert yields to masculine engineering:

> A dreamer comes—as dreamers will—
> To watch the swirling torrents spill
> Between the steep, black lava walls,
> And on the foaming, crashing falls.
> He sees the desert, vast and grand,
> Give way before a man-made land,
> The sparkling streams flash here and there,
> And life is springing everywhere.[65]

With the desert's greening comes feminine influence; DeMary's "children gather flowers as they may," while Grissom's irrigated landscape is dotted "with houses set in misty green, / And church spires lifted high."[66] These gendered portrayals defined the position of women's clubs on the irrigated frontier. First, men tamed the desert with engineering marvels. Then, women "settled" the new "garden" by introducing the elements of civilization—children, homes, and churches.[67] DeMary's work consciously built upon an irrigated women's literary tradition; her personal library contained copies of Mary Hallock Foote's *The Chosen Valley*, Irene Welch Grissom's collection of poems entitled *The Passing of the Desert*, and Bess Foster Smith's anthology of Idaho poetry, *Sunlit Peaks*.[68]

In providing a forum for women's views, supporting women's literacy and education, and by sponsoring women's creative practices, the Culture Club indirectly supported other Progressive reforms, including suffrage. No evidence exists that the club openly endorsed national suffrage. Indeed, many Minidoka settlers viewed the group as narrow and elitist, and many clubwomen, like Mary Hallock Foote, did not support suffrage. Foote wrote in an 1887 letter that she did not "care to contribute towards the campaign for municipal suffrage, not being entirely in sympathy with it as a means towards the progress of woman."[69] But, as the first women's organization on the Minidoka project, the Culture Club inspired a host of other organizations that supported more radical reforms. The Federation of Women's Clubs endorsed suffrage at its 1910 national convention.[70] A photograph of the Rupert Square, taken during the early 1910s, reveals that the reclamation community hosted a suffragette parade. Finely dressed women march down the dusty street, carrying signs with slogans such as "Rupert for Suffrage" and "Votes for Women." The parade appears to be well attended; rows of men and women line the streets of the square. Minidoka project suffragettes already possessed the right to vote, because Idaho became the fourth state to grant that right in 1896. Rupert's suffrage parade suggests that women in states and communities that already had the vote were essential in securing the Nineteenth Amendment in 1920. They actively lobbied for a right that they already possessed, so that women who could not safely fight for that right would eventually possess it as well. Many of the women who already had the vote lived in the arid West, the area served by the Reclamation Act. Wyoming (1869), Utah (1870), Colorado (1893), Washington (1910), California (1911), Oregon (1912), Arizona (1912), Montana (1914), and Nevada (1914) all granted full suffrage to women before 1920. Women in reclamation communities used their unique relationship with the federal government to support national suffrage. Reclamation communities received unprecedented federal attention; suffrage advocates used this attention to lobby for women's voting rights.[71]

The Culture Club's influence extended beyond the cultural landscape to the built environment. Rupert's central green, the only town square in the state of Idaho, recalled the city squares of small Illinois towns, where both DeMarys spent their childhoods. The Reclamation Service platted Rupert in 1904; by 1905 businesses had sprung up on four streets facing a square, where reclamation officials planned to dig the first well on the Minidoka tract. Settlers called the town Wellfirst, or Wetfirst, until the service officially changed the name to Rupert.[72] The earliest businesses to locate on the town square did so illegally, as the lots were not appraised and sold until 1907 and 1908. Pressure from concerned citizen groups, including the Culture Club, helped maintain the integrity of the square throughout 1905 and 1906, despite problems with squatters and a lack of water.[73] When, during the spring of 1906 an enterprising businessman attempted to erect a building in the center of the square, a group of concerned citizens formed a committee to halt the construction. Albin C. DeMary's Commercial Club participated in the group, which convinced Cal Masterson to move his building, and collected six dollars in donations to help defray the cost of relocation.[74]

In June 1907, with the first irrigation water in sight, Rupert surveyed, cleared, and graded its streets and planted poplar trees throughout the central green. "In the center will be a circle of 75 feet in diameter surrounded by trees," the paper explained, "in which seats will be placed for summer lounging, and to which walks will lead diagonally from each corner, and one from each side of the four side centers." To further enhance the irrigated landscape of the town square, town trustees forbade carriage traffic on the immediate side streets, so that women would not have to step over steaming clumps of manure, and instituted an ordinance requiring teams to be "properly tied either to a hitching post or suitable weight." In 1910, Rupert's trustees procured contracts to build sidewalks around the square; the town voted to pave its streets in 1919. By 1947, the *Minidoka County News* declared, "no city of comparable size in Idaho has as many hard-surfaced streets as the City of Rupert, and every one of them oiled since 1919!" The Rupert town square remains a testament to the Edenic idealism of reclamation settlers. An elite corps of Rupert founders, headed by the DeMarys, managed to make the city green a priority, even when water was scarce and intended for crop irrigation, not aesthetic use. In January 2001 the National Park Service listed the Rupert town square and its surrounding historic district on the National Register of Historic Places.[75] Cultural improvements accompanied the infrastructure improvements. By the early 1920s the original opera house was replaced by the Wilson Theater, a grand building on one of the town square's corners. Its construction cemented the cultural centrality of Rupert, while its architecture, described by the current restoration architect as a mix of Art Nouveau and Farm Egyptian, combined the ideals of Progressive urbanity with agrarian values. The terra-cotta decorative elements feature wheat and other agricultural products.[76]

Unlike many of her private irrigation and Carey Act predecessors, Elizabeth DeMary remained in Rupert, Idaho, until the end of her life; she died in 1942. Her club remained active until World War I when, like many federated women's clubs, it disbanded. Competition from other women's organizations, the transfer of club goals from cultural advancement to the support of the war effort, the debate over women's suffrage and pacifism, and a perceived linkage between socialist groups and organized women's clubs hurt attendance nationwide.[77] The demise of the Culture Club also signaled political and social change in irrigated settlement communities. As competition for Snake River water increased, and the Reclamation Service became more focused on generating hydroelectric power, the relative authority of organizations in settlement communities declined.[78] The service became the Bureau of Reclamation in

1923, introducing an increasingly bureaucratic era in which the agency shifted its focus from small farm settlement and town development to dam building and hydroelectric power.[79]

As settlement areas expanded, moreover, their population demographics changed. The introduction of sugar beet factories, for example, and increased labor needs on irrigated farms, by the 1920s, attracted large immigrant populations. German, Russian, and Hispanic newcomers embraced the kind of opportunity advocated by Progressive women's clubs, but at the same time their presence diluted the influence of the original elite Protestant settlers. Moreover, these new immigrants could not afford to adhere to the domestic and cultural standards maintained by clubwomen. By the 1920s, the Idaho State Federation of Women's Clubs was advocating a firm stance on the issue of immigration and Idaho communities. "Throughout the Federation this term emphasis was on Americanization," the federation's historian explained, "for war had shown the need for assimilating into American life the foreign born upon her shores."[80] These changes heralded the end of the irrigation settlement era and led to disillusionment among the early settlers.[81] Elizabeth DeMary's 1931 poem, "O Little Town," expressed her frustration at the demise of the utopian irrigation vision:

> O Little Town, why must you always wear
> That homely dress of changeless gray content?
> Are there no flaming flowers for your hair,
> No orange sash from distant China sent?
> Is there no Spanish shawl for which you yearn,
> Nor fairy filmy gauze from Paris gleaned?
> Why must you ever look so plain and stern?
> Are you from gay and lovely things quite weaned?
> Now would you not to one mad dance and wild
> Your staid and quiet person truly give?
> Are you to humdrum days so reconciled
> That now you know not what it is to live?
> I slowly turned, then saw what kept life sweet,
> Two blissful loves passed me on the street.[82]

Between 1870 and 1920, however, middle-class women created a network of female interaction that both reflected and created the nature of irrigated communities. DeMary's club work is not anomalous, but indicative of a literary, civic-minded culture created by middle-class women in irrigated settlement areas in southern Idaho. Perhaps because of the fragility of their enterprise and the mobility of the irrigated settlement population, middle-class settlers cultivated and maintained the cultural networks that women's clubs created. Women's associations provided the intellectual and physical space necessary for middle-class women to engage in literary activity and civic practices and, in turn, to define and shape the cultural and social landscapes of the arid West. Women like Elizabeth Layton DeMary used a sisterhood of middle-class clubwomen to cultivate the culture of the sagebrush plains and to reconcile their place on the degraded frontier. DeMary and her peers, moreover, created a distinctly western version of New Womanhood. DeMary came to Idaho with a vision of gender formed by her time at the Illinois Female College and by her association with the emergent middle-class in Jacksonville, Illinois. She translated her ideas about womanhood to a new landscape where she used them to challenge the rugged, crude, pioneer model of white womanhood that had already become part of Idaho's regional identity. And in her gendered portrayal of the irrigated landscape, DeMary reacted against the sanguine promise of pastoral living found in middle-class booster literature of the early-twentieth-century West. DeMary's New Woman was both a pioneer and a Progressive. She was an idealist about the future and a realist about the present, where frontier circumstances often confounded her work. The New Womanhood of the late settlement period in the arid West created the ideology of the New West, where industrial irrigation, cultured settlements, and feminine organization would replace the violent economy and masculine individualism of the Old West.

ACKNOWLEDGMENTS

The author gratefully acknowledges the Redd Center of Western Studies at Brigham Young University, and the Faculty Research and Humanties and Social Sciences Research Committees at Idaho State University, for support of this research. Dee Garceau-Hagen provided invaluable editing and vastly improved the manuscript.

NOTES

1. This large, undated photograph resides in a frame on top of a bookshelf in the DeMary Reading Room at the DeMary Memorial Library, Rupert, Idaho. The photographer was most likely Albin C. DeMary, the husband of Elizabeth DeMary, and the homeowner of the house and yard featured in the photo. DeMary collected government documents, personal photographs and letters, newspaper articles, and publications on Idaho and the Rocky Mountain West until his death in 1977. He donated the funds for the construction of Rupert's city library, built in 1958, which houses the manuscript collection and the library that he compiled and also donated. Elizabeth DeMary's papers are also held at the city library, as well as her personal book collection. Elizabeth died in 1942; after her death, Rupert's history became DeMary's focus and passion. Madelyn Player

was extremely generous in allowing me access to her private library and manuscript collection, which also aided in the research for this paper. DeMary Manuscript Collection (DMC), DeMary Memorial Library, Rupert, Idaho.

2. This research includes Lillian Schlissel, *Women's Diaries of the Westward Journey*, preface by Carl N. Degler (New York: Schocken Books, 1992); Ruth B. Moynihan, Susan Armitage, and Christiane Fischer Dichamp, eds., *So Much to Be Done: Women Settlers on the Mining and Ranching Frontier* (Lincoln: University of Nebraska Press, 1990); Julie Roy Jeffrey, *Frontier Women: The Trans-Mississippi West, 1840–1880* (New York: Hill and Wang, 1979); and Ronald M. James and C. Elizabeth Raymond, eds., *Comstock Women: The Making of a Mining Community* (Reno/Las Vegas: University of Nevada Press, 1998).

3. By the end of the nineteenth century the imagined view of the West as a wild and masculine place was well established in American culture. This perception manifested itself in the emergence of the popular western novel and in the popularity of Buffalo Bill Cody's Wild West Show. See Richard White, *"It's Your Misfortune and None of My Own": A New History of the American West* (Norman: University of Oklahoma Press, 1991), 613–17.

4. U.S. Congress, Fifty-Seventh Session, *Reclamation Act/Newlands Act of 1902* (qtn.); full-text entry accessed through the Center for Columbia River History, http://www.ccrh.org.

5. David M. Wrobel, *Promised Lands: Promotion, Memory, and the Creation of the American West* (Lawrence: University Press of Kansas, 2002), 131.

6. Lee Whipple-Haslam, *Early Days in California: Scenes and Events of the '50s as I Remember Them, Written by Mrs. Lee Whipple-Haslam* (Jamestown, California, c. 1925?), accessed via Library of Congress *American Memory* web-site, http://memory.loc.gov.

7. Wrobel, *Promised Lands*, 131; Barbara Welter, "The Cult of True Womanhood, 1820–1860," *American Quarterly* XVIII (1966): 151–74.

8. Ideologies of place and regionalism currently figure prominently in historical studies of the western United States. William G. Robbins, Mark Spence, and Sara Dant Ewert discuss the implications of the new *bioregionalism* in "Beyond Place: A Forum," *Oregon Historical Quarterly* 104, no. 4 (winter 2002): 414–51.

9. The house with the arbor is still standing in Rupert, Idaho. The wooden arbor was replaced by a vinyl one by the current owners in 2004, but Elizabeth Layton DeMary's gardens remain.

10. Information about the history of Jacksonville, Illinois, was taken from "History of the City," City of Jacksonville Official Website, www.jacksonvilleil.com/.

11. Carroll Smith-Rosenberg, *Disorderly Conduct: Visions of Gender in Victorian America* (New York: Oxford University Press, 1985), 247.

12. As quoted in the Official Home Page of MacMurray College, Illinois, "MacMurray Campus History," www.mac.edu/campus/camp_history.html. All information about the history of MacMurray College was taken from this site. See also Walter B. Hendrickson, *Forward in the Second Century of MacMurray College: A History of 125 Years* (Jacksonville: MacMurray College, 1972).

13. Official Home Page of MacMurray College, Illinois, "MacMurray Campus History," www.mac.edu/campus/camp_history.html.

14. All biographical information for Elizabeth Layton and Albin Charles DeMary in this section comes from Minidoka County Historical Society, *A History of Minidoka County and Its People* (Dallas, TX: Taylor Publishing Company, 1985), 185–86.

15. *Ibid.*

16. Illinois Female College did not award baccalaureate degrees until 1909.

17. Hogsett, *The Golden Years: A History of the Idaho Federation of Women's Clubs* (Caldwell, ID: Caxton Printers, 1955), 307 (qtn.); Minidoka County Historical Society, *A History of Minidoka County and Its People*, 185. For a discussion of the ideology of Progressive urban planning, or "positive environmentalism," and its relationship to social control, see Paul Boyer, *Urban Masses and Moral Order in America, 1820–1920* (Cambridge, Massachusetts: Harvard University Press, 1978), especially 220–32.

18. Helen K. Priest, "History [of] Southside Improvement Club," January 1954, Southside Improvement Club Records, MS 2/1171, Idaho State Historical Society Library, Boise, Idaho; Hogsett, *The Golden Years*, 307.

19. As quoted in Susan E. Williams', "An Urban Study of Rupert, Idaho" (unpublished master's thesis, Kent State University, March 1963), 54–57. See also "Minidoka County Grew Fast after 'Late Start' in Idaho," in Minidoka County News, *The Minidoka Story: The Land and the People* (Rupert, Idaho: Minidoka County News, 1963; Reprint, 2001), 1–2. *The Minidoka Story* is comprised of reprinted newspaper articles from the *Rupert Pioneer* and other early papers. I will give page citations for the reprint, rather than citations for the individual articles.

20. Minidoka County Historical Society, *A History of Minidoka County and Its People*, 186.

21. "Photograph of Elizabeth and Dorothy DeMary," circa 1906, DeMary Photograph Collection, DMC.

22. There were, of course, exceptions to this pattern of failure. The Carey Act, passed by Congress in 1894, provided that each state containing "desert land," as defined by the Desert Land Act (1877), could select up to one million acres for reclamation. The land would be held by states in trust for homesteaders; the land was available as long as the states found a way to irrigate it. States could either construct their own irrigation projects or hire private companies to do the work, for a price per acre set by the state. One of the Carey Act's greatest successes occurred in Twin Falls, Idaho, located approximately forty-five miles west of Rupert. There, Ira B. Perrine headed the largest private irrigation project in the United States. Indeed, Idaho eventually contained three-fifths of all land irrigated under the provisions of the Carey Act. For an overview of the Desert Land and Carey acts, see Donald J. Pisani, *To Reclaim a Divided West: Water, Law, and Public Policy 1848–1902*, Histories of the American Frontier, Ray Allen Billington, ed. (Albuquerque, NM: University of New Mexico Press, 1992), 88–89, 251–72; and Tim Palmer, *The Snake River: Window to the West* (Washington, DC: Island Press, 1991), 53–111. For a brief examination of pre-1902 irrigation projects in Idaho, see Carlos A. Schwantes, *In Mountain Shadows: A History of Idaho* (Lincoln: University of Nebraska Press, 1991), 163–66. For a contemporary observer's comparison of the Minidoka Reclamation Project with the Twin Falls Project, see Richard Lowitt and Judith Fabry, eds., *Henry A. Wallace's Irrigation Frontier: On the Trail of the Corn Belt Farmer, 1909* (Norman: University of Oklahoma Press, 1991), 158–66. Minidoka County News, *The Minidoka Story*, 1; Congress, Senate, "National Irrigation Policy—Its Development and Significance," 76th Cong., 1st Sess., Senate Document No. 36, 2, DMC; Department of Interior, *21st Annual Report of the Reclamation Service* (Washington, DC: Government Printing Office, 1922), 63, DMC.

23. For a detailed examination of the politics surrounding passage of the Newlands Act, see Pisani, *To Reclaim a Divided West*, 273–325. The full text of the Reclamation Act can be accessed through the Center for Columbia River History website, located at http://www.ccrh.org/content.htm.

24. Burley Irrigation District Home Page, *Burley Irrigation District History*, http://www.cyberhighway.net/~bid/history.htm; Eric A. Stene, "The Minidoka Project," Fifth Draft, Bureau of Reclamation History Program, Research on Historic Reclamation Projects, 1997, Bureau of Reclamation DataWeb, http://dataweb.usbr.gov/html/

minidoka1.html; DeMary, *History of Rupert, 1905–1922,* February 22, 1912, March 14, 1912, April 4, 1912, DMC; Minidoka County News, *The Minidoka Story,* 1.

25. DeMary, *History of Rupert 1905–1922,* November 9, 1905, December 28, 1905, October 19, 1905, February 15, 1906, DMC.

26. For an overview of the development of the Wild West stereotype, see Richard W. Etulain, *Re-Imagining the Modern American West: A Century of Fiction, History, and Art* (Tucson: University of Arizona Press, 1996), 5–30.

27. Karen Blair, *The Clubwoman as Feminist: True Womanhood Redefined, 1868–1914* (New York: Holmes & Meier Publishers, 1980), 57–71.

28. Vernetta Hogsett, *The Golden Years,* 1–7; 98; Sandra Haarsager, *Organized Womanhood: Cultural Politics in the Pacific Northwest, 1840–1920* (Norman: University of Oklahoma Press, 1997), 179–82.

29. Lori Merish, *Sentimental Materialism: Gender, Commodity Culture, and Nineteenth-Century American Literature* (Durham: Duke University Press, 2000), 18–19; Gillian Brown, *Domestic Individualism: Imagining Self in Nineteenth-Century America* (Berkeley: University of California Press, 1990), 20–21.

30. Charles E. Sargent, *Our Home, Or Influences Emanating from the Hearthstone* (Springfield, MA: King-Richardson Company, 1899), 367.

31. Merish, *Sentimental Materialism,* 20–22; Abigail Scott Duniway, *Edna and John: A Romance of Idaho Flat,* ed. Debra Shein (Pullman: Washington State University Press, 2000).

32. Women on the sagebrush flats knew what they were missing. Montgomery Ward and Sears Roebuck mail-order catalogs advertised the newest gadgets and served as a model of ideal domesticity. Thomas J. Schlereth, *Artifacts and the American Past* (Nashville, TN: American Association for State and Local History, 1980), 48–65.

33. Unknown Photographer, "W. R. Pickle's original homestead dwelling on the North Platte Project, Nebraska and Wyoming," circa 1910, Photographs of Irrigation Projects of the Bureau of Reclamation, Series J, Record Group 115, National Archives and Records Administration—Rocky Mountain Branch, Denver, Colorado.

34. See Lori Merish, *Sentimental Materialism,* 1–27.

35. Lori D. Ginzberg, *Women and the Work of Benevolence: Morality, Politics, and Class in the 19th-Century United States* (New Haven: Yale University Press, 1990), 10.

36. Blair, *The Clubwoman as Feminist,* 60–61.

37. The often antipastoral tone of women's creative work in irrigated communities demonstrates that an antiprogress narrative existed within the ranks of the so-called conquerors from the beginning of settlement, contrary to the ideological underpinnings of the new western history movement. A reassessment of the new western history is currently underway, by both its adherents and its critics. See Patricia Nelson Limerick, *Something in the Soil: Legacies and Reckonings in the New West* (New York: Norton, 2000), and Forrest G. Robinson, *The New Western History: The Territory Ahead* (Tucson: University of Arizona, 1998).

38. A pathologist, quoted in T. J. Jackson Lears, "Champions and Critics of Modernity," in *The Industrial Revolution in America,* ed. Gary J. Kornblith, Problems in American Civilization Series (Boston: Houghton Mifflin Company, 1998), 170.

39. William E. Smythe as quoted in *The Conquest of Urban America,* excerpted in Clyde A. Milner II, Anne M. Butler, and David Rich Lewis, *Major Problems in the History of the American West,* second edition (Boston: Houghton Mifflin Company, 1997), 385.

40. Anne Rugles Gere, *Intimate Practices: Literacy and Cultural Work in U.S. Women's Clubs, 1880–1920* (Urbana: University of Illinois Press, 1997), 1–16.

41. Krista Comer, "Literature, Gender Studies, and the New Western History," in *The New Western History: The Territory Ahead,* ed. Forrest G. Robinson, (Tucson: University of Arizona Press, 1997), 118.

42. On the difficulty of leaving family obligations for club work, see M.L.N., "Another Plan for Women's Clubs," in *The Century: A Popular Quarterly* 29, no. 3 (January 1885): 474.

43. The area Arthur Foote identified as an appropriate location for a dam is now the site of Arrowrock Dam, completed by the Reclamation Service in 1915. When constructed, it was the tallest concrete dam in the world. Bureau of Reclamation, "Boise Project, Idaho and Oregon," in Bureau of Reclamation, "DataWeb: Managing Water in the American West," http://dataweb.usbr.gov/html/boise.html, 3.

44. Mary Hallock Foote, "The Irrigating Ditch: Pictures of the Far West, VII," in *Century: A Popular Quarterly* 38, no. 2 (June 1889): 298.

45. Ibid., 299. Mark Fiege analyzed Mary Hallock Foote's illustration of *The Irrigating Ditch* in *Irrigated Eden: The Making of an Agricultural Landscape in the American West* (Seattle: Unversity of Washington Press, 1999), 186.

46. Foote, "The Irrigating Ditch," 300.

47. Foote, *The Chosen Valley*, in *Century: A Popular Quarterly* 44, no. 6 (October 1892): 833.

48. *The Chosen Valley* was serialized in *Century* magazine. For the first serial, see Mary Hallock Foote, *The Chosen Valley*, in *Century: A Popular Quarterly* 44, no. 1 (May 1892): 106–20.

49. Annie Pike Greenwood, Foreword by Jo Ann Ruckman, *We Sagebrush Folks* (Moscow: University of Idaho Press, 1988), 119.

50. Ibid., 122.

51. Ibid., 116.

52. Ibid., 116.

53. Ibid., 113.

54. A. C. DeMary, "Rupert Culture Club," January 3, 1907, *History of Rupert, 1905–1922*, DMC.

55. DeMary, *History of Rupert, 1905–1922*, October 19, 1905, DMC; Minidoka County News, *The Minidoka Story*, 2; Vernetta Murchison Hogsett, *The Golden Years*, 365; Haarsager, *Organized Womanhood*, 161–65.

56. DeMary, *History of Rupert, 1905–1922*, December 23, 1915, DMC; Minidoka County News, *The Minidoka Story*, 2.

57. Gail McDonald, "The Mind a Department Store: Reconfiguring Space in the Gilded Age," *Modern Language Quarterly* 63 (June 2002): 227–50.

58. "Joe Ruggles' Was First Play at New Opera House in Rupert," *Rupert Pioneer*, November 23, 1905, reprinted in Minidoka County News, *The Minidoka Story*, 31.

59. Lowitt and Fabry, *Henry A. Wallace's Irrigation Frontier*, 144–52.

60. DeMary, *History of Rupert, 1905–1922*, September 20, 1906, DMC.

61. The measure passed by a vote of 274 to 107 in Rupert. See Minidoka County Historical Society, *A History of Minidoka County and Its People*, 12.

62. Haarsager, *Organized Womanhood*, 148, 332–36. Details of the Culture Club's first annual banquet can be found in DeMary, *History of Rupert, 1905–1922*, January 3, 1907, DMC.

63. Elizabeth DeMary as quoted in U.S. Bureau of Reclamation, *Reclamation Record* 7 (February 1916): 60–61; also quoted in Mark Fiege, *Irrigated Eden*, 222 n. 1.

64. *Irrigation* was published in the Reclamation Service's journal, *Reclamation Era*. I found it taped to the inside cover of Elizabeth DeMary's book *Sunlit Peaks*, DMC.

65. Irene Welch Grissom, *The Passing of the Desert* (Garden City, New York: Country Life Press, 1924), 2.

66. From *The Mirage*, in Grissom, *The Passing of the Desert*, 3.

67. Mark Fiege discusses the various cultural myths associated with irrigation in *Irrigated Eden*, 171–202.

68. Titles from the Personal Library of Elizabeth Layton DeMary, Elizabeth Layton DeMary Collection, DMC.
69. Mary Hallock Foote to Alice B. Stockham, M.D., August 15, 1887, from Boise, Idaho, MSS 223, Albertsons Library, Boise State University, Boise, Idaho.
70. Hogsett, *The Golden Years*, 41.
71. The photograph of the suffrage parade is the private property of the James Goodman family, Rupert, Idaho. The photograph is reproduced in Minidoka County News, *The Minidoka Story*, 8. For more about the founding of Rupert's Methodist Church, see A. M. Lambert, "Church History on Project," *History of Rupert, 1905–1922*, DMC. For information about another of Rupert's social clubs, the Pansy Club, see Mrs. C. B. Burgher, "Flowers Nurtured in Sheltered Spot Gave Pansy Club Its Name," *The Minidoka Story*, 10. The Pansy Club supported the Boise Children's Home and the American Red Cross.
72. The source of Rupert's name has been cause for much speculation by regional historians. The Reclamation Service did not keep a record of the sources for all of its place names. Contemporary historians suggested that it was named for a prominent writer of the time period, Rupert Hughes, though Hughes later denied the assertion. Another theory suggested that it was named for Prince Rupert of the Hudson Bay Company. Albin C. DeMary unsuccessfully attempted to uncover the origins of the town's name during the 1940s by writing to retired reclamation officials. See Minidoka County News, *The Minidoka Story*, 2; J. T. Burke to A. C. DeMary, October 25, 1944, *Letter Scrapbook*, DMC.
73. "Early Rupert Scenes," in Minidoka County News, *The Minidoka Story*, 39; Minidoka County Historical Society, *Scrapbook of Rupert, Idaho: Articles and Pictures*, 5, Minidoka County Musuem, Rupert, Idaho.
74. "Early Rupert Scenes," in Minidoka County News, *The Minidoka Story*, 39; Minidoka County Historical Society, *Scrapbook of Rupert, Idaho: Articles and Pictures*, 5.
75. DeMary, *History of Rupert, 1905–1922*, June 6, 1907, June 13, 1907, DMC; Minidoka County Historical Society, *Scrapbook of Rupert, Idaho*, 5; "Rupert Square Had Sidewalks Built in 1910," in Minidoka County News, *The Minidoka Story*, 14; U.S., Department of the Interior, National Park Service, "National Register of Historic Places Listings," January 26, 2001, http://www.cr.nps.gov/NR/listings/20010126.htm.
76. Interview with Jerry Meyers, Restoration Architect, Rupert Renaissance Project, August 19, 2003, Pocatello City Hall, Pocatello, Idaho.
77. Hogsett, *The Golden Years*, 98.
78. For an extensive discussion of the Snake River Committee of Nine and other cooperative organizations, see Fiege, *Irrigated Eden*, 25–27; 81–116.
79. Linenberger, *Dams, Dynamos, and Development*, 24–25.
80. Hogsett, *The Golden Years*, 90.
81. Williams, "An Urban Study of Rupert, Idaho," 59. Leonard J. Arrington addresses the population growth of Idaho's twentieth-century agricultural communities in *History of Idaho*, Volume I (Moscow: University of Idaho Press, 1994), 471–532.
82. Bess Foster Smith, *Sunlit Peaks: An Anthology of Idaho Verse* (Caldwell, ID: Caxton Printers, 1931), 73.

CONTRIBUTORS

June Johnson Bube is a Senior Lecturer of English at Seattle University. She holds a B.A. in English and an M.A. in education from Stanford University. She earned her Ph.D. in nineteenth-century American literature from the University of Washington. She has written about women's dime novel westerns in "From Sensational Dime Novel to Feminist Western: Adapting Genre, Transforming Gender" in *Change in the American West: Exploring the Human Dimension*, edited by Stephen Tchudi (University of Nevada Press, 1996). In addition to her published work on rhetoric and composition, June's recent Americanist research has focused on Native American women writers, women's reform fiction of the nineteenth century, and the rise of the mass market in the nineteenth century.

Anne M. Butler is Trustee Professor, Emeritus, from Utah State University. She served for fourteen years as associate editor, coeditor, or senior editor of the *Western Historical Quarterly*. A scholar of the American West, Butler has published extensively concerning several aspects of social history, especially those that involve the experiences of women in the late nineteenth and early twentieth centuries. Her publications include, *Daughters of Joy, Sisters of Misery: Prostitutes in the American West* and *Gendered Justice in the American West: Women Prisoners in Men's Penitentiaries*. Her current research deals with Roman Catholic Sisters in the West, and she is coeditor, with Michael E. Engh, S.J. and Thomas W. Spalding, C.F.X., of *The Frontiers and Catholic Identities*. Her article, "Western Spaces, Catholic Places," won the 2001 religious history Arrington-Prucha prize of the Western History Association.

Natalia A. Dykstra is an Assistant Professor of English at Hope College in Holland, Michigan. She has received a NEH Fellowship, 2005–2006, for her book project on Marian "Clover" Adams, amateur photography, and nineteenth-century American visual culture.

Dee Garceau-Hagen is an Associate Professor of History and Chair of Women's Studies at Rhodes College, where she teaches courses on gender in the American West. She is the author of *The Important Things of Life: Women, Work and Family in Sweetwater County, Wyoming, 1880–1929* (University of Nebraska Press, 1997), and coeditor with Matt Basso and Laura McCall of *Across the Great Divide: Cultures of Manhood in the American West* (Routledge 2001). Her essay on Mourning Dove appears in *Sifters: Native American Women's Lives*, ed. Theda Perdue (Oxford University Press, 2001), and she coproduced the short documentary film, "A Capitol Beat," (2002) with graduate students at the Center for Documentary Film, George Washington University. She lives in Memphis, Tennessee with her husband, Ron Hagen.

Lynn M. Hudson is an Associate Professor in the History Department of California Polytechnic State University, San Luis Obispo, where she teaches courses in Women's Studies. She is the author of *The Making of 'Mammy Pleasant': A Black Entrepreneur in Nineteenth Century San Francisco* (University of Illinois Press, 2003).

Ruthanne Lum McCunn writes about Chinese on both sides of the Pacific. Besides *Thousand Pieces of Gold*, her award-winning books include *The Moon Pearl, Wooden Fish Songs, Chinese American Portraits*, and *Sole Survivor*. McCunn's work has been translated into nine languages, published in sixteen countries, and adapted for stage and screen. A former librarian and teacher, McCunn often lectures at schools, universities, libraries, and community organizations. She lives in San Francisco with her husband and two cats.

Linda Peavy and Ursula Smith are independent scholars whose special area of interest is western women's history. Their co-authored works include *The Gold Rush Widows of Little Falls, Women in Waiting in the Westward Movement, Pioneer Women* and *Frontier Children*. They served as senior historical consultants for the PBS mini-series *Frontier House* and, with producer Simon Shaw, wrote the companion book for that series. Their forthcoming book on the girls' basketball team from Fort Shaw Indian School has been greatly enriched by memories and memorabilia shared by descendants and tribal kin of the players.

Rose Stremlau is a Ph.D. candidate in the Department of History at the University of North Carolina at Chapel Hill. She specializes in Native American and American women's history. She currently is completing her dissertation on the resilience of Cherokee familial organization and values during the allotment era.

Laura Woodworth-Ney is an Assistant Professor of History and Codirector of Women's Studies at Idaho State University. She is the author of *Mapping Identity: The Creation of the Coeur d'Alene Indian Reservation, 1805–1902* (University Press of Colorado, 2004) and editor of *Idaho Yesterdays: The Journal of Idaho History.* She is currently writing a book entitled *Reclaiming Culture: Women, Ideology, and the Settlement of the Irrigated West, 1870–1924,* under contract with the University of Arizona Press. She lives in Pocatello, Idaho, with her husband, son, and two cats.

INDEX